GW01403322

European Foundations of the Welfare State

European Foundations of the Welfare State

Franz-Xaver Kaufmann

Translated from the German by John Veit-Wilson
with the assistance of Thomas Skelton-Robinson

Berghahn Books
New York • Oxford

Published in 2012 by
Berghahn Books
www.berghahnbooks.com

©2012 Franz-Xaver Kaufmann

Library of Congress Cataloging-in-Publication Data

Kaufmann, Franz-Xaver.
European foundations of the welfare state / Franz-Xaver Kaufmann ; translated from
the German by John Veit-Wilson, with the assistance of Thomas Skelton-Robinson.
p. cm.
Includes bibliographical references and index.
ISBN 978-0-85745-476-8 (hbk. : alk. paper) — ISBN 978-0-85745-477-5 (ebook :
alk. paper)
1. Welfare state—Europe. 2. Public welfare—Europe. I. Veit Wilson, John H.
II. Skelton-Robinson, Thomas. III. Title.
HN373.K38 2012
330.12'6094—dc23

2011040758

British Library Cataloguing in Publication Data

A catalogue record for this book is available from the British Library

Printed in the United States on acid-free paper.

ISBN 978-0-85745-476-8 (hardback)
ISBN 978-0-85745-477-5 (ebook)

To my beloved wife Karin – in the fifty-third year of our sharing life

Contents

FIGURES

FOREWORD

When Professor Kaufmann kindly asked me to write this foreword, he probably did not know that one of my first jobs, some fifty years ago, between school and university, was in an institution of the German welfare state: the Alsterdorfer Anstalten in Hamburg. Working as a Hilfspfleger (care assistant) did not allow much time for reading, and I learned little about the history or logic of continental welfare. Moreover, despite this unusual start for a British academic economist, my knowledge has remained deficient. It is therefore with great pleasure and benefit that I have read this collection of Professor Kaufmann's essays, translated from German by Professor Veit-Wilson. This book renders accessible a rich set of essays on the past and future development of the welfare state in Europe.

As the introduction to the 2010 *Oxford Handbook of the Welfare State* (Castles et al., 2010) points out, only the 'tip of the iceberg' of the non-English-language literature on the welfare state is translated into English. As an economist, I have been doubly handicapped. My economics course in Cambridge in the mid 1960s not only required me to read Smith, Ricardo, Marshall and Keynes but not List, Menger or the German historical school, but it also taught little about even the English-language literature on the welfare state. (Marshall was Alfred, not T.H.—although I did meet the latter at the home of James Meade). More recently, economists have discovered the welfare state but tend to view it from their own particular perspective of its functions and dysfunctions in the context of a market economy. This brings me to the first lesson I drew from reading Professor Kaufmann's impressive and wide-ranging book.

As the author says, the book 'offers a way of thinking about the welfare state that may not be familiar to an international audience', which is also a way of thinking different from that of mainstream economics. To quote from chapter 1, 'the development of systems of public provision of welfare are not only a by-product of industrialization, compensating for some dysfunctions of processes of economic and social change, but an essential factor in the constitution of modern European societies'. I still believe, as I argued in my Geneva Association annual lecture twenty years ago, that the all-or-nothing nature of industrial employment (which means that people who fall sick or become unemployed can lose all their income) was one of the reasons why social insurance came into being, but I recognize that this is only part of the story. As Professor Kaufmann says, social policies are essential for cultural, political and social integration. It is no accident that new political entities of the nineteenth century like Germany and New Zealand were in the lead. This is also relevant to the 'European Social Model', a term that has little meaning when used to analyse the past history of national welfare provisions but resonates in contemporary debate about future social policy: to quote from chapter 10, 'the rhetoric of a European social model becomes more credible if we consider it as a discourse within the framework of the search for a European identity'.

The book contains many rich themes, and I can highlight only a few. One of these themes is the emphasis, in chapter 3, on the influence of religious movements on the development of the European welfare state. In the case of Britain he refers to R.H. Tawney, and one can also cite empirical social investigators such as Seebohm Rowntree, whose findings about poverty were so influential. Another is the stress Professor Kaufmann places on international influences on the emergence of social rights (chapter 4). With references to the ILO Declaration of Philadelphia in 1944 and to the roles of Eleanor Roosevelt, H.G. Wells and others, he argues that 1945 was a watershed in the development of fundamental social rights. This in turn had important consequences for national welfare states. In Britain, the post-war Beveridge-based social security legislation was less revolutionary than often claimed (being largely a rationalization of existing schemes), but it broke new ground in its espousal of universalism and in linking social security to the wider issues of employment, education and health (fighting the five 'Giant Evils' of want, disease, ignorance, squalor and idleness).

I hope that these brief remarks have whetted the reader's appetite. Professor Kaufmann ends chapter 10 by observing that the future politics of the welfare state 'will resemble more the attempt to steer a sailing ship dependent on fair winds than to command a steamer dependent on the power of its own engine. It is the task of social science to redefine and explore empirically the boundaries between the dynamics of markets and their social consequences in a multi-tiered political system'. The present volume is essential reading for all who seek to rise to this challenge.

Anthony B. Atkinson, May 2011

Translator's Preface

Scholarship is a triumph of the human mind because it is capable of imposing order and pattern on the unruly material of human experience.
—Noel Annan, "Lytton Strachey and His Critics"[1]

What is a welfare state? The question has many disparate answers, and the term itself is treated as having many meanings across the spectrum of debate, from the most punctilious and intensive scholarship to the crudities of everyday party-political argument. Some meanings have positive associations in some countries and ideologies, some negative, but debate rarely extends to examination of the underlying and often conflicting assumptions and diverse histories that the exchanges take for granted. For that reason, I was not only honoured but pleased to be asked to help Franz-Xaver Kaufmann translate his book so that, to complement their own understandings, the English-reading public could be offered an introduction to the meanings and intellectual roots of the concept of the welfare state as understood from the European continental perspective.

The disagreement about meanings goes far deeper than mere semantics or ideology: it is rooted in differences in the national cultures of intellectual and scholarly approaches to the subject. In his seminal essay on intellectual styles, the sociologist Johan Galtung (1981: 817–856)[2] analysed some of the contentious issues, and among the ideal-type styles he distinguished, two are relevant to this translation – the saxonic (roughly speaking, the Anglo-Saxon intellectual style that can be distinguished into UK and US versions) and the teutonic intellectual style (which is not confined to Germans). Regarding ideas of 'the welfare state', an oversimplified distinction suggests that from a saxonic perspective, all states and their governments carry out some sort of social policies for some citizens, but by no means should all of them be called welfare states. The seminal work on the idea of a welfare state by such English writers as Richard

Titmuss, Dorothy Wedderburn, or Asa Briggs exemplifies this position.[3] In complete contrast to this approach, a common European continental assumption is that all modern industrial states are welfare states, but not all of them carry out social policies. This has led, not surprisingly, to some mutual incomprehension.

This is no place for a fuller explanation, but the confusion is not helped either by the saxonic tendency to seek empirical evidence to trace the development of social policy and welfare institutions to the point where they might be conceptualized as a welfare state, or by the teutonic preference for logic- and theory-based normative approaches that start from the assumption that modern states must be welfare states because they are by definition concerned with the welfare of all their subjects, whether or not the empirical evidence supports this belief. Much hangs on the qualitative meanings of the term 'welfare' and whose meanings they are – those of all the people in question or those only of the observer, as illustrated by the mutually contradictory connotations of the term 'subject'. From the teutonic perspective, in which the state always exists (exemplified by whatever form of rule it has), the great emancipation of the individual was from the status of an object at the disposition of the ruler to that of a subject of the state, to be treated with consideration. But from other intellectual perspectives, the individual was always the subject of the state until emancipation enabled the emergence of the autonomous citizen. As the Nordics put it, 'it's not "the state" against us (subjects); we are the citizens and it's our state'.

This book is therefore indispensable as a tool with which to dispel the confusion. In responding to Franz-Xaver Kaufmann's invitation to translate chapters he had written in German and edit some he had written in English, I came to the process with a good deal of diffidence as I was mindful of my previous experience of translating and editing densely written German scholarship into English. On that occasion, the (different) German academic author commented to me after the process was completed that he had felt it necessary to change some of my 'plain English because it had not sufficiently conveyed the complexity of his German thought'. As Galtung implied about the teutonic style of academic exposition and argument, complexity and profundity are inseparably intermingled and thus hard to translate, but in practice a greater problem was one to which the philosopher Karl Popper referred in his memoirs:

> Everybody who has done some translating, and who has thought about it, knows that there is no such thing as a grammatically correct and also almost literal translation of any interesting text. Every good translation is

an *interpretation* of the original text; and I would even go so far as to say that every good translation of a nontrivial text must be a theoretical re-construction. Thus it will even incorporate bits of a commentary. Every good translation must be, at the same time, close *and* free.... Incidentally, it is a mistake to think that in an attempt to translate a piece of purely theoretical writing, aesthetic considerations are not important.... In any case, although a translation may be bad because it is not *sufficiently* precise, a *precise* translation of a difficult text simply does not exist. And if the two languages have a different structure, some theories may be almost untrans-latable. (Popper 1982: 23–24, emphasis in original)

Experience showed me that Popper's demanding criteria could not be met if the translation was to be precise and was not to be my theoretical reconstruction of the author's text. The demand for German conceptual precision sometimes jarred with clarity of English expression, and even technical dictionaries failed to provide equivalents for some expressions in German, a language where scholars commonly convey conceptual in-novation and complexity by coining polysyllabic neologisms. Since my objective was an English version of Kaufmann's work without obtrusive evidence of my own views on either substance or style, and since we agreed that the process of translation was to be collaborative and itera-tive, I tried to work through stages, from an initial broad-brush transla-tion of the German to an English version that reflects not only the pre-cise substantive details of the argument but even some of the texture and terminology of the style of the original. The final text thus owes as much to the author's own views on how his argument should be expressed in English as it does to my views, as faithfully as he and I could achieve it together.

I want to express my appreciation and thanks to all those who made this translation possible. The Hanse Institute for Advanced Studies in Delmenhorst generously granted me a research fellowship for five months in 2008 and 2009 to enable me to work there on the translation and to pursue my own research, and I greatly valued the kind support of its staff. I very much appreciated the help Thomas Skelton-Robinson gave me with five chapters. The additional costs of the translation were also generously supported by Franz-Xaver Kaufmann and by the Bielefelder Universitätsgesellschaft. I am particularly grateful to Stephan Leibfried for his friendly help and encouragement throughout the project.

John Veit-Wilson
Newcastle University, May 2010.

Notes

1. Broadcast on BBC Third Programme on 5 May 1949, reprinted in Morris (1956: 149).
2. I am indebted to Andreas Busch for drawing this highly relevant paper to my attention.
3. The references are given in an essay and a response (Veit-Wilson 2000, 2002) in which I tried to outline some of these issues.

ACKNOWLEDGEMENTS

This book would not exist without the repeated urging of Stephan Leib-fried (Bremen) and Lutz Leisering (Bielefeld) to publish some of my work in English, and without their intellectual and administrative support. This is how I understand friendship.

It was my great chance that John Veit-Wilson decided to charge himself for translating the chapters written in German and to amend the few written in English. I am sure that he has underestimated the time it would cost to him to complete this job. He was a sensible and judicious interpreter of my thought, and I am highly indebted to his patience and generosity.

I thank all copyright holders for permissions to reprint material in this book.

Chapter 1, 'Pioneers of Social Reformism: Sismondi, List, Mill', is a translation of 'Vorläufer wohlfahrtsstaatlichen Denkens: Sismondi, List, Mill', published in Thomas Drepper, Andreas Göbel and Hans Nokielski (eds), *Sozialer Wandel und Kulturelle Innovation. Historische und systematische Perspektiven. Eckardt Pankoke zum 65. Geburtstag* (Sozialwissenschaftliche Schriften, Heft 40), Verlag Duncker & Humblot, Berlin, 2005, 43–69, © by the author.

Chapter 2, 'German Origins of a Theory of Social Reform: Hegel, Stein and the Idea of Social Policy', is a translation of the first chapter from my *Sozialpolitisches Denken – Die deutsche Tradition*, © Suhrkamp Verlag, Frankfurt a. M., 2003, 13–39, completed by a new introduction. A prior version was published in Bundesministerium für Arbeit und Soziales und Bundesarchiv (eds.), *Geschichte der Sozialpolitik in Deutschland seit 1945*, vol. 1, © Nomos-Verlag, Baden-Baden, 2001, 15–23.

Chapter 3, 'Christian Influences on Social Reform,' is a translation of 'Christentum und Wohlfahrtsstaat', published in *Zeitschrift für Sozialreform* 34 (1988): 65–89, © by the author.

Chapter 4, 'Welfare Internationalism before the Welfare State: The Emergence of Human Social Rights', is a somewhat shortened translation of *Die Entstehung sozialer Grundrechte und die wohlfahrtsstaatliche Entwicklung* (Nordrhein-Westfälische Akademie der Wissenschaften, Vorträge G 387), © Verlag Ferdinand Schöningh, Paderborn, 2003; annex to chapter 4, © Verlag Stämpfli & Cie AG, Bern, and C.H. Beck'sche Verlagsbuchhandlung, Munich.

Chapter 5, 'Social Security: The Leading Idea and Its Problems', is a somewhat extended version of 'Social Security', in Neil S. Smelser and Paul B. Baltes (eds.), *International Encyclopedia of the Social and Behavioral Sciences*, vol. 21, © Elsevier Publishers, 2001, 14435–14439.

Chapter 6, 'Social Policy Intervention: Elements of a Sociological Theory', is a translation of 'Elemente einer soziologischen Theorie sozialpolitischer Intervention' (1982) in the revised version as published in my *Sozialpolitik und Sozialstaat: Soziologische Analysen*, 2nd, enl. ed., © VS-Verlag, Wiesbaden, 2005, 69–106.

Chapter 7, 'First-Order and Second-Order Social Policies', is a translation of 'Der Sozialstaat als Prozeß – Für eine Sozialpolitik zweiter Ordnung', in Franz Ruland, Bernd Baron von Maydell and Hans-Jürgen Papier (eds), *Verfassung, Theorie und Praxis des Sozialstaates. Festschrift für Hans F. Zacher zum 70. Geburtstag*, Verlag C.F. Müller, Heidelberg, 1998, 307–322, © by the author.

Chapter 8, 'The State and the Production of Welfare', is a translation of 'Staat und Wohlfahrtsproduktion', in Hans-Ulrich Derlien, Uta Gerhard and Fritz. W. Scharpf (eds), *Systemrationalität und Partialinteresse. Festschrift für Renate Mayntz*, © Nomos-Verlagsgesellschaft, Baden-Baden, 1994, 357–380.

Chapter 9, 'National Welfare State Traditions and the European Social Model', is a substantially enlarged and revised translation of 'Nationale Traditionen der Wohlfahrtsstaatlichkeit und das "Europäische Sozialmodell"', in Klaus Busch (ed.), *Wandel der Wohlfahrtsstaaten in Europa*, © Nomos-Verlagsgesellschaft, Baden-Baden, 2008, 17–27. Substantial enlarging parts are translated extracts from my *Varianten des Wohlfahrtsstaats*, 5th ed. © Suhrkamp-Verlag, Frankfurt am Main, 2003 [5th ed. 2006].

Chapter 10, 'Towards a Theory of the Welfare State', was first published in *European Review: An Interdisciplinary Journal of the Academia Europea* and then reprinted in Stephan Leibfried (ed.), *Welfare State Futures*, © Cambridge University Press, Cambridge, 2001, 15–36.

Chapter 11, 'The Welfare State Achievements and Continuing Problems', is a translation of chapters 4 and 5 of my *Herausforderungen des Sozialstaates*, © Suhrkamp Verlag, Frankfurt a. M., 1997 (6th ed., 2004), 34–68, complemented by new considerations on the issue of justice.

Chapter 12, 'Human Assets and Demographic Challenges to the Welfare State', is a translation of 'Humanvermögen: Eine neue Kategorie der Sozialstaatstheorie', in Herbert Obinger and Elmar Rieger (eds), *Wohlfahrtsstaatlichkeit in entwickelten Demokratien: Herausforderungen, Reformen und Perspektiven*, Frankfurt and New York: Campus-Verlag, 2009, 95–117, © by the author.

Chapter 13, 'Solidarity and Redistribution under the Pressure of International Competition', is a translation of 'Sozialstaatliche Solidarität und Umverteilung im internationalen Wettbewerb' in Jens Beckert et al. (eds), *Transnationale Solidarität – Chancen und Grenzen*, Frankfurt and New York: Campus Verlag, 2004, 51–70, © by the author.

Chapter 14, 'What Comes after the Classic Welfare State?' is a translation of 'Diskurse über Staatsaufgaben', in Dieter Grimm (ed.), *Staatsaufgaben*, © Nomos-Verlagsgesellschaft, Baden-Baden, 1994, 15–41.

Chapters 6, 7, 8, 12, 13 and 14 have been published in German also in Franz-Xaver Kaufmann, *Sozialpolitik und Sozialstaat: Soziologische Analysen*, 3rd, enl. ed., © VS-Verlag Wiesbaden 2009.

All originals have been revised and sometimes updated to fit into the line of argument of this volume.

A SOCIOLOGICAL PERSPECTIVE

If we want to know where to go, we have to know where we came from. Nowadays social welfare programmes are spreading throughout the world, often shaped by international organizations like the International Labour Organisation and the World Bank. However, the more far-reaching notion of a political responsibility for the basic well-being of all members of a political society, which originated in the Western idea of a welfare state, is by no means spreading worldwide but remains more or less a feature of Europe and the former British Commonwealth. The welfare state in the European sense is not simply an administrative arrangement of various measures of social protection but a political project embedded in distinct cultural traditions and giving rise to a distinct path of modernization.

This book aims to review the intellectual foundations that underpinned the road towards the European welfare state, and to formulate some basic concepts for understanding it. The point of departure is, to put it briefly, that the necessity of collective provision for basic welfare is a consequence of the loss of accessible natural goods for everyone, which either custom or natural opportunity offered throughout the world in premodern times. It was not industrialization but the privatization and marketization of the former opportunities for self-sufficiency that opened the basic modernizing breach in the economic history of mankind. Rousseau and Marx were right to claim that the enclosures of the commons and the laws against begging switched the way of life to 'industrialization' – which originally meant *to make men industrious*, not in their own interests but for those of their employers. The exclusion of the poor from the original appropriation of natural goods challenged a culture shaped by Christian traditions and the humanistic enlightenment, which claimed the basic equality of all, in the context of societies assuming national identities and having political institutions strong enough to assume some responsibility for their members.

In this framework, the European welfare state emerged and now has to cope with the new challenges of open frontiers, global competition and demographic ageing if not population decline. Of course, the challenge of the privatization and marketization of natural resources is still spreading throughout the world, though it does not offer work for all but often only deprives people of what had secured their subsistence so far – most evidently, globally, in the case of water resources. And it remains an open question if and where cultural convictions and political institutions will eventually emerge to secure the basics of life and human rights for those deprived if not actually starving. In short, modernizing countries that have developed as welfare states commit themselves to including virtually all their residents in the basic provisions of life, whereas other modernizing countries tend to exclude substantial parts of their population from the fruits of economic and cultural progress. What are the implications of this difference?

In Search of a Theory of and for the Welfare State

Though the general idea of a welfare state seems to be accepted by majorities in all Western European countries, its legitimating reasons, specific goals and institutional realizations vary. In the international arena, Nordic and Anglo-Saxon interpretations dominate the scene, while the French and the German traditions remain peripheral. The author of this book, of Swiss origin, is more or less familiar with them all, though he studied chiefly the German institutions and intellectual traditions, which were seminal for the theoretical understanding of social policy. The present selection of revised and coordinated essays and chapters, most of which were originally written in German and translated by John Veit-Wilson with some assistance from Thomas Skelton-Robinson, therefore offers a way of thinking about the welfare state that may not be familiar to an international audience. However, the German tradition of reasoning about the welfare state has something to say to further international debate about this subject. It is a fact that the distinction between state and society and the question of their productive interaction, which is also currently emerging in international debate, has driven the German debate about social policy since its beginnings in the 1840s. These ideas are also seminal for the studies in this book.

The perspective on the welfare state that is central to this book therefore does not focus primarily on the various systems of public provision of welfare or on the ideological differences between various welfare states, as is customary in comparative research on welfare state regimes following Esping-Andersen (1990). It is neither 'quantitative' in the economic nor 'institutionalist' in the legal sense. Rather, it is sociological in the sense that it starts by considering the development of welfare states in the cultural and structural context of the great transformations of society and their aftermath, which we usually call *modernization*. It maintains that the social policies and the development of systems of public welfare provision are not only a by-product of industrialization, compensating for some dysfunctions of processes of economic and social change, but an essential factor in the constitution of modern European societies. Social policies are not only a way of redistributing income that may be considered as benevolent or as harming economic growth. Social policies, and their complex effects in the form of the developed welfare state in particular, are essential for cultural political and social integration, for the orientation of private lives and, finally, also for economic productivity. In this sense, so far not all countries in the West are welfare states, and those with emerging economies in East Asia even less so.

A theory of the welfare state has to work out the reason or 'logic' implicit in these developments. As to the relationship between politics and economy, it is possible to distinguish three 'ideal types' that have been tried historically in the context of modernization:

1. The separation of polity and economy, politics leaving economic activity largely unbounded in the sense of the liberal faith in the benevolent forces of market coordination, or *liberal capitalism*;
2. The merger of polity and economy, most explicit in the connection of the public budget with the planned economy, or *socialism*;
3. The coordination of mutually dependent political and economic systems that are structurally differentiated, or the *welfare state*.

Whereas both liberal capitalism and socialism display some degree of simple functional logic of markets or hierarchies respectively, the institutional arrangements of welfare states are more complex. So far it is unclear why the welfare state has been a historical success and under what conditions it can endure into the future.

Social policies are considered here as neither part nor counterpart of economic policies; their impact on the economy remains contingent on various factors. Social policies are not operated solely by the political authorities or solely by business or private bodies. Rather, they are the synthesis resulting from interaction between politics, economy, associations and private households. It is therefore the task of government (and of the social sciences) to devise regulations to further synergies between them. It is a specific feature of the European foundations of the welfare state that the welfare under consideration is primarily individual welfare; collective 'welfare of the people' can also be found in dictatorial regimes. It follows that *a focus on the life chances of individuals* has to be central to a theory of the welfare state in the European sense. However, the collective utility of social policies is not to be underestimated. A theory of the welfare state has to devise concepts, hypotheses and perspectives for analysing the implications of welfare policies, from the perspective of not only the individual but also collective utility.

What is usually termed the welfare state has its precarious scientific existence without theory of its own in the space between jurisprudence, economics, sociology and political science, not to overlook social philosophy. In the German-speaking world, from 1873 the activity of the Verein für Socialpolitik (Association for Social Policy) offered an academic foundation for practical social policy. In Britain the relevant questions became subsumed under the heading of a distinct discipline, social administration, but the Association of Social Administration has actually changed its name in UK Association for Social Policy. For the British the term welfare state chiefly means the British system of social protection as originally established in the aftermath of the Second World War. In Britain as well as in other countries, scholarly discussions have focused on history, institutions, consequences and the reform of particular systems of social protection at the national level. It is only since the 1980s and 1990s that one can see attempts to study comparatively the overall developments in social and economic policies that the British call the *welfare state*, the Germans *Sozialstaat*, the French *l'état providence*, the Dutch *Verzorgingsstat* and the Swedes *välfärdsstat* or *folkhemmet*. US Americans, on the other hand, understand welfare only as poor relief and distrust a welfare state for creating dependency. Of course, other condensed terms such as 'social security' or 'social services' are used too, but none mobilize political passions or academic scrutiny as do 'welfare state' and its equivalents in other languages.

Since social policies evolved independently in different nations, they differed in their legitimations, in the political issues that came into focus, and in the shape of the institutions that emerged from the political controversies. The same may be said about democracy or even about market capitalism: they all exhibit national or at least different cultural characteristics. Although there is extensive international debate about the operative concept of democracy or of market economy, no comparable discussion concerns the conception of the welfare state (Veit-Wilson 2000; Kaube 2003). Comparative studies are dominated by the inductive method, and comparisons focus almost entirely on easily comparable issues such as social budgets or legal norms. Personal social services as such and their organization, let alone the ways and means of their coordination, are rarely compared.

To this day, there have been few systematic attempts to connect social welfare issues with theories of the state, the economic order, political management, social structure, household economics or ethics, and to the extent that such an attempt has been made, it has usually had a characteristic disciplinary one-sidedness. Moreover, the scientific treatment of issues often suffers from political and ideological biases. Liberal authors mistrust state intervention a priori, while social-democratic and Christian-democratic authors all too easily take social problems as evidence of the state's responsibility and capacity to solve them, without considering the constraints of administrative policy or the demands of the economic system, let alone foreseeable side effects.

The European Continental and the Anglo-Saxon Perspectives on the Welfare State

Various reasons can be suggested for this ambiguous assessment of social policies and the welfare state. The most important reason – in the political and economic sciences alike – is itself of a theoretical nature and results from an inadequate conceptualization of the societal context. Legal and political scholars distinguish between the 'state' and 'society' while economists distinguish between the 'market economy' and the 'state'; these fields thus do not share the same concept of the state. Hegel, to whom we owe the seminal distinction between the 'state' and 'civil society', identified a third principle of association, namely the 'family'. Yet both leading perspectives conceptually ignore the welfare-creating services of private households. The manifold services of private associations, as well as corporatism, fit equally poorly into the scheme of *Politics against Markets* (Esping-Andersen 1985). The dominance of legal and economic thought has led to the development of an abstract antithesis between the 'market' and the 'state' that serves as the starting point for all debates about systematic economic policy today. However, modern societies command a greater arsenal of principles of control and welfare production, and 'good' societies depend on the complementarity of these principles.

A less obvious reason for the dominance of the sterile opposition be-tween market and state stems from economic, political and cultural dif-ferences between the United States of America and continental Europe (Alber 2001: 62ff., Kaufmann 2003c, see also chapter 9). To put it briefly, the U.S. was never so dependent economically on industrial production as Europe was, so worker movements never gained comparable influence. Moreover, American workers were often black, and in the U.S. the basic social cleavage was not class but race; consequently social inequality and exclusion remained more 'legitimate' in the U.S. Politically, the fragmen-tation of the American political system made for greater organizational difficulty. From the perspective of religion, Calvinism did not inhibit competition and striving for maximum gain, nor did it provide particular legitimation to the political authorities. Catholicism, on the other hand, opposed not only socialism but also capitalism, and Lutheranism empha-sized a conception of the state as a moral institution.

At the heart of different attitudes towards the welfare state are funda-mentally different conceptions of 'state' and 'society', as well as of 'public' and 'private'. Indeed, these terms are essential for the identification of modern societies. The Americans' individualistic idea of society is based on living with the experience of the Frontier, going west, and the re-peated necessity of forming a political community from the bottom up. In Europe, by contrast, the state, including an efficient state administra-tion, preceded the liberalization of markets and also democratization. An exception is Britain, where the civil service was not built up until almost two centuries after the Glorious Revolution. As is well known, the politi-cal administration in the United States is very unevenly professionalized, even to this day. The experience of a reliable political administration is an element of European political culture, despite continuous complaints about bureaucracy. Another cultural difference is the lack of impact of Roman law on the English-speaking countries. The distinction between public and private law stems from Roman law and is central to the conti-nental understanding of the political system.

It is worth recalling the origins of this distinction as described by the Roman jurist Ulpian: 'Public law looks at what is common to Romans. Private law looks at what is of individual utility' (Ulpian: *De justitia et jure* 1,1; FXK's translation). Public and private are not conceived as separate domains but as different perspectives, applying in various combinations to the social, economic and political realities. The 'purely public' (e.g. constitutional decision-making) and the 'purely private' matters (e.g. gambling or love) are limiting cases, whereas most parts of social life may be considered more from a public or more from a private perspective. The predominance of one or another is a normative and often contested political issue. This applies also to matters of social policy: from a (German) juridical perspective, social policies always exhibit a mixture of public and private law. This confirms the original idea of *Sozialpolitik* being the outcome of a *mediation* between 'state' and 'civil society' in the Hegelian sense. And with the current shift in many European welfare states from public service provision to independent or even 'private' bodies under public regulation, the hybridization of the welfare state becomes no longer only a German but also an international phenomenon (Gilbert 1983: 6ff., 2002; Berner 2009).

Thus the concept of 'the state' is not as universal in European history as hitherto assumed, but instead stems essentially from the continental European tradition (Bendix 1964; Dyson 1980). This is not only true for the emergence of institutions relating to positive law and stemming from the tradition of Roman law, but also applies to the history of political ideas: the Anglo-Saxon tradition, after taming the Hobbesian Leviathan, was more concerned with constitutional issues than with the interdependent operation of the now separated powers of parliament, the executive and the judiciary.

The continental notion of the state has to be considered as the consequence of both institution building and formulation of theories of the state (Grimm 1986). Thus the continental state is

> a generalizing, integrating and legitimating concept … the most integrated form of political society, emphasis being placed on its association with the ideal of collectivity and the general good, and its combination of socio-cultural with a legal dimension. As an aggregate concept the state stresses the interdependency and integration of institutions as opposed to the structural differentiation typical of 'civil' society and so beloved of modern Anglo-American political science. (Dyson 1980: 208f.)

The Anglo-Saxon concepts of government and Crown have a narrower scope, are more centred on people than on institutions, and place less emphasis on the unity of the public sector, including the judiciary. Nettl (1968) therefore considers Britain and (to a lesser degree) the United States as 'stateless societies' and shows that the Anglo-Saxon social sciences consequently differ from the European tradition in their statelessness. However, matters seem to have changed in recent decades, so this presentation of a more 'continental' perspective[1] may be of interest to British and American readers as well.

The British literature on the welfare state focuses on 'social administration' or, more recently, on policies and not on politics. Keeping the differences in political concepts in mind, the conceptual weakness of British thought about the welfare state becomes comprehensible. This mode of thought refers only to one sector within which political power is exercised and not to the unifying effect of the political institutions per se. But in fact social problems and welfare issues form only a part of political activity: it is the same government that decides on pollution control, tax reform, economic policy, defence and social security, and there are not two separate entities, one called welfare state (*Sozialstaat*) and the other called political or constitutional state (*Rechtsstaat*). We therefore call the realm of governmental as well as nongovernmental social services the *welfare sector* and not the welfare state (see chapter 10). The welfare sector is part of the public sector, that is, the institutional outcome of a growing interdependence of polity and economy (Kaufmann, Majone and Ostrom 1986; Kaufmann 1991b). A more comprehensive perspective shows that the promotion of welfare cannot be restricted to social administration but is also involved in, for example, full employment policy and defence, as Beveridge was clearly aware (see Beveridge 1943: 98ff.).

Just as the continental European and the Anglo-Saxon political cultures display characteristic differences in terms of their conception of the state, so they also differ in the degree of trust they place in the ability of politics to solve problems. In continental Europe there is greater acceptance of arguments based on public interest (if defined as requiring government intervention) and, consequently, of the legitimacy of collective action and political intervention. This book puts forward a perspective on the welfare state that aims to transcend the idiosyncrasies of national or ideological perspectives. Our basic concept is not the welfare *state*, but the political responsibility for the *production of welfare for all*, which may be performed by households, associations and markets, and by political provisions as well (see chapter 8). The empirical question, then, is what consequences may be anticipated and observed arising from specific institutional arrangements and public interventions.

The Welfare State: A Preliminary Sketch

The first recorded use of the English term 'welfare state' is generally attributed to Archbishop William Temple, who used it in the pamphlet *Citizen and Churchmen* in 1941 (Gregg 1967: 3). As Edgerton (2006: 59f.) shows, however, the political scientist Alfred E. Zimmern had coined the term previously in 1934, though in the more general sense of a 'classic liberal democracy'.[2] In 1941, Roosevelt and Churchill proclaimed the Atlantic Charter and called for 'freedom from fear and want' in a new society after their victorious end to the Second World War. The Beveridge Report, widely considered a landmark in offering a programme for the welfare state, was published in the following year. In 1948 the Universal Declaration of Human Rights affirmed not only civil but also social rights, such as the rights to social security, work and recreation, a decent standard of living and the protection of mothers as well as the right to education and to cultural participation (see chapter 4, Annex).

It is conventional to consider most if not all industrialized countries as welfare states. But while economic growth fuelled by industrialization is believed to be a precondition for the development of nationwide social or welfare policies, by no means do all industrialized countries actually accept the programme implied by the Universal Declaration of Human Rights in either their policies or their institutions. It is therefore misleading to treat all members of the OECD, for example, as welfare states, even if this is common practice in welfare state research. The approach in this book tries to offer evidence for a more precise understanding of welfare states.

If one considers the welfare state as a kind of consensual definition of a society's 'legal and therefore formal and explicit responsibility for the basic well-being of all of its members' (Girvetz 1968: 512),[3] it makes sense to say that in the Anglo-Saxon world the welfare state has emerged during and since the Second World War, despite some formative innovations beginning with the Elizabethan Poor Laws (1597/1601), the British Factory Act of 1833, the Public Health Act of 1848, the Education Act of 1870, the Workmen's Compensation Act of 1897 and the Old Age Pensions Act of 1908.

Although Great Britain (and to some extent also France) led in the industrialization process of the nineteenth century and first experienced the social problems of transition to industrial work (Polanyi's commentary (1944) is still impressive), it was not Britain but Germany that played a pioneering role in the intellectual analysis of the new society and of its problems, as well as in the creation of political measures to deal with these problems. In the 1830s and 1840s a keen awareness of the new character of industrial misery (as distinct from pre-industrial poverty) was found in such leading theorists as Franz von Baader (1835), Robert von Mohl (1835), Lorenz von Stein (1842, 1850) and Karl Marx (first in 1844, see Marx 1968). It is striking how these thinkers, who range across the spectrum of political thought from conservative (Baader) to liberal (Mohl), reformist (Stein) and revolutionary (Marx), converge in the diagnosis of industrial misery as stemming from a social division between the wealthier people who are able to participate in the development of the new economic opportunities, and the 'proletarians without property' (Baader) who are forced to sell their ability to work for whatever price and under whatever working conditions they can get.

The network of these new economic opportunities was called – following Hegel (1821) – the (civil) society, and was differentiated from the state, that is, the constitution of self-contained legal power. The new opportunities for industrialization were seen as a consequence of the liberal state's withdrawal from economic tutelage. Industrialization's social consequences were thus attributed to the separation between state and society and the abolition of the feudal order that accounted for economic backwardness as well as offering a basic protection to the bondsmen, and other early forms of social security such as guilds, local and ecclesiastical assistance, and the like. It is in that context that the term *Sozialpolitik* (meaning either social politics or social policies or both) emerged in the social sciences to denote the problem of mediating between state and society, to resolve the social problems of early capitalism (see chapter 2).

The institutional aspects of the programmatic term *Sozialpolitik* emerged slowly during the second part of the nineteenth century, given academic support by the Verein für Sozialpolitik, the association of social scientists founded in 1873 to promote social reform through state intervention. With the unification of the German Reich in 1870/71 under the auspices of the King of Prussia, the *étatistic* approach to solving social problems became stronger. The introduction of the first nationwide social security system for industrial workers in the 1880s is rightly considered a landmark in the creation of modern social policies.

The widespread tendency to describe modern states as welfare states suggests that there has been a very similar political evolution in all Western countries and in other parts of the world. As the works of some comparative researchers show,[4] it is, however, difficult to ascertain a common pattern in the development of the social legislation and services. The genesis of welfare policies cannot be validly explained by any one or even compound factor theories. There is also no consensus with respect to the core institutions of the welfare state. In the Anglo-Saxon discussion, the welfare state is widely identified with the existence of certain social services. In the United States the term social services designates five main domains of welfare institutions: education, health, income maintenance, housing and employment. In British classifications the last domain seems to be excluded. British authors, however, tend to add the newer domain of social work and counselling as 'personal social services'. In the German discussion there is some tendency to identify the *Sozialstaat* with *Sozialpolitik*. The latter term emphasizes workers' protection and social security, that is, those activities of the central state regulated under the auspices of the Ministry of Labour, which has important corporate relationships with the employers and the unions. Whereas health and housing are sometimes included, education has hitherto been regularly excluded from the concept of *Sozialpolitik*, though there is currently a tendency among scholars to include it, as well as other local services. The international *Handbook of the Welfare State*, which was published after this book was written, has the makings of becoming the standard work for years to come (Castles et al. 2010). It deals with the following policies: Social expenditure and revenues, old-age Pensions, health, long-term care, work accident and sickness benefits, disability, unemployment insurance, labour market activation, social assistance, family benefits and services, housing, and education. This broad approach converges with the understanding of the welfare sector in this book.

The specific problem of European welfare states is not their lack of power to intervene but the consequences of their success. Existing systems of support change the aspirations of the population, the systems develop their own dynamic, and they become more and more costly. They therefore need continuous political management and control in order to carry out their tasks under changing circumstances. Thus constraints on their costs and efficiency repeatedly become issues of public concern. The welfare state program does not promise a fool's paradise, nor is it a substitute for religious hopes. It concerns only the protection and promotion of particular defined aspects of individual welfare that are public concerns, through politically determined arrangements for the production of welfare. However, what is of public concern remains controversial. Some arguments for the collective utility of the welfare state from societies' overall perspectives are put forward in what follows.

The legitimacy and efficiency of the welfare state has principally been called into question by authors from the United States (e.g. Murray 1984, 1988; Popenoe 1988). The inefficiency of American programs for 'welfare' seems to follow more from structural competition between Washington and individual states than from the fragmentation and instability of the programs and their frequent modification. Moreover, administration at the local level often lacks continuity and professionalization (see for instance Pressman and Wildavsky 1973). The failure of many social policies seems to be caused by the lack of specific U.S. federal competences at state level, such as legal foundations, a professionalized public service, or judicial control of the public services.

One basic distinction may be drawn from the preceding considerations. In the Anglo-Saxon context, 'welfare state' denotes above all a complex of institutionalized policies, as described above. In the continental and especially German context, the 'social state' means above all a political commonwealth's normative commitment to welfare, as expressed for instance by constitutional aims or international agreements. From an analytical perspective the British concept of welfare state focuses on structural or organizational aspects, the German concept of social state on cultural or programmatic aspects of the welfare state. In order to distinguish between them for analytical purposes, I shall use the term *welfare sector* to denote the structural-organizational aspect, that is, the welfare state in the conventional empirical sense of social administration or social services. And I speak about the *welfare aims* to denote the normative aspects of the welfare state in the sense of social rights, inclusion or aims and values legitimizing sociopolitical intervention.[5] The exciting issues for politics as well as for research on social policies and the welfare state lie, in my opinion, in the empirical overlap between the two spheres of welfare sector and welfare aims.[6]

Modernity, Modernization and the Welfare State

An adequate theory of the welfare state must refer not only to politics and public institutions, but to the relationship between this political core and the 'rest of society' – to the mediation between state and civil society in the sense meant by Lorenz von Stein (see chapter 2). It is now necessary to abandon everyday language and to become more precise, since one cannot speak scientifically about 'society' without opting for a certain conception of it. I start with the traditional Aristotelian concept of a political community, one that has marked Anglo-Saxon political theory until recent times. Whereas for Hegel and his German followers 'society' described only a part of the social relationships of a commonwealth (the economic relationships in the case of Hegel, or the associative relationships in the case of Robert von Mohl), I follow the tradition of reserving the name of society for the totality of social relationships of an imagined or empirical commonwealth. I start therefore with the idea that the processes of differentiation between the polity, the economy and the family, which Hegel (1821) focused on first, are operating within or rather transforming society. We denote these processes as modernization.[7] The remainder of society is not, however, composed only of the economy and the family. Modern societies expand and specialize in a growing number of subsystems or spheres of communication and organized action, such as religion, science, the media and law, not forgetting education and health. Such systems consist of networks of organizations united by common or complementary concerns, relating to different aspects of social life that are identified by specific codes.[8] What is called globalization points to the expansion of such partial systems of communication and exchange beyond national borders, thereby limiting national politics' powers of control.

A broad consensus among historians as well as sociologists asserts that the timely coincidence of cultural change (secularization, enlightenment), of technical innovations (such as the invention of the steam engine or the production of steel) and of political revolution (constitutionalism, nationalism) in the second half of the eighteenth century formed the threshold between traditional and modern society in Western Europe. The social sciences have developed through intellectual dispute about these changes. The term modernization was introduced in the late 1950s only to establish links between the various partial aspects and processes that had been discussed hitherto, such as rationalization, secularization, industrialization, democratization and individualization (Lerner 1968). And debate persists about the degree of uniformity or diversity of the trajectories (see Eisenstadt 2000).

Modernity as Legitimation of Change

We follow the sociological mainstream by distinguishing cultural from structural aspects of modernization, and relating both to the acceleration of social change. From a cultural perspective, the direction was set by the *Querelle des Anciens et des Modernes*, a literary debate among European intellectuals at the end of the seventeenth century. The issue concerned aesthetics, namely the question whether the ideals of antiquity were irrevocable or whether – as the 'Moderns' claimed – new aesthetic forms could also become exemplary. In the same period the sense of history and of temporality, the distinction between past, present, and future, began to emerge. Whereas traditional societies were oriented towards authorities established in the past and thought to be binding on the future as well, the Enlightenment put aside traditional authorities and oriented reason towards a new and better future. However, hopes for progress ended in the atrocities of *La Terreur* in the aftermath of the French revolution, and since then social change has become ambivalent and contested in mainstream thought, though the experience and consciousness of inevitable change remains fundamental.[9] It follows that

> Modernity here will be defined culturally, as an epoch turned to the future, conceived as likely to be different from and possibly better than the present.... Modernity ends when words like progress, advance, development, emancipation, liberation, growth, accumulation, enlightenment, embetterment, avant-garde, lose their attraction and their function as guides to social action. (Therborn 1995: 4)

From a cultural point of view, modernity is the legitimation of lasting change; it bears 'the spirit of permanent revision' (Jacob Burckhardt).

As the future is always unknown, modern societies are confronted with the issue of insecurity, that is, the challenge of reducing the opacity and uncertainty of the future (see chapter 5). Though many critics and social movements oppose certain forms of innovation and change, only small minorities (like the Amish) are opposed to the dynamics of modern societies in principle.

Functional Differentiation, Inclusion and Exchange

The dominant macrosociological paradigm understands modernization as the shift from a rank-ordered and territorial structure of society to a functionally differentiated structure, disembedded from local ties. Obvious boundaries have been erected, between economics and politics (by the freedom of private property ownership and the ban on corruption), between the family and politics (by democratization and the ban on nepotism), between politics and religion (by secularization and the freedom of religion), and between the family and the economy (mainly by the separation of household and workplace and the emergence of big business). Historically, these limiting differentiations were often contested. The success of liberalization and modernization seem to depend on these apparent boundaries. The specialized realms of activities have developed their own skills and systems of knowledge, often even including specialized sciences such as economics, law, theology or political science. On the other side, social relationships have tended to become more extended and more equal.

From a structural point of view, we have to consider modernization as change at various levels. At the level of everyday life, the dissolution of the old feudal or administrative bonds opened the way for mobilization. People were no longer bound to a specific territory, stabilized by the right to use the natural resources of a particular soil, but were allowed to try out the newly emergent opportunities of industry and trade, though they lost the old securities of the past. At the level of social organization, the landlords' and political communities' overall responsibility for their subjects was dissolved and new forms of free association began to flourish, no longer distinguishing between members and outsiders for their whole lives but by choice – not by tradition but by decision. Among these new forms, the institution of factories hiring people for incidental tasks and firing them for incidental reasons became commonplace.

At the level of social communication, a separation of spheres of action through specialization eventually took place: political rule became constrained by constitutions and especially by fundamental rights. Economic activities became separated from households and were no longer based on subsistence but on market opportunities. The accumulation of knowledge was no longer restricted to 'learning by doing' but became formalized in schools and universities. Law no longer remained a matter of tradition defined by precedent but developed into manageable systems shaped and administered by professionalized jurists. Though many of these trends had their origins in the Middle Ages, organizational separation on the basis of different tasks and the intensification of specialized communication and knowledge were novel elements. The works of Niklas Luhmann most succinctly analyse the consequences of these trends: the structural differentiation of societal functions gives way to the autopoiesis of partial systems of society with their own codes defining selectivity and indifference towards everything external to the elements operating within the system.[10]

Subsystems or spheres of society are only systems of communication; they are not actors. They store knowledge that is essential for specialized decisions or actions. Social life is maintained through the decisions of organizations and the actions of persons. They also induce transfers across the boundaries of communication systems, transfers essential to individual as well as collective social life (Brock and Junge 1995). Most of these transfers take the form of marketized exchange, mediated by money and prices. But other forms of reciprocity also exist, for example in the realm of transfers within and between households or free associations, which are controlled by solidarity. And wherever hierarchical power relations exist, transfers by redistribution become established (Polanyi 1957; Etzioni 1971; Kaufmann and Krüsselberg 1984; Hegner 1991). It is a matter of interpretation whether such redistributive transfers are perceived as enforced, as altruistic, or as embodying extended reciprocity through political intervention. The latter is the argument for the welfare state.

Though modern societies exhibit highly complex institutional arrangements guiding the decision-making rules of organizations, nothing will move without 'natural actors'– human beings with their desires, needs, emotions, values, skills, abilities and limited knowledge – who on the one hand participate as citizens, members or clients of various organizations in collective life, and on the other live their private lives as individuals. Both spheres are more interconnected at the individual level than most theories admit: private life depends on the scope of inclusion into the roles and benefits of organizations, and participation in organizations is shaped by the private interests, preferences and motives of not only the individual but also the leaders of existing organizations. As far as there is no *right* of entry and participation, this remains a completely contingent form of social inclusion.[11]

In traditional societies people were – strictly speaking – not isolated individuals but members of one and only one collectivity.[12] They resembled companies of actors with permanent personnel meeting every day in the same place but in different plays, with varying roles such as father and mother, landlord or labourer, servant or participant in social events. Modern man resembles a player on tour, changing places and companies as well as the plays.[13] As no one lives and acts in the context of one partial system alone, and as nobody is any longer dependent on one organization alone, individuals today are confronted by the challenge of structural plurality, and in coping with structural plurality one is forced to become a person, a centre of decision in its own right, since no one can resolve the conflicting claims with which he or she is confronted. Norbert Elias (1994) paraphrases the *Civilising Process* with respect to the individual as *Gesellschaftlicher Zwang zum Selbstzwang*, structural constraint to develop self-management and personal identity.[14] From a sociological point of view, man's much-beloved freedom is nothing for himself alone but results from his optimizing multiple social roles and dependencies.

By no means do the conditions of modernity assure this process of becoming oneself, of developing individual and social identity. From Durkheim onwards sociologists have emphasized and explored the dangers of anomie and deviant behaviour. Modern sociology speaks about the need for empowerment in order to cope with the risks and opportunities of modern life. Social inequality is not primarily inequality of income but inequality of empowerment, often due to social deprivation in childhood. And from the normative perspective of freedom, no one can exercise liberty without some basic intellectual and material resources.[15]

Hegel's dissolution of the millenarian notion of a social unity constituted by political authority into the difference between state, civil society and family represents the beginning of a theory of the functional differentiation in modern society, which has become one of the most important paradigms of modern social theory, notably through the work of Parsons (1971) and especially Luhmann (1977, 1997). Modern society, in Luhmann's view, is structured by a multiplicity of functional systems such as the economy, politics, law, science, religion, mass media and so on. Individuals no longer belong to these systems by birth or class but take part in them by law, contract or association. Functional systems therefore tend to be highly discriminating about individuals and about specific categories of persons as well. According to Luhmann, the welfare state's central task is to secure every individual's inclusion in each functional system to the degree he or she needs its benefits. This also corresponds to the idea of economic social and cultural rights in the United Nations' Declaration of Human Rights (1948) and its aftermath (see chapter 4). It was at that time that the British sociologist T.H. Marshall (1950) raised the threefold conception of human rights in this declaration and conceived citizenship as the combination of civil, political and social rights. In recent times the binary perspective on inclusion and exclusion has become a focus for issues of social inequality (Stichweh and Windolf 2009; Gestrich, Raphael and Uerlings 2009).

Though the normative goal of welfare states is to include everyone who is legally resident[16] in the sense of enabling access to life's basic necessities, nevertheless social inequality persists to substantial degrees, and even equality of opportunities for inclusion, let alone exchange, are in practice seldom secure. The consequences of transactions in the welfare sector seldom meet the standards of the welfare aims. These problems, however, cannot be dealt with at the level of a general theory of the welfare state but only at the level of national social policies.

Welfare Policies Responding to the Functional Differentiation of Society

The historical process of functional differentiation reached its first threshold in the struggle over the investiture of bishops, the 'Papal Revolution' (1075–1122) and its aftermath (Berman 1983). In 1122, emperor and pope agreed that the pope should confer the spiritual powers on the bishops, while the emperor should confer the secular powers. Thus for the first time the cultural difference between spiritual and secular became defined and shaped the structural difference between ecclesiastical and secular powers, a tension finally resolved by Napoleon Bonaparte's secularization of ecclesiastical wealth throughout continental Europe.

The structural differentiation between polity and economy began with trade over long distances and became effective as a consequence of the bourgeois revolutions. Its cultural basis became the doctrine of free trade, originating with Adam Smith but persisting in a more complex form in neo-liberalism. The structural difference between the market economy and the household economy developed as work became spatially separated from private living. The cultural basis for the latter developed with ideas of romantic love and of privacy.

Three factors can define the constellation that made social policies and the welfare state necessary for successful modernization. First was the structural differentiation of the polity and the economy: the liberal creed of *laissez-faire* (government shall not interfere), which won supremacy in the nineteenth century beginning in Britain, was the cultural stabilization of the structural emancipation of trade and industry from governmental tutelage. The second factor was the abolition of subjects' former rights to subsistence in their place of origin or settlement or the place to which they were bound.[17] Whereas the landlord and other masters had been responsible for their labourers even during illness or disability, free labour became independent but unprotected. Industrialization, though a remedy for preindustrial poverty, attracted landless people to new, risky situations, as Sismondi was the first to acknowledge (see chapter 1). The third factor was the industrial immiseration in the settlements of the working or work-seeking poor, generally distinct from bourgeois cities, which became the most immediate motor for sociopolitical intervention.

The state first entered into industrial regulation to protect children from working conditions that were obviously not conducive to securing their vital interests, and whose deficiencies became obvious not only through the protests of 'moral entrepreneurs' but also in statistical reports by recruitment officers seeking vigorous soldiers. Once the ban on interference was broken, the evidence of practices damaging health and other aspects of workers' lives became stronger and led to the expansion and intensification of public intervention.[18] The protection of labour, or social policies more broadly in the context of production, became the first realm of welfare state activities.

Despite industrial growth, poverty remained a persistent challenge to modern societies. This was obvious in the case of those who were unable to earn their living by work, the 'deserving poor'. The care of the poor, who were generally also sick or disabled, was an old Christian tradition that had devolved to secular bodies in Protestant regions. But what about the 'able-bodied poor' who for various reasons do not find work? This issue remains among the most contested to this day. Does joblessness depend on a lack of motivation to work or on economic and social conditions? Should there be a minimum income strategy paid from public budgets or a public system of social insurance, offering benefits above the minimum for subsistence to those who have earned their living for some time? Wherever a right to subsistence is acknowledged – and this is an essential feature of welfare states – systems of some kind are established to redistribute a substantial part of the national product to those who cannot participate in production for the market. Policies in the context of redistribution therefore form the second realm of welfare state activities.[19]

An individual's life chances do not depend on financial resources alone but also on rights, abilities and opportunities (see chapter 6). As the scope of welfare policies began to go beyond industrial workers, defining the whole population as potential objects of political responsibility, the hitherto neglected dimensions of abilities and opportunities gained more attention. The influence of the social sciences has increased awareness that personal social services such as school meals, health services, education, housing and counselling are public-benefit goods, meaning that their provision has side effects (beyond the subjective welfare of the recipients) that are beneficial for third parties. In other words, they produce positive or hinder negative external effects. This is particularly evident in the case of natural and social reproduction. As humans are mortal, every commonwealth needs younger generations to succeed to its positions. Since birth control has become almost normal in modern societies, individual reproduction is no longer assured. Meanwhile, in many countries the number of children has become a main cause of household poverty. Thus the dangers facing family welfare production have come into political focus, together with a growing public interest in the rising generations' qualifications (Kaufmann 1990, 2005; Esping-Andersen 2002), and the importance of regenerating human resources also becomes recognized from an economic perspective. Thus a third realm of welfare-state activities has gained strength in recent decades, namely, social policies in the realm of the reproduction and regeneration of human resources.[20]

The manifold organizations that implement social policies do not form a coherent system from a structural point of view. Though some policies in some countries have developed into networks of organizations exhibiting characteristics of order in the sense of a coherent system (e.g. social security, or a national health system), the provision of publicly regulated welfare follows different patterns not only between but also within nations. The totality of social services does not form a coherent system, but a unifying factor seems to exist and is commonly expressed by the term 'welfare state' or, from the analytical perspective presented above, welfare sector. From a structural perspective this welfare sector is often heterogeneous or 'clefted' (Berner 2009: 47). From a management perspective it is coordinated by various institutional forms such as hierarchies, markets, solidarity, professions and corporatism (Kaufmann 1991c: 228). What, then, constitutes the unity of the welfare sector?

It seems difficult to link the welfare sector with the sociological perspective of functional differentiation. It does not serve a particular societal function, and its output is multifunctional and relates to both individuals and social systems. The precursors of public welfare institutions originated in various parts of society: social insurance, for instance, followed from private insurance originating in the economy as well as in friendly societies and workers' associations, while health services originated in the realms of religion and the military. Most social policies did not start from scratch but instead generalized existing solutions to social problems that had previously been tested on a smaller scale (de Swaan 1988). As they evolved into publicly regulated systems, they seldom formed a part of the national administration, but rather of local government (as in Great Britain and Scandinavia), or existed as special agencies (as in France, Switzerland and Germany). Often the services are not administered by public officials but by representatives of various interests in the civil society, such as worker and employer unions, moral entrepreneurs or religious organizations. As we have already seen, the difference between public and private is blurred within the welfare sector (Kaufmann 1986).

What, then, accounts for the unity of the welfare sector? It is the goal of individual welfare that legitimizes the existence of the welfare sector and forms bonds between the institutions in it. What therefore specifically distinguishes the social services is the direct relationship of their output to individuals' life situations and fields of action. They provide individuals with rights, resources, opportunities and competences (see chapter 6). Though they may also serve many other interests, and though many side effects may not relate to individual welfare, there is no social policy without concern for individual welfare. As we have seen, functional differentiation leads to the loss of comprehensive social ties and to individualization, and it is in reaction to these trends that the search for social rights and inclusion has been articulated. The inherent logic of the welfare state assumes that furthering individual welfare also means furthering collective welfare. This assumption may of course be questionable in terms of particular measures and their impact, but on closer inspection the individual welfare of particular groups will not be pursued in democratic political struggles if no case can be made for accompanying collective utility.

The emergence of the welfare aspects of the modern state is generally seen as a late feature of political development (Marshall 1950; Rokkan 1975). As writers such as Flora et al. (1983) show, Rokkan's approach is a valuable heuristic aid but it cannot account for the multiplicity of historical steps of state formation in the various European countries. Absolutist and mercantile states such as France or Prussia in the eighteenth century already showed considerable concern for the welfare of their subjects. This concern was based on the assumption that the political and economic power of these political societies depended upon the health and education of their populations (see Dorwart 1971). This argument gains new importance with the concern for human resources and the concept of an 'enabling state' (Gilbert and Gilbert 1989). The concept of human capital or human resources is now used to explain such relationships (see chapter 12).

Beyond Redistribution: Integrating Societies

The classic focus on the welfare state adopts a redistributive perspective. Both neo-liberal (or, in U.S. terminology, conservative) critics of and social-democratic believers in the Keynesian welfare state support this perspective. It is, however, too narrow.

From the perspective of redistribution, the interventions of the welfare state look like a zero-sum game: what is given to some must be taken from others. Such a perspective restricts itself to a short-sighted focus that fails to take account of the impact and consequences of sociopolitical interventions. It is naturally difficult if not impossible to predict and evaluate the indirect consequences of particular interventions precisely. Every intervention is only one factor within a complex web of forces shaping the situations of individual lives and social changes, and whoever receives some benefits in cash or kind has the power to respond and to use them as he or she wishes and not according to the intentions of politicians and administrators. But it is the task of the social sciences to analyse empirically the processes of delivery and to evaluate the outcomes of sociopolitical interventions in order to improve our generalized knowledge about the impact of particular policies. The social sciences also have a theoretical task: to overcome the political actors' narrow views on redistribution by opening a broader perspective on the impact and consequences of welfare politics and policies. Welfare policies are not a zero-sum game: they can increase both self-reliance and dependence on state intervention; individual welfare for some may go along with collective welfare for all.

From a private property perspective, all public expenditure seems only to be burdensome. The state extracts income for its own purposes by means of taxes and contributions, thus depriving those who had gained income from work and from capital. But this is only the viewpoint of one of society's subsystems, the economic.[21] The same can be said of the legal perspective, as expressed in the saying *fiat justitia et pereat mundus*.[22] Further, the disciplinary perspectives of the different social sciences – e.g. economics, law, political science – follow the logics of their respective fields of communication and their one-sidedness, and they contribute to shaping this one-sidedness. It is the duty of a theory of society to reflect this variety of different communication systems and their consequences for the people who try to lead their lives subject to conflicting demands.

Modern societies consist of several partial systems of communication, each of them with a high degree of autonomy, shaping its own values and motivating organizations as well as individuals to behave or act according to their specific reasons or logics. Thus the logic of the economy is to increase one's stake in the markets, the logic of politics is to increase power, the logic of law is to force social behaviour to conform to the rule of law, the logic of science is to increase reliable knowledge, the logic of a family is to increase solidarity among those related to it, and so on. The logic of each of these systems is incompatible with the logic of others, and there is no hierarchy among them. They have to coexist in ambiguous and often conflicting relationships, and both individual and organized actors have to find ways of accommodating and reconciling the claims of the different logics in their actions. They are mutually dependent on each other even though no general rule coordinates their claims, except that modern constitutions have to resolve their irreconcilable differences through fundamental liberties (Luhmann 1965).

How then can the coherence of a modern commonwealth be conceptualized? Four connective bonds deserve to be noted (Kaufmann 1997c):

1. *Normative integration.* This is the classic answer in Western culture, ever since the faith of the Israelites in their God. Though secularization has weakened the religious roots of common values and morality, and pluralism is mushrooming, the belief in everyone's human dignity and the concomitant ethos of human rights are increasingly influential in international relations under the pressure towards globalization (see chapter 4).
2. *Interdependence of functional systems.* Though the specialized systems of communication diverge in their aims and legitimation, their interaction is unavoidable and is secured through organizational decisions that have to respect the rationalities of diverse systems.[23] Thus for instance the economy needs a reliable legal system and a policy of stable money in order to flourish, while government need a flourishing economy in order to finance its activities.
3. *Democratically constituted legal order.* This aspect is central for political communities that are themselves constituted by legal procedures and operate through legislation. As laws are passed subject to public control they have not only a functional but also a moral sense, which contributes to the identity of a commonwealth (Habermas 1992).
4. *Mutual respect for differences.* As modern societies are pluralistic in their value orientations and heterogeneous in their life contexts, human solidarity cannot be based on similarity alone. The respect for individual self-determination within the limits of law is therefore essential for peaceful coexistence.

Welfare policies in democratic welfare states are an expression of these basic requirements for political integration: they are founded on the acknowledgment of human rights, they result from democratic decisions, they respect – at least in principle – differences of values and life orientations among the population under the rule of law, and they subdue the stresses and conflicts that result from the tensions between the specialized systems of communication and the diverse claims of individuals.

Individual and Collective Utilities

The aim of this introductory chapter is to give an account of the ideas on which the understanding of the welfare state in this volume is based. The elements of theory elaborated in the chapters to come are more specific, with the exception of chapter 10, which is a complement to this introduction. The perspective put forward is a theory not only *of* but also *for* the welfare state, that is to say, I aim at a theory that not only generalizes empirically on the variety of national developments but also does so with a normative interest in its explanatory success. This corresponds to theories of market economy or democracy that are neither purely descriptive nor value-free. I hope to follow Max Weber, however, in avoiding the evaluation of different ideological positions on the welfare state or their semantics. The values implied here refer more to their *Kulturbedeutung* (cultural significance) in Weber's sense. It is absolutely clear that the understanding of modernization is of paramount cultural significance, and the central argument in this chapter runs that the institutional outcome of a society's 'legal and therefore formal and explicit responsibility for the basic well-being of all of its members' (Girvetz 1968: 512) has been and still is a constitutive factor in the success of European modernization. This perspective is more general than current political arguments for or against specific interpretations of the welfare state and leaves them open. And it places on the agenda the question to what extent alternative modes of modernization may be sustainable.

What, then, are the leading welfare policies and their functions with respect to modernization?[24]

1. Though capitalist markets had been evolving since the Middle Ages they remained essentially markets for trade that did not directly affect the processes of production. Markets themselves remained constrained by custom and political rule. The liberalization of labour and the marketization of land were the consequences of political decisions for shaping mobility. Adam Smith's battle against the Settlement Laws and his arguments for free trade throughout the British Empire were based on the idea that freeing the pursuit

of individual interest was also in the interest of the monarch, and from a democratic perspective it was in the collective interest. The most obvious impact of his doctrine was in Prussia, where economic liberalization was imposed directly from the top by political order. The resulting long-term growth of European industrial economies confirmed the liberal arguments. This progress produces negative externalities, which often provoke resistance to change. By coping with the risks of liberalization, social policies contribute to the acceptance of social change.

2. Unlike early capitalism in the United States and now in many 'underdeveloped' countries, capitalism in Europe was never unregulated politically. In addition to the rules for fair trade, laws were passed in the UK from an early stage, protecting the establishment of trade unions but also regulating their actions (1824/25) and providing for factory inspection (1833). Things evolved in a variety of ways in different countries, Britain remaining the most liberal among them – and its trade unions the most prepared to struggle. Beginning with the September Agreement in Denmark (1899), agreements between representatives of employers and trade unions opened the way to a balance between corporatistic and *étatistic* labour regulation. The stabilization of industrial labour and the establishment of peaceful industrial relations thereafter were fundamental to the success of a free economy.[25] Moreover, advances in labour protection often proved to increase labour productivity, so that instead of being a burden they acquired not only a social but also an economic value. As several comparative studies show, the extension of welfare provisions (or social budgets) is neither related to long-term reduction in economic growth nor does it hinder economic flexibility, which depend more on particular combinations of factors and the intelligence of governments (Pfaller, Gough and Therborn 1991; Scharpf and Schmidt 2000).

3. The acknowledgement of political responsibility for the welfare of citizens and the ensuing social policies were constitutive of the compatibility of capitalism and democracy in Europe.[26] In the early phases of industrial capitalism there was a consensus among the elites that workers should not be given the right to vote, and their fears of riots (if not revolutions) were not unfounded. Bismarck was right in assuming that social reform would contribute to reconciling industrial workers with the German Reich, though he was not successful in alienating them from socialism. Social Democrats, however, did not opt for revolution but for 'revisionism', thus integrating the working class into the political nation. It is also a wide-

spread observation that major social reforms succeeded only after political crises. Class conflict became tamed by social policies.

4. At first, social policies were reactions to actual grievances, but their accumulation followed characteristic national patterns. Early solutions set the path on which social reforms then progressed. Despite such national differences, the issues of concern were rather similar because they targeted typical problems individuals experience in industrializing and urbanizing settings: employment, protection against such risks as those of industrial work, health, housing, income maintenance, education and mobility. Whereas efforts by individuals remained contingent on their particular opportunities and were often without clear direction, social policies brought standardized and, in principle, comprehensive solutions. Social policies became a functional equivalent to former traditional patterns of life, giving a sense of direction while still remaining more anonymous and leaving more openings for individual choices. Legislation often refers to the chronological age of those concerned: age limits, for example, define school entry, working age, adulthood and the age of retirement. Thus the 'normal biography' is framed by public laws (Kohli 1985; Mayer and Müller 1989), and typical risks become covered by social security. Insofar as social policies create trust they also contribute to the emotional security of the citizens (see chapter 5). Together they frame the way to individualization and combat anomie if not deviant behaviour.

5. While class conflict has lost its challenge in most European countries, new challenges have emerged: globalization and demographic decline. Globalization intensifies international competition, not only for business but also for political communities such as the European Union, nations or even subnational political bodies (see chapter 13). The extension of welfare policies seems to be positively linked to the openness of a national economy (Rieger and Leibfried 2003). Thus governments become responsible for the position of their commonwealth in relation to others, which requires the promotion of synergies among economic and social policies.

6. Demographic ageing and decline threaten precisely that synergy, as does unemployment, which particularly affects unskilled workers. Thus the quantity and quality of human resources is becoming a new central focus for welfare policies of immediate economic relevance (see chapter 12). These problems cannot be solved by market mechanisms or anonymous businesses. They refer to 'people processing' and its institutions, the family, education and in particular the personal services.

Seen from the theory of functional differentiation, the emergence of a welfare state helps to stabilize the specialized structures by coping with their indifference to side effects, especially at the level of individual life situations. Social policies can be differentiated analytically from other fields of policymaking by reference to individual life situations. However, individual problems and expected individual utility alone are by no means sufficient to provoke political interest, let alone policies. Collective action can be motivated only by collective utilities. It is a task for social science in the field of social policies to explore and to establish links between individual and collective utilities.

This task has become more complicated in the context of what is sometimes called the 'crisis of the welfare state'. Indeed, the multiplication of sociopolitical interventions and the inherent cost dynamics of many social policies produce unanticipated second-order effects, such as inefficiencies due to overlapping interventions, the opacity of regulations or excess costs of social budgets. In coping with such challenges it is misleading to refer to individual welfare and the solution of social problems. These are problems at the level of public organization and fiscal politics, which refer only indirectly to individual welfare. Many of these interventions, such as cuts in social budgets, may look rather unsocial from the viewpoint of those affected. Distinguishing between first-order and second-order social policies may help to differentiate the problems (see chapter 7).

To sum up: from a sociological perspective, social or welfare policies first emerged as responses to the loss of the old securities of feudal order during the structural transformation of society that we call modernization. The inherent logic of the capitalist mode of production is reckless and inconsiderate to the life situations of those who are compelled to work under its conditions. The welfare state is the political project to construct a collective institutional framework protecting and furthering the individual welfare of all who belong to a certain commonwealth. Though political legislation and public regulation are essential elements of the idea of the welfare state, public administration of the services is not. The institutional framework remains open to be complemented by other forms of welfare production.

Overview

This book is organized in four parts. The first part focuses on ideas that have been seminal for the present understanding of the welfare state. The second considers social politics and policies from the theoretical perspective of intervention and discusses some of the implications. In historical terms this kind of theory is concerned with developments before the Second World War. The third part then considers the welfare state as the cumulative outcome of social policies and as a programme for political and social integration, as it emerged after the Second World War. The final part is concerned with perspectives for the future. The emphasis throughout the book is on ideas and theoretical concepts, not on institutional developments. I focus on the cultural – not the political, administrative or economic – side of welfare policies, and on the intellectual instruments for understanding what is going on in the historical process of institution building for the production of welfare in contemporary societies..

The first part of this book gives an account of the seminal ideas forming the intellectual foundations for understanding the modern welfare state. Of course, the issue of public welfare (*salus publica*) was already an aspect of political thought in premodern polities. But it is sensible to begin our inquiry with authors who reacted to the liberal theory of free markets as first formulated by Adam Smith. Although Smith considered political economy 'as a branch of the science of a statesman or legislator' (Smith 1776: *Book IV*, Introduction), the result of his teaching was the legitimation of the functional autonomy of the economic subsystem, in the sense described above. The unanticipated consequences of this autonomy formed the material that critics seized on, Sismondi (1773–1846) being the first among them. Chapter 1 sets out his arguments, which focus on the problem of the distribution of wealth and some external effects of the economic system. Karl Marx studied Sismondi very thoroughly but did not follow his reformist direction, and therefore Marx should not be included in a chapter on the origins of social reformism. A second early critic of Smith was the less well-known German Friedrich List (1789–1846). His critique of Smith is more fundamental, since he focused on the preconditions that make a market economy productive. His 'theory of productive forces' included the factor of human capital, which is of crucial importance for current approaches to the merits of the welfare state. The third critic, best known to an Anglo-Saxon audience, is John Stuart Mill (1806–73). I focus on one aspect of his multifaceted work, namely, the issue of political intervention, which is indispensable to all debates on social policy. These three authors naturally formulated their ideas before anyone was thinking about social policy, let alone the welfare state, but their ideas remain seminal for its theoretical understanding.

Chapter 2 focuses on the intellectual foundations of the German welfare state. The original thinker was Hegel, and his *Philosophy of Law* (or *of Right*, 1821) can be regarded as the first theory of a functionally differentiated society. It forms the starting point for this theoretical reconstruction of the welfare state. The original thinker on the German *Sozialstaat* (social state) was his follower Lorenz von Stein, whose ideas are presented in more detail. Finally, this chapter gives an account of the early history of the term *Socialpolitik* before the foundation of the Verein für Socialpolitik (1873). This early history of sociopolitical thinking has been forgotten even in the collective memory of German social policy. Some of the sources are discussed here for the first time.

The introduction of comprehensive social insurance for industrial workers in Germany (1881–89) is commonly attributed to anti-revolutionary conservatism. In other countries the sociopolitical movement is held to have been led by Social Democrats or similar parties. Before the substantial study by Kersbergen (1995), the influence of Christian movements was seldom mentioned. Chapter 3, 'Christian Influences on Social Reform', based on Kaufmann (1983) and first published in 1988, was thus a pioneering study of a subject that has received increased attention in recent years (Kersbergen and Manow 2009; Manow 2009). The unanimity of support for ensuring everyone a decent life, which characterizes the moral foundations of the European welfare state, is not explicable without reference to the Christian tradition.

From the perspective of this book, chapter 4, 'Welfare Internationalism before the Welfare State: The Emergence of Social Rights', is of central significance. Its main message is that the conventionally national perspective on welfare states is too narrow, even if it includes comparisons with several countries. A genuinely international or, rather, supranational movement and inspiration surrounded the cradle of the welfare state. The idea of economic, social and cultural rights (in addition to civil and political rights) took shape in the context of the foundation of the United Nations. Interestingly, this international context is almost absent from the writings of T.H. Marshall, who first introduced the issue to the theoretical debate about the welfare state, and it was rarely mentioned until recently by, in particular, Deacon (1997) and later by Leisering (2007a). Whereas specialists have elucidated the genesis of the Universal Declaration of Human Rights and its aftermath, the origins of the idea of social rights are, as far as I know, explored here for the first time.

Parts I and II of this book are bridged by chapter 5: 'Social Security: The Leading Idea and its Problems'. Whereas 'social security' operates in article 22 of the Universal Declaration of Human Rights as a kind of umbrella word, in 1934 it became the name for the social reforms President Roosevelt planned to introduce in the context of his 'New Deal'. This chapter analyses the emergence of the collective aim of security and its inherent values and relates it to the institutional ambivalences of social security.

From an analytical point of view the issues of social policies reflect patterns of intervention by the state in what is conventionally called civil society. This perspective presupposes the distinction between 'state' and 'society' that is very prominent in the German tradition and has also been recently adopted by Anglo-Saxon authors. It is by no means obvious that political ambitions to change social conditions will be successful, for social policies always interfere with social structures and particular interests. Chapter 6 takes the idea of intervention seriously and explores its implications for the success of social policies. This success is implemented in four dimensions of social policy effects: rights, economic resources, contextual opportunities and acquired abilities. The analytical framework developed in this chapter claims to consider social policies from the perspective of goal setting and evaluation.

It is conventional wisdom that sociopolitical interventions aim to solve social problems, and social problems concern individuals in their private or professional life situations. The origins of social policies reveal the identification of particular social problems: accidents at work, the inability to earn one's living, children in poverty and so on. With the intensification and accumulation of political interventions the original conceptual links between the definition of a problem and the means for its solution become more and more blurred. Interventions do not interact only with social conditions but also with other interventions. The most obvious interface concerns the budgets for specific measures. Insofar as their aggregate outgoings exceed some political threshold, so competition and coordination, trade-offs and cutbacks move to the centre of social politics. The interests of those affected become marginal to these debates, whereas the interests of stakeholders – bureaucrats, professionals and other members of one policy community or another – drive the political agenda. Chapter 7 therefore introduces the distinction between first- and second-order social policies, which may help to explain why social politics and the subsequent policies sometimes appear to be so 'unsocial'.

Parts III and IV of the book present some of the central ideas of my theory of the welfare state in greater depth. The basic idea of the welfare state is that political authority defines itself as responsible for basic aspects of the well-being of the members of its political community. Chapter 8 then analyses the problematic of this project by developing the concept of welfare production in its relationship to politics. The concept of 'welfare', examined here in the context of political and economic theory, reveals that both overlook non-monetary forms of welfare production, especially those within households and the family. A discussion of different concepts of welfare show that public discourses of welfare are not necessarily dependent on subjective definitions of well-being but may refer to culturally agreed elements of a 'good life'. The quality of social policies must be discussed from the perspective of furthering synergies between individual and collective benefits. From the perspective of a normative theory of the welfare state, issues of social policy need to be substantiated at the level of individual, intermediate and national welfare. This chapter may be my most original contribution to a theory of the welfare state.

The development of welfare states since the Second World War has been a national affair. What, then, is the influence of European integration? In asking this question Chapter 9 first summarizes a comparative historical study of the path of modernization in relation to welfare policies in the United States, the Soviet Union, Great Britain, Sweden, France and Germany. It gives reasons for excluding the U.S. and Soviet Union from the concept of the welfare state and thus explains it more precisely, revealing the high degree of its internal variety. This may be read as a historical complement to the more abstract perspective of this introduction. As to the impact of European integration, the outcome is that convergence still respects national traditions, but harmonization takes place through rulings by the European Court of Justice as well as by pragmatic coordination at the administrative level.

Chapter 10 outlines my theoretical perspective on the welfare state in context and is to be read as complementary to this introduction. It postulates the realization of fundamental social rights as the leading normative issue, and the preservation and reproduction of human assets as the basic functional issue for the welfare state. A political system may be said to be a welfare state if it is legitimized to use ongoing legal and organizational interventions to react to the undesired consequences of unfettered competition within the economic system and to exclusion from essential services. Diagnoses of a 'crisis of the welfare state' are discussed and reinterpreted, leading to the last part of this book.

Part IV concerns perspectives on issues surrounding the much-debated future of the welfare state. Chapter 11 starts by summarizing the successes of the welfare state in terms of economic and political benefits as well as its cultural and social significance. It goes on to develop the idea that some of the institutions of existing welfare states are losing their former power to solve problems and argues that they are ageing and why this is so. The renaissance of moral argument and demands for 'social justice' are symptoms of this deficiency.

Chapter 12 discusses a central problem for the future of the welfare state, namely demographic ageing and the reduction of the labour force, in terms of the concept of 'human assets'. This is a promising concept for linking individual and collective utility in the theory and practice of the welfare state. It reintroduces the anthropological perspective into the theory of society and thus paves the way for linking it to a theory of the welfare state.

Chapter 13 discusses the challenge of globalization, especially from the perspective of competitive pressures on national solidarities and political power to redistribute. It clarifies the notion of solidarity and its relationship to redistribution and discusses the impact of globalization on the realms of action of nation states, as well as the ambivalent function of the EU in this context. The welfare state's redistributive power loses its voluntary character and becomes dependent on the art of governance and political support for policies that give force to the attractions of a place or nation for economic investment. The synergy of economic and social policies moves into the centre of future welfare policies.

Finally, chapter 14 again takes up a historical perspective. It focuses on theories of the state and distinguishes four stages in discourse about the state as the self-description of the political system: (1) police state, (2) constitutional or legal state, (3) welfare state, (4) regulatory state. The book itself contributes to transcending the classical idea of the welfare state and puts forward concepts and arguments for a more all-embracing understanding of issues around what is conventionally called the welfare state. These converge with the perspective of a system regulatory state.

Notes

1. The development of the German theory of the state as an example of the continental perspective is presented in more detail in chapter 14.

2. In Germany, a distinguished member of the Verein für Sozialpolitik, Adolph Wagner (1876: 305), had already used the term Cultur- und Wohlfahrtsstaat to denote the extension of the activities of the state into the fields of culture and welfare, but it was seldom used in German political rhetoric; when it was, it was only in a somewhat pejorative sense to denote the Scandinavian model or more generally the danger of political and fiscal overload stemming from welfare politics. The positive German equivalent is Sozialstaat (social state), or from a more liberal perspective, Soziale Marktwirtschaft (social market economy). These ideas emerged only after 1945 (Kaufmann 2003b: 125ff.)

3. Veit-Wilson (2000) gives an extensive account of British argument over the concept of the 'welfare state' and proposes '"inclusion of the poor" as the key discriminator between welfare and unwelfare states'. This discriminator then is operationalized as a policy of 'minimum real income for all' (Veit-Wilson 2000: 12, 13). This conforms broadly with Girvetz's definition given above. For present purposes a strict definition seems unhelpful, since the goals of welfare states may go beyond anti-poverty policies, though the latter are essential for the distinction.

4. Seminal studies include Briggs (1961); Rimlinger (1971); Heclo (1974); de Laubier (1978a); Flora and Heidenheimer (1981); Alber (1982); Kohl (1985); Wilensky

(1985): Ashford (1986); Hepple (1986); de Swaan (1988); Ritter (1989); Baldwin (1990); Esping-Andersen (1990); and Zacher (1991).

5. In the German juridical interpretation of the constitutional term 'social' (in the sense of 'social state', see articles 20.I and 28.I of the German Constitution), the social is interpreted as *Staatsziel*, the aims of the state (Zacher 2004).

6. This then is the realm of social politics. Comparative research since the seminal work of Esping-Andersen (1990) has focused on the description and explanation of 'welfare state regimes', that is, on similarities and differences among national welfare sectors. I doubt that this line of thought will lead to fruitful generalization about welfare state issues. First, for methodological reasons, the number of cases is too small compared to the number of descriptive variables to be taken into account. Second, because the explanatory variables (e.g. class structure, political system, political power, religion and culture, etc.) are intrinsically complex, most explanatory approaches focus on one factor alone, in order to preserve the illusion of the explanatory power of the regime approach. The latest and more ambitious attempt by Kersbergen and Manow (2009) starts from the regime approach, but their study of the complex interaction between religion, class structure and party regime leads them to single-country studies, which exhibit greater explanatory power. Before the EU exerted pressure toward unification, the national development of welfare states in Europe remained highly idiosyncratic, in that development was driven by the interaction of national factors. For a comparative approach based on this premise see Kaufmann 2003c.

7. Therborn (1995: 3ff.) puts forward arguments, with which I agree, explaining why modernity and modernization are preferable terms for a theoretical approach to these transformations.

8. That modernization is related to growing specialization – from professions to structured macrosystems of communication – is now widely acknowledged in sociology. But the question Durkheim first asked in the preface to the second edition of his *Division of Labour in Society* (1960), namely, how growing heterogeneity becomes integrated into a functioning whole, in other words how a modern society is possible, remains a matter for debate in sociology. For Luhmann the precarious possibility of society constitutes sociology (1981c: 195). Talcott Parsons (e.g. 1971) was the first to introduce the subject into Anglo-Saxon sociology. It is impossible to summarize these discussions here; I refer only to my own interpretation (e.g. Kaufmann 1991a; 1997b; 2002a) and focus on the contribution of welfare state developments to the success of modernization. For the latter see also chapter 11.

9. From my perspective the best account of the Enlightenment's intellectual breakthrough and its conditions is given by Koselleck (1973).

10. See Luhmann (1997: chapter 4). For an overview and perceptive critique of Luhmann's theory of functional differentiation see Schwinn (1995).

11. The appropriation of formerly public realms through private interests sets in motion a process that is in fact similar to that of the privatization of the commons on the eve of industrialization (Rifkin 2000). Again, people become excluded or only selectively included by the extension of the private realm. This is the basic challenge to which the welfare state has to find solutions.

12. This is self-evident for segmentary societies such as clans or isolated communities. But even in rank-ordered societies, everyone knows where he or she belongs – or does not belong. Inclusion may be differentiated, however, according to one's rank. Vagrants are excluded on all dimensions so no reciprocity is expected on either side (Luhmann 1997: 622ff.).

13. Giddens (1990: 21) emphasizes the spatial aspect of functional structuring as disembedding. Thus disembedded individuals can participate in the benefits of the subsystems wherever they are. They no longer belong structurally only to one place and one group.

14. This circumstance was first noted by Simmel (1890). For more details see Kaufmann (1973: 169ff., 221ff.)

15. This aspect is highlighted by the work of Amartya Sen, who transcends the notion of utility in that of advantage and capability (Sen 1982; 1985).

16. Whereas the doctrine of human rights declares everyone is a bearer of rights, in almost every political community such universalism is restricted to those with a legal status, with the exception of the right to bare existence. This means that in practice 'inclusion' is a very diffuse concept subject to many particularly diverse interpretations (Leisering 2004a; Kaufmann 2009).

17. This argument overlooks ordinary vagrancy in premodern times. Vagrancy eventually facilitated free labour.

18. A comparative account of the making of labour law in Europe up to 1945 is given by Hepple (1986).

19. For an international overview see Atkinson (1989).

20. This field lacks comparative research (Alber 1995). More on human resources is offered in chapter 12.

21. From the economic perspective, the impact of social policies must be considered as the positive or negative external effects measured in cash terms. It is obvious that this does not address the essence of social policies that concern individuals' life situations and their consequences.

22. 'Let there be justice, though the world perish.'

23. This chiefly happens through internal differentiation within an organization. For example, governments have distinct ministries for the economy, science, law, education, etc., but government as a whole takes the final decisions under the pressure of political expediency. Business organizations also have their own specialized sections, e.g. for law and research.

24. Here I owe substantial inspiration to Huf (1998).

25. This argument can be criticized by pointing to the much less regulated industrial relations in the U.S., which did not hinder industrialization. The overall conditions there were so different, however, that it seems justified to exclude the U.S. from the range of welfare states and to ascribe them to a proper mode of modernization (see Kaufmann 2003c: 82ff. and chapter 9).

26. Huf 1998: 174. Again the U.S. differed, because democracy preceded capitalism.

Part I

Intellectual Foundations

Chapter 1

PIONEERS OF SOCIAL REFORMISM
Sismondi, List, Mill

Is There a Classical Way of Thinking about the Welfare State?

The best way to ascertain the nature of a cultural tradition is to reconstruct its history. That reveals the value of talking about 'classical authors', those who succinctly articulated the ideas that over time became accepted as leading and influencing a subject. The discussion of classical authors necessarily involves a discourse of historical reconstruction. Only later generations can decide the classical status of texts, which they do according to the perspectives of their own time and not those of the authors. And because the perspectives of those later generations change over time, the perceived value of the classical authors may swing widely.

Like the proverbial owl of Minerva, which spreads its wings only with the falling of the dusk, so systematic reflection on the social or welfare state first emerged in the context of diagnoses of its crisis. The discourse of the crisis of the welfare state arose in neo-Marxist circles at the beginning of the 1970s, but soon widened out after the collapse of the Bretton Woods agreement on exchange rates and the first oil crisis. Since the collapse of the Soviet system, the European model of the social welfare state has lost its role as midpoint between capitalism and socialism, and now has to defend itself against attack by both U.S.-inspired market approaches and the discourse of globalization, which predicts the inescapable demise of the European welfare state. The increasingly unbalanced demographic structure of many European states, especially Germany, adds further plausibility to the crisis scenario.

But what, besides exhausted social budgets, does it mean to talk about the social or welfare state? Jürgen Kaube recently diagnosed a 'deficit in reflection on the welfare state' despite some three decades of international welfare state research. What is lacking, he claimed, is

> a unitary prior or associated ideology something like the idea of contractual natural law or the doctrine of the dictatorship of the proletariat.... [Additionally, it lacks] any theoretical formulations of 'justice', 'solidarity' or 'welfare' equivalent to those of 'freedom' in the theory of natural law, or of 'equality' in democratic theory. (Kaube 2003: 44)

Incremental and pragmatic *reformism*, to which the development of the welfare state can above all be traced, seems to be less clearly delineated and permeated by ideology in comparison with the dominant arguments between the great streams of nineteenth-century ideas – liberalism, conservatism and socialism. Its idealistic foundations in Anglo-Saxon utilitarianism, in Christian Catholic and Lutheran (particularly pietistic) values, and not least in social-democratic reformism, remain heterogeneous and ideologically controversial. Even if there are solid grounds for talking about an international development of the welfare state after the Second World War, this was nationally path-dependent, each country identifying its individual 'social problems' and institutional responses based on assumptions reaching far back into its own unique history (Kaufmann 2003c). It is therefore hardly surprising that there is no internationally recognized 'ideology of the welfare state', even if the doctrine of fundamental social rights is at least a step in this direction that may become significant as a consequence of globalization (see chapter 4).

Kaube's observation that there is no coherent body of legitimating ideas and concepts for the welfare state has to be taken seriously. Nevertheless, I want to identify potential classic welfare state thinkers, those whose ideas and concepts should be taken into account in any current theory of the welfare state. To be brief, I mean authors who, in the course of the characteristic nineteenth-century dispute between liberalism and socialism (confidence in the market or in the state), sought a third way, giving credence to the advantages and necessity of both guiding principles, and who (at least implicitly) took account of the core issues of modernization theory, the differentiation and complementarity of society's functional systems. The history of ideas about national economy generally includes them under the concept of *interventionism*, which is doubtless an important aspect.[1] But this is misplaced, not only from a sociological perspective but also in the sense of the specificity of phenomena both in the market economy and in political events seen in their total social context. In what follows, the representatives of various disciplines will be referred to in the light of these perspectives.

German Authors

In terms of historical influence, Lorenz von Stein is fundamental, and in this connection his inspiration, Hegel, must not be overlooked (see chapter 2). The development of the welfare state had its origins in dealing with the consequences of liberalization and industrialization, in particular the problems of functional differentiation.[2] Modern thought on differentiation reaches back to Hegel. Stein was the first to seek out the agency of the 'state' and of 'civil society' disrupted by class conflict, although he and the other German social policy thinkers were similarly inattentive to the third factor of Hegelian differentiation, namely the family. Nevertheless, Lorenz von Stein was the founder of a theoretical perspective on society that nowadays seems indispensable for a theory of the welfare state.

As the second German classical welfare state thinker I want to propose the 'state socialist' Adolph Wagner (see Kaufmann 2003b: 49ff., 65ff.). Wagner's significance lies not only in his 'Speech on the Social Question' (1871), which led to the establishment of the Verein für Socialpolitik (Association for Social Policy), but chiefly in his exposition of the scientific foundations of public finance. Wagner systematically laid out the 'toolkit' of what von Stein had called 'the working state', paying particular and constant attention to its significance both for the fiscal economy and for social policy. To Wagner, social policy meant influencing the distributive conditions of the social economy in the interests of the disadvantaged classes. Wagner's science of public finance continues to be seminal for such basic ideas of the social state as progressive income tax and the significance of publicly funded services.

The social democratic jurist Hugo Sinzheimer has almost been excluded from social policy discourse (see Kaufmann 2003b: 87ff.). He did not move in social policy circles, and although it is true that at the time some connections were being made between social law and welfare state development (though hardly with labour law), little support can be expected from jurisprudence. Sinzheimer's groundbreaking contribution consisted in overcoming the individualistic interpretation of the labour contract as envisaged by Roman law. Following Karl Marx, he described the labour contract as a 'legalised power relationship', and in line with German legal traditions he developed the legal model of the 'corporate agreement on labour standards' as it has become operative in German laws on labour relations and wage agreements. Sinzheimer was clear about law's social consequences and therefore promoted a 'legislative jurisprudence', or in today's terminology, a theory of legislation. If with hindsight we can say that Wagner justified the state's socially formative actions in terms of fiscal theory, Sinzheimer did so on the basis of legal theory.

In recent decades increasing attention has been paid to Eduard Heimann (see Kaufmann 2003b: 113ff.). Apparently unaware of Lorenz von Stein, Heimann published *Soziale Theorie des Kapitalismus* (*The Social Theory of Capitalism*), which again raised the problem of social theory and placed the dynamic of capitalism in the context of social and intellectual history. Heimann saw social policy as 'the institutional sediment of the social idea in capitalism' (Heimann 1929: 167). He described the 'social idea' as the middle and working classes' common basic values, drawn from Christianity and the Enlightenment. We see here a clear perception of the challenge of capitalism as moulding society and its productive reconfiguration through social policy, though by contrast Heimann lacks a clear concept of the state. In later publications stretching into the 1960s, he examined the connections between cultural and economic development. He was among the first to show explicitly how the class problem would be superseded by the new challenges of capitalism, particularly through the depersonalizing effects of techno-economic rationalism and by environmental hazards.

Few social scientists in Germany after the Second World War interpreted the relations between state and society in the light of the widespread international development of the welfare state that was then taking place. However, Hans Achinger deserves mention, since among other things notably contributed to the integration of institutional welfare and social policy, thereby helping to overcoming the social policy fixation on problems of class and 'the workers question'. The thrust of his argument is clear from the title of his book, *Sozialpolitk als Gesellschaftspolitik – von der Arbeiterfrage zum Wohlfahrtsstaat* (*Social Policy as Societal Politics: From the Labour Question to the Welfare State*) (1958). His writings also sensitized readers to the undesirable side effects of the growing institutionalization of social policy, which were subsequently debated at length under the headings of 'juridification' and 'bureaucratization'. Finally, Achinger (1966) contributed significantly to a *sociological* engagement with social policy, and outlined important items for a research agenda.

This account of German authors to be assigned to the history of social policy is incomplete without a reference to Friedrich List, the campaigner for the German Tariff Union. List's theoretical work was in part only rediscovered decades after his death and, perhaps for that reason, has led a shadowy existence in the histories of the various social sciences – unjustly, as will be shown below.

Foreign Authors

Nominations to the list of classical writers on welfare state thought must, of course, also include names from abroad, although until the end of the Weimar Republic the German tradition was at the international forefront of social policy theory. Without doubt this list must include the names of the two Swedish economists Alva and Gunnar Myrdal and the British sociologist, Thomas H. Marshall. The Myrdals were among the first to point to the relationship between demographic trends and social policy, and supported a connection between gender politics and family policy (Myrdal and Myrdal 1934; A. Myrdal 1945). Furthermore, Gunnar Myrdal directed attention to fundamental problems of social policy, in addition to pioneering social policy perspectives on the problems of developing countries (G. Myrdal 1960). In more recent years, Marshall's theory of 'citizenship' and, in this context, its emphasis on social rights as the foundation of social inclusion (1950, 1964), has also been adopted in Germany (Rieger 1992a).

Rather than add further names from this period, I now want to focus in greater detail on three pioneers of welfare state thinking who belonged to a generation in which no mention was made of 'social policy' or even of 'welfare state'.[3] Apart from Friedrich List (mentioned above), they are the Swiss Sismondi, highly influential chiefly in francophone circles, and the Englishman John Stuart Mill. None of the three can be ascribed to any particular discipline or was tied to one by university life; rather, they all pursued the Enlightenment ideal of the polymath. In addition, all three developed their relevant social science positions *in reaction to Adam Smith and his followers*. That is a crucial criterion for inclusion in my list of classical authors, since the governmental and mercantilistic welfare doctrines of the seventeenth and eighteenth centuries were already aware of the relationship between princely policies, the well-being of the subjects and economic and political success; to that extent, reference to the 'preliberal welfare state' is entirely justified (Dorwart 1971; see chapter 14). What they lacked was awareness of the growing problems that emerge from the increasing independence of the business sphere from the state. This tension, first conceptualized by Hegel, between civil society, the state and the family, is nevertheless theoretically constitutive of all the contemporary problems of what is meant by a welfare state.

Simonde de Sismondi:
Distributive Problematics and External Effects

Jean Charles Léonard Simonde was born in Geneva in 1773 and died there in 1842. Throughout his life he was a private scholar and could afford to decline the invitations he received to the universities of Vienna and Paris. To draw attention to his Italian ancestry he added the surname of de Sismondi, and it is under this name that he is known in social science, chiefly as a historian and scholar of political economy. The title of his book (which in this context must be rated a classic), *Nouveaux principes d'économie politique: Ou, de las richesse dans ses rapports avec la population* (*New Principles of Political Economy: Of Wealth in its Relationship to the Population*) (1819),[4] alluded to David Ricardo's *Principles of Political Economy*, which had been published two years earlier and represented the first critical discussion of the Adam Smith school. Besides Ricardo, the next significant representative was the Frenchman Jean-Baptiste Say, and together with him Sismondi initially propagated the ideas of Adam Smith in French-speaking circles, in a paper published in 1803. In his later book *New Principles of Political Economy* (referred to above) he again addressed the ideas of this school, but now in certain respects as a critic:

> I separated myself from friends with whom I shared political opinions – I pointed to the dangers of innovations they recommended – I showed that many institutions they had attacked for a long time as evil, had beneficial consequences – and finally, on more than one occasion, I called for the intervention of the state to regulate the progress of wealth, instead of reducing political economy to the simplest and apparently most liberal motto of *laisser faire et laisser passer*. (Sismondi 1991: 7)

Sismondi's diagnostic insight was that, under the influence of the first industrial crisis of overproduction in England, he showed the contradictory character of the bourgeois industrial economy: the growing economic change brought about by industrial capital was presented as a threat to the harmonic picture of a civil society of equals. His main contribution to a theory of political economy consists of the systematic differentiation of the problems of production on the one hand and of distribution on the other, which has become seminal for most proposals for social reform. Political economy meant to him 'the investigation of the means by which the greatest number of men in a given state may participate in the highest degree of physical happiness, so far as it depends on the government' (Sismondi 1991: 511), and he saw it as the state's responsibility to ensure a just distribution of the wealth produced. He even professed the principles of Adam Smith's political economy and explained very clearly its superiority to the mercantile system and the teachings of the physiocrats. But he distanced himself from Smith on one decisive point: that it was not just the gross value of the social product that determined people's welfare, but *the relationship between its size and its distribution*. Thus the distinctiveness of distributive issues from allocative issues was first articulated, and on this point a theory of the welfare state is very clearly different from the economics of welfare, since the latter's reference to Pareto optimalization is concerned only with allocative and not with distributive aspects of economic processes; indeed, the difference is still often not recognized (Sen 1970).

The significance of Sismondi's argument for social theory resulted from bringing three insights together:

1. That left to its own devices the industrial system tends to overproduction because it concentrates the dominant share of the profits in the hands of some few capitalists while the vast mass of the population receive too little in wages to be able to buy the products. The industrial system continually expands the range of goods on offer while simultaneously bringing about unemployment through the competition for jobs and thus reducing demand. This became the basis of the demands for state involvement in income distribution.

2. Sismondi opposed Malthus's claim that there was an immanent tendency towards overpopulation, but argued instead that the large size of proletarian families (and here he used the adjective in its original Latin sense) could be ascribed to their poverty, which negated all possibility of security or plans for the future. Sismondi pleaded for a wider distribution of productive resources and support for small business, which would of itself generate a rationalization of reproduction and thus a reduction in population growth.

3. The exploitation of workers – and here Sismondi, in the state of economic development of the time, was thinking of agricultural as well as industrial workers – was the consequence of the dissolution of the ancient obligations of solidarity and mutual protection as they had been laid down both in the feudal system and by the guilds. This 'emancipation' enabled employers to overload their workers and to externalize the costs of their illness and disability, since these consequences were now to be the responsibility of the community. Thus Sismondi exposed the problem of the negative external effects of production in the market economy and proposed, as a solution, the internalization of costs.[5]

The relevance of Sismondi's argument to social theory becomes apparent only when these three insights are drawn together. Abolishing the ranked restrictions on economic activity led to the unleashing of competition and thus to extreme developments – overproduction here, population growth and rising poverty there – between which yawned the totally unnecessary contradiction of the distributive problem. The proposed state interventions could thus not only produce immediate effects on distributive policy but could also lead to social consequences, resulting in the solution of the 'social question'. Sismondi predicted the abolition of want among the population living at subsistence level through the combined effects of several measures. First, inheritance laws designed to force the breaking up of large fortunes should prevent great wealth being accumulated and broaden the smaller land-owning and artisan strata of society. In addition, legislation should

> give the master a monetary and political incentive to bind his workers ever closer to himself, to hire them for longer periods, to have them share in his profits, and then, perhaps, will private interests, better guided, mend on their own the injuries that private interests have inflicted on society. Then the heads of manufactures would occupy their minds with schemes to lift their workers to their level, to interest them in ownership and economy, to make of them finally men and citizens, whereas today they labour incessantly to turn them into machines. (Sismondi 1991: 585)

The operational integration of the lower classes would give them a perspective on life that could also lead to a more rational approach to reproductive behaviour, and thus the pressure of the growing superfluous youthful labour force, Marx's 'industrial reserve army', would disappear by itself.

The logic of Sismondi's programme is that the development of production would take place more slowly than under unrestricted capitalism. 'Without a doubt, such an extensive change in legislation … would soon reveal that many manufacturers, believed to be profitable, are really losers, because the help given each year to their workers by society amounts to more than their profits' (Sismondi 1991: 586). As the record shows, this idea has not prevailed against the dynamic of 'enrich yourselves' ('enrichissez-vous' as Guizot, the French finance minister of the time, put it), but the demand for social policy measures in favour of workers can be persuasively based on Sismondi's thought. Moreover, his arguments gain greater credibility in the face of the impending ecological catastrophe. Similarly, Sismondi was the first to recognize that rising well-being was superior to Malthus's 'moral restraint' as a device for rationalizing the reproductive behaviour of the lower classes.

Although Marx viewed Sismondi as a 'petty-bourgeois economist', he valued him comparatively highly: 'key ideas with which Marx foretold the collapse of capitalism: concentration of ownership, over-production, under-consumption, immiseration and social disintegration, stem from Sismondi, which Marx fully acknowledged in significant places' (Jonas 1976: 219). Nevertheless, Marx criticized Sismondi for trying to bridge the gap between a crudely profit-oriented economy and a state focused on the welfare of citizens. Sismondi actually had not developed this theoretically but had only made some more or less plausible suggestions – which from today's standpoint, however, do contain the idea of striving for deliberate control of institutional change; further, Sismondi considered the state capable of altering such institutional arrangements. But his elaboration of this idea remained rudimentary, and he did not also consider to what extent and why the state might be in a position to change the institutional conditions of human behaviour. Marx thus rejected this aspiration and therefore relied on the proletarian revolution. By contrast, for Lorenz von Stein the question of the state's capacity for action remained a central issue.

In terms of historical consequences, Sismondi has been most influential in France, although his thought – as mediated by Marx and Rodbertus – has also influenced the German interpretation of social questions (Gide and Rist 1948: 210ff.). Mill's independent treatment of the distributive problem (see below) was provoked by the 'speculations of the St Simonians' (Mill 1909: xxii), among whom Sismondi should also be included.

Friedrich List: The State and Productive Forces

Friedrich List called Adam Smith's concept of the causes of the 'Wealth of Nations' into question in a more radical manner than Sismondi had done. For List, it was not just the division of labour and competition that increased the productivity of labour, but a considerably broader complex of 'productive forces' that were the basis of people's well-being. List (1789–1846) was a Swabian autodidact and for a brief period the professor of public administration at the University of Tübingen; he later became a politician and unpopular emigrant. Economist and inspiration of national protectionism, railway pioneer in America and campaigner for the political unification of Germany, List depended on publicity work for his living for most of his life and ended what became an increasingly wretched life by his own hand. His political and publicity activities, as well as his opposition to liberal economy and his lack of an academic base, doubtless contributed to his being recorded in history more for his political activities than on the basis of his academic achievements.[6] One must add that two of his most important papers, namely his essays submitted to the Prize Competition of the Paris Académie des Sciences Morales et Politiques (Academy of the Moral and Political Sciences) in 1837, were first rediscovered in, respectively, 1913 and 1983.[7] Moreover, List cannot be allocated to any school of thought and is thus only worth a footnote to the economists, while the sociologists totally ignore him.

List's analysis took as its starting point Germany's regional fragmentation and economic backwardness after the Congress of Vienna (1815). He
stood for liberal and constitutional forms of government and strove for
the unification of the German states into a unitary economic area. This
was chiefly because of his perception of technical, economic and political
domination by England, whose products flooded the continent once the
Napoleonic blockade was lifted. List's academic thought was deeply influenced by this contemporary situation but is more than a mere reaction
to it, and he gave it – principally in *Das natürliche System der politischen
Ökonomie* (*The Natural System of Political Economy*; see List 1927) – a completely autonomous theoretical basis. Its systematic structure consisted of
three elements: a theory of economic development, a theory of productive
forces, and a political theory. It started from the problem of how economic
development could catch up, or to be precise, how Germany could best
reach the stage of progressive development that England had achieved.

According to List, a country's economic development is chiefly dependent on the degree of evolution of its productive forces. A government
would therefore do best not to promote trade in the first instance but
to build up its nation's productive forces. List understood this to mean
primarily the real capital in the economy, particularly as created by industrialization, and to allow this to grow free of foreign competition he
recommended protectionist tariff policies.[8] But this is only the preliminary aspect of the problem. In arguing the matter, above all against Adam
Smith, List pointed out that Smith ascribed the causes of public well-being
to the productivity of labour but did not enable labour productivity itself
to be explained:

> The power of producing wealth is therefore infinitely more important than
> wealth itself.… We ask, can it be deemed scientific reasoning if we assign
> as the cause of a phenomenon that which in itself is the result of a number
> of more deep-seated causes? … what is it that induces these heads, arms,
> and hands to produce, and calls into activity these exertions? What else
> can it be than the spirit which animates the individuals, the social order
> which renders their energy fruitful, and the forces of nature which they are
> in a position to make use of?' (List 1928: chap. 12)

Labour productivity is, in List's view, not just a natural phenomenon
but the central problem of a nation's chances of development, and he saw
it as depending on four key factors:

1. Environmental factors such as climate, soil conditions, mineral resources and the conditions for communication (such as rivers or
   obstructive mountains);

2. Individual resources in the form of socialization, education and experience, seen as the individual's and nation's human capital;
3. The institutional conditions for productivity, by which List meant a nation's entire cultural, juridical and organizational resources;[9]
4. Economic forces in the narrower sense, in particular those of agricultural and manufacturing production; in other words, the degree of economic development of agriculture and industry. List ascribed to trade only a limited influence on the development of productive forces (see List 1927: chap. 19).

From the perspective of differentiation theory, List's theory of productive forces concerns itself not only with factors operative within the economic system, but also the contributions of other parts of the social system, especially law and politics but also including the family and the educational services. He particularly emphasized the cultural and political conditions whose economic value is scarcely calculable in any detail but on which the opportunities for economic development may depend decisively. And he gave the relevant qualities of the individual a broader scope than the concept of human capital assumes, in that he also included both social values and capabilities ('cultural and social capital').

List's theory thus concerns 'the forces and capabilities which are active and contribute to production, but not those objects themselves which are produced and as such have an exchange value' (List 1927: 91). The latter is the subject of the 'cosmopolitan economics' of Smith and his followers, which by passing over the 'national economy' that List emphasized, directly equated 'individual economics' with 'the economics of mankind'. By contrast, List's theory clearly depicts a national state that in his view bears the responsibility for the development of productive forces. This does not call the significance of the market economy itself into question, but only the concept in classical economic theory, following Smith, of a politically independent market economy. What was important for List was, to put it in modern terms, the synergy between the state and the market. He also gave consideration to the role of the family in creating value, in contrast to almost all other nineteenth-century economists.

Admittedly, List inclined towards overemphasizing the directive power of the state. To be precise, he had not given systematic consideration to the problem of the unintended side effects of state intervention at all, to which John Stuart Mill drew attention. He had, however, already posed the question of the conditions under which state economic policies can be effective. That is the spirit of his theory of development.[10] State policies have various functions at different stages of development. List recommended protectionist policies (for which he is generally assumed to be the invariable champion) only for the transitional stage from a purely agrarian economy to a national industrial economy, whereas in the transition from this internal market-centred third stage to the fourth stage of development (substantial international exchange), protectionism is to be given up in favour of free trade. What is particularly decisive is 'that the restrictive trade policies can only be effective insofar as they are underpinned by cultural progress and the free institutions of the state'.[11]

As regards a theory of the welfare state, List is ground-breaking in his emphasis on the responsibility of the state for the institutional parameters of economic activity and as guarantor of the development of human resources, and he saw both of these perspectives in conjunction: 'History also teaches that individuals derive the greater part of their productive powers from the social institutions and conditions under which they are placed' (List 1928: chap. 10). But both types of 'productive forces' are outside the purview of classical economics, and List commented polemically but with justification, 'The man who breeds pigs is, according to this school, a productive member of the community, but he who educates men is merely non-productive.... A Newton, a Watt, or a Kepler is not so productive as a donkey, a horse or a draught-ox'.[12] We can therefore describe List above all as the mastermind of human capital theory. It is true that many nineteenth-century authors, in particular those of the two so-called German historical schools, drew attention to the neglect of cultural and social forces in economic theory and on that basis developed an 'ethical dimension' in social economy that leads directly to social policy. But that mode of thought remained theoretically weak and set the 'social' and the 'cultural' in antithetical opposition to 'economics'. List was by contrast the first to clarify the economic value of the state's social and cultural policies, and thereby to some extent overcame the sterile contradiction between market economy and state intervention. He thus became a pioneer of the current concerns of a social economics that attempts to reconstitute society's productive capacities in their interaction in a variety of social contexts. List's theory is dynamic and pragmatic. He was not so much concerned with the peculiarities of the different stages of development but with the strategies by which development from one stage to another could be achieved. That is his significance today for the concept of the development of the Third World (see Senghaas 1975, 1989).

On the other hand, one can hardly find any social policy argument in the proper sense in List's work. Admittedly he did not misjudge the hardship of his times, but in industrialization he saw not the cause but the solution to the problem (Seidel 1971). It was not the factories that created the poor, but the poor who built the factories, he wrote to King Wilhelm I of Württemberg. His principal goal was the rapid industrialization of

Germany, which he also expected to resolve the 'social question'. In this creative optimism he resembled our final author.

John Stuart Mill:
Self-Help and the Problem of Intervention

In the history of ideas he was a blue-eyed liberal and in later life he described himself as a socialist, but the history of political thought treats him as a sceptical democrat. John Stuart Mill (1806–73) was a child prodigy whose father, James Mill, raised his son according to the principles of his friend Jeremy Bentham. As a result, the young Mill was influenced by most of the intellectual trends of the first half of the nineteenth century, and many therefore see him as an eclectic. His reputation was above all built on *A System of Logic* (1843), his *Principles of Political Economy* (1848), and his political papers *On Liberty* (1859) and *Considerations on Representative Government* (1861). As an official and later pensioner of the East India Company, he was lifelong free of concern about his earning his daily bread.[13] World-famous during his lifetime, his star was almost extinguished in the first half of the twentieth century. However, since 1970 he has had something of a renaissance in the English-speaking world.

Mill is pertinent here because of his theory of state intervention, developed in his *Principles of Political Economy* and discussed there in the fifth volume, 'On the Influence of Government'. This is, however, more broadly related to his concern for a political order of the greatest possible freedom *and* social justice.[14] And this was no mere theoretical matter. Mill was a member of parliament from 1865 to 1868 and seems to have contributed to the recognition that influential circles in the Liberal party gave to social policy in the last decades of the nineteenth century, which itself was the precondition for the great Liberal social reforms in the UK between 1905 and 1920.

What follows concerns itself principally with Mill, although his significant but contentious position can only be fully understood in the context of his interaction with Jeremy Bentham. Bentham was the first 'theoretician of political intervention' to earn the title,[15] and Mill's distinct position on state intervention was at heart a liberal response to Bentham's authoritarian collectivism, even if combined with a generous dose of sympathy for 'socialist' ideas, what today would rather be called social or cooperative ideas.[16] Mill aimed to develop principles to distinguish between justified and unjustified state interventions. He was thus the first to formulate a theoretical problem that continues to lie at the heart of most argument about social policy and the welfare state to the present day.

Bentham's starting point was the insight that the individual is driven by his 'pains and pleasures' to behaviour which is not compatible with the greatest happiness of society. This is above all the case when society lacks sanctions to direct the individual towards right behaviour, or when the individual does not or will not understand his best interests.' (Keller 1945: 48)

In Bentham's view, unlike that of liberalism, there was no 'hidden hand' bringing harmony between individual and collective interests, as in Adam Smith's metaphor. Rather, it was the task of the legislator to design rational instruments, that is to say, rules by which individuals could, on the basis of the advantages and disadvantages associated with them, maintain their pain/pleasure balance in such a way that their actions were in the collective interest. Bentham developed systematic proposals for political institutions to meet these requirements. He did not see freedom as something to which people have some sort of natural right, but as a purely functional question. More important than freedom would be the reliability of such laws within whose bonds freedom could develop. The degree of freedom would be decided by the legislator in accordance with the principle of maximizing the happiness of the greatest number. Bentham was fully aware of the unpredictability of the consequences of legislation and therefore developed not only the notion of codification (that is, the assertion and systematization of all legal norms) but also allowed for the possibility of their revision, and thus brought both its stability and variability into his concept of rational law. The ground-breaking innovation of Bentham's teaching was that law is not derived from nature or mere custom but is the product of rational construction and revisable political decisions. In terms of its consequences this can justly be compared with Adam Smith's discovery of the laws of the market, and thus law, too, can be basically understood as a mechanism for collective learning.

Mill adopted Bentham's state-theoretical orientation and confronted it with the classical economic theories that to him had become unquestionable truths.[17] His critique of Bentham chiefly addressed his methods, his undifferentiated concept of utility and his crude understanding of democracy, which treated majority rule as its sole criterion for decision-taking. What above all distinguishes Mill from Bentham is his insight into the elementary significance of freedom for human progress:

> It is desirable, in short, that in things which do not primarily concern others, individuality should assert itself. Where, not the person's own character, but the traditions or customs of other people are the rule of conduct, there is wanting one of the principal ingredients of human happiness, and quite the chief ingredient of individual and social progress. (Mill 1992: 55)

For Mill, 'the desire for freedom and autonomy was one of the strongest wishes of human nature'.[18] He developed a kind of 'sociology of freedom', which meant that the extent to which people themselves had possibilities for choosing and thus developing their capacities depended on the forms of human institutions. He was equally concerned to ensure the openings for innovative minorities and a potentially broad variety of perspectives to confront the oppressive power of majority opinion towards conformity. It was precisely this variety, and the safeguarding of oppositional argument in public opinion and parliament alike, that Mill saw as indispensable to the goal of human progress and therefore a precept of the utility principle.

This is the sense in which Mill's engagement in the emancipation of the working class has to be understood. In his view it applied not only to the workers in the narrow sense but already particularly to women, and he entered parliament not just to achieve publicity for their right to vote but to achieve it politically. Mill dealt with the labour question in a number of places in his *Principles of Political Economy*, principally in Book IV, 'Influence of the Progress of Society on Production and Distribution'. Just as Sismondi had done, he treated the distributive question as independent of the question of production. He interpreted the dependency of the working classes as purely a question of power, which could be overcome with increasing education and the growth of intelligence and self-organization that would follow. Class conflict struck him as an unproductive condition that contradicted the criterion of utility and therefore had to be overcome. To this end, he proposed cooperative producer associations as forms of co-management as much as for the division of capital and profits. The cooperative principle struck him as the most appropriate for helping workers to become independent autonomous beings, and he described relevant experiments at length.

Mill's position on the politics of the welfare state is treated as controversial in the literature (see Ekelund and Tollison 1987, and Kurer 1991b). He explicitly encouraged state intervention for combating the immiseration of the lower classes, for their education and training since they could not afford school fees, and for extending their ownership of property. Apart from that, his social policy proposals were more strongly directed at the promotion of self-sufficiency among the underprivileged classes. His overall aim was to improve equality of opportunity, but not thereby an equalization of the outcomes of productive activity. As far as the problem of state intervention was concerned, Mill oriented himself on the Benthamite distinction between 'agenda' and 'non-agenda', as judged by the relationship between the costs and benefits of state intervention, that is, increasing or damaging the general welfare. Unlike Bentham, Mill was not satisfied with this maxim but in lengthy and at times almost casu-istical arguments he tried to elaborate criteria to distinguish appropriate from dysfunctional interventions by the state.[19]

Mill distinguished between 'necessary and optional functions of gov-ernment' (Mill 1909: 795ff.). As 'necessary' he saw those state functions whose general utility is not treated as contentious in their time – in other words, about which there is agreement on their appropriateness. He saw the unequivocal judgement of majority public opinion as decisive in iden-tifying 'necessity'. Among the necessary state functions of his time he included the collection of taxes and the assurance of general security, as well as lawmaking and the administration of justice. In consequence, he took trouble to develop general principles of taxation that would include an inheritance tax on large fortunes in order to counteract the concentra-tion of wealth. His guiding principle in this was the guarantee of a sub-sistence minimum free of both direct and indirect taxation, while above this level the aim should be a proportional though not progressive income tax burden.

As far as the optional functions were concerned, Mill regretfully noted that there were almost no rules by which, in dubious cases, to distinguish between the responsibility or incompetence of the state. The tenth and eleventh chapters of Book V of his *Principles* are consequently devoted exclusively to the development of such rules. At first he rejects state in-tervention in all those cases where the political aims are considered ob-jectionable or the means of achieving them ineffectual. These are thus categorical judgements against, for instance, restrictions on the expres-sion of public opinion or the freedom of the press, or protectionist trade policies, or the facilitation of monopolies or attempts by state interven-tion to invalidate free price-fixing. The theoretically interesting question, then, concerns those state interventions in which a clear distinction can-not be made on the basis of general principles, but where instead it is a matter of the relationship between the benefits that derive from state interventions and the dysfunctional consequences of such interventions. At this point Mill launches into extended sophistry. Nevertheless, his basic principle is founded on the idea of freedom: the supporters of any state intervention must have grounds to believe that it brings greater benefits than disadvantages. Every state intervention must be considered wrong if it does not on balance bring greater benefit.

The greater part of the discussion then focuses on criteria by which the benefits of a state intervention can be considered a priori plausible: 'they are so many that rather than supporting the principle they explode it' (Keller 1945: 155). The state should intervene especially when it might believe that individuals may not fully understand their own interests, or may not really be able to judge the means by which to satisfy their needs, as is the case with children (hence compulsory school attendance). Furthermore, in all cases where a third party acts on behalf of the interests of particular individuals, as may be the case for welfare and, not least, many commercial services, private measures were by no means a priori superior in Mill's view. He even foresaw the problems of externality effects, whether positive or negative. Finally – and this qualification takes on the character of a general condition – there are objects of public concern, which government must therefore put right if for some reason the private sector has not done so, even if in principle it could be done by the private sector. The examples given here are harbours, canals, drinking water systems, hospitals or universities.

If one wants to draw conclusions from this multiplicity of perspectives, these optional functions are best served by the concept of subsidiarity: government should intervene where – and only where – specific grounds exist in that objectives that have been judged to be in the public interest are not being sufficiently achieved by private initiatives. However, wherever feasible, the private initiatives or decentralized collective solutions should always be given priority:

> The greatest dissemination of power consistent with efficiency; but the greatest possible centralization of information, and diffusion of it from the centre.… the rules themselves should be laid down by the legislature; the central administrative authority only watching over their execution. (Mill 1992: 109)

These precepts represent the earliest contemporary consideration of the transition from a 'welfare state' to a 'regulatory state' (see chapter 14).

However, a necessary corollary of utilitarian thought is that the public interest cannot be assumed to have an inherently unchanging form; what it is can only be established in the context of political argument. Mill distinguished himself from Bentham in this respect: while Bentham wanted to make the evaluation of the public interest dependent solely on majority decisions, what mattered most to Mill was that this was a process in the course of which the largest number of disparate points of view on political opinions and decision-making procedures could best be revealed, so that in this way the learning capacity of the political system could be maximized.

To conclude, four cases can be distinguished in respect of state intervention:

(1) Duties of the state over which there is general consensus about their usefulness, and which can therefore be described as 'necessary';

(2) Tasks and objectives that appear to be achievable by political as well as private means; here the principle of the subsidiarity of state interventions is applicable;

(3) Objectives whose pursuit by state means is rejected because their import is held to be objectionable;

(4) Tasks whose implementation by the state is rejected because the resources it needs for their successful achievement cannot be identified.

In the light of Mill's deliberations it becomes clearer why, from a theoretical perspective, social reformist positions often appear unsatisfying and merely pragmatic. The principal standpoints adopted for and against state intervention, by the liberal side on one hand or, conversely, on the conservative or socialist side, cannot replace a more detailed assessment of the benefits and disadvantages of state interventions. Nevertheless, Mill's sophisticated solution is not totally convincing. In most cases there can of course be different opinions about the effects and side effects of specific state interventions, which thus arrive at divergent conclusions on the basis of straightforwardly utilitarian views.[20] This is precisely what continues to underlie arguments to the present day.

Mill's contribution to a theory of the reformist position lies less in his utilitarian utterances than in the conclusions he drew from them. Most importantly, in the light of the great uncertainties about the consequences of intervention, as wide an evaluative capacity as possible should be established, by means of proportional representation and genuinely inclusive voting rights (including women). This would lead to the formation of a public who would benefit and with whose help the ability to learn can be augmented in the process of taking democratic decisions.

In the German world, Mill and the utilitarian positions he represents have never become influential. His sociopolitical conception of the primary elements of 'self-help' versus 'state help' nevertheless correspond broadly to those of Lujo Brentano (1879), who was strongly oriented towards Britain. The renewed interest in Mill in the English-speaking world may be related to the renaissance of liberal ideas of self-help and the increasingly obvious limits to state provision in general.

Conclusion

It is not only economic beliefs but also perspectives on social policy that today promote ideas about distributive categories. That is obvious from the individual's point of view, since everyone wants to know how one will be affected by the outcomes of political decisions. Seen this way, welfare state politics appear as a zero-sum game: what is given to one must be taken away from another, whether directly in the form of taxes and benefits, or indirectly when the bills for the state's indebted beneficence have to be paid.

By contrast, most political discourses of the welfare state try to explain the collective advantages and disadvantages of particular policy measures in order to arrive at conclusions beyond merely individual trade-offs. The advantaged and the burdened are not just two groups regularly confronting each other; they are both minorities that must try to attract the political support of the majority. At that stage it is not individual interest claims that count but the case for collective advantage or the so-called public benefit. Scholarly discourses can offer an arena for wrestling with the credibility of such arguments.

Clearly there is still no body of received criteria for determining collective benefit. Enquiry into the ideas of the classical welfare state authors is above all a search for arguments of lasting validity, which might in the process expose useful material for theory-building in some fortunate cases. From Sismondi we can gain an insight into the autonomy of the distributive sphere and the subjection of external effects to institutional regulation. Friedrich List can make us aware of the significance of procedural benefits and the creation of human capital. John Stuart Mill can be thanked for incisively formulating the intervention problem and for pointing to the procedural elements of the search for collective welfare through social policy, and the consequent legitimation of parliamentary democracy. All three come together in proposing the cultivation of the abilities of the lower social classes in particular as a prerequisite for lasting progress towards freedom and equality. We could treat the arguments as fragments or even as building blocks of an all-embracing analysis that today, when the limits and dysfunctions of state distributive policies are increasingly apparent, might contribute to recollecting what is the essential aim of the welfare state.

Notes

1. See Keller (1945); also as an unsurpassed standard reference Gide and Rist (1948).
2. Huf (1998) is succinct on this.
3. The semantic connection between 'policy' and 'social' first developed in Germany in the setting of the 1848 events; a coded reference to 'social policy' can first be evidenced in the context of the Bismarckian social reforms. The international spread of

the concept only followed the Second World War. Lorenz von Stein was the first to speak of a 'social state', and Adolph Wagner of a 'welfare state', but even these descriptions embedded themselves in a codified form in Germany only after the Second World War, and actually only achieved a significantly wider circulation in the 1970s in connection with discussion of the crisis of the welfare state.

4. An English translation of the second edition (1827) was eventually published (Sismondi 1991). On Sismondi, see de Laubier (1978b) and Gide and Rist (1948: 184ff.).

5. 'It is quite clear that if the trades could be reconstituted as guilds, for charitable purposes only, and if the master of the trades were under the obligation to provide help to all the poor of their trade, on precisely the same footing on which the parishes furnish such help in England, one would soon set a limit to the sufferings to which the working class finds itself exposed' (Sismondi 1991: 583). This is precisely what the *Berufsgenossenschaften* (a kind of social insurance scheme against accidents at work funded exclusively by the employers of each branch of industry) in Germany achieved in the field of industrial injuries.

6. For List's life and work, see Heuss, Salin and Schumpeter (1965), and Henderson (1983); for the most up-to-date record of research on List, see Stadt Reutlingen (1989). For List's theoretical system, see Randak (1972).

7. Published as List (1927) and (1985). Up to that time, List's academic work was mainly known in the German-speaking world only through his book *Das nationale System der politischen Ökonomie (The National System of Political Economy)*, first published in 1841 (List 1928).

8. 'A nation which possesses only an agriculture which is dependent on other countries, but which is enabled by its moral qualities or the nature of its terrain to set up and multiply its manufacturing capacity by introducing duties and taxes, may at that moment sacrifice many values, because it brings forth industries which produce almost only expensive and incomplete goods. However, this will secure a considerable body of productive forces for the future, provided that the division of labour is then introduced on a large scale among the workers and that an active reciprocity between agriculture and industry is permanently assured; that would then lead to a lasting progressive growth of general well-being' (List 1927: 195).

9.. 'The Christian religion, monogamy, abolition of slavery and of vassalage, heritability of the throne, invention of printing, of the press, of the postal system, of money weights and measures, of the calendar, of watches, of police, the introduction of the principle of freehold property, of means of transport, are rich sources of productive power' (List 1928: chap. 12).

10. List's theory of development is most elaborated as a theory of successive stages in his *Natural System* of 1837 (List 1927: chaps. 9–13, also 18). His later works contain occasional variant versions, as for instance in the introduction to his *National System* (List 1928). In this connection the details are unimportant.

11. List 1928: 155. He also remarks in another place: 'Import duties should not be introduced in order to raise cash for the state coffers, since they may be extremely damaging to the productive forces of the nation.... They should be introduced with the aim of protecting and significantly increasing the nation's productive forces' (1927: 195).

12. List (1928: chap. 12). Incidentally, List's polemic here was directed not just against the neglect of household production, but against the classical economists' thesis that only manufacture was productive but services were not.

13. An excellent introduction to J.S. Mill's life, works and impact can be found in Stafford (1998). Kurer (1991a) offers a reconstruction of Mill's social philosophy. There is, of course, a large literature on Mill in English.
14. It is no accident that Mill gave his *Principles of Political Economy* the subtitle 'With Some of their Applications to Social Philosophy' (Mill 1909). One cannot exaggerate the influence of this textbook, which in edition after edition set Mill's social concerns out clearly; it extended to thirty-two editions in the nineteenth century (see Stafford 1998: 9).
15. See Keller (1945: 60ff.). Neither Bentham nor Mill has been taken very seriously on the continent, particularly not in Germany, and the same is true of the ideas of Hegel and Lorenz von Stein in Britain. This is not just because of different intellectual traditions but is based on structural realities: in the eighteenth century England was a comparatively liberal society in which the government had only limited influence, while in Germany the state remained the all-powerful reality.
16. In the nineteenth century most of the social reform movements were described as 'socialist'. The conceptual relationship to Marxism was not taken for granted until the twentieth century.
17. However, as distinguished from Ricardo and his school, that applies only with historical reservations. On Auguste Comte's considerable influence here, see Ashley (1969: xvff.).
18. Rinderle (2000: 141). What needs to be added in this connection is the circumstances of the time: Mill's chief opposition was to the traditionalism and paternalism of the Victorian age, against which he asserted the freedom and potential for self-determination of all, including the workers. This also explains his scepticism about state measures to protect adults.
19. See Mill (1909: Book V, chaps. 1 and 11), and also *On Liberty* (Mill 1992: 104ff.).
20. Kurer (1991a: 194) draws a similar conclusion: 'Mill's approach leads to a particular difficulty, that of incompatible ends. This is reflected in his discussion about practical politics, and is responsible to a large degree for the traditional view of Mill as an incoherent thinker. There is however no such confusion on Mill's part, the problem is one inherent in the complexities of his aims'.

Chapter 2

GERMAN ORIGINS OF
A THEORY OF SOCIAL REFORM
Hegel, Stein and the Idea of 'Social Policy'

The word 'social' first found its way into the German language in the 1830s (Geck 1963) and rapidly came into use in the 1840s, giving rise to a multiplicity of compound and associated terms. Those of particular interest here include 'the social question', social movement, socialism, social science, social reform, 'the social state' and social policy. Most of these terms arose independently of each other, but in the 1850s and 1860s they converged into a semantic field whose specific characteristic was indicated by the adjective 'social' (Pankoke 1970). This chapter aims to reconstruct the development of the concept and meaning of 'social policy'.

Contrary to general assumptions, this concept was not first used in the context of Bismarckian social insurance (1881–89). Nor is it attributable to the foundation of the Verein für Sozialpolitik (the Association for Social Policy, 1873), an association of reform-oriented social scientists and practitioners that remains the leading scholarly association in its field in Germany. The Bismarckian social legislation certainly did popularize the idea of 'social policy', but compared to the original conception this was in the much more limited sense of the state's approach to the *Arbeiterfrage* (the problem of the working class). This circumscription was not narrowly party-political but had its grounds in political thought, since the foundation of the German Reich had given the overall idea of society a nationalistic and simultaneously state-centred connotation.

The distinction between 'the state' and 'civil society' that had been elaborated in the wake of Hegel's development of 'a science of society' was lost once again. However, in this situation the idea of 'social policy' arose to mean a mediation between state and civil society – in other words, a kind of interaction between the order-creating power of the state on the one hand and, on the other, the dynamic of concurrent ideas, technical innovations and capitalistic competition that drove civil society.

'Social policy' (in its German usage) thus originated as a concept in social science that has gradually made a practical career in politics. Until the end of the Weimar Republic, social policy remained above all an academic label for the study of institutional developments that were being implemented under other names. Its introduction to practice followed mainly after the Second World War. The concept burgeoned only after 1970, and in doing so pushed older descriptions such as 'social administration' into the background.

In German, the concept of *Sozialpolitik* embodies three meanings that are distinguished in English. The first is the struggle for the implementation of social reform (social politics), while the second is the implementation of statutory and administrative reforms (social policies). The third sees social policy as a basic conceptual field within social science – similar to social administration in the UK – which in Germany gained considerable independence, principally during the Weimar period. After the Second World War social policy virtually became a specialized branch of economics. Today, though dominated by sociology, it is a much more interdisciplinary subject to which jurists, political scientists, social philosophers and economists also contribute.[1]

This chapter addresses the early history of these concepts and meanings of social policy. In those days the concept was still firmly anchored in theories about society itself and not confined only to inductive systematizations and generalizations about practical social reforms. This older concept may have more to teach us than what it has become since the time of Bismarck.

Social – Socialism – The Study of Society

In the 1840s, the tensions between the declining epoch of agrarian feudalism and the rising epochs of liberalization and industrialization were reaching their peak. Famine, labour unrest, revolts and civil wars formed the emotional basis for the scholarly search for understanding and the debates on political ideas of the time. In the process, the political problems of nationalism and constitutionalism became closely wrapped up with the problems of pauperism, urbanization and the immiseration of the workers. Accordingly, the emerging strands of social thought were subject to the various disparate expressions of the "zeitgeist". This was especially true of the two countries undergoing the greatest social change, Britain (Pinker 1971; Metz 1985) and France (Donzelot 1984; Castel 1995). Industrialization remained underdeveloped in the as-yet disunited German-speaking countries, even in hindsight, and for that reason the German social thinkers drew on conditions in England and France for examples. They thus had a detached perspective on the new conditions, which aided the development of an autonomous social science. As far as social science was concerned, German speakers were the leading thinkers in the nineteenth century, and it is this fact that justifies a full account of these early connections.

The 'Social' as an Expression of Secularization

The word *social* can be traced back to the Latin *socialis*, which even in the age of Seneca was associated with thinking about society. He translated the Aristotelian *zoon politicon* into *animal sociale*, and from then on the Latin word *socialis* served to describe a person's specifically political or social status. Medieval philosophy gave this conception a theological elaboration: human coexistence resulted from mankind's divinely given capacity for reason, which enabled humans to recognize the laws nature had laid down. This Christian interpretation was called into question in the seventeenth century by the novel doctrine of natural law. In this tradition of thought, founded by Hugo Grotius and Samuel Pufendorf, the concept *socialis*, together with its respective derivations *socialitas* and *sociabilitas*, acquired a definitive character to describe human coexistence as well as enquiry into its origins (Schieder 1984: 924; Müller 1967: 23–46). In accordance with the self-secularizing view of the world, the human tendency to live communally and seek political cohesion could no longer be treated as deriving from divinely given human reason but demanded a specific justification. Moreover, this explanatory burden became heavier as the idea of natural law became more strongly tied to Enlightenment notions of individualism.[2]

Since the end of the eighteenth century, 'the foreign term "socialist" [has been] adopted into the German conceptual vocabulary as the totally value-free description of the social philosophy based on natural law of the schools of Grotius and Pufendorf' (Schieder 1984: 930). 'Socialist' was the name given to those philosophers who first posed the question of human order in purely secular terms, and did so primarily under political auspices. They can be distinguished from those thinkers collectively labelled as 'socialists' from the mid 1830s on – particularly Robert Owen, Saint-Simon and Fourier – chiefly in that the latter saw a solution to the problems of human order less in political reform or revolution than in changes in society, especially in a transformation of property relations. This shift in the conceptualization of the problem is closely related to the development of an independent 'science of society', detached from political or juridical philosophy.

The term 'social' became embedded in German following the transmutation of the word *Gesellschaft* (society), a change worth noting briefly (see Riedel 1979). Until the turn of the nineteenth century, the word *Gesellschaft* was the dominant translation of the Latin *societas* and covered virtually all forms of human coexistence. A more specific use in German terminology was the description *bürgerliche Gesellschaft,* 'civil society', which referred to the Aristotelian notion of the political form of human association. Civil society was even understood as organized domination, which, following modern ideas of natural law, displaced the legitimating foundations of domination from theological ideas to theories of social contract.

The older forms of domination must still be understood as relating power in the household to political power; the only legally competent citizens in pre-revolutionary society (*societas civilis cum imperio*) were the heads of households, who for their part held power over their powerless (in the legal sense) household members. In spite of numerous changes in the power relationships between political heads (kings, princes, magistrates) and household heads, as well as their collective associations (estates and corporations), these intermediary structures remained characteristic of sociopolitical relations in the greater part of Europe from ancient times up to the French Revolution. In political hindsight it was precisely the abolition of all *corps intermédiares* (intermediary bodies) and the granting of civil rights to all (males) that were the most revolutionary events of 1789, although even here women and dependent servants remained excluded. However, when the monarchy was restored in 1814, voting rights were restricted to the wealthiest property owners.

The granting of civil rights and thus the abolition of ancient duties of protection and subservience rapidly extended – not least as a consequence of the Napoleonic wars – throughout Europe. By contrast, the extension of rights to political participation to non-property-owning sections of the population as well as to women was long delayed and became a key theme in political debate until the First World War. But the fight against political inequality was soon joined by that against social inequality, though the relationship between these two forms of inequality was seen in very different ways, depending on political perspective. These differences in viewpoint were frequently expressed by the concepts of 'political' versus 'social' *reform* (see Dipper 1992). The representatives of social reform formulated their diagnosis with clarity as early as 1837 in a motion proposed by Franz-Josef von Buss, a member of the parliament of the Grand Duchy of Baden: 'Since the insecure legal and political position of the workers is above all rooted in their unfavourable economic situation, so it is in legal and political respects that aid towards the betterment of the economic conditions of the workers is to be expected' (Kuczynski 1960: 248). Or in more materialistic terms, 'what does the constitution give the people? Rights, but no bread, no work, no education. Rights are stones, and not everyone receives these stones; whoever has not paid at the very least 20 gulden in taxes, who has not even got bread, will not receive a single stone of these rights' (Grün 1845: 19).

The Differentiation between the Political and the Social: G.W.F. Hegel

The conceptual distinction between state and (civil) society (*societas civilis sine imperio*), in other words between the political and the social, had been implied by the critics of absolutism since the time of Montesquieu (1745) but first found clear expression in Hegel's *Philosophy of Right*. The political and the social appeared here for the first time as two distinct fields, each dominated by different legal principles, whose relationship consequently became the fundamental problem of social policy.[3]

The novelty in the nascent science of society was the internal, autonomous dynamics of the social sphere, which was, to use Adam Smith's metaphor, governed by an invisible hand and not just by the visible hand of government. Just as political power came to be governed by the rule of law and circumscribed by constitutional rights to freedom at the same time that the abolition of feudal ties released individuals into freedom and the pressure to compete, a new invincible dynamic developed, which – according to liberal principles of state self-restraint – ought not to be restricted. This was expressed in many ways: as an expansion of economic competition, as a flight from the countryside into urbanization, as industrial growth and the destruction of proto-industrial domestic industries, and in a general population growth stimulated by falling mortality as well as the abolition of restrictions on marriage. Thus the number of uprooted workers seeking paid work, who often no longer had settled residence anywhere, grew very rapidly. This very obvious change in the conditions of life was debated in the 1820s and 1830s mainly under the heading of pauperism, but from 1840 a new name started to embed itself – the 'social question'. This renaming signified a new consciousness of the problem. It was no longer a matter of the treatment of the poor, but of the relationship between the 'ranks' (or 'estates' in the feudal ranking of society) or 'classes' – it was, in other words, a question of the *structure of society*.

The content of the new study of society was disputed throughout the nineteenth century, as was the object of the nascent 'science of society', or 'social science' (see Pankoke 1991; Jonas 1976: vol. 1). In the present context, the only relevant traditions of thought are those that systematically reflected the distinction between state and (economic) society.

Hegel dissolved the millenarian notion of a social unity constituted by political authority into the difference between state, civil society and family. This represents the beginning of a theory of functional differentiation in modern society that has become one of the most important paradigms of modern social theory, especially through the work of Talcott Parsons and Niklas Luhmann (see Luhmann 1977, 1985a). Hegel's concept of civil society was focused – following modern terminology – on the economic sector of society, whose conceptualization as a self-organizing market-mediated system of labour specialization had already been developed by Adam Smith, Jean Baptiste Say and David Ricardo. While human liberty in the state expressed itself, according to Hegel, as the free affirmation of a legal order that also secured the liberty of one's fellow men and found the moral conditions of its development within the family, in civil society it expressed itself as the unrestricted drive towards the satisfaction of needs. This drive manifested itself as work, which in the context of civil society was chiefly work for the satisfaction of other people's needs as the condition for the satisfaction of one's own (Hegel 1821/2008: §§ 182–207; Siep 1997; Priddat 1990).

In contrast to economic theory, Hegel conceptualized economic relations not as processes of exchange moderated by market prices, but as relations between individuals. His thought started not from products but from the needs of economic man and his work. Nevertheless, these complementary needs did not simply lead to a 'needs system' as imagined by liberal theory; instead, the reciprocally advantageous arbitration of needs was produced by the guarantee of private property and the legal security of contractual conditions – in other words, by state action. Hegel understood the juridification of political power, the constitutional state, as the historical realization of reason. Thus in Hegel's theory of society the individual appeared in two civil roles: as a citizen (*citoyen*) of the state and as a member (*bourgeois*) of civil society.

Hegel emphasized the contingency and arbitrariness of conditions in civil society. This is not a natural condition but the consequence of individuals each pursuing their own interests capriciously. For Hegel, the social inequality of persons was thus a *constitutive* element of civic society. By contrast with the fundamental equality of civil rights in the constitutional state, in civil society the 'inequality in ability, wealth, and even in intellectual and moral education' among individuals resulted in 'an inequality of humans ... inherent in the idea ... [and] countering it with the demand for *equality* is feeble-minded' (Hegel 1821: § 200). The social inequality of individuals thus became for Hegel a constitutive force in civil society.[4] In due course Karl Marx and Lorenz von Stein took up this insight in the context of class theory and related it to the diagnoses of the early socialists in various ways.

It must be clear from the outset that Hegel's social theory was the first to conceptualize significant features of modern industrial-capitalistic society and thus also the implicit tension between its socio-economic inequalities and the ideal of political equality. Hegel enables 'society' to become aware of itself, so to speak. The general public perceived the idea of the 'social question' first as the tension between the political idea of civil equality and the realities of social development, which, chiefly in France, was acted out in the form of repeated violent revolts. But in German-speaking countries as well, the uprisings by the weavers in Bohemia and Silesia (1844) gave the social question public resonance and thus stimulated the desire for a better understanding of modern society.

By contrast with the mainly descriptive use of 'social' in French and English, the word *sozial* in German usage generally held a normative meaning, whether valued as positive or as critically negative, and this immediately linked the idea closely to the problem of poverty and later to the question of the workers (Müller 1967). In this way, 'the social' was often posed as a contradiction to 'the individual', whereupon it appears as what is lacking in civil society in the liberal sense (Gurvitch 1932; Donzelot 1984). However, this lack does not appear as a constitutive defect of capitalism, as Karl Marx maintained, but as something remediable through social reform or social policy. This specific semantic usage assumes not only the distinction between 'political' and 'social' but, similarly, between 'social' and 'economic', although this latter distinction is not yet present in Hegel's concept of civil society. The subject of a specific 'science of society', one that could be distinguished from political science and also from political economy, was first introduced into the debate by Robert von Mohl (1851). What Mohl criticized in the social scientists of his day was that, following the fictions of the French Revolution, they conceived society in too individualistic a manner. Instead, he postulated the entire realm of the intermediary corporations and associations between the individual and the state as the topic of the study of society. As a result, there was no bridge between the class theory of society and the corporatist concepts, even though both of these approaches had long-lasting influence on sociopolitical thought.

The close connection between 'social' and 'socialism' can be explained by the fact that until the very end of the nineteenth century, this concept was in no way locked into the Marx-Engels approach. Rather, it served sometimes to generalize and sometimes to distinguish the many streams of social movements and social reform, as well as providing their intellectual 'social science' foundations. This relationship between social science analysis and political engagement, which were often lumped together as 'socialism', provides the enduring context for the development of 'social policy'.

The Social Question – Social Reform – Social Policy

From the 1840s up to the First World War, the term 'the social question' (roughly equivalent to 'social problems') constituted the dominant subject matter of social reform and of social policy.[5] In the context of German conditions, until around 1850 the social question was identified with the problems of pauperism, while under the conditions in England and France the focus was on the problems of the industrial workers. The earliest German example of the problems of the industrial proletariat being expressed in the language of the social is found in the work of Franz von Baader (1835).

Science of Society and Social Reform: Lorenz von Stein

It was the writings of Lorenz von Stein that were decisive for the development in Germany of a firm connection between the problem of the workers, social science or the science of society, and the demands for social reform.[6] Stein drew connections between the French socialists' critical diagnosis of capitalism and Hegel's theory of society, thereby arriving first at a diagnosis amazingly similar to that later made by Karl Marx and Friedrich Engels about the inevitability of class conflict under the conditions of liberal capitalism. However, he distinguished himself from these authors in terms of possible escape routes – for him, the way out of proletarian misery was not the revolutionary overthrow of the conditions of the ownership of property but social reform based on the responsibility of a state rising neutrally above the contradictions of class conflict.

In terms of their difference, Stein's conceptual advance beyond Hegel's thought is evident in his articulation of the tension between the 'pure' concepts of the state and of society on the one hand, and their real relationship on the other. According to this concept, the state is the protector of the collective interests of a people, and this protection is accomplished by representation in the person of the prince and by work in the form of administration. Against this, society stands conceptually as a moral order and as the locus for the development of personality, as well as of interests under the given conditions of property ownership. While state and society are clearly distinct as ideas, in historical reality they continuously interpenetrate one another and in this way give rise to different forms of society (Stein 1856: 22ff.).

A further conceptual advance of Stein's consists in the dynamic conception of the distinction between state and society, as realized in the French revolutionary constitution of 1789. The extension of civil rights to all creates a 'civic society' in which social inequality no longer depends on difference in legal rights but only on that of property. Wealth ownership thereby gains a wider social significance for individuals and their communities, becoming a principal mark of their social status. Work and wealth now become the structural indicators of the 'economic society' developed on the basis of legal equality for everyone (Stein 1850: vol. 1, 451ff.). Ideally this offers everyone the opportunity for social advancement and gaining wealth, but in practice the effects of generalized competition and existing differences in wealth leads to the solidification of social classes and thereby to 'industrial society', in other words to capitalism as Marx understood it (Stein 1850: vol. 2, 55ff.; Hegner 1976).

The goal of Stein's social theory was, first, to elaborate on the formation of the proletariat as a class and the inherently insoluble class conflict of industrial society, which – as Stein demonstrated in his analysis of conditions in France – tended towards civil war. Next, it aimed to show that a constructive solution was possible, namely by mediating between the conflicting, yet at the same time mutually interdependent, class interests of labour and capital with the help of a neutral third party, which Stein initially referred to as the 'monarchy of social reform'. His central concern, however, was the 'realisation of the principle of the state' (Böckenförde 1976c: 162). Stein had – following Hegel – considerable reservations about the forms of democracy that he was aware of at that time, since he feared that in this type of state class conflict would be introduced into politics, thus damaging the required neutrality of the state. Nevertheless, what was for him the core issue was not the form of the state but *the achievement of a productive compromise between the classes*. Stein conceived this compromise as the general recognition of the constitutional guarantee of property rights for the wealth-owning classes on the one hand and, on the other, the furtherance of the social emancipation of the working class and its consequential political emancipation through free association (social movements) and social administration.[7]

Even in the administrative science that dominated his later work, Stein remained faithful to his earlier formulation of 'social reform'. But he focused instead on a part of the problem, that of social administration, in the course of which he ran up against the problem that was to become central for the subsequent conceptual history of social policy: does the idea of social administration refer to a specific field within public administration? Or alternatively, does it refer to a particular aim or orientation for state intervention in social situations? In the 1876 edition of his *Handbuch der Verwaltungslehre* (*Handbook of Administrative Science*) he tried to address these differences through the distinction between 'societal administration' and 'social administration'. By contrast, in the 1887/88 edition, the concept of social administration appeared alongside legal and commercial administration as a specific field whose obligations, subject to a corresponding legal duty, were 'to determine the relations between capital and labour so that beside the maintenance of acquired capital, the capital-building powers of labour would similarly be maintained' (Stein 1888: 35).

The concept of social policy first appeared in Stein's work in the 1888 edition, in the form of a subcategory of 'general social administration' and on a level with the 'social police'. 'Social policy ... takes place where the general principle of social administration is implemented in individual fields of administration, such as in departments and ministries for specific subjects. It embraces the totality of those measures through which the individual parts of the administrative apparatus enable the free and equal development of the labour force for all, without regard to capital and income' (Stein 1888: 46). Against this, the social police were responsible for safeguarding property relations, for which Stein nevertheless explicitly rejected special privileges in the sense of the Bismarckian socialist laws.[8]

Stein was the first to adopt a theoretical position corresponding to today's dominant understanding of the regulatory politics of the social or welfare state. His 'social state' had the task of both protecting the conditions for private property and hence the development of an independent entrepreneurial capacity, and improving the working and living conditions of labour. This also implies a self-limitation of the state role in the sense of the principle of subsidiarity, though one that is less restrictive than in the liberal assumptions:

> The state through its administration must never nor in any circumstances offer any more than to produce those conditions for personal, economic

and social development which the individual cannot manage for himself, and must then leave it to the individual exercising his free will to shape and develop his own life by the use of those conditions. (Stein 1876: 59)

Thus for Stein social policy meant a defined intention by 'the working state', that is, the administration. It was not a reference to the political process through which social reforms were carried out, which in Stein's work generally remained unelucidated. The recognition of the necessity of social reforms to be undertaken by the state, that is, by the established authorities, seems to have been sufficient for him as a historical driving force. And the dissemination of this recognition was one of Stein's central concerns.[9] Apart from this politico-democratic deficit – which of course reflected the reality of the Habsburg and Hohenzollern social policy regimes – we can already find in Stein most of the insights that are important to the foundations of modern social policy, in particular the idea of human capital and the argument for social order.

The Emergence of the Term Sozialpolitik

Paired associations between the words 'political' and 'social' date from the middle of the 1840s, but they only became widely used in the context of 'the year of revolutions', 1848. A significant French influence also coloured these word associations, as Germans who had emigrated to France or Belgium often brought the semantics of the social into the German language.

Noteworthy in the emergence of German word associations is a study by the radical democrat Julius Fröbel (1847). As an exile from Prussia living in Zürich, he first published Neue Politik (New Politics) in 1846 under the pseudonym of Junius, then retitled the second edition as System der socialen Politik (A System of Social Politics). The text of the book is identical in both editions and contains the word 'social' only sporadically and without a connection to 'political'. However, in the foreword to the second edition the two paired words are used in a quite taken-for-granted manner:

> For all social and political problems – including economic problems – there is only one criterion, and that is the moral criterion … and if the world wants to adopt a new politico-social form, it must first make advances in moral consciousness by which the new form will be conditioned…. The advances must be absolutely clear in their association if … there is to be deliberate work on the form of a better politico-social order. I have therefore founded my social politics on a new reworking of ethics, or rather, that is what it is. (Fröbel 1847: iv)

As this passage shows, Fröbel's text stands more on a level with Kant than with Hegel. What is lacking is a theory of the social, which in general he understood as being entirely dependent on the political. The change in the choice of words between the two editions of Fröbel's *New Politics* allows us to assume that the pairing of 'social' and 'political' emerged during the years 1844 to 1846, that is, at the time of the weavers' uprisings and the Cabinet Order of Friedrich Wilhelm IV reacting against it.

In a manner similar to that of Fröbel the word association 'social-political' is found in a polemical paper attacking liberal radicalism that was apparently written in the spring of 1848: 'This party is the actual leader of the revolutionary movement stretching out from Paris across Europe. It is the socialist-political publicist, the bearer and distributor of social-political ideas and doctrines through which the world shakes and shatters, through which absolutism will be destroyed in order to make way for the socialist-democratic republic' (E. Hofmann 1848: 9). The connection between the words social and political here is meant to suggest a link between the democratic and the socialist movements.

A crucial contribution to the spread of the pairing 'social-political' came from the Prussian local administrator and 'social scientist' M. von Lavergne-Peguilhen. In his opinion, 'politics should proceed from the standpoint of the societal cosmos, and the politics which derives from that is German social policy' (Lavergne-Peguilhen 1863: iv). He juxtaposed this concept with the individualism and political centralism of French politics, and as a result emphasized the principle of the monarchy and the estates:

> Certain laws are founded on important aspects of life in society; by dint of political arithmetic these aspects must be allowed to have an effect, in the same way as state reforms have effects etc. Social policy draws the conclusions of these scientific axioms and builds its doctrines on those foundations, in that it seeks to test and confirm them in practice; alongside the rights and interests of the individual, it represents society and strives to set up its rights; it believes it cannot better serve the individual, or better protect the interests of the peoples, as through the assiduous study of the statutes on which the existence and the development of society depends, through state treatment of society according to the statutory measures, and with regard to people's Christian calling. That is the perspective of this young science, hardly in its first stages of development, but which because of this perspective nonetheless has a rich future significance. (Lavergne-Peguilhen 1863: 173)

This is a belated formulation of ideas which go back a long way. Lavergne-Peguilhen appeared as the champion of a 'science of society' as early as 1838 (Lavergne-Peguilhen 1838–41). In 1849 he presented a proposal in the Prussian First Chamber for 'the establishment of a central institute for social policy, whose task will be to study social conditions on a continuous basis; on that basis, to prepare or to report on proposals for legislation or practical measures; to provide support for the development of the science of society into an empirical science; to offer all an organisational centre for efforts directed towards the recognition and reform of society and to keep the government in regular mutual contact with the development of society' (quoted by Geck 1950: 14). Seldom has the scientific task of social policy been expressed more succinctly.

The clashes of 1848 and 1849 already involved all the political positions that have continued to dominate debates on social policy to the present day. The liberals expected the conquest of poverty through the self-healing powers of the market and the strengthening of the potential for self-help (first expressed by Mohl 1835). The revolutionaries around Marx and Engels predicted the overthrow of the capitalist system because of its inherent contradictions. Conservatives demanded the re-creation of solidaristic bonds as a reflection of the traditional ethos of feudal society. The reformist position hoped to stabilize the political and social system permanently by means of institutional reform. The word associations 'social policy' and 'social reform' were used chiefly by representatives of the conservative and institutional reformist positions, and only occasionally by the liberals, while the revolutionaries soon struck the term 'social reform', which they had initially used, out of their vocabularies. As a result, for the working-class movement the alternatives 'revolution or reform' became the battlefront for its internal arguments (Dipper 1992: 228ff.).

Defining the Concept

The collapse of the political movement of 1848 caused the question of political reform to retreat into the background, and the term 'social reform' was increasingly used in the political sense of a conservative programmatic formula of a reform that excluded subjects of the state from political rights. To some extent the concept of social policy fell into the same pool of ideas.

The first attempt to define the concept was made by W. H. Riehl, whose programme for 'a conservative social policy' defined it as follows:

> It is essential to render the whole body of individual insights derived from the natural history of peoples intellectually useful for the idea of the state, and practically useful for the expansion of our constitutional and administrative state and for the reconstruction of the rotten civil society. These

facts of natural history must be used as a weapon and protector against the biased party doctrines which want to cut our political life to fit their preconceived pattern. This is what I call social policy. Because of these facts of natural history, the science of the state must be broadened, and an independent part of it placed as the science of society beside public law and the study of administration. (Riehl 1854: 21)

Riehl posed the solution to the social question, seen as the problem of the working class, as a matter of the incorporation of the proletariat into the corporative structure of social ranks or estates. In that way he tried to solve what he fully recognized were new problems in the framework of a traditional rank-ordered view of society.

By contrast, a paper first published in June 1848 by Karl Marlo, an economist who thought in 'state-socialist' terms, was forward-looking. It already reveals a consistent distinction between the 'social' and the 'political' aspects of life:

The word 'social' embraces in the widest sense all the conditions which arise from people living together, though in the narrower sense only those which do not arise from the exercise of state power. We shall invariably use it in the latter sense. By contrast, what we understand by 'society' is the entirety of all those people linked to a state. In this sense the life of society has a political and a social aspect.… But in making this distinction one must keep in mind that the state … gives order to the social side of life, and so even the social situation of a people wherever they are is dependent on their political circumstances. (Marlo 1850: 5ff.)

Here the concept of society is the overarching concept, an idea that persists in the current image of a national society, whereas the distinction made by Hegel (and following him, Stein) emphasized the difference between the state and (civil) society instead of this unity. But the distinction between the political and the social was retained and already implied their interdependence.

A concise summary of thought during this earliest period of conceptual history, when the tensions in the Hegelian distinction between state and civil society were being worked out, is given by the earliest article dedicated to the very concept of social policy:

The embodiment of the conditions among one people by which the advantages of birth, of property and of knowledge are distributed, as well as respect and status stemming from these advantages, is called society. Until the beginning of this century no one had ever treated these conditions as material for scientific examination. Once science has conquered this material it can never surrender it again. We live as citizens of two worlds, that

of the state and that of society. The determination of the relations between
these two worlds will in future be the principal task of political research.
There can in the future be no other politics but social policy. (Meyer 1864:
319)

Social policy is seen here as a science laying the foundations for the politics of societal formation, one whose point of departure from a study of
social conditions is from the perspective of their embedded patterns of distribution. By contrast, Riehl saw the main role of 'the science of society'
as the more accurate description of human communal life through ethno-
graphic study. Both ideas converge in that only a government that fully
understands the conditions of its society can pursue purposive policies.

The Nationalist Diminution of Social Policy

In conclusion, it must be kept in mind that at the level of the political
controversies between 1789 and 1848 the nascent social science or science of society was already working with a sociologically based concept of
social policy, but nevertheless one whose social assumptions varied widely
according to author. In particular, Lorenz von Stein had already given
substance to social policy in the sense of administrative interventions
by the state. In this process, a markedly dialectical relationship between
'state' and 'society' became apparent, which with regard to Hegel became
described as 'mediation'. However, these theoretical perspectives on society did not become influential in the history of the concept that followed.
Under the impetus of the national unification of Germany, ideas about
functional differentiation that were decisive for a deeper theoretical understanding of social policy again faded into the background. A lasting
contribution to this trend was made in particular by the Prussian historian
Heinrich von Treitschke, who criticized the proposal for an independent
science of society yet used the description 'socio-political' for the political
science of which he was an exponent: 'The whole of political science is
socio-political; it must show how the beliefs of the people as a whole are
realized in the diversity of their individual aspirations' (Treitschke 1859:
82ff.).

Thus Gustav Schmoller, the founder of the Verein für Sozialpolitik in
1873 and its long-standing chairman, could note in a review of Stein's
Administrative Science: 'He has created a true system for the first time,
but has discovered that the overwhelming majority of economists understand his books as little as if they were written in Chinese' (Schmoller
1867: 269). Up to the end of the First World War, the concept of social

policy developed under the influence of Bismarckian social reforms was so strongly premised upon the idea of national unification under *political* direction that the autonomous dynamic of the 'social' was forgotten.

Notes

1. The following can be recommended as standard sources: Lampert and Althammer (2007); M.G. Schmidt (2005); Lessenich (2003); Leibfried and Wagschal (2000). Detailed historical presentations of practical social policy in Germany are given by Stolleis (2011) for the earlier period and Frerich and Frey (1996) for the period after 1945, and most exhaustively by *Bundesministerium für Arbeit und Soziales und Bundesachiv* (Federal Ministry for Labour and Social Affairs in collaboration with the Federal Archives) eds., *Geschichte der Sozialpolitik in Deutschland seit 1945* (*History of Social Policy in Germany since 1945*), 11 volumes , Baden-Baden, 2001 - 2008. Volume 1 is published in English as series in 2012 under the headline *German Social Policy* by Springer publishers, Heidelberg.
2. These explanatory problematics gave rise not only to modern political philosophy but also to sociology. Luhmann (1981c: 195) describes 'the insecure potential of sociability itself' as 'the problem which constitutes the discipline'.
3. This distinction was not made by English-speaking writers until very recently. It is connected with the continental adoption of the distinction in Roman law between public and private law, in which the state is ruled by public law and civil society by private law. See at length Dyson (1980) and the introduction above.
4. Hegel did not overlook the problematic aspects of the contemporary impoverishment, which is far less explicitly expressed in his published work (see Hegel 1821: § 243ff.) than in the transcripts of the lectures he gave in 1819–20: 'The creation of poverty is chiefly a consequence of civil society, and it necessarily arises from this source. Wealth is accumulated without measures or limits on the one hand, and want and suffering on the other. The expansion of wealth and of poverty march in step with one another. The inevitability of this process lies in the fact that the work needed to satisfy needs becomes more abstracted … and in place of the abstracted work, as we have seen, comes the machine. In this way the effects of abstracted work are propagated.… In all these ways want and poverty are multiplied. Likewise, individuals become even more dependent because of the division of labour.' Hegel draws social policy conclusions directly from this diagnosis (though without using the term): 'This is the greater task which falls upon the administration. It must see to it that the individual is given the opportunity to earn through work what is due to him. If people are unemployed, they have a right to demand that work is found for them.' (After Pankoke 1991: 1050ff.).
5. The literature of the 1840s features the term 'social reform', chiefly following Stein (1842). For material on social policy before the concept became fixed see Philippovich (1908) and Reidegeld (1996: 65–150).
6. Stein revised his ground-breaking book *Der Sozialismus und Communismus des heutigen Frankreich* (*Socialism and Communism in Contemporary France*, 1842), then published an enlarged edition in two volumes (1848), and published it in a definitive three-

volume edition under the title *Die Geschichte der sozialen Bewegungen in Frankreich von 1789 bis auf unsere Tage* (*The History of the Social Movements in France from 1789 up to Our Day*) in 1850. For an abridged English version see Stein (1964). Recommended interpretations of the social science content of Stein's work are given by Böckenförde (1976c), Quesel (1989), Koslowski (1995) and in English by Roth (1968).

7. 'If, however, the propertied class exercises the administration of the state in the spirit of the non-propertied classes to alleviate the lot of the workers, provides for their education, and offers the possibility of acquiring capital, even if only slowly, this class will be more indifferent towards the form of the constitution to the extent that its interests are being more strongly promoted. Under such an administration monarchy, dictatorship, aristocracy and democracy are equally possible, precisely because in the end the acquired property makes unfreedom impossible, and because the promotion of paid work becomes the promotion of liberty.... The transition of democracy to that new form is already indicated in the slogan of "social democracy". As of yet the content of that idea is unclear. If it does not emerge from its lack of clarity, it will vanish. If it wants to escape from it, it must become a science of society. Then the future will belong to it' (Stein 1850: vol. 3 , 207).

8. 'The real danger to civil society thus does not lie in socialist teaching but in the unemployment of labour. Consequently the persecution by the police of socialist doctrines and diverse opinions leads to misunderstandings about the nature of the social threat and the role of the police, that is, as long as there is no direct call for the use of physical force against the existing order' (Stein 1888: 75).

9. It was Heimann (1929) who first systematically analyzed the significance of the moral impetus for social policy, the 'social ideal' as the motive force of sociopolitical development. By social ideal he understood the historically influential complex of normative patterns of life in freedom and dignity that, based on Christian traditions and Enlightenment designs for a free society, evolved following the development of capitalism. In his view the labour movement was an important bearer of the social ideal, though it did not in the first place draw on its own ideals but on those of the liberal bourgeoisie in order to demand a similar freedom and dignity for the individual in working life. The gradual transformation of capitalism and of the class conflict it generated were enabled by means of social policy, according to Heimann, because both the working and middle classes shared the same basic values. For further discussion see Kaufmann (2003b: 113ff.).

Chapter 3

CHRISTIAN INFLUENCES
ON SOCIAL REFORM

The question of the significance of Christianity for the emergence of the welfare state was first posed in 1983 by the German-American sociologist Arnold Heidenheimer. In a brilliant essay, he imagined a dialogue between the great sociologist Max Weber and Ernst Troeltsch, a leading theologian of liberal Protestantism in Germany.

In reality, Weber and Troeltsch had actually undertaken a study tour together in the U.S. in 1904. Their aim was to examine the social forms of Protestant Christianity there, to which end they had developed the twin concepts of 'church' and 'sect'. In the course of this tour they visited the World's Fair in St Louis, which is where Heidenheimer placed his imaginary dialogue. It revolved around the question why Germany was the first country to introduce a state-regulated social security system, which in the context of international comparisons is taken today as one of the most important indicators of welfare state development. The Scandinavian countries followed around 1900, while the more strongly industrialized countries – the U.K., France, the Netherlands and the U.S. did so only very gradually (and in the case of U.S. to the present day, only in a very incomplete manner). Germany and the Scandinavian countries were dominated by a strong Lutheran state church, whereas historically Britain, the Netherlands and the U.S. had been much more influenced by Calvinism, which had developed a strongly distanced relationship to state power. Was this – so they asked in Heidenheimer's imaginary dia-

logue – an explanation for the disparate rates of welfare state development (Heidenheimer 1983)?

Quite apart from the possible answers, the underlying question deserves attention. In the broad field of research into the history of social
policy and the development of the welfare state, the influence of religious factors was scarcely recognized until recent times. The general assumption was that the welfare state was brought into being above all by
a social democratic mindset and social democratic parties. In 1970, for
instance, a much-cited *Intellectual History of the Social Movement in the 19th
and 20th Centuries* was published that did not even make a single reference
to Christian social ideas. 'The highest peak and centre point of the intellectual history of the social movement is ... generally agreed to be Marx's
theory, so one can simply talk about before and after Marx's theory' is
how Werner Hofmann (1970: 13) grounded his approach. The dominant
picture of the 'social movement' treats both the romantic and also the
later Christian social movements of both confessions as part of the pre-
Enlightenment era, or else puts them in the sphere of 'bourgeois social reform', where they obviously do not belong, in order to define them out of
'the social movement'. Under the influence of the Scandinavian model,
the welfare state is even treated internationally as characteristically social
democratic (Castles 1978).

It is of course hard to deny that liberal and social democratic thought
can on the whole be credited with more originality and analytical power,
in relation to understanding the new era of industrialization, than can
Christian social thought. By contrast, it was precisely in the pioneering
country of Germany that the Christian social movement was very important for the practical development of social policy and state welfare.
While the motives for Bismarckian social insurance arose primarily from a
conservatism coloured by Protestantism, the demands for state regulation
of factory work in the spirit of equal justice for labour and capital was an
ongoing theme of the Catholic Christian social movement. It began with
Franz Buss's 'Factory Speech' in the Baden Parliament (1837), continued
in the Catholic Party's post-1877 initiatives against Bismarck's rejection
of labour protection, manifested itself in the economic and social policy
foundations of the Weimar Constitution, and even led to the workers'
participation legislation after the Second World War.

Morris Janowitz was among the few early writers who took a position on
the significance and functions of ideas and activities inspired by Christian
belief for the development of the welfare state. He described religious and
altruistic forces as effective but only at the second stage, and he traced the
origins to connections between Protestantism and socialism. Organized
religion had added an integrative ethos to socialist aspirations (Janowitz

1976: 20ff.). Heidenheimer's and Janowitz's conjectures will be examined and explained below, starting with Heidenheimer's assumption that there was no single Christian influence on the development of state welfare but that a variety of Christian influences can be traced, depending on confessional denominations and relationships between church and state.[1]

The Welfare State

From the perspective of social theory, the welfare state appears as a politically determined form of social organization that aspires to guarantee all members of a community a chance to participate in the important aspects of social life – in other words, social inclusion. From this viewpoint, the development of a welfare state starts where state action intervenes to ensure that extra-local begging is not simply suppressed but is socially integrated. Milestones along this road are the Elizabethan Poor Laws in England (1597–1601) and the Prussian General State Law of 1794, and building on that, its introduction of a Settlement Law in the 1842 legislation. The factory acts and the creation of a social security system also appeared from this standpoint as measures to assure the industrial worker of a recognized social status both in and outside the productive process. Even more obviously, publicly regulated social services such as education, health and social welfare contribute to social inclusion.

How to explain the relative stability of a social formation constituted on welfare state lines, where the economically powerful and socially influential are compelled to surrender some of their powers and to carry the greater part of the financial costs? An explanation based on democratic theory, which relies on the growing political influence of disadvantaged groups in society, is clearly insufficient to explain the stability of the arrangement. It is more likely that the substantial economic success and social stability from which the propertied and influential social classes profited was a consequence of the state welfare arrangements themselves. In retrospect, the welfare state has not only solved the problem of social inclusion but ensured social peace with a minimum of state repression and, not least, the broad-based evolution of human capabilities both within and outside the economic sphere, something that today provides the foundations for the productivity of the most developed countries on earth.

What has religion – and Christianity in particular – to do with the emergence of this form of social organization? Theories of the sociology of religion suggest that a principal social function of religion lies in the guarantee of social integration. The novel mechanisms of social inclusion outlined above have obviously contributed to the collective social integration of 'modern society', and one can consequently assume that they have something to do with religion. But how? Could the legitimation of the welfare state perhaps represent a new religion, a so-called civil religion that supersedes an obsolescent Christianity? Or does it show that Christianity was a major force both in the genesis of the welfare state and may also perhaps be for its future?

The answer is, as can only be expected from such broad questions, multifaceted and not in the least unequivocal. I must confine answering this question to outlining a central chain of argument.

The Influence of Christianity

If European societies on the way to modernization did not break down over the contradictions of liberalism and socialism but instead found their way to the solution of state social politics on a new integrated level, it is largely thanks to the effects of the Christian mindset and to people and social movements motivated by Christianity. Three strands of ideas will be argued to support this proposition. In intellectual history, the fundamental belief in man being made in the image of God, together with the institutionalized stabilization of the equal powers of kaiser and pope, formed a central precondition for the doctrine of human rights, modern social differentiation and state social inclusion. British development manifestly exemplifies the social ethical effectiveness of religious protest. The German example represents the eventual interaction of conservative-Protestant conceptions of the state with Christian social movements characterized by Catholicism. Political and pragmatic considerations, then, emerge as more important than church doctrines, which nevertheless rejected, on Christian grounds, both liberalism's atomistic social assumptions and class conflict, in favour of social integrative strategies based on the state.

Conceptual Factors

The fact that the social forms of the welfare state arose only in those parts of Europe in which the Western tradition remained unbroken and in which Christianity thus remained uncontested as the principal religion for 1,500 years, and spread thence to colonies elsewhere in the world, suggests a strong a priori case for a connection. Although Max Weber and Ernst Troeltsch held that the development processes that led to modern society chiefly started with the Reformation, modern sociological and social history research suggests preconditions reaching back into the eleventh century. Eugen Rosenstock-Huessy (1938) described Pope Gregory VII's papal decree of 1075, his revolt against continuing dominance by the emperor as in the recently separated (1054) eastern Byzantine Church, as the first Western revolution. In particular, the great sociolegal study by Berman (1983), together with Nelson's researches (1977), manifests the breakthrough in both principle and institutional practice that occurred in the twelfth century through the conflict and eventual stabilization of different functions and status equivalence between emperor and pope – namely, the development of rival doctrines of law, scholastic philosophy and universities, as well as the assumption of independence by medieval cities and the consequent growth in trade. Within a few decades this laid the foundations for a new and differentiated form of society. Its inner dynamic brought forth the very processes of rationalization and modernization whose many aspects the social sciences have tried to explain from their outset.

The specific effects of Christianity are of course hard to isolate in the context of this unique Western path, and in any case the ways in which the churches practised Christian ideas were by no means always in conformity. If one interprets Western history as the unfolding of growing freedoms, then the achievement of institutionalized church liberty in the 'investiture controversy' (1075–1125) marks a significant switch in direction towards a functional differentiation of religion and society (Kaufmann 1989: 77ff.). As a result, it was chiefly the religious movements, in somewhat strained relationships with the dominant church, that carried forward the idea of freedom. A decisive moment was the emigration of the puritan Dissenters to the New World, where the libertarian aspects of modern constitutions were first voiced (Morgan 1988). 'In the conviction that there was a right to conscience independent of the state, the point was found from which the variety of inalienable individual rights grow' (Jellineck 1904: 51). The belief that the individual is endowed 'by God and Nature' with specific rights that do not derive from the state is the basis of the American Bill of Rights and the democratic postulates that follow from it. And although the Catholic Church tenaciously struggled against the liberal doctrines of human rights in the nineteenth century, its opposition to absolutist state demands precisely in Catholic states acted de facto to set limits to the state, thus strengthening the development of a differentiated liberal form of society.[2]

The idea of universal human rights, derived from the 'natural law' of early modernity and now part of the normative assumptions of at least the Western world, was consequently revolutionary because it ascribed such rights to each individual irrespective of his or her social and political allegiances. This radical idea of fundamental human equality, which goes beyond the concept of *aequalitas* as related to the conditions for virtue in Stoic philosophy, originates in the Christian doctrine of the equality of all men on the basis of their creation in the image of God and salvation through Jesus Christ. Even if church theology began to legitimate social inequality once again in the period after Constantine, the belief in Christian equality was retained chiefly in the monastic orders and the poverty movements of the late Middle Ages. Luther revived the idea again, though only in the sense of inner intrinsic equal value, not outward social equality. That conclusion began to be drawn only during the Enlightenment (Dann 1975: 1001 ff).

The fundamental belief in the equal worth of all human beings is the only basis for understanding the power of those processes that are associated with the idea of increasing inclusion. We all know that exclusion, humiliation, impoverishment or even the deliberate liquidation of entire human groups have historically been the rule rather than the exception, up to the present day. This is the background against which the historical weight of the continuing expansion of everyman's (and nowadays every woman's) opportunities for involvement and participation becomes comprehensible in the process of welfare state evolution. Thus a universalistic ethos shattering group and class barriers, as Christianity had laid down from the very beginning, materialized itself institutionally. Even today its effective power does not seem to have diminished, notwithstanding that its origins in Christianity have been widely forgotten. In this context the sociology of religion refers to an implicit Christianity that has materialized in the structures of the welfare state.[3] As the originally moral demands have increasingly acquired the character of legal conditions, so their Christian content has become hard to see. Further, the German religious welfare organizations Caritas (Catholic) and Diakonie (Lutheran), displaced from their traditional charitable position by the development of state welfare, have had to decide on their new role in society (Coughlin 1965; Gabriel 2001). From this perspective the development of the welfare state appears as the correlate of those processes that we are used to identifying with the concept of secularization.

For those sociologists who offer no apologia for Christianity but seek a preferably non-partisan societal development, lines of development stretching over centuries, such as sketched out above, present major risks of interpretation that can be ameliorated only by appropriate studies of social, theoretical and conceptual history. The approach outlined above is relatively secure: for instance, the historian Benjamin Nelson, an authority who cannot be suspected of an exaggeratedly evolution-theory interpretation, arrives in his pursuit of Weber's question at the conclusion that 'an especially important' key to understanding the unique Western path lies in 'the different reactions of east and west to the pressures imposed by the drive to greater brotherhood and universality' (Nelson 1977: ix). As far as the present day is concerned, the study by Rieger and Leibfried (2004) incisively demonstrates the disparate 'social theologies' of Christianity and Confucianism, and their consequences in the lack of provisions qualifying as welfare states in East Asia.

Here one must recall a second line of argument that became known through Max Weber's celebrated study of *The Protestant Ethic and the Spirit of Capitalism*: the positive value Christianity places on physical work as a condition of the labour discipline process in early modern times. In any case, more recent research has placed the significance of the Reformation into relative context; the positive value placed on work and occupation prevailed during the late Middle Ages, and the rational approach was already a product of the Renaissance (Delumeau 1967). The puritan assurance of salvation through work is now seen more as an exception in a significantly broader movement towards religiously legitimated social discipline, which in practice was imposed by the exercise of power or the pressures of competition.[4] In any case, the stabilization of regular, well-disciplined labour capacity was a significant condition for the success of industrialization and, building on that, the growth of the social sector. And the growth of the social sector itself contributed to the stabilization of labour capacity and – as became increasingly important over time – to the stock of labour skills.

Intervention by the State as the Central Issue

These general connections do not, however, quite answer the question of the specific contribution that Christianity has made to the development of the welfare state in modern society. As suggested in the introduction, the dominant interpretation assumes that on the whole it was pressure from the socialist labour movement that set social policy reforms into motion, even where bourgeois governments implemented them.[5] It is doubtless true that fear of the rising socialist movement was a significant condition for the political practicability of Bismarckian social insurance legislation. And it must be asserted that as a rule, social reforms presuppose a substantial pressure from problems that the simple existence of misery, social inequality and the exploitation of the socially weak cannot explain. Only when unjust social conditions are problematized as such, and when organized minorities at least arouse among the rulers awareness that the status quo cannot be maintained, can one expect opportunities for change. In this sense it is indisputable that the existence of a revolutionary wing in the German workers' movement, as well as internationally, contributed to raising the pressure of the political problem, and thus to reducing established political groups' resistance to proposals for reform as the lesser of evils.

The Western European welfare states, however, are obviously not the child of revolution but the outcome of a mass of sociopolitical reforms whose cumulative effects can only in retrospect be seen to have a progressive orientation, one that at the time of the struggle over these reforms was generally the aim of only a minority of those involved. Further, the historical development that this successful evolutionary path has followed cannot be taken for granted. A ruthless class struggle or a systematic oppression, never mind the eradication of all rebellious elements and the enslavement of the remainder, might not have been any less likely, judging by human historical experience so far.[6]

In the nineteenth century, the ideologies of liberalism and socialism stood irreconcilably opposed on the central questions of the ownership of the means of production and on economic freedom, even if in some respects they seemed to resemble each other, such as in rejecting state intervention for the solution of the social question. But it was precisely this path that proved to be successful.

If from this perspective we ask what brought about the state-induced solution of the social question in the nineteenth century, we find above all individuals, groups and movements for whom the Christian mindset meant more than the legitimation of submission to authority and reactionary traditionalism. It would be premature to identify this with the Christian socialist movement, since its adherents often engaged their Christian commitment with both conservative and liberal political tendencies. It would also be too simplistic to ascribe a single view of the state to all these Christians, or to assert that they alone helped to bring about the measures that we retrospectively recognize as significant for the development of the welfare state. Circumstances varied from country to country: in Scandinavia, Christian motives seem to have played a lesser role in welfare state development than in Britain and Western Europe.[7] This study will focus on the pioneering countries Britain and Germany, which also have the most extensive research material for use.[8]

Britain

Up to the First World War, the political situation in the U.K. was marked by the opposition of Liberals and Conservatives, but no clear social policy battle lines were thereby exposed. Social policy advances were, rather, the outcome of coalitions cutting across party lines that often brought quite ideologically disparate groups together (Frazer 1984: 13). What is demonstrable is the persistent influence of religious movements, mainly at arm's length from the High Church association of Crown and Cross.[9]

Anglican clergymen began to campaign against child labour as early as the beginning of the nineteenth century, and as a result many social reformers were close to the evangelical wing of the Anglican church, from which many initiatives for social and caring action stemmed (Bradley 1976; Heclo 1974: 159, 165ff.). Many social reformers came from the free churches and were close to the business world, which was itself mainly oriented towards Nonconformism.[10] The deep-seated and widespread moral outrage over the growing distress in the factories drew its strength primarily from religious convictions. Quite apart from the Poor Laws, in which Bentham's suggestions were implemented through empirically based socio-technical legislation, the chief argument for strengthening state activity was the protection of the socially weak, particularly women and children. The social reforms in the mid-nineteenth century arose from the connection between the conservative idea of a 'paternalistic government' and the idea of a 'reforming state' (Roberts 1979; Briggs 1978: 274ff.; Frazer 1984: 15ff.). A specifically religious influence is clearly discernible in the later social reforms as well. One example is the Liberal Lloyd George, whose legislation (1908–20) is seen as laying the foundations of the welfare state; the earth-shattering electoral triumph of the Liberals in 1906 was brought about, inter alia, by collaboration with English Nonconformism (Koss 1975). Another example is the historian Richard H. Tawney (1880–1962), a Christian who was very influential in the Labour Party. But no religious motivation can be detected in the social reforms following the Second World War.

German Protestantism

While an extensive literature treats both of the great Christian confessions in Germany, it tends to be somewhat one-sided and sometimes even biased in the treatment of its own contribution to the solution of the social question.[11] Only a few works examine the connections between Christianity and social policy from a bi-confessional perspective (Blackburn 1980; Brakelmann 1971; Greschat 1980; Kaufmann 1983; Lampert and Althammer 1987: 67ff.; Schneider 1982). And there is a total absence of studies that evaluate the significance of social reform ideas inspired by Christian beliefs, together with social movements based on them, as against other influences. I must confine myself here to a few tentative characterizations.

In the Lutheran sphere the tension is notable, as in Britain, between the rule of the established state church and the movement for pietistic revival, which was itself based on the earlier conditions in the Pietistic movement of Halle in the eighteenth century (Hinrichs 1977; M. Schmidt 1978). A significant number of Prussian state employees were influenced by Pietism, and some had actually been educated in Halle. The most prominent nineteenth-century social reformers were Protestants sympathetic to Pietism with strongly expressed religious views. Examples include the Reichsfreiherr Karl vom und zum Stein, who initiated peasant emancipation and the Prussian local government constitution (Schnabel 1965: 51ff.); Ernst von Bodelschwingh, the Prussian minister of the interior and also Oberpräsident (highest official) of the Rheinland, who introduced the first child protection legislation and the 1845 Prussian Factory Act (Shanahan 1962: 194ff.); or Theodor Lohmann, the senior civil servant to whom, as effectively its leading spirit, the Reich's entire social legislation from 1880 to 1906 must be credited (Rothfels 1927).[12]

However, while this person-centred perspective is easy to pursue, it can only illustrate the influence of Protestantism on the developing trend towards the welfare state; it cannot explain it. What was decisive was the Prussian state's fundamental identification with the predominantly Lutheran state church.[13] The idea of a 'Christian state' as represented by Friedrich Wilhelm IV and the influential conservative philosopher of the state, Friedrich Julius Stahl, was simply the visible pinnacle of a concept of the state whose clear anti-revolutionary and anti-enlightenment tones dominated the entire century, which explains the socialist workers' movement's antagonism to Christianity. Stahl's philosophy of the state influenced even Bismarck, for whom the concerns of social legislation were the direct expression of 'a state socialism which was above all the outcome of the modern Christian concept of the state' (Tennstedt 1981b: 668). This belief in the social responsibility of the 'Christian state' clearly distinguished the conservative from the liberal wing of German Protestantism, although even within conservative Protestantism no notable interest in the social question developed in the second half of the nineteenth century. It was chiefly individuals, such as Theodor Fliedner, Johann Hinrich Wiechern, Rudolf Todt, Adolf Stöcker and Friedrich Naumann, who developed a wider awareness of social issues through their personal contacts in influential political circles. In general, the Protestant Christian social movement remained weak, and its lasting contribution has been in the field of Diakonie, the denominational social services, rather than in national social policy (Brakelmann 1966; Beyreuther 1962). Much more influential in this field was the Verein für Sozialpolitik, whose prominent members included numerous politically engaged Protestants such as Adolph Wagner and Lujo Brentano.

Since the Conservative Party followed Bismarck and later Wilhelm II, together with the Catholic Party (the Zentrum) they formed the parliamentary majority for social legislation up to the First World War. But this happened less through engagement with the idea of social policy than because of 'loyalty to the Kaiser and the Reich', which has been described as 'a taken-for-granted assumption about the state based on a scarcely distinguishable mixture of idealistic state theory and the Lutheran doctrine of submission to authority' (Schick 1970: 121).

The Catholic Social Movement and the Zentrum

Even the comparatively detailed *Social History of Social Policy in Germany* by Florian Tennstedt refers to the Christian social movement only as an 'also-ran'. For example, the 1889 Ruhr miners' strike is treated as a key event, with the additional comment that

> [a]mong the principal participants were Catholic mineworkers, relatively colourless politically, and as Ultramontanes not gladly welcomed in Bismarck's Reich, but the ostracised Social Democrats could not be blamed as instigators. What was both striking and alarming about this miners' strike was precisely that it combined massively disruptive work stoppages with loyalty to the state. (Tennstedt 1981a: 228)

To describe the Catholic social movement as politically colourless is to attribute colour only to extremes. That is not a fair description: as the name of the associated political party Zentrum shows, the movement stood in the centre and was thus open to coalitions on all sides, and it demonstrated the most reliable and continuous support for social policy development towards the welfare state.

By clear contrast with Protestantism, the social movement in German Catholicism became, if not a dominant power, a politically influential one. At the heart of the so-called social Catholicism was the Volksverein für das katholische Deutschland (People's Association for a Catholic Germany), founded in 1890, which at its peak shortly before the First World War numbered no fewer than 800,000 members. The association, based in Mönchengladbach, described itself as a 'promotional society for Christian social reform' (Heitzer 1979: 24), combining a programme of work with adult education and the formation of leadership in the Catholic social movement. Sociologically speaking, it can be credited with a key position because – as was also the case with the Zentrum – it recruited from all social classes, in other words effectively trying to bridge the chasm between the middle and working classes that had been deepening ever since the 1860s. The People's Association and its associated Catholic social movement were thus not simply a bourgeois movement like the Christian social movement around Stöcker and Naumann.[14] The Catholic sphere was far more effective in that it neutralized the rampant class conflict and replaced it with a programme of social reform combined with action whose goal was, in the words of Franz Hitze, 'the complete incorporation of the working class into the organs of society' (Mockenhaupt 1977: 175).

The idea that it was the church – not the state – that was called upon to solve the 'social question' of the disinherited classes and was positioned to do so was widely held by Catholics in the nineteenth century and particularly influenced Catholic social thought in France and Belgium (Greschat 1980: 113ff., 178ff.). The switch to state social policy in German Catholicism is thus remarkable and was a characteristic of the Zentrum, not only following the Bismarckian initiatives but ever since its foundation. The electoral programme in Essen in 1870 demanded 'elimination of the social injustices sustaining the moral and physical ruin of the workers, and the promotion of the interests of the working class through sound Christian legislation', while early in 1871 a policy statement by Bishop von Ketteler of Mainz concretized these demands in the form of a wide-ranging social policy programme.

What became decisive for the state-friendly orientation of the Catholic social movement in Germany was Bishop von Ketteler's change of attitude, since his previous writings had anticipated the solution of the 'social question' through church charitable work and guild-type associations, and even by producers' cooperatives on the Lassalle model (Jostock 1965; Greschat 1980: 134–35; Wattler 1978: 18ff.). In any case, there were also typical divisions within the movement on how far state influence was desirable. These differences crystallized around Bismarck's plan for state subventions to the proposed workers' contributory pension scheme (1889). The majority of the Zentrum rejected this as a form of 'state socialism', but thanks to the support of the Zentrum's minority it was passed by the Reichstag. Following corporatist doctrine, the majority favoured pensions financed exclusively by agreement between employers and employees on a self-management basis. But the minority view was expressed by Peter Reichensperger in terms that reflected the spirit of the welfare state: 'The state is, for us, the organised association of the people caring for all material and spiritual resources, and that ought also to be realised here' (Bachem 1929: 71).

At the theoretical level of debate, the principal figures were Georg von Hertling, representing a restrictive and solely legalistic approach to the state, and on the other hand Franz Hitze, standing for 'state compulsion to implement a just social order' (Bachem 1929: 20). The 'Mönchengladbach line' in Catholic social thought stood firmly on the basis of parliamentarianism and, later, democracy, by contrast with the 'Vienna line' around Carl von Vogelsang, which favoured the re-establishment of a corporate political system.[15] The Mönchengladbach corporatism was confined to the economic sphere, where a solution to the social question was envisaged from the collaboration of employers and workers on a number of levels. These ideas found concrete expression in the consultative committee system under the Weimar Constitution and the Betriebsrätegesetz (Works' Council Act) of 1920, as well as in the Federal Republic's Betriebsverfassungsgesetz (Industrial Constitution Act) of 1953.

All in all, one must not exaggerate the logical consistency of the leading ideas of the Catholic social movement of that time. The members of the People's Association and of the *Zentrum* Party were first of all practical men – politicians, popular educators and organizers. There were few Catholic scholars at that time, and even after the end of the *Kulturkampf*[16] cultural Protestantism ruled the academic field. Not until after the First World War did Catholic scholarly reflection became weightier – and with it the associated academic arguments over social policy, disregarding the pressing problems of the time (Briefs 1925; Kaufmann 2003b: 98ff.). Apart from the monumental creation of a solidaristic economics (Pesch 1920–26) that clarified the theoretical contribution of Catholic corporatism, the positive content of the expanding Catholic social thought lay mainly in scholarly interpretation of papal encyclicals; only rarely did it find its way to the analysis of actual empirical problems.

In the Reichstag, the Zentrum evolved into the group that most emphatically promoted the politics of labour protection and workers' political and social emancipation in the framework of the existing political order (Stegmann 1978). In terms of what it contained, the Zentrum's social policy programme largely coincided with demands also made by the Social Democrats, but by contrast with the Social Democrats the Zentrum pursued a pragmatic politics (modern political scientists would call it incrementalist) of ameliorating the workers' conditions. The Zentrum was even prepared to reach compromises when more thoroughgoing demands could not be achieved.[17] Against this, up to the First World War the Social Democrats followed an uncompromising political line, permitting the defeat of much social legislation because they could not force their wider political objectives through. At that time this attracted criticism that they were more interested in revolution than in the improvement of workers' conditions.

Following the fall of Bismarck, the Catholics began to gain influence in the social policy sections of the Ministries of the Interior and Commerce.

From 1906 they also took part in government, and after the First World War the ministerial responsibility for social policy went, after a short interim Social Democratic period, to the Zentrum in the person of the priest Heinrich Brauns, who became minister for labour in the cabinets of twelve governments between 1920 and 1928 (Mockenhaupt 1977). According to Ludwig Preller, the spiritual foundations of social reform were less inspired by Catholic thought but 'representatives of Catholicism developed … an influence on the [practical] design of social policy which cannot be overestimated'. Evangelical thought, by contrast, left 'no detectable impression on post-war social policy' (Preller 1949: 221, 225).

In short, it is clear that chiefly two forces drove the development of German national social policy: Reich Chancellor Bismarck together with some of the conservatives who stood behind him, and the Zentrum. The social policy perspectives of these two forces were not identical, however. Out of a sense of Christian responsibility and political zeal, Bismarck wanted to prevent the workers' descent into poverty, and he saw his social insurance policies mainly as a new form of paternalistic poverty policy that would satisfy the workers and profit the Reich. He thus opposed on economic grounds all attempts to strengthen workers' protections and guarantee their rights at work. However, the thrust of the Zentrum's social policies lay in this second field. The principal goal of Catholic social policy was to bring about state provisions for the improvement of relations between employers and employees and thus avoid an escalation of class conflict. Furthermore, the Zentrum's federalistic approach distinguished it from Bismarck's centralizing politics. This was expressed in legislation chiefly as the decentralization of administration, so that while Bismarck aimed for a national centralized organization for industrial injuries insurance and old age pensions, the Zentrum's opposition led on the contrary to the establishment of the occupational and locally based social insurance schemes that still existed at the end of the twentieth century.

Taken as a whole, it is evident that the current form of the German welfare state largely corresponds to the Zentrum's earlier political vision. On the one hand, a strong central state function in the sphere of legislation does not disdain intervention in economic processes; this is the anti-liberal component. On the other hand, the stabilization and pacification of the conflicts of interest between employers and employees without the involvement of the state is nowadays widely expressed in occupational wage bargaining and the self-management of social insurance funds, which comprises the corporatist and anti-socialist element of these policies. Finally, the emphasis on federalism and the right to independent social services – in short the solution, in principle, of the decentralization problem (which Catholic social thought conceptualized as the principle of subsidiarity) – is the anti-statist component that in the early stages ran counter to Prussian and Bismarckian centralism. This principle of plurality and the relative autonomy of the organizations involved in social policy, together with trust in the potential for finding decentralized solutions to problems, is what distinguishes the structure of the German welfare state very clearly from that of the British.

The policies and the approach of the Zentrum contributed significantly to Pope Leo XIII's adoption of a positive view on the democratic state and his final assent to Catholic political action independent of the church hierarchy (Bachem 1929: 208). Even the first papal encyclical on the social question, *Rerum Novarum* (1891), was deeply influenced by German Catholicism's experience in social politics (Bachem 1929: 125ff.). The transition from church and rank to state methods of combating problems was thus less programmatic than pragmatic.

The circumstance of the Catholics' embroilment in the *Kulturkampf* after the foundation of the German Reich in 1871 enabled the formation of a representative denominational party that, on the basis of its almost complete dedication to Church concerns, managed to overcome almost all Church reservations. To the extent that external pressures allowed and the Zentrum became a politically powerful force, the tensions within Catholicism themselves also became apparent, even though at this time the historical decision in favour of the welfare state model had already been taken.

Conclusion

To conclude, let us return to the theory of the welfare state. Its most convincing foundations can be traced to Lorenz von Stein in the mid-nineteenth century and to Eduard Heimann in the 1920s. While von Stein made a thorough analysis of the necessity for state intervention in social conditions in order to regulate class contradictions (see chapter 2), Heimann (1929) introduced a new aspect, that one cannot assume that the state alone has either the insight or the power to solve the social problem. Only a social movement acting in the name of a social vision (Heimann meant the realization of liberal rights to freedom and human dignity even for the working class) and using the political means available to it to change social conditions can activate the state's social policy potentialities. Even if social policy on a national scale remains limited by capitalism's current productive potential, the social movement is effective, though in the sense of a gradual transformation of capitalism.

What is needed is to draw out the organisational and technical creativity of capitalism and build it into a free social order.... Social policy is the institutionalised insertion of the social idea into capitalism.... It is the realisation of the social idea in capitalism against that capitalism. The peculiar significance of social policy is its double status both as an alien intruder and as a component of the capitalist system, that's social policy's double identity as conservative and revolutionary. (Heimann 1929: 158, 167–68)

The transformation of the socially unstable early and high capitalism into the societal welfare statist form would not have been possible without idealistic foundations. These resulted from a synthesis of conservative, liberal and socialist intellectual sources, an admittedly unstable and politically variable synthesis that is more likely to be attained from a Christian perspective than by other political and ideological currents.

This Christian social perspective did not, however, generally correspond to the dominant assumptions of the various Christian denominations to which the protagonists of social policies belonged. This expresses a more generalized characteristic of the Judaeo-Western religious tradition: that its vitality and openness to change derive from the tension between the institution and the individual. The prophet stands before the king; Jesus against the Jewish establishment; the medieval movements for religious poverty and the modern religious revival movements against the ruling power of the church. Even the German Catholic social movement could only follow its chosen path after dramatic confrontations with sections of the German episcopate and the maximum of diplomatic tact in relations with Rome (see Anderson 1981).

In the German case presented here, ideas, associations and activities motivated by Christian belief seem to have been highly significant in the breakthrough to the welfare state. That does not diminish the significance of liberalism for the development of the market economy – a prerequisite to generating affluence – nor of socialism as the highly effective opposition to the tyranny in the relations of production. Between the conflicting demands of these great forces, even more powerful in political hindsight, the function of the various initiatives inspired by Christian belief in this field can best be described as catalytic, enabling a process to take place while other forces move it.

The so-called crisis of the welfare state often debated nowadays seems primarily a matter of perception. Hopes that the welfare state would solve all the problems of human coexistence, raised in the decades following the Second World War, have crumbled away. The welfare state is not a salvation but only a fairly effective institutional arrangement constantly requiring that its capacity for reform be put to the test.

Would revived religious motives help this process? The question leads into the broad field of the contemporary diagnosis of Christianity and perspectives on its future (Kaufmann 2000b). In view of the fact that even in the past it was only minorities in the churches whose actions raised social issues, the weakening of popular involvement in the churches is not a counterargument. If the relative significance of Christian engagement is seen in its catalytic rather than interpretative or political effects, then the growing socio-ethical complexity of conditions in our society is no insurmountable barrier.

Moral arguments, which in Europe derive their power from the body of implicitly Christian ideas in modern constitutions and humanistic value systems, may best legitimate a perspective embracing particular interests. The model of the individual responsible before God still seems to be among the strongest sources of individual responsibility, even though in pluralistic societies with their multiple and often contradictory demands, where long-term considerations clash with short-term interests, an unprejudiced evaluation of the balance of interests cannot be assured (Kaufmann 1992). The effect of Christian involvement in all these cases is very diffuse and thus hard to identify in individual instances. This seems to be a general characteristic of the current cultural situation: the plurality of values and the inevitable selectivity of decision-making drive the past and pre-existent implicit normativity of the decision process into the background, compared with the consciously situated viewpoint.

As long and as far as the moral minimum of a general recognition of freedom and social rights for all and their reasonable protection (that is, the basic principle of inclusion based on the values of freedom, equality and security) is not permanently damaged, the debates about social policy in the foreseeable future will probably be carried on without apparent religious fervour. The influence of Christianity remains implicit here in the presuppositions of decision-making. The explicit appearance of religious energies in social movements or policy programmes can be expected only where serious and lasting problematic situations become defined as collective problems in opposition to the manifest postulates of some or most Christian traditions.

Notes

1. The substance of this chapter was first published as Kaufmann (1988a). Kersbergen (1995) has produced an important further study that focuses on the influence of

Christian parties in Europe. Manow (2002) offers a critique of the neglect of confessional factors in Esping-Andersen's typology (1990). An overview of the discussion about various religions' impact on the welfare state, which has intensified in recent times, can be found in Opielka (2008). See also Kahl (2005, 2006); Manow (2009); Kersbergen and Manow (2009).

2. In this context the significant representatives of late medieval Spanish scholasticism should also be mentioned, such as F. Vittoria, F. Suarez or J. De Mariana, who insisted on people's natural rights and defended them equally against both imperial and papal domination (Dempf 1937; Hamilton 1963). The practical consequences of these doctrines can be found especially in the ethic of Spanish colonialism (Höffner 1972).

3. As shown in the history of the origins of the Universal Declaration of the United Nations (see chapter 4), explicitly Christian perspectives played only a subordinate role, most clearly by Jacques Maritain and René Cassin. That this subject even reached the agenda of the United Nations against the reluctance of the U.S. government on this contentious question can be ascribed above all to the human rights movements in the United States supported mainly by Christian and Jewish initiatives (De la Chapelle 1967: 19ff.).

4. On discipline through imposed power see Sachße and Tennstedt (1986); on discipline through competition see Elias (1969). The widening of perspective that this suggests was, moreover, already Max Weber's intention: see Schluchter (1979: 204ff.).

5. These circumstances have subsequently been studied in considerably differentiated detail: see Kersbergen and Manow (2009).

6. The civil wars in Russia and Finland and the only-just-avoided civil war in Germany at the end of the First World War show that we are not dealing with mere abstract considerations here.

7. In Scandinavia, the basic rules of poor relief seem to reach back into the period before Christianization (see Ratzinger 1884: 412ff.). In addition, Christianity's influence on these countries' traditions and culture does not seem to have been as great as in the rest of Europe (see Ebertz and Schultheis 1986: 141ff.). In Sweden and Norway the influence of social democracy was dominant in the development of the welfare state. In Denmark the 'radical liberals' had a similar key effect, as the centre had in Germany (see Flora 1986: 5ff., 120ff., 175ff., 297ff.). In recent decades it seems that something of a Christian reaction has been forming politically against growing secularization (see Madeley 1977).

8. At the time when this article was originally written (1987) only a few cross-national studies existed (Moody 1953; Fogarty 1957; Scholl 1966; Greschat 1980). It is, of course, not enough just to show the existence and activities of Christian ideas and movements, whose relative significance must be evaluated in the context of the national state politics of different countries. On the significance of the relationship between church and state for the formation of confessional parties see Madeley (1982) and Kersbergen and Manow (2009).

9. See Greschat (1980: 11ff.) and Baker (1975). On the history of High Church attitudes towards social questions, see Norman (1976). This study suggests that the Anglican hierarchy was generally involved with the actual contemporary trends. However, even Archbishop William Temple, a leading figure in the Christian social movement, remained reluctant to support political and administrative solutions to social problems, although he is often credited with the first use in Britain of the term 'welfare state' (Temple 1941).

10. Of the fifteen *Founders of the Welfare State* named by Barker (1984), eight clearly have a religious background. Besides that, the ideological motivation generally shows signs of a belief in Benthamite scientific utilitarianism. Marx's ideas seem to have had little impact in spite of his long residence in England.

11. The literature on the Catholic contribution is immense. Summaries can be found in Bauer (1931), Alexander (1953), E. Ritter (1954), Heitzer (1979), Rauscher (1981/82) and Schneider (1981). On the Protestant sphere, see especially Shanahan (1962), Opitz (1969), Schick (1970), Brakelmann (1977) and Kouri (1984).

12. Further reference should be made to the influence of German Protestants on the principle of the 'social market economy' after the Second World War (Manow 2001).

13. The Lutheran and Reformed (Calvinist) provincial churches had already been amalgamated into the Prussian national church during the Restoration period under Friedrich Wilhelm III. The Prussian kings thereafter became head of the unitary Protestant Church.

14. This is also evident in the high level of organization among workers. In 1913, the Catholic workers' associations led by clergymen had 626,000 members consisting mainly of Catholics, while the non-denominational Christian trades unions had 342,000 members (E. Ritter 1954: 328).

15. On their differences, see Alexander (1953), Bachem (1929: 125ff.) and E. Ritter (1954: 56ff.).

16. The '*Kulturkampf*' (cultural struggle) broke out as a political and administrative conflict in Prussia under Bismarck against the Catholic Church as a consequence of the decisions of the first Vatican Council (1870), comparable with what was later waged in the anti-socialist legislation of 1878.

17. The Centre's readiness to compromise over social policy matters naturally also arose from the inherent plurality of interests in a party representing a wide range of class interests.

Chapter 4

WELFARE INTERNATIONALISM BEFORE THE WELFARE STATE
The Emergence of Human Social Rights

Cross-national comparative studies of welfare state development expose not only many similarities in institutional development but also differences for which there is so far no agreed terminology. This is not surprising, since the welfare state development has been achieved – or so it seems at first sight from the perspective of the various national histories – as a political process within the framework of the national state. Welfare state development has its unique points of departure in each country: their political arguments were inflamed by disparate problems, and earlier institutional solutions determined further advances. As a result, the social sciences nowadays refer to the extensive 'path dependency' of national welfare-state development. It follows that under the heading of a country's 'welfare state development' falls not only the dynamic of its institutional growth but also the cultural and political value context that through legitimation and criticism drives the institutional dynamic. The interaction between political conflict (politics) and institutional development (policies) almost inescapably affects the idiosyncratic national characteristics of welfare state development (Kaufmann 2003c: 30ff.).

A large body of comparative welfare-state studies has developed in the past thirty years, one that has taken the common aspects of the focus countries studied as given, thus implying an international concept of 'the welfare state' that is nevertheless rarely explicit. If one looks more closely, it appears that the international comparative studies are concerned almost exclusively with social expenditure, and in particular with the state or quasi-state systems of income maintenance known as 'social security'. The regulation of labour relations and the personal social services rarely fall under comparative scrutiny. The likely reason is that few things are easier to compare than statistics in units of money. The proportion of public expenditure on social services or social protection is commonly used as an acceptable operationalization of the extent of a welfare state, and thus Eurostat (the EU statistical services) and more recently the OECD are making significant efforts to improve the underlying national statistics for the purpose of cross-national comparison, though in that process they inevitably run up against the variety of institutional constraints in each individual country. To use these data uncritically is to implicitly assume that all EU member states – or, what is more problematic, the entire body of OECD countries – can be described as welfare states with comparable social welfare structures.

If, however, one starts from the nationally differentiated developments, it is difficult to reach a single, nationally impartial concept of the welfare state. Currently dominant in research to deal with this problem are trends towards creating typologies of welfare states, following Esping-Andersen (1990), but so far the approach has not led to convincing solutions (Kaufmann 2003c: 21ff.).

The focus in this chapter, however, is another approach to cross-national studies of welfare state development, one that concerns itself not with comparative national developments but with developments at the international level. Efforts to achieve international social policy, and especially programmes of transnational social and economic policies, are vital for a common prior understanding of welfare state development, even if their legal enforceability remains weak. Studying international developments allows one to draw firmer theoretical conclusions about the social or welfare state than can be reached by inductive generalization based on studying national developments. In the international arena, national characteristics are discursively generalized, not just by scientific researchers but by the participating national politicians and their experts, thus leading in part to new concepts. These international discursive processes act on preconceptions of the nature of welfare states, something that is rarely seen in cross-national comparative welfare state studies so far.

The period in which the welfare state was constituted is generally seen as what the French call 'les trente glorieuses', the thirty glorious years between the end of the Second World War in 1945 and the subsequent long period of growth in Western economies, up to the collapse of the Bretton Woods monetary system and the first international oil crisis. Of course there had been many social policy reforms before that, not least the pioneering German social insurance legislation of the 1880s associated with the name of Reich Chancellor von Bismarck. It was at that time that an idea emerged under the name of 'social policy', but only in German, which conceptualized state activity in the interests of the disadvantaged classes, in the sense of a key political theme (Kaufmann 2003b; see also chapter 2). At the international level, concepts like social policy or welfare state originated only after the Second World War and the developments outlined below.

The idea of labour protection became internationally accepted at the start of the twentieth century, but it was less a political programme than a painstaking attempt to make isolated provisions internationally binding. Only the Allies' concern about the aims of the Second World War enabled U.S. President Franklin D Roosevelt and British Prime Minister Winston Churchill, meeting on the high seas, to formulate the leading ideas of the post-war settlement, as noted by the press release of 14 August 1941. This so-called Atlantic Charter, which was not even signed by the participants, was intended as little more than a brief public explanation primarily for propaganda purposes. As a result, it nevertheless symbolized the start of international welfare state activity, which reached its programmatic peak in the United Nations' Universal Declaration of Human Rights in 1948. The heart of this chapter traces these achievements, taking for granted the much-described evolution of the idea of universal human rights in the second half of the eighteenth century; it focuses solely on the emergence of the idea of human social rights, to be understood initially in the concrete sense of 'economic, social and cultural rights' in the spirit of articles 22–27 of the UN's Universal Declaration of Human Rights.

Primitive forms of human social rights in the form of a state's objectives or its obligations to care for its citizens can be traced back to early modern ideas of the state, and were first given voice at the constitutional level in article 21 of the Jacobin constitution of 1793 in France.[1] Although the presumption of state responsibility for care was already being discussed in the context of the 1789 French constitution, the consequence was that human social rights became widely associated with the regime of terror by the Comité du salut public (Committee of Public Safety, meaning well-being), and thus discredited (Krause 1981). This can only be mentioned briefly as introduction, since our focus is on international developments in the first half of the twentieth century and the emergence of a specific pattern of politico-social responsibility, namely the form of universal human rights. The discussion will present not only the political processes and institutional outcomes but also three writers who had a lasting influence on the generation of the idea of social rights: the British writer H.G. Wells, the French philosopher Jacques Maritain and the Russian-French sociologist Georges Gurvitch. The conclusion will offer some reflections on current issues around human social rights.

International Social Policy and the Emergence of Welfare State Programmatics

The Internationalization of Social Policy Problems and the International Labour Office

The movement that later attracted the label of 'social policy' originated in the suffering of children exploited to the point of exhaustion in the early stages of industrialization. Even the earliest proponent of labour protection laws for children, the Scottish mill owner Robert Owen, not only initiated a Parliamentary prohibition on the employment of children under the age of nine in Britain, but also pressed for an international solution to the problem. As early as 1818 he made recommendations for the protection of women and children in two memoranda to governments in Europe.

It was Switzerland, above all, that subsequently became engaged in internationalizing labour protection. The cantons of Zürich and Glarus were among the global pioneers of labour protection laws, and at the Confederal level the most extensive factory legislation in the world was passed in 1877. The principal provisions were a prohibition on child labour for those under the age of fourteen, an eleven-hour standard working day, maternity leave, restrictions on night working, factory inspection and the regulation of labour contract law.[2]

The reason for Switzerland's international policy initiative, alongside the humane motives expressed by the movement for social policy, was concern about the international competitiveness of Swiss industry, since it seemed to be threatened because of its strict labour protection standards. But precisely on these competition grounds, the diplomatic initiatives for international factory legislation, or at least for an international, collectively financed labour office, had almost no success. However, it became possible to found a non-governmental organization in 1900, the Internationalen Vereinigung für gesetzlichen Arbeitsschutz (the International Association for Labour Legislation), which set up an International Labour Office in Basel as its organizational base. Though synonymous with the International Labour Office founded after the First World War, this first initiative was no 'office' in the conventional sense but rather an international amalgamation of civil reformers in national sections, among whom the German Gesellschaft für Soziale Reform (Association for Social Reform) and the American Association for Labor Legislation were among the leading members.[3] Before the First World War Basel had organized several international government conferences, which led to two multilateral agreements with social policy implications, namely the prohibition of women's night work and of white phosphorus in match manufacture. The adoption and ratification of further agreements was blocked by the outbreak of the First World War. In general and with few exceptions, these agreements were ratified only by states that had themselves already legislated internally for the corresponding prohibitions. Thus the instrument of international agreements had indeed been set up and tested before the First World War, but it led to real progress in social policy in only a few instances. Most states followed the declared interests of their domestic industries without recognizing that the improvement of labour protection is advantageous economically and often also in the interests of business. It was not by chance that the labour protection standards, once achieved, were not again questioned at times of economic crisis.

The First World War led to a strengthening of the labour movement in most industrial nations, and also to an expansion of trades unions' international activities. Congresses in Leeds (1916) and Bern (1917 and 1919) set out the labour movement's wide-ranging demands for international labour legislation (Heyde 1919; Tczerclas von Tilly 1924: 24–42). These initiatives converged with those of the bourgeois social reformers. But even at government level, under the pressure of the Russian revolution there was growing recognition of the need for the internationalization of labour protection, so much so that the topic became an important item at the Versailles Peace Conference that ended the First World War.

In any case, neither the substantive demands of the international trade union movement nor the proposals of the German government could ensure that decisions taken by the international organization would lay an immediate duty on signatory governments. Rather, section XIII of the Versailles Peace Treaty of 1919, dedicated to the subject of labour, chiefly contained legal rules pertaining to the foundation, organization and operational modes of the International Labour Organisation (ILO) as a facility of the League of Nations, nowadays the United Nations. An International Labour Office set up in Geneva as its executive body, now constituted under international law, immediately took over as successor to the non-governmental International Labour Office in Basel. Substantial objectives for the ILO were outlined in the concluding article 427, but without implying any immediate obligations for the signatory states.

By comparison with any agreements made under international law during the era of national states, section XIII of the Versailles Peace Treaty displayed a number of unusual characteristics:

1. A very detailed code of procedure, containing the rudiments of an international control mechanism;
2. The creation of a permanent organization in the form of the annual representative general meeting of the signatory states, and an administration under international law in the form of the International Labour Office mentioned above, the latter being under a management council on which the chief industrial nations were permanently represented;
3. The tripartite composition of the ILO's structure. Each country was represented by four delegates with one vote each, of whom two represented the current national labour ministry and one each represented the trades unions and the employers' organizations. This pattern of representation, unusual in international organizations, emphasized the importance of its recognition by the representatives of capital and labour in the solution of the social problem. Until then, progress in social policy had usually been achieved only as the result of productive compromises between the power holders of industrial production in society. However, the foundation of the ILO did not merely reflect an international political revaluation of trades unions and employers' associations, but also an upgrading of the ministries in national states concerned with labour and social problems, in the sense that these could now negotiate international social policy issues directly, without going through the usual foreign policy channels (Wallin 1969: 51);
4. The lack of any powers of veto by either nations or specific groups. Voting was not weighted by group interests but by the votes cast by those actually present, so that a variety of different combinations of majorities might be achieved. Decisions were, as a rule, taken on the basis of simple majorities of those representatives present, but a more qualified majority was required for particularly important decisions, such as the adoption of proposals for conventions.

All in all, this was at that time a novel and path-breaking procedure for arriving at decisions under international law. In any case, the regulations did not require the ILO member states to incorporate the standards adopted by the ILO into their domestic law. They were only obliged to bring the relevant rules to the attention of the nationally responsible bodies (generally the parliaments) for decision on their implementation. The obligation under international law was thus confined to consideration of the matters proposed but not their statutory implementation, so that national sovereignty in giving assent was not affected.

The ILO's activities were carried out on two levels. One was the political level of the general assembly, which by a qualified majority of two thirds of the votes cast could adopt defined social policy standards either as 'proposals' (non-binding suggestions for nationally legislated norms) or as 'schemes for international agreement', which would become binding under international law if they were ratified by national governments.[4] The significant effect of the ILO consisted of its capacity to define purposive standards at all, and then to render them acceptable both to governments and to the social partners, thereby confronting national parliaments with well-balanced proposals that they could accept or reject but that they could not eradicate from the agenda.[5] But independent of ratification, in many countries the ILO's proposals and standards acted as models and were to some extent incorporated into national legislative processes. The effect of the standards was naturally greater in countries experiencing increasing industrialization. In countries with well-developed labour- and social legislation that exceeded the ILO standards, the ratification of the covenants implied at the very least a prohibition on falling back, which had practical effects during the global economic crisis.

Furthermore, the ILO looked after the administrative and operational tasks of the International Labour Office. In its early days its dominant tasks were the collection and dissemination of information about working conditions in member states, as well as making the arrangements for annual general assemblies, including submissions for decision. Since the incorporation of the ILO into the United Nations, technical advice and educational assistance to countries with lower social standards have grown significantly, to the extent that today these operations are at least as important among the ILO's activities as are the preparation of new standards (Jenks 1970; Senti 2002).

Until the Second World War the ILO worked on problems and standards that almost exclusively related to the working conditions and social security of industrial workers and marine employees. After the war and following reorientation towards the much broader ambit of the United Nations, the covenants' subject fields expanded towards affecting the living conditions of basically all population groups. This transition – from international social policy aimed at the labour question to welfare state responsibility fundamentally affecting the entire population – marks a deep-seated break whose origins and processes call for examination.

From the Atlantic Charter to the Foundation of the United Nations

It has to be reiterated that until the Second World War both national and international social policy was almost exclusively concerned with the problems of poverty, of women and children, and of the industrial labour force. Social policy measures were basically selective, with the priorities varying from one country to another. This generally reflected the persisting dominance in most European societies of nineteenth-century attitudes towards class and rank. The process of fundamental democratization that marked the second half of the twentieth century was activated by the widespread shared sense of fear in trenches and air raid shelters, and can be traced back to the growing influence of both socialist and American democratic ideas throughout the world, which from this perspective appear as converging. The concept of the welfare state as 'the institutional outcome of the assumption by a society of legal and therefore formal and explicit responsibility for the basic well-being of all of its members' (Girvetz 1968: 512) is valid as a political expression of this fundamental democratization. But at the outbreak of war it was still unborn, at any rate in Western societies. How then did it arise? That question must now be addressed.

Hitler's attack on Poland shocked England and France, but their duty of support immediately forced them into the growing conflict of the Second World War without their having given further thought to their war aims. The extraordinary initial success of the Axis powers drove the rapprochement between U.S. President Franklin D. Roosevelt and British Prime Minister Winston S. Churchill, who was aiming to bring the U.S. into the war. The first meeting between these two statesmen took place under almost conspiratorial circumstances in a Newfoundland bay between 9 and 12 August 1941, and it ended with a joint declaration that was published simultaneously on 14 August in London and Washington.[6] It was a British newspaper, the *Daily Herald*, that first called the joint declaration 'the Atlantic Charter' (Wilson 1969: 222), and this is the name under which it has gone into history.[7]

Editing the joint declaration took up a considerable part of the talks. If, following Roosevelt's invitation to present a draft, Churchill tried to commit the U.S. to base its policies on shared principles 'in the face of Nazi and German aggression and of the dangers to all peoples arising therefrom' (Wilson 1969: 187), so for his part Roosevelt tried to bind Churchill to the principles of global free trade and thus to giving up the British Commonwealth preferential trade system after the war. In hindsight the story of the process of editing the declaration reveals an increasing convergence on broad principles for 'a better future for the world', as the preamble put it. It was precisely this principled characteristic and its avoidance of any political commitments that gave effective power to the Atlantic Charter as the declared programme for a post-war settlement.[8] The Allied nations pursuing the war acceded to this declaration as early as 24 September 1941, and after the U.S. joined the world war following Pearl Harbour, the text became the programmatic element of the Joint Declaration by the United Nations on 1 January 1942, binding the twenty-six governments opposing the Triple Alliance into concerted action.[9] The group of the later United Nations was composed of those assenting to this Joint Declaration, so that the principles expressed in the Atlantic Charter could thenceforward become valid as the official Allied post-war settlement aims.

In this connection, points 5 and 6 of the Atlantic Charter are of interest. Point 5, 'They desire to bring about the fullest collaboration between all nations in the economic field with the object of securing, for all, improved labour standards, economic advancement, and social security', was only introduced into the text by the British in the final round of negotiations but was nevertheless impulsively accepted by Roosevelt, possibly because he had himself promoted the concept of social security in 1934 (see chapter 5). Point 5 was the first expression of the idea of an international responsibility for welfare, which as a result found its place as articles 55 and 56 of the UN Charter (see appendix 3).[10] Point 6 of the Joint Declaration focuses on the aim of 'freedom from fear and want', two of the 'four essential human freedoms' that Roosevelt had already emphasized in a message to the U.S. Congress early in 1941.[11] Even if international legitimation for welfare state development had already been articulated in this way, clearly there was no mention of social rights here but only of political aims that governments ought to pursue, by international cooperation but of course also on the basis of their own national methods. At the time of the Atlantic Charter Roosevelt rejected the idea of a successor organization to the League of Nations and supposed that post-war order would be maintained by a monopoly of power exercised by the Americans and the British, while the remainder of the nations on earth should focus on exploiting their resources and provide for the welfare of their citizens (Lash 1976: 399).

The ILO Declaration of Philadelphia (1944) as the Manifesto of the Welfare State

As a result of the Second World War, the League of Nations was effectively dead. This represented a serious threat to the existence of the International Labour Office, which had been closely connected to the League. Point 5 of the Atlantic Charter offered a link for the ILO, which had in the mean time relocated from Geneva to Montreal, to readjust its own profile to the changed conditions and to present itself as the champion of social affairs in the post-war world (Alcock 1971: chaps. 9–11; Lee 1994). In October 1941, an extraordinary conference called by the ILO in New York gave its support to the Atlantic Charter, and thus surrendered its neutrality towards the parties engaged in the war. At the same time, the ILO put itself forward as ready to collaborate in post-war planning of specialized provisions for social matters. This should not be interpreted as simply a self-interested attempt to save an institution threatened by the demise of the League of Nations, for it had a solid political background. It appeared, to the trades unions and the employers' associations who were represented as full members of the ILO, that in the framework of international relations it was an ideal instrument designed for exercising direct influence on post-war planning. The representative trades unions were particularly emphatic on the continued existence of the ILO, and in this the British government supported them.

It was in this context that the term 'social' first appeared on the international organizational scene as a programmatic concept. The ILO called for

a *social* mandate.... This mandate should include the elimination of unemployment, the establishment of machinery for placing, vocational training and retraining workers, improving social insurance in all its fields and its extension to all workers, the institution of a wage policy aimed at securing a just share of the fruits of progress for the worker, a minimum wage for those too weak to secure it for themselves, measures to promote better nutrition, adequate housing and facilities for recreation and culture, improved conditions of work, an international public works policy, the organisation of migration, and the collaboration of employers and workers in the initiation and application of economic and social measures. (Alcock 1971: 165ff.; emphasis added)

This ambitious programme went far beyond the ILO's previous activities, above all in the belief, furthered by the global economic crisis, that labour protection alone could not improve workers' living conditions. However, the programme was restricted to 'workers'; it was not directed towards 'all human beings', though in view of the attention given to living conditions, the focus on 'better nutrition, adequate housing and facilities for recreation and culture' (where the absence of health issues is striking) clearly went beyond the sphere of production alone. This new systematic or societal policy perspective is particularly noticeable in a paper by Harold Butler, the director of the International Labour Office at that time:

Today the programme is far wider both in scope and in origin. It covers not only the comparatively narrow domain of conditions of work but the infinitely more extensive area of conditions of life. It has its origin not in the demand of one section of the community for the satisfaction of a series of claims for concessions to be made by another section, but in a widespread conviction that aims at a better organization of the life of the community as a whole in the interests of the community as a whole. (Lee 1994: 469)

This attempt at popularity by the ILO ran up against the opposition of the USSR, which had been excluded from the League of Nations after its invasion of Finland in 1940 and was therefore treated as a non-member by the ILO. Additionally, the tensions between the represented and non-represented trades unions and between the disparate political orientations within the labour movement all played a role. The ILO was not included in the increasingly intensive preparations for the organizational constitution of the UN from 1943 onwards. In an attempt to justify its existence and shore up its sense of purpose, the International Labour Office called a new international conference in Philadelphia in April 1944, issuing a declaration that subsequently became part of the revised constitution of the ILO in 1946.

The Declaration of Philadelphia can be counted as the birth of a comprehensive welfare state programme at the international organizational level.[12] It was arranged in five parts. Part 1 reconfirms the basic clauses of the foundation document of 1919 in condensed form, while part 2 develops a new, wide-ranging and universalistic agenda for the organization (see appendix 2). Part 3 then contains a concretization of these broad ideas on the basis of aims for social policy, for instance the promotion of full employment and the improvement of living conditions, the traditional goal of labour protection, the guarantee of collective negotiation, the assurance of minimum wages and comprehensive health protection, besides '[h] provision for child welfare and maternity protection; [i] the provision of adequate nutrition, housing and facilities for recreation and culture; [j] the assurance of equality of educational and vocational opportunity'. The final parts 4 and 5 underlined these proposals with emphatic declarations. In conclusion, the conference affirmed

> that the principles set forth in this declaration are fully applicable to all peoples everywhere, and that, while the manner of their application must be determined with due regard to the stage of social and economic development reached by each people, their progressive application to peoples who are still dependent, as well as to those who have already achieved self-government, is a matter of concern to the whole civilised world.

This passage clearly reveals the universalistic orientation of the proposed tasks and their all-embracing welfare perspective. It is true that regard must be paid to 'the stage of social and economic development reached by each people', but at the same time it proposes decolonization and lays an international responsibility on 'the whole civilised world'. For the first time, the passage in appendix 2 also contains the formulation 'All human beings ... have the right' (emphasis added), even though they do not refer to specific rights but to striving towards 'their material well-being and their spiritual development in conditions of freedom and dignity, of economic security and equal opportunity'. The term 'right' used here thus still bears a metaphorical connotation.

The constitution (Charter) of the United Nations that was published in June 1945 refers to questions of responsibility for welfare and human rights only in very general terms.[13] The preamble emphasizes 'belief in fundamental human rights, in the dignity and worth of the human personality' and the aim 'to promote social progress and a better standard of living in greater freedom'. Besides furthering world peace and international security, article 1 also aims 'to bring about international cooperation to solve international economic, social cultural and human problems, and to pay regard to and secure human rights and fundamental freedoms for all, without distinction of race, gender, language or religion.' The United Nations instrument created to pursue these goals of international cooperation in the economic and social spheres was the Economic and Social Council (ECOSOC), which was also given the task of promoting human rights.[14]

The Genesis of the General Declaration of Human Rights, Especially the Concepts of Economic, Social and Cultural Rights

As soon as the United Nations Charter had been drafted, the criticism was heard – primarily in the U.S. – that it evaded giving any substantive expression to human rights (De la Chapelle 1967: 19ff.). Considering the charter's characteristic of international legal duties, this could have meant a much stronger obligation on states than did the UN Universal Declaration of Human Rights (UDHR), finally passed by the General Assembly in December 1948, which, from a juridical viewpoint, represented nothing more than a non-binding resolution. But as the drawn-out negotiations on the wording of the UDHR and its obligations showed, imposing such duties probably exceeded the collective intentions of the UN's founding members.

Significance

In spite of its legally unenforceable character, the historical significance of the UDHR can hardly be exaggerated. This was the first international expression of a substantive list of human rights claiming global validity, adopted by almost all the countries in the United Nations, whose contents were consequently to be specified in legally binding covenants, but also increasingly recognized independently as a constituent part of international law. Even this global consensus was implied from the outset by the idea of human rights, whose roots go back to the Greeks and Romans as well as to Christian universalism. The articulation of the idea of human rights is nevertheless a product of early modern ideas of natural law and the Enlightenment. The proposition that 'human rights ... first emerged as politico-legal concepts in the modern era' (Bielefeldt 1998: 25) is also acceptable on the basis of social theory. To be more precise, it was only as a consequence of the institutionalized autonomy of politics in the form of the modern juridical and constitutional state that the ethical intuitions or convictions associated with the recognition of human dignity could achieve the form of subjective rights (Luhmann 1981b). To the extent that this recognition was extended to every human being – and in this generalization the modern ethos of human rights extends beyond that of classical antiquity – the idea of human rights immediately conflicts with the form in which it was first associated with the institution of the national state.

A political concretization of the idea of human rights was first achieved in the U.S. Bill of Rights (1789, based on the model of Virginia, 1776) and in the French Declaration of the Rights of Man and the Citizen of 1789, incorporated into the constitution of 1791. The double expression used here – 'man and the citizen' – already points towards European nation-states' adoption of the idea of human rights, which in nineteenth-century constitutions reduced human rights to the rights of the citizens of each state. It was the experience of the First World War and of the ruthless totalitarian powers of the Nazi and Stalinist regimes that destroyed trust in the sovereign nation state in Europe and blazed the way for national law subject to international standards, i.e., a binding supranational ethos of human rights. These human rights aspirations combined with the above-mentioned idea, particularly promoted by Britain, of an international responsibility for global welfare development (*welfare internationalism*). It led through the achievement of the UDHR to a concept of human rights that embraced cultural, economic and social rights in addition to the rights to liberty and political participation. Nevertheless, a significant difference was introduced: while the right to liberty and political rights imposed unconditional validity, the guarantee of the social rights was left to the 'organisation and resources of each state' – in other words, to national conditions.

Context

The UDHR follows the tradition of the U.S. Bill of Rights by expressing, to start with, the individual's right to liberty and political activity as rights that restrict the autonomy of the state (articles 2–21). At the national level the rights to liberty and political activity express (even if in sometimes varying formulations) an aspect of already widely recognized tradition. However, since the UDHR is an international document, it is directed at binding national sovereignty under international law following transnational principles.

In this context, I shall focus on the new element of economic, social and cultural rights (articles 22–27), which until then had rarely been explicit at the national level, and which for brevity I shall describe here as human social rights (see appendix 4). Although the welfare-state agenda naturally assumes the rights to liberty and political activity, these human social rights have become intrinsic to the legitimation of welfare state development.

What was decisive for the acceptance of social rights onto the list of human rights was the perception, which became widespread under the Allies, that the dramatic extent of the global economic crisis (including its political consequences) could to a considerable extent be ascribed to failures of international economic cooperation and to national protectionism in the interwar period. Accordingly, the re-establishment of full employment was rated as the most urgent goal of post-war economic policy, to be best achieved through international cooperation. From the outset the U.S., which was pressing for the project as Britain was too, did not conceive of the UN as simply as the agent of international security policy but also as the agency for international economic and welfare policy. Consequently the original plans for the UN organization envisaged it having its own central body for dealing with economic questions (Russell 1958: 333ff.). In the event, ECOSOC was created as one of six major UN bodies, but obviously with less power than the Security Council. Because the political experience of fascism and the destruction of freedom and democracy were interpreted as the consequences of economic instability, the human rights question and economic development were seen as closely related. For this reason the responsibility for human rights issues was allocated to the competence of ECOSOC.[15]

The U.S. State Department had been considering a Bill of Rights as a component part of the UN constitution since early in the planning process. However, preparations came to a stop in the summer of 1943 when it became apparent that it would be hard to reach political consensus on a form of wording for state obligations with regard to the classical rights to 'life, liberty, property, enterprise, and employment', as well as regarding a right to education and the prohibition of discrimination on the grounds of religion, gender or race (Russell 1958: 312ff.). Only under pressure from a broad human rights movement in U.S. did the State Department, in the run-up to the San Francisco Conference (1945) at which the UN Charter was passed, renew its interest in the topic of human rights and gain the support of the other Great Powers for the project of a declaration of human rights. Thus the topic entered the political debate only after the foundation of the UN, in the form of the Commission on Human Rights that ECOSOC set up in February 1946.

This commission was led by Eleanor Roosevelt, widow of the great U.S. president, who in this connection set herself the goal of implementing the programme of the Four Essential Human Freedoms of 1941, including 'freedom from want'. The influential members of the commission included the later Nobel Peace Prize winner René Cassin from France, the Lebanese delegate Charles Malik and the Chinese delegate P.C. Chang, who as a result also became members of the committee responsible for drafting decisions in the General Assembly. One would not have guessed from its origins that the UDHR was an exclusively Western production. The broad resonance that belief in human rights struck at that time also infused a UNESCO symposium in 1947. To be more precise, one might say that an ethos of recognizing every individual as 'human' could have developed outside the sphere of influence of Western Christianity and the Enlightenment, but that the specific expression of this ethos in the form of individual rights was rooted in Western culture.[16]

The Emergence of the Text[17]

The Commission on Human Rights was supported by a Division of Human Rights, set up by the UN General Secretariat and for many years directed by the Canadian John P. Humphrey, which collected and sifted the many proposals submitted and also drew up a first draft. Through intensive consultations the Commission on Human Rights drafted a proposal, which was then redrafted by the General Assembly's Third Committee responsible for it. The UN General Assembly then passed it in Paris on 10 December 1948 without a dissenting vote, though the Eastern bloc countries abstained, as did Saudi Arabia and South Africa.

The economic, social and cultural rights that concern us here had not been explicitly stated in the terms of reference ECOSOC laid down for the Commission on Human Rights upon its establishment in 1946 (Köhler 1987: 166). They initially appeared in the first draft elaborated under Humphrey's direction, but not in the British alternative draft. Humphrey had almost exclusively used English-language texts from Western and Latin American countries for his rough draft, while the later documentation from the UN Secretariat drew on a considerably wider range of sources (Verdoot 1964: 42ff.). An exhaustive catalogue of welfare-relevant demands was presented in articles 35–44 under the heading of 'positive freedoms', while defensive rights were labelled as 'negative freedoms' in articles 3–34 (Wronka 1992: 90).

The rough draft was tightened up and reworked by a drafting committee chaired by the French international jurist René Cassin. The final result represented the success of the structure that Cassin had proposed, which displayed a clear gradation between the classical rights to liberty and the new human social rights. Thus, for instance, the latter were not explicitly mentioned in the declaration's opening paragraphs.[18] Without describing the editing process in detail, the significant aspects of disagreement are sketched below.

As stated, from the outset the Americans and the British believed that there was a connection between future world peace and economic development, so that a consensual agreement on the UN's responsibility for welfare existed in principle and was also expressed in the relevant passages of the UN Charter. However, the U.S. Bill of Rights recognized only rights to liberty, and hitherto the dominant tendency of the Western human rights tradition had not recognized economic and social rights. It is therefore not surprising that they were not contained in the original draft of the Commission on Human Rights.

During the commission's consultations the Soviet delegate was foremost among those who supported social rights, though at the same time he questioned the draft's liberal view that the individual could be the juridical subject of international law. The argument about social rights thus became confused with the tensions over the Cold War, which was already looming. From the Soviet perspective, social rights were the achievements of the socialist state that had already been realized, as a result of which the contradiction between the individual and the state had in principle been resolved. By contrast, from the point of view of the Western representatives of the ethos of freedom, the irresolvable tension between the state's authoritarian demands and individual liberty was the very reason for the necessity of human rights guaranteed by international law. While the socialist view saw the individual as the product of social conditions, the liberal version postulated a human freedom derived 'from God' or 'from nature' and preceding any institutional order. This notion cannot, however, be used for economic and social rights because they necessarily depend on certain levels of social and economic development, and because guaranteeing them presupposes not merely a negative abstention but a positive intervention by the state. That poses the question how far states can have duties imposed on them at all without regard to their degree of development for those purposes.

A third position was that adopted by several Latin American nations. They had united around an American Declaration of the Rights and Duties of Men in 1948, before the United Nations, whose early drafts were also submitted to the UN Commission on Human Rights. The Latin American declaration contained social rights but did not distinguish them categorically from rights to liberty and participation, much in the way Roosevelt had already included freedom from want among the four essential human freedoms. In this case education, work and social security were not only included among the fundamental human rights but placed higher on the list than liberties and political rights. While a distinction could be drawn between the rights to liberty and to participation on both socialist and liberal grounds, even if with contradictory emphasis, from the Latin American perspective this distinction was seen as less important than the individual's all-embracing claim both to liberty *and* to 'social security'. At the heart of this argument stands *the complementary character of liberty and social rights*, while the variety of conditions surrounding implementation are not ascribed with any systematic status. According to the account given by Humphrey, the human rights commission's secretary, this position particularly influenced his early draft, which in turn had a decisive influence on the progress of the consultations (Verdoot 1964: 58).

Examining the compromise that was achieved after difficult negotiations on the agreed statement (Köhler 1987: 274ff.) reveals that the fundamental social rights form a clearly detached, shorter second part of the UDHR. Both parts of the UDHR are introduced by a programmatic article, articles 3 and 22. While article 3 unconditionally states, in lapidary style, 'Everybody has the right to life, liberty and personal security', article 22 puts forward the following compromise formula proposed by René Cassin:

> Everyone, as a member of society, has the right to social security and is entitled to realization, through national effort and international co-operation and in accordance with the organization and resources of each State, of the economic, social and cultural rights indispensable for his dignity and the free development of his personality.

This article precedes the list of the individual rights, namely the right to work and appropriate remuneration as well as to professional association (article 23), to recreation and leisure (article 24), to social protection (article 25), to education (article 26) and to participation in cultural life (article 27) (see appendix 4). The 'right to social security' implies a wide-ranging right to take part in what society can offer.[19] But at the same time this subjective right of participation was placed under the restrictive condition 'in accordance with the organization and resources of each State'. What is notable is the concluding recourse to 'national effort and international co-operation', by which the programme inserted international responsibility for welfare into the UDHR.

Here article 28 is worth a brief mention. The improbable and almost utopian 'demand for a social and international order in which the rights and freedoms offered by this declaration can be fully realised' showed itself in time to be the forerunner of a new common understanding of human rights, one that was concretized particularly in the 'right to development' declared in 1986.[20] In recent discussion of human rights, the economic, social and cultural rights count as 'second generation' rights, while demands for institutional guarantees of 'third generation' rights continue to be negotiated (Köhler 1987: 1063; Wronka 1992: 120ff.). They will not be pursued further here.

Welfare State Aims

In that social rights in the UDHR are on the one hand individually formed, by analogy with the rights to liberty and political participation, and at the same time the extent of the entitlements that follow are tied to the political capabilities of each individual state, a tension-filled agenda emerges whose dynamic can only ever develop in the context of existing power relations. However, this wording makes it clear that neither the liberal nor the socialist view prevailed, but rather that a legitimating basis for new institutional developments 'between the market and the state' was being created, which characterizes welfare state trends ever since (see chapter 10).

For the most part in Western Europe, between the Cold War's conflicting poles, an institutional configuration has been carried through, often after bitter national political argument, which is clearly equally distinct from both the socialist model of centralized integrated planning of production and consumption, and the private capitalist model, where by definition the coordination of production and consumption takes place only indirectly, through markets. To be more precise, elements of both models are stressfully integrated into a single entity. What the private capitalist model (as roughly realized in the U.S.) shares with the social or welfare state model is the option of independence of the entrepreneurial function and coordination of production on the basis of markets. But business and markets are not independent of the state since they are subject to public inspection, especially in the fields of competition and labour law. What the socialist model as practised particularly in USSR (but with limited success) shares with the welfare state model is the recognition of social rights for everybody, even if the way they are guaranteed varies from country to country.

In many countries this strained compromise has in practice been carved out. Deep-seated conflicts between employers' associations and trades unions have in many places led to explicit compromises, first in Denmark (the September Agreement of 1899) and then in the collapsing German Reich (the Stinnes-Legien Agreement of November 1918). In the distress of the global economic crisis Switzerland achieved the Peace Agreement, which is still currently updated, and Sweden reached the Saltsjöbaden Agreement. France reached the Matignon Agreement in 1936, though this did not last long, and then in 1968 the Accords de Grenelle, which are still in force today. These agreements were similar in many respects, such as the employers' recognition of trades union rights and the intervention of the social state, and the trades unions' recognition of the private economic entrepreneurial sphere and restrictions on the right to strike. These agreements were put on a stable footing by mutual recognition of the social partners as joint negotiators.

The Origins of the Idea of Human Social Rights

The League of Nations assembly that took place as part of the Versailles Peace Treaty did not refer to the idea of human rights, even though relevant proposals existed at the time. A concise list of binding state obligations produced by the Institut de Droit International (Institute of International Law) attracted little response; only American international jurists took it up (De la Chapelle 1967: 18). Besides, it still lacked any hint of state responsibility for welfare. The earliest explicit reference to human *social* rights can be found in the Complément à la Déclaration des Droits de l'homme (Addendum to the Declaration of the Rights of Man), which was resolved by a League of the Rights of Man in Dijon in 1936.[21] A variety of drafts and proposals were put forward in the early 1940s, some of which were also among the material available to the Commission on Human Rights (Verdoot 1964: 41ff.). Lauterpacht's (1945) particularly incisive proposal covered in its article 13 'the right to work, to education and to public assistance in case of unemployment, old age, sickness, disablement and other cases of undeserved want'. This text, together with H.G. Wells's proposal discussed below, were among the materials that were considered in the context of an informal pre-meeting before the establishment of the Commission on Human Rights (Wronka 1992: 87ff.).

The centre of this complex human rights movement clearly lay in the U.S., where much attention was focused on the 'four essential human freedoms' enunciated by Roosevelt. The movement received lasting support from both Christian churches and from Jewish representatives. A joint declaration, 'Patterns for Peace', on 7 October 1943 by the Christian and Jewish authorities was widely disseminated and seems to have mobilized public opinion especially for the international realization of human rights (De la Chapelle 1967: 19ff.).

In view of the contingent nature of historical events it makes sense to treat the question of the origins of the idea of human social rights narrowly, and refer only to authors whose key concepts stand out in the immediate foreground of the above-mentioned processes. In the rationale they offer, we immediately come across older sources. My view is that this is a case involving three people – the British writer and political publicist Herbert George Wells, the French philosopher Jacques Maritain, and the Russian emigrant sociologist working mainly in France, Georges Gurvitch. That is not to say that it was only these three men who historically advanced the idea of fundamental social rights. The Second World War generation had a clear idea of the connection between economic and political crises, so the relationship between human rights and their social conditions appeared credible. What marks out the authors named is the clarity of their concepts and their focus on the idea of fundamental social rights as analogous to the rights to liberty and participation.

H.G. Wells (1866–1946)

A versatile publicist and glittering personality on the British cultural scene, Wells was among the first who, shortly after the outbreak of war, questioned the purpose of war and thereby developed some far-reaching visions. By January 1940 he had already published a booklet entitled *The New World Order: Whether It Is Attainable, How It Can Be Attained, and What Sort of World a World at Peace Will Have To Be* (Wells 1940a). It offers the vision of a federal world order and the social diagnosis of growing collectivism in the economic sphere.[22] Just as the old rights to liberty had grown out of reaction against the growing political power of rulers tending to absolutism, Wells argued, the necessity of protecting human rights grew against the accumulation of economic power. His initial draft of a declaration of human rights contained in first place rights to health, to education, to paid work, to property and trade, and to private life, concluding with a range of rights in the same tradition as the right to liberty. In the second version (in the widely published form of a 'Penguin Special' entitled *The Rights of Man, Or What Are We Fighting For?* [Wells 1940b]) he put the rights to protection against state power foremost and left the rights concerned with material existence to follow.[23] What moved his contemporaries was not the want caused by the global economic crisis but the unrestrained barbarity of the Nazi regime (Wells 1940b: 31). Disappointment over the failure of the League of Nations and horror at how a supposedly civilized nation was capable of acting in this way were the principal forces driving the international human rights movement during the Second World War, as many other commentaries have shown.

Wells's vision of future economic policy was liberal socialism, and to that extent history has not supported him. Welfare state development remained based on freedom of economic enterprise and decentralized market coordination of economic life, and the social rights he proposed were implemented through compensatory measures of income maintenance in the absence of employment, and public financing of education and health services beside the market economy. But his vision of the future world order, which depended on the universal recognition of human rights inclusive of fundamental social rights, set the tone for the years that followed. It is uncertain whether Wells was aware of Kant's *Zum Ewigen Frieden* (*On Eternal Peace*) (Kant 1795). In any case, this may have been the original vision that the League of Nations strove for and that was furthered by the United Nations.

Wells wrote to President Roosevelt on 29 October 1940 about his thoughts on a declaration of human rights and his vision of the war aims (Wilson 1969: 177ff.). Whether or not Roosevelt was inspired by these ethical war aims in formulating his four freedoms seems unclear, but the very short interval of only two months is striking. Wells's draft was also among the eighteen submissions that the Secretariat of the Commission on Human Rights considered while it was composing the first draft of the Declaration of Human Rights (Verdoot 1967: 41, 58).

Jacques Maritain (1882–1973)

Like Wells, the Catholic French philosopher Maritain reacted immediately to the outbreak of war. During the first weeks of war he published a number of articles that chiefly concerned a federal order in Germany and Europe after the war, and the necessity of moral renewal on the basis of a Christianity free of paternalism (Maritain 1940). He emigrated to the U.S. in 1940, and there in 1942 he published the seminal book in this context, *Les droits de l'homme et la loi naturelle* (*The Rights of Man and Natural Law*).[24]

Starting from Thomas Aquinas's doctrine of natural law, Maritain developed a dynamic concept of human rights founded on each human being's unchangeable dignity as God's creation but whose specific form depends on current cultural and material circumstances (Maritain 1942: 663ff.). Taking account of Roosevelt's four essential human freedoms, he interpreted them as natural law postulates for a civilized world. He saw the fundamental social rights in industrial society as a consequence of human dignity founded on natural law. Hence he emphasized the individual's right to work, preferably in a freely chosen occupation, and posed this as a criterion of a just economic order.

In short, Maritain distinguished three kinds of human rights:

1. Rights of the human being as such, particularly the right to existence and bodily integrity, as well as various rights to liberty;
2. Rights as a citizen, particularly the right to national self-determination and universal suffrage;
3. Rights as a social person, and especially also as a working person, particularly the right to work and the free choice of occupation, the right to association, the right to fair wages and co-management, the right to community assistance in the event of need, unemployment, illness and old age, as well as the right to inalienable participation in civilisation's fundamental material and cultural resources according to society's capacity to offer them. (Maritain 1942: 690ff.)

The British sociologist T.H. Marshall subsequently (1950) elaborated a closely related tripartite division under the heading of civil, political and social rights, and it is in this form that they are found in recent welfare state discourse. Moreover, the structure of the UDHR as designed by Robert Cassin strikingly follows these distinctions.

Maritain bases his concept of fundamental social rights on the tradition of natural law that goes back to Antigone, the Stoa and Christianity, though his principal source is Thomas Aquinas. From 1940 to 1944 Maritain stayed in the U.S., where he acquired considerable influence. He was briefly the French ambassador to the Holy See, and after 1945 he led the French delegation at UNESCO, which was trying to influence the preparation of the UDHR through a symposium of leading thinkers from throughout the world (UNESCO 1951). Maritain wrote the introduction to this report and thereby emphasized that agreement on the wording of human rights was possible in principle quite independently of the variety of ideological positions adopted by the participants. The Commission on Human Rights did not, however, want to deal with UNESCO's report (Verdoot 1964: 62ff.). Maritain's influence on the creation of the text seems to have been indirect at best, as René Cassin, who had drafted the text, was presumably acquainted with his writings.

Georges Gurvitch (1894–1965)

The French (since 1929) sociologist George Gurvitch, who was of Russian origin, deserves special credit for the historical foundations of human *social* rights. When Maritain emigrated to New York, Gurvitch published a study there, *La declaration des droits sociaux* (*The Declaration of Social Rights*), in a series edited by Maritain. This study analysed the origins of social rights and put forward an independent list.[25] At least as interesting as its contents are its sociological foundations.

Gurvitch had published two books on the idea of social law as early as 1931/32 (Gurvitch 1931, 1932). The idea of social law was not to be understood in today's social policy form, but as the concept of law integrating individual and collective interests. What Gurvitch meant by 'social law' were the norms people accept in a society (he was also referring to the French idea of solidarity) that affect certain shared values. In theory it is the opposite of the individualistic law of contract in the Roman law tradition. According to the theory of social law, commitment to norms is not based on self-interested acts of will but in shared conviction; one could even speak of shared ethos. It is feasible for the state to express and to sanction such norms, but the concept does not depend on that, and Gurvitch did not even consider it conceptually typical. The examples he gave of social law were international law or collective labour law.

The growing complexity of society, Gurvitch thought, would exceed the state's capacity to regulate it, and liberty could be achieved only by structurally differentiating social spheres serving different values. For that reason he sought alternatives, regulatory forms independent of the state. The economic sphere in particular deserved state-free regulation, not only by market forces but also by law. His project for a declaration of social rights consequently focused chiefly on the economic sphere, in which he distinguished between the rights of the individual as such, the citizen, the producer and the consumer (Gurvitch 1946: 85ff.). The role of the declaration consisted in the explicit formulation of an ethos for industrial society, one that could be articulated at both national and international levels. Gurvitch justified this assumed international consensus by calling on the tradition of socialist thought from the Jacobin constitution of 1793 to the Soviet constitution of 1936, but also by referring to the Weimar constitution, other legal codes and the activities of the International Labour Office, as well as the American discussion about Roosevelt's declaration of the four essential freedoms.

The essence of his approach is the distinction between the state and political economy. The latter should be subject to a 'National Economic Council' as the highest arbitrating authority, while economic management should be overseen by corporatist structures and as large a degree as possible of co-determination between producers and consumers. Proposals in the Weimar constitution are recognizable inspirations here. As far as producers' rights were concerned, Gurvitch adopted trades unions' demands in their entirety, while employers' rights remained obscure. Consumers' rights are more creative: they start with a right to subsistence income as well as to social protection in the event of need, illness, invalidity and old age. Then comes a right to take part in price and rent control bodies, and also self-managed social insurance. Consumers should also be represented on the managements of the productive economy in their capacity as customers, and the same applies to territorial economic councils. Gurvitch's kind of economy seems to be based on a mixture of public services and private production, one that firmly guarantees private property rights and equally emphasizes social duties. Human rights as such seem to refer above all to the rights of children and those not yet born, to family protection and to equality for women, as well as to children born out of wedlock, and finally to the right to the development of the individual's abilities and school education, and to free choice of occupation.

Gurvitch's sweeping proposals for a declaration of social rights totalling fifty-eight articles is more impressive for the breadth of its vision than for the precision of its individual provisions. As a theoretical advance, the instructive distinction between the social obligations or goals of the state on the one hand, and individual rights on the other, is worth attention. These rights still lack juridical credentials, just as the function of the state remains entirely obscure in Gurvitch's social blueprint (Sinzheimer 1976: 177ff.). By contrast, Gurvitch's interpretation of social law corresponds closely to the actual function that the UN discharges through the UDHR: it puts forward a worldwide ethos of human rights – the model of 'the good society' – that can be approximated by actual states in various ways for economic and political reasons. Although from a normative juridical perspective they are non-binding, the UDHR is 'an important expression of confidence in human rights by the community of nations' (Zacher 1976: xxvii).

A comparison of the views of these three authors with articles 23–27 of the UDHR shows that their contents are virtually all included but their proposals were more far-reaching, as were also those of the ILO Philadelphia conference mentioned above. The UN Commission on Human Rights emphasized among the many proposals the ground-breaking aspects of the right to work, to health and recreation, to social security, to family protection, to education and to participation in cultural life, and from them it constructed a framework open to further specifications and interpretations.

It would be wrong to see fundamental social rights in isolation. They are credible only as elements in a model that also embraces rights to liberty and political rights in a peaceful global society composed of democratically ruled states, to be emphasized by some concluding remarks below.

The Problem of Human Social Rights

The Role of Human Rights in Social Theory

It is apparent that sociological and social policy literature seldom pays attention to the idea of human rights, nor does the idea play a role in the vast body of comparative research into welfare state development. This is chiefly because, after the foundation of the UN, the global perspectives that had inspired the Allies' planning ever since the Atlantic Charter quickly ebbed away and were replaced by the East-West conflict on the one hand and by a rebirth of nationalist emotions following decolonization on the other. Accordingly, those outside the circle of activists seem to have considered the UN's preparation and passing of the UDHR as a rather peripheral achievement. As an example, in a history of the UN (Luard 1982) the preparation and passing of the UDHR was not mentioned even once.

Accordingly, even theorizing about fundamental social rights has taken place only in national contexts. From a social science perspective, the publication of T.H. Marshall's *Social Class and Citizenship* (1950) was seminal. Marshall developed the idea of a gradual unfolding of the status of citizen through the creation and general recognition first of civil, then political and finally social rights, solely on the basis of evidence from British history. As far as the social rights were concerned, he related them chiefly to the immediate post-war reforms based on the Beveridge Report (Beveridge 1942). In fact, the Beveridge Report can be interpreted as a wide-ranging blueprint for welfare state policies, thus giving tangible form in Britain to the promise of the Atlantic Charter, and the overwhelming support that it received from the British population may have contributed significantly to the success of the welfare state idea (Bremme 1961: 39ff.). Beveridge himself explicitly referred to his plan being founded on the Atlantic Charter:

> The Atlantic Charter, among other aims, speaks of securing for all 'improved labour standards, economic advancement and social security.' The Security Plan in my Report is a plan for turning the last two words 'social security' from words into deeds, for securing that no one in Britain willing to work, while he can, is without income sufficient to meet at all times the essential needs of himself and of his family. (Beveridge 1943: 53)

It must, however, be noted that Marshall never based social rights on the UDHR, even if from today's perspective it enabled the juridical character of social entitlements to be built on far firmer foundations.

The subsequent discussion of fundamental social rights in social theory led to Marshall's ideas being accepted by Talcott Parsons, who embellished the problem of the attainment of full citizenship status with the concept of inclusion (Parsons 1971: 20ff., 1977: 250ff.). Parsons's social theory, especially his concept of social community, was manifestly based on the nation state, and it was therefore the three dimensions of citizenship in Marshall's sense that inclusion in the social community should guarantee. Thus it could almost be taken for granted that fundamental social rights related to problems of national integration, not just in welfare state practice but also in social theory. Even Niklas Luhmann, whose social theory is based on the proposition of global society, gave insufficient thought to the consequences for social inclusion theory (Luhmann 1981a; Kaufmann 1997b: 11ff.).

However, to the extent that nation states lose control over their borders, and goods, capital, persons and ideas circulate freely throughout the world, the constitutive constellation changes:

> It is obvious that this model of double political inclusion [by political and social rights: FXK] which is standardised and codified in the concept of citizen, is today collapsing. We observe a deterritorialisation of politics and a depoliticisation of territories.... If politics ... has anything to do with collective binding decisions, then it becomes increasingly unclear what collectivity it is which in fact is tied by these decisions or ought to be. (Stichweh 2000: 167)

In any case, the consequences of so-called globalization for politics and social theory are not at all clear and are probably far more complex than has so far been assumed. In that regard, it is very likely that the nation states will not disappear but will instead undergo a change of function (Leibfried and Zürn 2005; Genschel and Zangl 2008; Hurrelmann et al. 2008).

It is already plain today that as nation states' strategies of legitimating their exclusive competence to political decisions lose their credibility, thus the concept of society loses its identification with the nation state. The emergence of a global public has given human rights an extraordinary boost in importance in the past two decades, one that extends into questions of war and peace and the justification of interventions under international law. The idea of human rights presupposes the inclusion of all human beings in a complex form of emergent global society. Individual human rights, especially fundamental political and social rights, are already recognizably derived from various functional systems of modern society, and their further elaboration will have to express this relationship more openly. Stichweh's thesis (2000: 161ff.) is supported in that many functional systems develop an inherent tendency to ever greater inclusion of the global population in training their members and the public for complementary roles. But this inclusion remains specific to that partial system, and it is unlikely that a political complex, similar to the nation state but at the global level, will be created to protect the rights to liberty, to enable political participation and to guarantee the social conditions for the unhindered development of personality, in principle for all human beings.

In place of the waning role of national citizen, the idea of human rights alone upholds the relationship between liberty, political participation and social protection, and it thereby gives a normative direction to global development worthy of the name of global society. In itself, the idea of human rights on its own is a very weak social bond, one that only gains relevance by means of the entirety of communicative, economic and political processes of global socialization. But it would be hard to deny it the function of a legitimating catalyst and normative standard. Human rights form the core of a 'global ethos of liberty' (Bielefeldt 1998), without which a humanistic development perspective on the process of modernization and globalization would be unthinkable.

Difficulties in Implementing Fundamental Human Rights under International Law

From the outset, the proponents of human rights in the UN pressed for human rights not only to be framed in a generally consensual manner but also to be embodied in the form of a convention, to be ratified by the UN member states, that would be binding under international law. The original intention was to draft and pass this convention at the same time as the UDHR, but the work on the UDHR turned out to be so demanding of time and effort that the relevant commissions soon decided to defer the convention and, in the light of the beginning Cold War, at least to get the UDHR through.

The plan was at first to have a single convention for all the rights conveyed by the UDHR, for there was a powerful sense of the interdependence of the right to liberty and the social rights arising from the living memory of global economic crisis and the horrors of the Nazi regime. The UN General Assembly declared in 1950 that 'the enjoyment of civic and political freedoms and of economic, social and cultural rights are interconnected and interdependent ... when deprived of economic, social and cultural rights, man does not represent the human person whom the Universal Declaration regards as the ideal of the free man' (Köhler 1987: 913).

However, in the subsequent deliberations of the ECOSOC Third Committee responsible for the human rights question, the majority view was that the conditions for implementing the rights to liberty and political participation on the one hand and economic, social and cultural rights on the other were too different from each other. It therefore proposed that two separate international conventions be drawn up, an International Covenant for Civil and Political Rights, and an International Covenant for Economic, Social and Cultural Rights.[26] The principal argument can be summarized as stating, in effect, that civil and political rights are considered to be pre-constitutional and unconditional, while economic, social and cultural rights can only be addressed by an actual state entity and implemented as seems feasible in the context of its current resource capabilities. After nearly twenty years of negotiations, both covenants were unanimously adopted by the General Assembly in 1966. Ten years later they came into force when a sufficient number of national ratifications had taken place. Thus a qualitative jump was made from 'the traditional interpretation of international law as a system regulating the coexistence of states, to the acknowledgement that international law also protected the individual' (Köhler 1987: 908ff.). The Federal Republic of Germany ratified the two covenants on 23 March and 3 January 1976 respectively. The United States has declined to ratify the covenant on social rights to the present day.

The long interval of twenty-eight years between passage of the UDHR and the coming into force of the two conventions itself emphasizes the difficulties that are involved in any political juridification of grand projects, whether on the national or international level.[27] This remains the case, just as in both covenants the scope of monitoring remains weak and sanctions for compliance are lacking. These are well-known weaknesses of international law. In the era of the Cold War, the arrangements for reporting procedures simply led to constant political argument. But as the evolution of interpretations of international law in recent years has shown, serious breaches of human rights by governments have increasingly served as grounds for military intervention, such that commitment to human rights arising from the covenants does seem to be growing. 'The fact that, in spite of conflict, the idea of human rights is rarely questioned any longer, is a sign that the language of human rights has become a leading pattern of thought, the choice of which is hardly ever noticed' (Heintz, Müller and Schiener 2006: 442). Even the more restricted field of human social rights shows some signs of progress (Nußberger 2005). This progress does not operate so much through political action as through the changing perception of the issues by jurists and social scientists. For instance, the *Limburg Principles on the Implementation of the International Covenant on Economic Social and Cultural Rights* (1986) have been complemented by the *Maastricht Guidelines on Violations of Economic, Social and Cultural*

Rights (1997), which declare that 'states are as responsible for violations of economic, social and cultural rights as they are for violations of civil and political rights' (article 4 cited by Veit-Wilson 2007: 66).

The separation of rights between liberty, civil and political rights on one side and social rights on the other was subsequently replicated at the level of the Council of Europe. The 1950 European Convention on Human Rights, which established a Court of Justice and effective individual rights of appeal, did not, however, include social rights. These were embedded in the European Social Charter (1961), which provided only for reporting procedures, and therefore negotiations between the Council of Europe and governments, but did not offer any facilities for individual appeals (Schambeck 1969; Wiebringhaus 1982). Even the proposed European constitution did not explicitly allow for fundamental social rights.[28]

Although it must not be overlooked that in the sphere of economic and social policy states have great difficulty acknowledging those of their commitments under international law that do not correspond precisely with their national legislation, the significance of the idea of human social rights should not be underestimated. It is among the guiding principles of international social development and has thereby contributed considerably to the legitimation of welfare state development at the national level. Admittedly the various national interpretative perspectives have to be taken into account as well (Kaufmann 2003c). In conclusion, the example of the Federal Republic of Germany will be used to outline the situation briefly.

The German Social State and the Idea of Fundamental Social Rights

In German jurisprudence the term 'social rights' means rights to statutory social benefits, but not human or fundamental social rights (*soziale Grundrechte*) as discussed above. Most German-language publications on the subject of fundamental social rights were not written by authors from the Federal Republic but by Austrian, Swiss and Dutch authors. The German Social Democratic Party devoted a conference to the subject in 1980, but it was alone in this (Böckenförde et al. 1981). Three factors affected German reluctance to accept the idea of fundamental social rights. First, the international campaign for the recognition of universal human rights was promoted by the Allied war opponents of Germany without its participation, and Germany only joined the UN in 1973. Germany therefore lacked the memory of historical emotion that in the post-war period helped to launch the idea of human rights. Second, Germany can look back on its own independent history of social policy evolution, labour law and social rights, which could in many ways act as a model for later international state welfare developments. Finally, perhaps the most influential factor was the ambivalent juridical experience of the economic and social law provisions of the Weimar constitution, where only part of the numerous provisions for ordering economic life were observed at the time, while others remained a dead letter. This allowed the parliamentary council preparing the *Grundgesetz* (Basic Law, also known as the constitution) to leave provisions for economic order broadly open in the Basic Law, and in allocating competences to leave the social order to two general clauses in the Basic Law, article 20, paragraph I: 'The Federal Republic of Germany is a democratic and social federal state', and article 28, paragraph I opening sentence: 'Constitutional order in the *Länder* must correspond to the principles of the republican, democratic and social constitutional state in the spirit of this Basic Law.' These two constitutional provisions have become known as the 'social state clauses'. Even so, it took lengthy discussions on constitutional law and a great many judgements by the Federal Constitutional Court to clarify the meaning of the social state clauses in practice (Zacher 1980, 2004).

According to Hans F. Zacher, the scholar most deeply engaged in this particular subject, the immediate practical regulatory impact of the social state principle has tended to be neutral. Nevertheless, it is not totally ineffective.

> It is (1) an incentive and an argument, invested with the most weighty constitutional law, affecting all political action and it legitimates governmental and administrative action, as long as this is not subject to some statutory proviso. It is (2) an argument for use in interpreting law and, as far as permissible – chiefly in the judge's hands – for its amendment. It is (3) a standard by which ... to judge statutory law ... (4) Finally, the principle of the social state is a restraint on the constitutional legislator. (Zacher 1977:159)

In this context, this means that the social state principle comprises no fundamental social rights but is, rather, a matter of a highly abstract state aim that is not fleshed out in the constitution and whose substantiation is therefore assigned to provisions at levels below the Basic Law. This includes primarily the legislator's social policy activities so far, which is to say that the aims of the social state are embodied in political discourses about social problems and in achievable legislative objectives. However, the aims of the social state are more systematically revealed through the Federal Republic's obligations in the social sphere under international law, in particular through the documents referred to above: the UN Covenant on Economic, Social and Cultural Rights and the European Social Charter. However, the ILO arrangements are generally so specific that they give less guidance on more far-reaching interpretations of the aims than does national legislation.

Indeed, the European Social Charter in particular with its many targets, some specific and some abstract, offers pointers to the interpretation of social state aims but does not, however, allow analysis down to that kind of individual norms. The inherent openness of the social state clauses in the German constitution has the advantage of allowing room to keep the political articulation and processing of new social problems open: 'Social law as social policy law is ... intrinsically self-amending law. And the social state principle as the constitutional "accumulator" of this law must uphold the openness to and permanence of change' (Zacher 1977: 158). Following this interpretation, the social state principle is intended as an argument for the maintenance of the status quo of vested social rights only to a very limited degree. As the judgements of the Federal Constitutional Court in recent decades have shown, the social state principle nowadays seems concerned above all with demanding the reduction of the material disadvantages suffered by parents who come off badly under the existing provisions of the social security system.

To sum up, it must be emphasized that the German Basic Law does not contain any explicit fundamental social rights. Their introduction was rejected at an early stage as well as during the debates on the reunification of the two German states. Accordingly, German jurisprudence also takes a sceptical or even negative stance towards it. However, the social state principle does admittedly represent a functional equivalent to fundamental social rights. It takes account of the circumstance that the priority of some and the realization of all fundamental social rights remain dependent on specific and historically malleable circumstances. That is why the specification and realization of fundamental social rights, unlike the right to liberty, is not regulated at constitutional level but is left to the appropriate legislator.

Appendices: Seminal Statements[29]

Appendix 1: Atlantic Charter (1941)

Joint declaration of the President of the United States of America and the Prime Minister, Mr. Churchill ... being met together, deem it right to make known certain common principles in the national policies of their respective countries on which they base their hopes for a better future for the world.

First, their countries seek no aggrandizement, territorial or other;

Second, they desire to see no territorial changes that do not accord with the freely expressed wishes of the peoples concerned;

Third, they respect the right of all peoples to choose the form of government under which they will live; and they wish to see sovereign rights and self-government restored to those who have been forcibly deprived of them;

Fourth, they will endeavor, with due respect for their existing obligations, to further the enjoyment by all States, great or small, victor or vanquished, of access, on equal terms, to the trade and to the raw materials of the world which are needed for their economic prosperity;

Fifth, they desire to bring about the fullest collaboration between all nations in the economic field with the object of securing, for all, improved labor standards, economic advancement, and social security;

Sixth, after the final destruction of the Nazi tyranny, they hope to see established a peace which will afford to all nations the means of dwelling in safety within their own boundaries, and which will afford assurance that all the men in all the lands may live out their lives in freedom from fear and want;

Seventh, such a peace should enable all men to traverse the high seas and oceans without hindrance;

Eighth, they believe that all of the nations of the world, for realistic as well as spiritual reasons, must come to the abandonment of the use of force....

(Volume I/1, Document 1, slightly shortened)

Appendix 2: Declaration of Philadelphia by the International Labour Organisation (1944)

(Part II) Believing that experience has fully demonstrated the truth of the statement in the Constitution of the International Labour Organisation that lasting peace can be established only if it is based on social justice, the Conference affirms that:

(a) all human beings, irrespective of race, creed or sex, have the right to pursue both their material well-being and their spiritual development in conditions of freedom and dignity, of economic security and equal opportunity;

(b) the attainment of the conditions in which this shall be possible must constitute the central aim of national and international policy;

(c) all national and international policies and measures, in particular those of an economic and financial character, should be judged in this light and accepted only in so far as they may be held to promote and not to hinder the achievement of this fundamental objective;

(d) it is a responsibility of the International Labour Organisation to examine and consider all international economic and financial policies and measures in the light of this fundamental objective;

(e) in discharging the task entrusted to it the International Labour Organisation, having considered all relevant economic and financial factors, may include in its decisions and recommendations any provisions which it considers appropriate.

(Part V) The Conference affirms that the principles set forth in this Declaration are fully applicable to all peoples everywhere and that, while the manner of their application must be determined with due regard to the stage of social and economic development reached by each people, their progressive application to peoples who are still dependent, as well as to those who have already achieved self-government, is a matter of concern to the whole civilized world.

(Volume I/2, Document 117, Annex, extract)

Appendix 3: Charter of the United Nations (1945)

Chapter IX: International economic and social cooperation

(Article 55) With a view to the creation of conditions of stability and well-being which are necessary for peaceful and friendly relations among nations based on respect for the principle of equal rights and self-determination of peoples, the United Nations shall promote:

(a) higher standards of living, full employment, and conditions of economic and social progress and development;

(b) solutions of international economic, social, health, and related problems; and international cultural and educational cooperation; and

(c) universal respect for, and observance of, human rights and fundamental freedoms for all without distinction as to race, sex, language, or religion.

(Article 56) All members pledge themselves to take joint and separate action in cooperation with the Organization for the achievement of the purposes set forth in Article 55.

(Volume I/1, Document 4, extract)

Appendix 4: Universal Declaration of Human Rights (1948)

Article 22

Everyone, as a member of society, has the right to social security and is entitled to realization, through national effort and international co-operation and in accordance with the organization and resources of each State, of the economic, social and cultural rights indispensable for his dignity and the free development of his personality.

Article 23

1. Everyone has the right to work, to free choice of employment, to just and favourable conditions of work and to protection against unemployment.
2. Everyone, without any discrimination, has the right to equal pay for equal work.
3. Everyone who works has the right to just and favourable remuneration ensuring for himself and his family an existence worthy of human dignity, and supplemented, if necessary, by other means of social protection.
4. Everyone has the right to form and to join trade unions for the protection of his interests.

Article 24

Everyone has the right to rest and leisure, including reasonable limitation of working hours and periodic holidays with pay.

Article 25

1. Everyone has the right to a standard of living adequate for the health and well-being of himself and of his family, including food, clothing, housing and medical care and necessary social services, and the right to security in the event of unemployment, sickness, disability, widowhood, old age or other lack of livelihood in circumstances beyond his control.
2. Motherhood and childhood are entitled to special care and assistance. All children, whether born in or out of wedlock, shall enjoy the same social protection.

Article 26

1. Everyone has the right to education. Education shall be free, at least in the elementary and fundamental stages. Elementary education shall be compulsory. Technical and professional education shall be made generally available and higher education shall be equally accessible to all on the basis of merit.

2. Education shall be directed to the full development of the human personality and to the strengthening of respect for human rights and fundamental freedoms. It shall promote understanding, tolerance and friendship among all nations, racial or religious groups, and shall further the activities of the United Nations for the maintenance of peace.
3. Parents have a prior right to choose the kind of education that shall be given to their children.

Article 27

1. Everyone has the right freely to participate in the cultural life of the community, to enjoy the arts and to share in scientific advancements and its benefits.
2. Everyone has the right to the protection of the moral and material interests resulting from any scientific, literary or artistic production of which he is the author.

Article 28

Everyone is entitled to a social and international order in which the rights and freedoms set forth in this Declaration can be fully realized.

(Volume I/1, Document 23, extract)

Notes

1. A review of the early history of social rights can be found in Gurvitch (1946: chap. 2).
2. Tczerclas von Tilly (1924) and E.P. Stolleis (1931) both give good introductions to the development of international labour protection.
3. On the German Association for Social Reform see vom Bruch (1985: 130–152); on the American Association for Labor Legislation see Skocpol (1992: 160–204).
4. In its first fifty years the ILO adopted 132 covenants, of which 116 came into effect through the required minimum number of ratifications. By 1970, a total of 121 member states had ratified an average of 29 covenants each (Johnston 1970: 308ff.).
5. At any rate, that was the intention. But because covenants under international law lack effective sanctions for compliance, regulation of rule observance was confined to reporting and the related publicity given to breaches of the rules. Since as a rule at least one of the social partners had an interest in the application of the ILO's agreed standards, the notification of rule-breaking was more likely than breaches of covenants, which involved only governments. On the topic of the supervision and effectiveness of the ILO standards, see the brief references in Johnston (1970: 97–106) and, at greater length, Valticos (1969).
6. On the details of the antecedents and consequences, see Wilson (1969); for background see Russell (1958: 34ff.) and Lash (1976: 398ff.).
7. The text of the Atlantic Charter is to be found in appendix 1.

8. 'It is a statement of basic principles and fundamental ideas and policies that are universal in their practical application', as U.S. Secretary of State Cordell Hull later expressed it (Wilson 1969: 261).

9. See Mangoldt and Rittberger (1995: vol. 1/1, document 2).

10. On the origins of these articles, see Köhler (1987: 155ff.).

11. Roosevelt, vol. 9, no. 152, 6 January 1941. In addition to freedom from fear and want, this declaration also contained freedom of speech and religion. Roosevelt subsequently tried to present these two latter freedoms as elements of the Atlantic Charter, for example in Roosevelt, vol. 11, no. 33, 12 March 1942.

12. The text can be found in Mangoldt and Rittberger (1995: vol. 1/2, document 117). An extract is also given in appendix 2.

13. The text can be found in Mangoldt and Rittberger (1995: vol. 1/1, document 4).

14. See articles 55 (appendix 3) and 62 of the UN Charter. On the preceding period, during which the political problems of implementing social rights were already apparent, see Russell (1958: chap. 30) and Köhler (1987: 155ff.).

15. See article 62 part 3 of the UN Charter. On ECOSOC's working methods see Sharp (1969) and Köhler (1987: 182ff.). As a result, ECOSOC's effectiveness was restricted not only by East-West tensions but by organizational sluggishness and the reluctance of many states to commit themselves to international economic and social policy.

16. The history of the idea of human rights is reconstructed in a variety of ways according to cultural context and, accordingly, significance attributed to different historical forces. H. Hofmann offers a brief account (1999: 18ff.) that reconstructs 'the discovery of human rights through the association and mutual interpenetration of three forces: 1. The juridical formative element derives from freedom charters under medieval feudal law. … 2. … the specific esteem accorded by European culture to the human personality is fed by a variety of disparate sources, such as Stoic pantheism, Christian creation theology, mysticism, Renaissance humanism and the philosophy of the Enlightenment and its idealism. The concept of human dignity characterises its apogee, humans as ends in themselves. 3. But only an additional element acting catalytically turns the human being to be protected into the autonomous subject of law, and the many different kinds of freedoms into one principle of equal freedom with a range of particular applications.… The catalytic role was played by the early modern social model of so-called "methodological individualism" with its specific manifestations of the state of nature and social contract theory. At the same time, this radical individualism, operating in the background up to the UDHR, has from some Third World perspectives led to certain cultural problems of acceptance.' For recent discussion of the intercultural differences and acceptability of human rights, see for instance Voigt (1998), 'Dignity of the Human Being and Human Rights' (1999), and Bielefeldt (1998) with particular reference to Islam.

17. Studies on the origins of the UDHR: Verdoot (1964); De la Chapelle (1967: 11–204); Köhler (1987: 265–286); Wronka (1992: 85–112); additionally from the perspective of the participants, Cassin (1951) and Humphrey (1979, 1984).

18. A request, chiefly by Latin American countries, to reword what is now article 3, 'Everyone has the right to life, liberty and the security of person', as follows: 'Everyone has the right to life, honour, liberty, physical integrity, and to the legal, economic and social security which is necessary to the full development of human personality' was rejected by the Third Committee because the key passage for social rights, 'economic and social security which is necessary to the full development of human personality', received only 20 votes, with 21 against and 7 abstentions (Köhler 1987: 276).

19. 'Social security' is thus understood in the broad way of the Latin American declaration, and not in the technical sense of a system of social protection. This also expresses the feelings that had become associated with the words 'social security' in the 1930s and 1940s (see chapter 5).
20. For the text see Mangoldt and Rittberger (1995: vol. 1/1, document 23).
21. The text can be found in Wells (1940b: 84ff.). The wording is very flowery and goes beyond the UDHR's postulates, in particular in the right to workers' participation in management and through qualified restriction of the right to property. Regrettably, even the *Encyclopedia of Human Rights* published by Edward Lawson (1991) omits further information about the league referred to.
22. See also Wells (1941) and Wagar (1961).
23. Wronka (1992: 88) comments on the distribution: 'This draft was eventually translated into ten languages and dropped by microfilm to the Resistance in occupied Europe and distributed worldwide to 300 editors in 48 countries. The final version of this World Declaration was undoubtedly a forerunner of the Universal Declaration of Human Rights'. It is reminiscent of the action undertaken by the Club of Rome with its study *The Limits of Growth* in 1972.
24. Maritain (1942). On Maritain in summary see McInerny (1995).
25. The collection published in Paris (1946) also contains 'Remarques preliminaires' (preliminary remarks).
26. Both texts are in Mangoldt and Rittberger (1995: vol. 1/1, document 4, 871–911 and 937–959). The legal interpretation is given in 'Economic, Social and Cultural Rights: Limburg Principles', in Lawson (1991: 416–421).
27. The example of law relating to women is emphasized by Heintz, Müller and Schiener (2006).
28. For discussion see Veit-Wilson (2007).
29. All texts are drawn from *The United Nation System and its Predecessors, Volume 1: The United Nations System* (Mangoldt and Rittberger 1995) with permission of the publishers.

Part II

Theory of Social Policy

Chapter 5

SOCIAL SECURITY
The Leading Idea and its Problems

'Social security' denotes both a complex of public institutions to protect individuals against common life risks and the programmatic idea that a commonwealth should provide all of its members with such protection that they feel secure within that commonwealth. This concept is broader than 'social insurance' and narrower than 'welfare state', but refers to similar problems.[1]

The Emergence of the Concept

'Security' (*securitas* in Latin) has a long-standing tradition in political rhetoric in Europe since the Roman Empire. In early modern times it was often used together with 'welfare' and 'felicity' to summarize a prince's duties to care for his subjects (see chapter 14). Thomas Hobbes made 'the safety of the people' a central task for his *Leviathan*, and this idea became seminal for modern political theory and constitutional practice. Wilhelm von Humboldt (1792) was the first to distinguish clearly between 'safety/security' and 'welfare'. He restricted the task of the state to the provision of 'safety/security', that is, on the one hand the protection of citizens' freedom from external threats, and on the other hand the internal protection of citizens' commitments and rights by the judiciary and police. 'Welfare' by contrast was now assigned to the private realm as the individual pursuit of happiness, in which the state was not to interfere. This became the liberal creed. In the nineteenth century the idea of public safety and security became restricted to the defence and protection of individual rights, and the latter became differentiated between security within the public realm and the protection of individual rights. But in the twentieth century the idea of security became paramount and was related to psychology and psychoanalysis, to the theory of cognition, to industrial and technical safety and to the reliability of the legal system, as well as to social security.

The specific context of the emergence of the term 'social security' was the Great Depression in the United States. In American pragmatism 'the quest for certainty' was abandoned and superseded by 'the search for security' (Dewey 1929). Inspired by the 'four wishes' of William I. Thomas (1966: 123ff.), first published in 1928, the 'desire for security' became a basic assumption about human motives and 'insecurity' a commonplace attribute of the zeitgeist, but also a substantial diagnosis of a crisis of orientation, especially among the middle classes (Lynd and Lynd 1937).

The invention of the expression 'social security' is commonly attributed to Franklin Delano Roosevelt or to his entourage. Roosevelt used it first in a Message to Congress on 30 September 1934, after having created a Committee on Economic Security to prepare the Social Security Act on 29 June 1934. However, a voluntary association promoting old age security renamed itself the American Association for Social Security in 1933 and changed the title of its journal from *Old Age Security Herald* to *Social Security* because the association's programme had been expanded from old age pensions to all branches of social insurance (Rubinow 1934: iii, 279).

In any case, the expression quickly gained strength, first embodied in the U.S. Social Security Act 1935 (SSA). It then appeared in the Atlantic Charter of 1941, became the catchword for the ILO's 1944 Declaration of Philadelphia and by 1948 had found its way into article 22 of the United Nations' Universal Declaration of Human Rights (see chapter 4). After the Second World War, social security had internationally become the leading term in programmes for the development of welfare states. Its specific meaning, however, remained vague.

Institutional Developments

At the time when the SSA was drafted, a public commitment to income maintenance for people in need was by no means a new idea. At the end of the nineteenth century two models were competing in Europe: public subsidization of mutual benefit associations (called the Ghent system), and social insurance along the lines of the German (Bismarck) model. The British social reforms introduced two new principles: payment of non-contributory old age pensions to deserving poor people (1908), and a contributory unemployment insurance system paying flat rate benefits (1911). In 1913 Sweden introduced the first universal system securing income in old age. After the Russian Revolution the Bolsheviks drafted a comprehensive system of social protection against all the major contingencies of life, following a concept that Lenin had already publicized in 1912; however, in practice the Stalinist system of social protection remained highly selective. Starting in France (1932), employers' payments of child allowances that had been voluntary were made obligatory, which ushered in a new model of administration: using private organizations to achieve public social policy ends. Thus social insurance for dependent workers was already competing with other models of social protection. The victory of the term 'social security' over 'social insurance' was a consequence of its vague meanings, which allowed it to include all kinds of public social protection. In 1947 the International Social Insurance Conference changed its name to the International Social Security Association and opened membership to state-administered systems (such as those of the U.K. and U.S.), which until then had been excluded.

The American SSA thus introduced a new name but hardly new ideas. However, it suffered from a problem not found in Europe, that of federalism. The U.S. Supreme Court had long held the federal government's attempts to introduce measures of social protection to be unconstitutional. Only after a positive Supreme Court ruling on the SSA in 1937 did federal social policies take shape, including policies to combat the risks of death of the breadwinner and of disability. Besides a federal system of old age insurance, the SSA introduced a new federal instrument into American politics: matching grants to individual states, which aimed to induce them to abolish the old forms of poor law, to introduce or to improve a system of unemployment compensation, and to provide better care for the blind as well as mothers and children (Committee on Economic Security 1937; Burns 1956). Thus the hitherto strictly separated domains of the federal and state governments became linked for the first time, only to remain a continued subject of controversy in the American polity with lasting consequences for the structure of social protection. A two-tiered system exists, consisting of 'social security' on the federal and 'welfare' on the state level (Cohen and Friedman 1972; Weir, Orloff and Skocpol 1988b; Arnold, Graetz and Munell 1998). The first programme, protecting most of the employed population, is well administered, highly stable and positively valued. The second, providing help only as a last resort, has remained an ever-contested object of repeated reforms. It is unevenly administered at the local level and its recipients remain stigmatized (Noble 1997).

What was innovative about the concept of social security was first developed in a 1942 report to the British government by a commission chaired by William Beveridge, entitled *Social Insurance and Allied Services*. It was a programme for a comprehensive and unified system covering the whole population against all the basic risks of life – an idea that Beveridge had already formulated in 1924. The Beveridge Report was received by the British population with unprecedented enthusiasm and became the blueprint for social legislation after the war (George 1968; Lowe 1993).

The Beveridge Report also proved seminal for the creation of the French *Sécurité Sociale* (1946–48). But by contrast with the United Kingdom, the principle of administrative unification of the system met with strong resistance in France from various social groups that preferred to keep or create separate insurances meeting their specific needs and interests (Galant 1955). In Germany only the term was adopted; the structure of the existing dual system remained unchanged. Moreover, a semantic distinction was made between the institutional (*Soziale Sicherung*) and the normative (*Soziale Sicherheit*) aspects of social security. In Scandinavia the term social security was hardly adopted at all, although the social protection systems underwent substantial reforms towards universalism.

Although many industrialized countries had developed measures of social protection against certain risks even before the Second World War, their impact remained generally modest. Some groups, such as public employees or veterans, were privileged by non-contributory benefits paid from general taxation, while industrial workers received only modest benefits based on contributions. With the exception of Scandinavia, rural populations remained mostly excluded from existing systems. In most countries a multitude of funds existed, designed respectively for specific risks, groups and localities. Repeated economic crises culminating in the Great Depression often undermined the reliability of expected benefits.

After the Second World War, different countries accepted the new ideal of social security in various ways. Coverage provided by existing institutions was almost everywhere extended, or new institutions were created to protect all or most of the population against specific risks. Most countries amalgamated the regulatory frameworks of different systems covering the same risks, or integrated the systems. Finally, the risks covered by schemes underwent international standardization. ILO Convention 102 on Minimum Standards of Social Security (1951) distinguishes eight forms of benefit: old age benefits, survivor benefits, disability benefits, family allowances, unemployment benefits, sickness benefits, medical care, and maternity benefits. Of course most advanced industrial countries' social protection institutions do not exactly match this list of benefits, but nowadays they do indeed tend to cover all these risks, albeit with varying degrees of coverage and benefits.

From a structural perspective the social security institutions form a discrete system, though one that is not defined everywhere in the same way. Delimitation issues concern the forms of benefit (in cash or in kind), of administration (centralized or decentralized; public, quasi-public or private), and of entitlement (public provision, insurance, relief), as well as the groups included (privileged or underprivileged groups are sometimes excluded) and the risks covered (family allowances, for example, are often excluded from the concept).

Security and Social Security as Value Concepts

The administrative codification of social security as a complex of institutions that provide benefits in cash or kind should not obscure the fact that the success of the concept owes less to these institutions than to the value connotations of the concept. President Roosevelt evinced a keen sense of these connotations when he characterized social security as 'freedom from fear and want' (6 January 1941), and when he described social security as a functional equivalent of the earlier security that stemmed from 'the interdependence of members of families upon each other and of the families within a small community upon each other' (8 June 1934).

But what does security mean? And why did the concept become so prominent and pervasive in the most advanced industrial countries, whose populations were more distant from serious want than any previous generations? Security has become a cultural value concept, a generally accepted standard for something that is desired and that, if opposed, arouses irritation (Kaufmann 1973). For a long time, security was not included among Western culture's value concepts. It began its career only after the First World War and lacks historical emphasis by comparison with other political value concepts, such as freedom, liberty or justice. Cultural value concepts emerge in reaction to generalized experiences of vulnerability, which in this instance are shown as loss of direction or in anxiety. The more one has to lose and the less transparent the future appears to be, the greater is the demand for security. The worldwide economic crisis following the 1929 crash was obviously exacerbating such experiences.

Security relates to human attitudes towards the future, not to the present. Insecurity does not mean an imminent danger but the possibility of future damage whose probability remains uncertain. The search for security is a correlate of the growing complexity of society and the ensuing acceleration of social change, which contributes to the 'loss of certainty' (Dewey) attributed to traditional society. Insofar as social change became a matter of articulated experience (which first happened historically in reflections on the French Revolution and its aftermath), a sense of history and of temporality has emerged that defines the future as open and uncertain. The same may be said about growing complexity: 'As seen by an observer complexity always takes the form of uncertainty' (Morin 1974: 571). For that reason the essence of the modern ideal of security can be interpreted as the mastery of complexity and risk, as the production of guarantees about future events (Kaufmann 2003a). This implies a paradoxical relation to the future: whereas the future is defined as temporality – the realm of contingency and uncertainty – the claim for security demands the annihilation of the temporality of the future and the control of social change.

In practice, security is attributed to (or demanded of) complex systems such as machines, factories, the legal system or systems of transport. But on closer inspection such systems are at best safe and reliable. Whether they are considered as secure in the sense of being emotionally tranquillizing depends on the public or individual perception. The generalized problem of security does not relate to protection (which is more efficient than ever), but to the relationship between external and internal security. Thus security, as a value term, means not only protection but also its reliability and the subjective perception of or trust in the reliability of protection, as well as the ensuing feeling of peace of mind (Kaufmann 1973: 150ff.). The Achilles heel of security under complex conditions is not the amount of protection (which is only a problem of effort) but the absence of protective transparency.

Security or safety were also long-standing pillars of political order that had already been incorporated into many constitutional documents (Makropoulos 1995) and now were transposed into a new economic and social context by Roosevelt's demand for social security. Just as government had the duty to care for external and internal security, it now had to provide a framework to guarantee everyone the means of existence through full employment, social insurance or other forms of benefits or services. 'Social security' thus became the umbrella word for economic, social and cultural rights as expressed in the United Nations Universal Declaration of Human Rights, article 22:

> Everyone as a member of society, has the right to social security and is entitled to realisation through national effort and international co-operation and in accordance with the organization and resources of each state, of the

economic, social and cultural rights indispensable for his dignity and the free development of his personality.

These rights are then specified as the right to work (article 23); the right to rest and leisure (article 24); the right to health, well-being and social protection, with special emphasis on mothers and children (article 25); the right to education (article 26); and the right to participation in culture, science and the arts (article 27) (see chapter 4, appendix 4).

Thus social security became another name for welfare in its politico-philosophical sense. It became a key term in the international evolution of the welfare state after the Second World War, though at the national level it was adopted in a variety of forms. In most countries the institutional aspect has long been dominant. In the current context of the 'crisis' or 'reconstruction' of the welfare state, social security again displays its normative aspect: the reliability of social protection is at stake. To what extent are politicians free to alter political regulations that aim to stabilize all or some specific parts of the population's future economic protection? Social security means the right of everybody who belongs to a certain commonwealth to be included in basic protection against destitution and want. It also implies, moreover, that such provisions should take a coherent and clearly accessible form for everyone, so that people not only are legally protected but also have easy and reliable access to such protection; and that they can trust in the future reliability of protection.

Ambivalences

The general appreciation of security started after the First World War in reaction to the acceleration of social change. In a manner of speaking it aims to annihilate temporality and the resultant uncertainty about the future. This is of course utopian, but every collective value has its utopian kernel, for example, freedom as the unrestricted capability to act. Because the future as such remains uncertain, it is impossible to reach security as such. But it is possible to control certain risks, such as unwanted potential future developments, either by prevention or by insurance. Such security, however, fails to meet the idealized hopes for security.

To the extent that collective values serve to legitimize political arguments, they clash with other value concepts. Thus, while the ideological antinomy of freedom or liberty and security is widespread, in use it is always partial – the freedom of some may cause insecurity for others. In social politics this argument often comes up against issues of redistribution. Those who are better off feel restricted by taxes and contributions, whereas the claims of those who are worse off are legitimated by the insecurity of their material existence.

Thus the normative use of security remains highly ambivalent. In a psychological sense, emotional security may result from the perception of reliable protection, but also from the subjective capacity to bear the insecurity of risk. For that reason, psychology has abandoned the concept of security and replaced it with a number of more specific terms, such as tolerance of frustration or contingencies, self-assuredness, various emotions, and the like.

Seen from the perspective of trust, the ideal of security has three basic connotations:

1. *Security in the sense of familiarity.* This form dominates in archaic societies that culturally annihilate the apparent contingencies of life by referring to extraordinary powers (Gehlen 1964). It is also attributed to traditional forms of community, where risk and situations for help are 'embedded' (Giddens 1990). Familiarity means that the instruments for help in cases of misfortune are within people's reach, and that they can control their reliability. Though traditionally the factual capacities for help remained much more modest than those of modern societies, familiarity with the community and its rules evokes spontaneous trust and contributes to emotional security. In a more analytical sense this security results from the experience of a persisting order without change in essence; in temporal terms it derives from the assumed continuity of the present. This at least is the perspective of those who have lost this kind of traditional security, which had no name for those living under these conditions. Maybe traditional security is only a retrospective construction by modern, secularized people. If there was security at all, it derived rather more from trust in supernatural forces.

2. *Security as reliability of protective systems.* This is the paradigmatic form of security in modern societies, as outlined above. Through specialization, future contingencies are either incorporated as risks in an organization's programme and contribute to its complexity, or they are excluded from its programme, as can be seen in some private insurance companies' contractual conditions. But public systems of social protection are also 'disembedded' and remain complex and difficult to understand. It is typical of modern systems that knowledge about their operations is a matter for professionalized insiders, whereas outsiders affected as clients or the general public experience them as impenetrable. As this problem cannot be solved by means of information alone (which at best operates in specific

situations), trust is essential if their effect is to induce tranquillity. But such trust is of a different quality from trust resulting from familiarity. As we have shown empirically, the appropriate attitude has the quality of suppressing distrust (Kaufmann 1973: 198f.). In such situations trust does not depend primarily on objective but on subjective factors such as intelligence and self-assurance.

3. *Security as self-assurance.* This form of security results from the individual capacity to cope with anxieties and risks. It depends on both available resources and personal confidence – on trust in oneself. Personal confidence is an attitude towards the future that depends on the belief that one will be able to cope with future contingencies, and on considering oneself not as an object but as a subject acting on one's own fate. Our empirical study of the conditions for subjective security showed a fairly strong correlation between (a) formal education and professional experience and (b) the capacity to overcome subjective fatalism and anxiety. People with high scores on fatalism also showed high scores on distrust of social security organizations and at the same time were more demanding (Kaufmann 1973: 312ff., 347ff.).

From the perspective of social policy, and following these distinctions, a choice has to be made between (or to combine) two strategies for security – either to strengthen social protection systems to protect people against life's risks, or to enable people to cope with insecurity themselves, for instance through public education. These two strategies, however, point to political choices that have to be made in the face of social inequality. Those who profit from above-average education may be more interested in enabling strategies, while those with below-average education may be more interested in protective strategies. As a matter of fact, parties of the 'left' often vote for more social protection, while those of the 'right' vote for more education. From a detached perspective, the two strategies look more complementary than exclusive. In order to increase the subjective security of the population all three forms of trust are important, even familiarity. Some familiarity may result from the long-standing existence and proven efficiency of organizations for coping with particular risks. Sudden rule changes or even institutional changes are therefore probably detrimental to maintaining the population's trust.

Another ambivalence of social security concerns the organizations that provide protection. In Europe at least, trust in the stability of political institutions is higher than trust in economic institutions such as private insurance or wealth management. In Germany the population has twice experienced an almost complete depreciation of financial assets, whereas neither the U.S. dollar nor the British pound has ever been replaced by new currency. In Anglo-Saxon countries private insurance therefore earns greater trust than it does in Germany or in France, for instance. This issue concerns the reliability of social protection, a typical issue for modern social systems.

Controversial Issues

General Problems

From the perspective of the Universal Declaration of Human Rights as well as of William Beveridge or Pierre Laroque, the 'father of the French *sécurité sociale*', social security was not restricted to publicly organized re-distribution within populations at risk but also included policies of full employment and of minimum wages. There was a clear awareness of the trade-off between full employment and the possibilities for funding social protection sufficiently. As the goal of guaranteeing to the entire popu-lation the opportunity to participate in the economic and cultural life of its society, social security implies education and employment as the primary means, leaving compensatory social protection as only a 'second-best' solution. The reification of social security has obscured this original perspective and focuses public attention on processes of compensatory protection and on processes only of redistribution. The current trend to substitute 'work for welfare' for the able-bodied is quite in line with the original intention, provided that a decent minimum living standard is at any rate attainable. There is a strong divergence, however, with regard to whether the role of labour markets should be exclusive (as in the Anglo-Saxon world) or whether there should be a subsidiary public role (as in the Scandinavian and German-speaking countries) in employing the less productive sections of the active population.

From the perspective of the 'Chicago School' of economics, the exist-ing systems of social security are too expensive. They disguise the relation-ship between an individual's contributions and benefits, and they benefit the middle classes more than those who are truly in need. Economists of this school maintain that a negative income tax would better serve the poor. Such a 'rational' economic perspective does not, however, take into account the existing trust in public systems of reciprocal security in most countries. The 'deal' that pools the risks of the whole population (or most of it) in one scheme, and thus makes basic economic security a matter of democratic politics, seems to be largely accepted in most countries, even though many people are aware that they are likely to be among the net payers to the system.

Given the natural inequality of abilities and the social inequalities resulting from birth, education, labour markets, and competition in general, all political endeavours to foster social security – whether in the broader or narrower sense – face the problem of distributive effects. These relate not only to the amount of individual benefit and the forms of public financing but to the institutional arrangements as well. Strong political conflicts emerged in many countries around the issue of creating a single comprehensive system for certain provisions, or for maintaining a fragmented system differentiating between classes of populations at risk. A somewhat related problem concerns the issue of securing only minimum standards, or higher standards of benefits through public provision as well. Finally, an obvious political struggle in all countries concerns the level of redistribution and who should bear the costs of social protection.

Comparative research has focused mainly on the explanation of national differences in institutional design and distributive effects. Path dependency upon earlier national approaches seems to be an important explanatory factor for these variations, next to political power relations and cultural orientations. An interesting finding is that systems that provide high levels of protection also tend to protect minimum standards better. There is one exception, however: Switzerland combines reliable minimum standards with a marked inequality of incomes.

Sectoral Aspects

Most political controversies do not arise over the system of social security as a whole but only concerning particular issues. As the functional organization of social protection is different from country to country, it remains difficult to generalize about this, though some broad issues may be identified.

The paramount problem in the contemporary debate – particularly as a consequence of demographic ageing – is security of income in old age. A three-tiered system consisting of universal and state-administered protection of basic standards (first tier), employment-related (and often private) protection of advanced standards (second tier), and complementary forms of personal provision (third tier) seems to be a promising model for resisting the demographic and economic challenges of decades to come. In order to ensure income security in old age for all, some public regulation and supervision of the second and third tiers nevertheless remains important.

The second complex of risks relates to illness, industrial diseases and long-term disability. Here, benefits in cash and in kind are necessary, and coverage for these risks is organized quite differently in different countries. Essentially, there are two different institutional models: the national health service, or protection through social insurance. Both systems face the problem of containing the explosion of costs that has resulted from the compounding of a wide range of medical, technological, demographic and economic factors. Moreover, individual health behaviour depends not only on diseases but also on opportunity structures.

The third complex of social security relates to the protection of the family. Since child labour has been forbidden and education made compulsory, children are no longer an economic asset for their parents but instead a powerful source of social inequality. Moreover, systems of social security make the elderly less dependent on the support by their own children. It is still contested to what extent parents (and especially mothers) should be supported by public means beyond the generally accepted subsidy in cases of manifest poverty. The low birth rate in most European populations now gives more political weight to demands for improving the living conditions and social protection of persons who are raising children or caring for their permanently incapacitated parents (see chapter 12).

The most contested part of social security remains public provision for the unemployed. Here, the trade-off with labour market policies and full employment is obvious, and beliefs vary about how best to deal with this problem.

The issue of poverty cuts across these functional distinctions. The extent to which it emerges as a separate problem that must be addressed by specific measures depends to a large extent on the institutional approaches that a country has adopted in the realms of social security mentioned above (Atkinson 1989).

The issues discussed here are those generally attributed to the concept of social security. The concept of the welfare state covers additional services such as housing, education, and personal services.

Summary

Social security denotes a complex of public or semi-public institutions to protect individuals against common life risks, namely old age, survivorship, disability, sickness, unemployment, medical care, maternity and the cost of children. It also refers to the programmatic idea that a commonwealth should provide all its members with such protection that they feel secure within that commonwealth. The concept emerged in the context of Franklin D. Roosevelt's New Deal and found its way into the UN Universal Declaration of Human Rights (article 22). Since the Second World

War, social security has become a leading term internationally in programmes for the development of welfare states. Its impact on the emergence of national programmes was quite different, however. Ambiguities in the concept result from its double sense as an ideal and as institutional reality. Though the ideal remains ambivalent in confrontation with other ideal values such as freedom or justice, it makes sense to use it as a critical standard for detecting the weaknesses of existing institutions.

Notes

1. This chapter is the revised and extended version of an article 'Social Security', which was published in the *International Encyclopaedia of the Social and Behavioural Sciences* (2001). This explains the summary form of argument. As I have carried out extensive research on this subject (Kaufmann 1973, 2003a), I have supplemented the original article, devoted to the state of the art, with some more personal interpretations of the idea of security.

Chapter 6

SOCIAL POLICY INTERVENTION
Elements of a Sociological Theory

The conventional idea of social policy assumes that policies can achieve their objectives simply by actually spending the necessary resources. Only after the beginning of the 1960s – initially in the U.S. and then from 1969 onwards in the former West Germany – did a new understanding of policy began to assert itself, one that considers the realization of politically desirable effects as in fact representing a problem in itself. Policy was no longer conceptually constructed only in terms of action theory as the interaction of conditions, aim(s) and measure(s) but instead became understood in terms of systems theory, as a multistage policy process marked by a high degree of contingency between the specific phases. In the social sciences this new policy concept found expression in research trends that can only be referred to here by their headings – policy sciences, the social indicator movement, evaluation research, implementation research, and others. As a rule, these trends in research are based on the premise that single policy processes (e.g. 'political programmes') can be isolated from each other. This is still an oversimplified notion, one that recent research has sought to rectify with more sophisticated concepts of interdependent policy processes and programmes.

This development can be ascribed not only to advances in the scientific understanding of policy, but equally to concrete changes in policy. The long-term expansive tendencies of nation-state functions in the twentieth century have led to a continuous growth in the absolute size of state bureaucracies, leading to problems of control and coordination that continue to defy the conventional capacities of consensual politics. In the process, the growth of state functions in certain operational areas has likewise resulted in an increase in the sheer density of interventions, and correspondingly in the concrete interdependence of policy measures, whose effects have increasingly been allowed to reinforce or neutralize each other unchecked. In this way, the chains of effects of actual policy processes have become ever longer, and also ever more confused. The policy model of a single political actor setting a target, passing the necessary measures, and thereby achieving the politically intended outcomes corresponds to the historical conditions of absolutist feudal rule. In reality, however, this notion has long been superseded, even when applied to the decisions of democratically elected parliaments. The scope for innovative, goal-orientated policy is restricted not only by the clash of vested interests and opposing power structures but also, increasingly, by the significance of prior political decisions.

This situation presents great opportunities to social science. The coordination so vital to practical policy requires review and new processes; it demands systematization and generalization, the development of more complex ideas of effective connections in policy contexts, and analysis of the features of the various areas of impact influenced by policy. One might assume that the consequent need for policy consultation would have delivered new impulses to theoretical formulations and empirical research in the relevant disciplines. Instead, even allowing for resistance to applied research from within the academic system (an often legitimate concern, considering the vested interests in its political exploitation), the yield from the social sciences focused on policy remains disappointing, so far. This has left a wide gap open between critical attitudes, or to be more precise, highly abstract attempts at systematization on the theoretical side, and simply inductive attempts at generalization on the empirical side. What is lacking can be described as 'applied basic research' (Kaufmann 1977). The aim of applied basic research is not to make a direct contribution to the solution of practical problems, but rather to create the theoretical (i.e. conceptual and methodological) conditions in which concrete forms of scientific and practical empiricism can be applied to rational problem solving.

The limited success of social science efforts to interpret and systematize political administrative practice can be primarily explained not by the absence of research but instead by the vagaries of the research field itself. This is not a reference to the notorious reluctance of organizations and their members to allow themselves to be treated as 'research objects' by outsiders. Rather, the 'perversity of the object' lies in the concrete complexity mentioned above, its diversity and interdependence. It seems to be difficult to discover an intermediate plane of abstraction between the specifics of political administrative practice in individual cases and the generalization of a theory of the 'policy process', one that would ideally allow a simultaneous application of abstract social science concepts to reflect reality and a conscious transfer to policy problems posed in practice. The following reflections on the sociological conceptualization of social policy and the systematization of forms of social policy intervention represent steps to proceed further along these lines.

Social Policy Interventions as the Object of Sociological Theory

What are the common elements that justify the choice of precisely social policy (and not, for instance, social or domestic politics, or specific policies concerning family, health, social insurance or education) as the starting point for the application of sociological theory? The principal reasons can only be mentioned briefly here.

1. Etymologically, the term 'social policy' first appeared in the emerging social sciences in the middle of the nineteenth century, to describe the 'mediation' between the private sphere of market-based society and the public sphere of the constitutional state. The term thus already historically contains an explicit connection with social theory (chapter 2).
2. The term is embedded in both social science and practice, and has gained international acceptance over the last thirty years.
3. The term suggests an intermediate level of abstraction in political inquiry. It is neither as general as 'policy' or 'societal politics', nor as specific as the subsidiary parts that are immediately identifiable through their institutional delineations, such as family or youth policy, employment conditions, education or health services.
4. The various policies subsumed under 'social policy' show common sociological characteristics and concrete related effects that justify a theoretical formulation at this level.

The reasoning behind this last argument leads directly to the subject of these reflections: the search for a sociological perspective on the processes of social policy. Jurisprudence treats the variety of what is presented historically as social policy under the headings of industrial law and social law. Political economy speaks about it under the headings of distributive policy or transfer economics. In political science and sociology, however, 'social policy' seems to be adopted as the name of a field of research, but without a generally recognized theoretical perspective such as, say, distributive theory has in economics.

From the Normative Perspective to the Analysis of Effects

In comparing the existing sociological and political science approaches, there at first glance seems to be widespread agreement that 'social policy' can be conceived as a part or field of state governmental policy. But this cannot be taken for granted, because from a historical perspective social policy concerns the relationship between state and society (in the Hegelian sense), while discussion of occupational or communal social policy refers to non-governmental social policy agencies. Moreover, in German social policy statutory measures are largely implemented by non-governmental agencies, meaning bodies that are not directly managed by the national government (social insurance agencies, charitable welfare institutions, local authorities, etc.). In such situations the managerial relationship between state and society remains contested. Even if national governments or local authorities still dominate social policy provision in the remaining classical welfare states, the growing tendency in many other countries is also towards pluralism and partial privatization of the social service agency structures.

Nevertheless, in the context of a theoretical approach it makes sense to take the government as both the starting point and the point of political transition of social policy, because it allows us to analyse and construct the disputed scope of state control as the relation between the state and other social policy actors (and the vested social interests that lie behind them).

But how is social policy itself distinct from other forms of state policy? Why does it deserve to be examined separately? The diverse attempts at definition and interpretation by various authors show that opinion on these matters is deeply divided. Without further detailed semantic debate, in my view the following basic tendencies can be distinguished:

1. *Service-based categories.* These are most commonly found in the literature directly concerned with practice, predominantly related to questions of institutional responsibility. In terms of theory building, they are relevant only as an empirical touchstone for the validity of abstract positions.
2. *Goal or value-orientated categorizations.* Almost all the older generalizing attempts to define social policy referred to the normative orientation of social policy measures, and therefore defined social

policy as, for example, the sum of measures aimed at freedom, welfare, social security or social justice. Zwiedineck-Südenhorst, a leading theorist of social policy on the eve of the First World War, went even further in generalizing and abstracting from the substance of the goals; his definition was that social policy 'encompasses all goal-oriented thought and practical attempts towards the social' (Zwiedineck-Südenhorst 1911: 37).

3. Critics have rightly raised objections to such normative definitions of social policy, arguing that normative perspectives and goals are often contested among the political actors, and that even social scientists are not in a position to offer a convincing substantiation of the binding character of any normative perspective. Instead, the suggestion is that social policy be defined in terms of its societal function, that is in relation to those stabilizing effects that social policy provides within a specific societal form (concretely in the capitalist one). Sachße and Tennstedt (1988: 14), for instance, define social policy as 'the entirety of state measures aimed at producing, maintaining and securing the supply of a utilisable workforce in the specific form of wage labour'. Nevertheless, such functional attempts at definition can be countered by the argument that every functional definition is predicated on assumptions about the systematized context that determines the function. Any number of options are available to define such 'system references', which in turn can themselves only be limited by (often implicit) prior normative choices. The relative arbitrariness of such functional approaches becomes obvious when one considers, in the present definition, that the group of eligible benefit claimants increasingly includes self-employed earners or those incapable of work. Or to put it more generally, entitlements are increasingly linked to citizenship rather than to labour conditions. It may help the clarity of analysis to distinguish, with Luhmann (1981a: 81ff.), between function (as the relation of a subsystem to the greater entity of which it is considered a part) and service (as the relation of a subsystem to another subsystem). While social policy undoubtedly contributes to maintaining social connections, it does so not merely in the sense of stabilizing the relations of both production and reproduction, but also by transforming them (Heimann 1929). Because social policy consists of a combination of provisions from different functional societal subsystems with regard to the living conditions of the population, its function in respect of the entirety remains relatively diffuse or correspondingly complex. By contrast, its services can be described and empirically analysed.

4. The specific difference of social policy may be defined not only on the basis of normative but equally on cognitive assumptions, specifically through its sphere of consequences, by asking what concrete conditions social policy affects, or rather, claims to exert an effect upon. Attempts to define social policy in this way also have a long tradition. The economic perspective on social policy still harks back to Adolph Wagner's classic definition of 'the state policy which seeks to combat shortcomings in aspects of distributive processes by force of legislation' (1891: 4). However, Bortkiewicz's definition appears sociologically more fruitful: 'Social policy is ... the state's position on conflicting social forces, expressed in legislation and administration' (Bortkiewicz 1899: 334–35). Numerous social theorists have followed Bortkiewicz's line that social policy's field of action is the relation between different classes or social groups. As opposed to this, newer writers, more influenced by welfare thinking, argue that social policy's real field of impact is to be found in the social position or life situation of individuals or specific groups.[1] A comprehensive definition of 'life situation' is given by Weisser (1956: 635) as the 'scope that people's external circumstances offer for meeting their basic wants, as determined by unhindered and thorough contemplation of the meaning of their lives'.

From the perspective of more recent understandings of policy – those for which the realization of politically desired effects (and naturally the avoidance of unwanted effects) represents the problem – it is advisable to take this perspective of outcome and impact as the starting point for further theoretical considerations.

Social Policy as Governmental Intervention in Social Circumstances

When Sir Robert Peel's Factory Act of 1819 first imposed state regulation on industrial child labour in England, it was described as state interference. This is a description that, far more clearly than the term intervention, indicates that what we are dealing with here is not a subject-object relation. Rather, the procedures relate to a social context that they are intended to alter and that clearly can react to the relevant intentions. While the classic model of political behaviour (using the basic concepts of goal, context and means) conceives procedures as selective measures related to a fixed situation, the concept of intervention enables a more sophisticated reconstruction of the contexts in question.

The nineteenth-century founding fathers of the German social sciences (W.H. Riehl, Robert von Mohl, Karl Marx and Lorenz von Stein) differed from each other in terms of their social concepts and the means by which the 'social question' was to be resolved. Nevertheless, they were in considerable agreement in defining this social question as a problem of the social inequalities conditioned by differing property relations and the resultant impoverishment of the non-propertied classes of the population. It follows from this that social policy has to do with resolving the social question through the state's impact on social relations – an idea developed by von Mohl and von Stein, albeit with differing emphases.

As a consequence, however, it becomes apparent that the activation of the state's social policy potential depends in turn on the extent to which the socially disadvantaged groups themselves are able to gain influence within the state. This explains the central importance of universal suffrage, and therefore the definition of social policy as the mediation between state and society. A systematic theoretical perspective enables us to differentiate more clearly between the relations of (1) voters and politics, (2) politics and administration, (3) administration and the public, and thus to understand better the dual relationship between the state and various social forces. It also emphasizes the fact that those who influence the formulation of political programmes are not necessarily identical with those whom these programmes address.

The field of operation of a country's foreign policy is its international relations, or more precisely the political context in which they take place. The field of operation of economic policy can be taken to be the market-driven 'economic system', whereby economic policy can be treated as an isolated phenomenon precisely because the production and distribution of economic goods in capitalist societies have become differentiated into a market-driven subsystem. But how can the field of operation of social policy be similarly delimited? The apparent diffuseness of its field of operation is traceable to the fact that, unlike the economy, it lacks a unitary subsystem context. The targets of social policy measures are 'categories of people who are, either in absolute or relative terms, economically and/or socially weak' (Lampert and Althammer 2007: 4). These categories, however, are socially organized to varying degrees, and on closer examination they become targeted groups only in terms of specific characteristics such as workers, parents, patients, schoolchildren and so on, which are then identified as entitled to specific services.

Following common linguistic usage, we could describe social policy's field of operation as social circumstances; the equivalent German term, *soziale Verhältnisse*, neatly embraces both social conditions and social relations. 'Social circumstances' are taken to be the conditions of life of individuals from the perspective of their participation in the historically determined aspects of social opportunities, and in particular from the perspective of their comparability with one another. In terms of social theory, this postulated equalization of participatory opportunities is legitimated by means of the concept of inclusion:

> According to this concept, every person must be able to have access to all fields of functioning. Everyone must be entitled to start a family, to participate in exercising power or at least in managing it. Everyone must be educated at school, receive medical treatment as and when required, and be able to participate in economic transactions. The principle of inclusion supersedes all forms of solidarity based on a person belonging to one, and only one, social group. (Luhmann 1980: 30–31; see also Parsons 1971: 20ff.)

Luhmann (1981a) deduces from this that the entire dynamic of the welfare state is based on this principle of inclusion.

Like the Marxist concept of the conditions of production, the term social circumstances concerns conditions that are 'inevitable and irrespective of their will' (Marx 1859: 8). They are entered into by individuals to sustain their existence in the form of employment or tenant relations, as members of occupational associations or social insurance schemes and the like, or as the clientele of social services or administrations. The aspect of inevitability lies in the increasing disappearance of the possibilities for independent subsistence. The feudal agrarian system still afforded an opportunity to provide for oneself and one's family directly through natural subsistence, and the loss of this opportunity means that people have inevitably become dependent on the exchange conditions of the markets and the politically determined conditions of public provision (see introduction). What the Marxist stipulation conceals is that this change can also result in offering greater scope in the choice of such conditions, though in the light of the stereotyped forms of modern kinds of participation these conditions may still be qualified as 'irrespective of their will'.

In the process of the emergence of social policies, individuals become comparable according to categories of socially defined characteristics (status indicators) and of participatory opportunities (situational features such as employment, income, housing, health provision, claims and participatory rights, etc.). We refer to social policy measures when disadvantages in participatory opportunity can be attributed to specific status categories (which always implies a comparison either with a standard of normality or with other status groups), and when political interventions are aimed at remedying these disadvantages. There is therefore no contradiction between the older definition of the field of operation of social policy measures as the relations between social groups, and the newer definition as life situation. Instead, both determinants shed light upon different facets of a coherent phenomenon. The older expression related mainly to the 'workers' question', and it thus essentially thought of social policy as the enlargement of the participatory opportunities of workers, defined as a social class, as a collective entity. However, as the participatory opportunities linked to worker status improved, the class aspect disappeared from view. In other words, the greater complexity of social interconnections became apparent, allowing workers and non-workers to be conceptualized according to other status features such as 'having legal guardianship of a child' or 'being over sixty years old'.

The definitions outlined above primarily serve analytical purposes. It is easy to show that the explicit sense of most social policy measures is covered by our choice of definition, but obviously there are also other further outcomes and intentions that are linked to them. To the extent, for instance, that a status categorization relates to organized bodies of individuals, an improvement in their participatory opportunities can also have the political side effect of increasing group power, which may indeed be entirely intentional on the part of some actors. If we use the description social policy for those policy measures aimed at improving the participatory opportunities of socially disadvantaged groups of individuals, it follows that the primary field of operations of these policy measures lies in participatory opportunities. For example, in an economic stimulus programme aimed not only at improving the economic situation of enterprises but also at job creation, the creation of opportunities for participation can be qualified as social policy even if in terms of our analytical concepts these are a side effect of economic policy measures.

Social Policy Intervention as a Multistage Process

In addition to objections arising from perspectives other than the present one, which is oriented on the dimension of outcomes and impact, an additional highly relevant objection must be addressed: can state action have any impact on social circumstances at all? Is state action not essentially confined to influencing the social macro-conditions upon which, in a highly contingent manner, the social micro-conditions merely depend? It must also be noted that whereas during the early period of social policy, state interventions took place in largely state-free social space, in the course of its development social policy has altered the relations between social classes and groups. Social policy measures transform social relations, and with them the social policy demands. Evolved social policies themselves become an aspect of social circumstances (Achinger 1958). Thus in some sense the already existing social policy institutions themselves become the object of further state intervention, in that they can be expanded, reprogrammed or even discontinued (chapter 7). The service providers come to exercise considerable influence over political decision-making processes, in a similar manner to the organized groups addressed by social policies.

The analytical problems elaborated under this heading can be successfully tackled by combining two of the theoretical perspectives introduced above, namely the insight of political science into the multistage nature of policy processes, and the sociological differentiation between various levels of societal reality.

The idea of a multistage policy process emerged in connection with the system theory treatment of policy pioneered by Easton (1965a, 1965b). Fundamental to this idea, and already embodied in the principle of the separation of powers, is the concept that despite the structural division between politics and administration, the two are nevertheless highly interconnected in procedural terms through data processing methods. The output of the political system (e.g. a law) becomes the input of the administrative system. However, the former simultaneously relies on the information and performance of the latter, which in its turn can be conceived of either as inputs into the political decision-making process or as feedback mechanisms (Deutsch 1963).

This two-stage perspective can be enhanced to a multistage one to the extent that structurally distinct subsystems (e.g. departments or subordinate authorities) can be identified within the political and administrative systems that are interconnected through output-input and feedback relations. This problem was initially recognized in the context of planning theory and identified as a problem of multistage planning (Ozbekhan 1969). Since then the role played by this problem in the process of policy production has received greater emphasis, raising awareness of the fact that not only are state measures formulated and adopted under multiple influences, but as a rule the agencies and authorities who implement them are not those who decided on them in the first place (first expressed by Pressman and Wildavsky 1973; Scharpf, Reissert and Schnabel 1976).

This has led to a change in perspective towards older normative views. The political concept, focused on behavioural theory and goal-oriented policy ideas, has been superseded by the (inter-) systems theory idea of multistage political processes. This latter idea identifies two forces simultaneously at work within these processes. First, overlapping political concepts (goals, programmes) are analysed in detail and translated into effective measures. Second, supplementary influences that could potentially give rise to goal displacement, implementation deficits or side effects are taken into account at each and every stage, referring to every system involved. This question is generally dealt with under the heading of implementation research (Mazmanian and Sabatier 1981).

The empirical examination of political processes has also shown that the separation of political planning from implementation can be exaggerated, in that the effectiveness of policy also ultimately rests on there being sufficient linkages and feedbacks between the two. This is why the attempt was subsequently undertaken to convert the implementation problem in turn into an overarching control theory formulation of the policy problem (Kaufmann, Majone and Ostrom 1986b; Kaufmann 1991b; Mayntz and Scharpf 1995).

The sociological conceptualization of social reality as a multilevel phenomenon originated in structural-functionalist studies. Thus Talcott Parsons distinguished between four 'organisational levels of the social structure', each of them analysed in terms of the functional requisites of the AGIL-model (detailed more precisely in Johnson 1961: 214ff.). For Parsons these organizational levels stood in a relation of hierarchical determination: structures and processes at the societal level determine what is feasible at the institutional level, which in turn determines the managerial level, with the managerial determining the 'technical' or 'primary' level. In other words, according to Parsons the overall societal level in modern societies expresses itself primarily in politics and no longer through religion, and a kind of regulatory primacy over general society, whose normative and factual power is not problematized, is ascribed to the political system. This is analogous to the older political theory.

Niklas Luhmann's social theory is based on Parson's proposition but differs from it in its formulation of key social integration mechanisms. Luhmann postulates the relative autonomy of the differentiated functional systems that have crystallized in the process of social evolution (he refers to the state, law, economy, religion, science, education and art), as well as an increasing independence of the different levels of social structure, discussed by him as the societal, organizational and interaction levels (Luhmann 1975). This expresses the same urge to formulate more complex theoretical contexts that is encountered in, for example, the theory of political processes. In what follows, I shall make use of Luhmann's concept of three levels, even though I consider both Parsons's institutional level and a supplementary focus on the personal level to be indispensable to the framework of complex sociological analysis (cf. Kaufmann 1982: 256ff.).

The concept and practice of the social state by no means require the political powers to take the provision of social services into public ownership, as is clearly shown in the case of Germany. However, the national and international stipulation of social rights indicates precisely what constitutes the core of the welfare state programme: 'Everyone ... has a right to social security and is entitled to realization, through additional effort and in co-operation and in accordance with the organization of each State, of the economic, political and cultural rights indispensable for his dignity and the free development of his personality'.[2] What this essentially involves is not compensation for an economic or social disadvantage, but a participation that corresponds to the idea of inclusion. The correct assertion that the state's powers to intervene to guarantee social rights are in fact limited does not absolve the state from its obligations as guarantor.

Because state services are typically services for other societal subsystems, from the multistage intervention perspective the problem for social policy can be expressed as follows: how, in keeping with the postulate of inclusion, can state interventions be designed in such a way as to influence the operations of organizations whose services are important for the lives of individuals? The sociological analysis of social policy processes reconstructs them as (1) the connections between numerous state interventions at the institutional level, with respect to (2) public, semi-private and private agencies at an organizational level, viewed from the aspect of (3) the participatory opportunities of individuals at the interactive level. In this way, the concept of a multistage social policy process can be combined with the idea of different levels of social reality.

Methodological Implications of the Concept of Intervention

The concept of intervention does not take the perspective of the operator, but instead adopts the perspective of a scientific observer of the operations. It follows that the action-oriented concept of intervention can be reconstructed in a more complex form, as (a) the (focal) actor who, on the basis of (b) specific intentions and (c) certain assumptions about the consequences of his or her behaviour, intervenes in (d) a defined situation using (e) specific measures in order to alter the situation (Kaufmann 1987). It should be emphasized that it is not only a specific behaviour on the part of the agent that is of relevance to this perspective, but also certain characteristics of the agent him or herself, for instance knowledge, situational assessments, resources, etc. Thus the question is not only what appropriate measures are needed to alter a situation to meet specified goals, but also how far an agent is capable of achieving a specific goal using the available resources. This constitutes the perspective from which political and administrative actors are observed within the framework of a sociology of social intervention.

What must similarly be taken into consideration in the observation are the characteristics of the field of intervention, in other words the structural circumstances to be affected by the actor. This is of central importance in social interventions that aim to change the social conditions and relations of individuals. In this case the field of intervention is itself constituted by actors who are capable of both examining and reacting to the objectives of the focal actor. Their acceptance or rejection of what they perceive to be the aims of the intervening actor depends on the way the intervening actor behaves, and they may express conformity or react with unforeseen dissent in respect of any measures. Thus social interventions do not concern clearly identifiable situations, but instead apply to a more or less opaque context, one whose reactions only become apparent to the intervening actor in the course of the intervention itself.

Social interventions are not generally carried out by a single actor. Instead they involve multiple actors who are usually active in a multistage intervention process. It is of course perfectly possible to conceive of a single action (such as giving an injection, providing advice, or deciding on about a claim for financial aid) as an intervention at a personal level, but strictly speaking these involve fairly trivial cases and moreover, as a rule, do not by themselves resolve any serious problems. Only in exceptional cases does one isolated intervention wholly bring about the curing of a patient's diseases, useful careers advice, the solution of family problems or the payment of social security. Taking complicated surgery as an example – and even more so in the case of entire social policy programmes – the multistage character of interventions and the involvement of numerous individual actors (in the latter case corporate actors as well) become obvious.

In keeping with the observer-centred concept, it follows that what can be defined in contextual examination as an intervention is determined by the scientific observers, and not by the intervening actors. This means that the focus no longer lies in what are often the manifold motives and imprecise intentions of the actors. Instead, the constitutive intention for the reconstruction of the intervention process is postulated by the observer, who must take the visible output at the level of the conjectural or explicit meaning into account, for instance by referring to the legal or medical context of the action. Social intervention is thus a basic analytical concept in the social science reconstruction of targeted actions to modify social contexts. The degree of sophistication involved in reconstructing the process of intervention, and the explanatory power that results from it, depend on the scope of the connections assumed by the scientific observer (Kaufmann and Strohmeier 1981).

But what is the point of such an explicit concept of intervention? If the involvement of multiple actors in social intervention processes represents the norm, then it can be assumed that their insights into the connections under consideration are limited and their own behavioural perspectives are biased. Scientific reconstruction enables the inclusion of the different perspectives of the various actors, therefore enabling the actors to gain a better sense of what makes for successful actions, and a better understanding of their context. The development of more complex intervention models, and thus correspondingly of more complex impact models, is consequently an essential part of collective learning processes. In order for the social reform standpoint to remain credible, the potential and success of such models must be subjected to examination.

The Ambiguity of Social Policy Intervention

The object of a sociological theory of social policy is the intervention of the state in social circumstances, or to be more precise, in the structural conditions under which people lead their everyday lives. This includes the area of production (work) as well as that of reproduction (socialization, regeneration of human capital, the time available for non-economic ends).

In this context three basic aspects require elucidation:

1. Social policy always involves the intervention of the state in pre-existing structured social fields. What becomes of these governmental measures depends on the characteristics of the field. This is where a sociological position most clearly diverges from that of the political sciences, which orient their thinking exclusively to the government. Thus the sociological approach must take into account the perspectives of all actors involved in an intervention process, including their alternative possibilities of action and their constraints. It is precisely the combination of these multiple perspectives in the sociological approach that affords its insights.

2. Social policy always involves intervention legitimized by the individual welfare of target groups. Regardless of individual political actors' underlying motives to support a measure that has been declared social policy (e.g. to win an election, to stymie an attempted revolution, or to create jobs for unemployed academics), the 'official' reason given is a situational improvement for either everyone or specific groups of inhabitants, and as a rule some sort of plausible connection exists between the adopted measures and the explicit aims.[3]

3. Besides the assumption of individual benefit, it is always crucial to examine the collective implications of social policy measures.[4] Pub-

lic intervention is not to be legitimized by meeting each and every individual's personal needs, even when spread over large numbers of people. The presupposition is more one of 'public interest', although the arguments for it can often be quite various, and in extreme cases even contradictory. There are three basic justifications of public interest:

a) The theory of public goods concerns public needs or collective benefits, the satisfaction of which cannot be guaranteed by purely market-driven production. In this case, social policy goods typically belong to the class of merit goods that may generate individually distributed benefits (e.g. school education) but nevertheless simultaneously yield external effects (e.g. vocational qualifications) that are in the general public interest (Head 1969). Public interest therefore focuses on the conjectured consequences resulting from the fulfilment or non-fulfilment of individual needs. In the process, economic theory primarily examines the productional and distributional aspects of specific goods, or rather the economic benefits and cost aspects of external effects. Nevertheless, this is only one aspect of collective advantage.

b) The sociological theory of social problems reveals other perspectives. Not every form of personal suffering or social deviation is immediately treated as a social problem. Instead, a collective definition process must elevate specific social circumstances to the status of social problems. By omitting the more superficial attempts to make social problems evident and demanding solid substantiation of both the definition and, above all, the pondering of social problems, one encounters ideas of social disorder that subsume both normative perspectives and quasi-theories of generic events and their causes or consequences. The choice of different defining perspectives (e.g. the majority of the population, government representatives, sociologists or recipients) can reflect differences in opinion in terms of both normative perspectives and quasi-theories (Gronemeyer 2007). In this process, the ability to form a consensus on the definition of social problems depends on the extent to which ideas of social order are generally shared. From this perspective, the public interest does not confine itself simply to cost-benefit calculations, but instead makes assumptions based on ideas about potential threats to proper social order. The ideal characteristics of this social order, in turn, serve as the criteria to evaluate the concrete circumstances of a problem. However, social problems are constituted not only through normative but also through cognitive arguments. Cognitive selection criteria could, for instance, be the number of people affected by the concrete circumstance of a problem, the intensity of the burdens, or the extent of the predictable detrimental consequences.

c) Finally, from the perspective of political science, the public interest may also be defined, in terms of immediate political interests, as the pursuit of political support for (or at least the consolidation of) a constantly somewhat precarious public order or mass loyalty. Whereas in the previous train of thought the intervention in social circumstances appeared, as it were, as an end in itself, here the explicit or implicit assumption is that governmental attempts to engage with social problems have a payback effect for the political actors.

In summarizing these three perspectives on social policy intervention it becomes apparent how and why the introduction and implementation of social policy measures touches on different interests. All three of the typical attempts at definition share an assumption about the collective implications of promoting individual welfare, but this collective implication may be evaluated differently from different political stances. Depending on the structured potential influence of these interests, they can take on a lesser or greater prominence in the process of programme formulation or implementation.

Social policy intervention therefore always remains ambiguous. One can neither assume that social policy measures always primarily result from the interests of the explicit target groups, nor can it even be expected that 'benevolent' governmental measures always meet with the approval of those affected by them. The effective organizational, cognitive and normative structures within the sphere of intervention cause attempted state interventions to mutate, both in terms of their interpretation and in terms of their intended outcomes.

This mutation is not to be treated simply as policy failure. The supposition is that mutations like these (which can also be understood as an expression of the contingency of social policy processes) do not simply emerge coincidentally or in uncontrollable forms. If this were the case, then any interest in a theory of social policy regulation would be fatuous. In any event there are good reasons to assume considerable consensus on the manifest goals or intended outcomes of specific social policy measures, and to accept that not all forms of governmental intervention have similar effects or must expect arbitrary mutations.

Dimensions of Social Participation

On the basis of the foregoing, we can assume that the regulation of social policy interventions by politics alone is necessarily insufficient. It is true that politics is the locus for taking decisions about the choice of problems to tackle politically, and also for formulating the basic conditions for implementing social policy measures. However, this says little about how they work and still less about their tangible outcomes. What follows is a tentative attempt to give structure to some of the typical forms of effective social policy intervention, to allow an outcome-based analysis of social policy to be theoretically substantiated.

Because the social policy context is complex, as suggested above, a theoretical treatment can only be undertaken on the basis of simplifications. To put it more precisely, the heuristic value of a theory is determined by the choice and consistent application of simplifying initial assumptions. The starting point is how and under what conditions ascertainable effects can be attained by state-induced measures acting on social circumstances, or in everyday terms, in relation to the working and living conditions of the population. This question appears to have practical relevance and is sufficiently generalized and susceptible of analysis using sociological concepts and methods.

Next, one must find features under which both the variety and experience of social policy measures can be arranged comparatively. I shall assume that social policy measures can be systematized according to their types of effects, which in keeping with my theme I shall take as their impact on the problem of social inclusion. Thus the aim of theorizing is to develop organizing principles, according to which existing or potential experiences of the effects of social policy measures can be collated comparatively, offering a tool to facilitate systematic generalizations. To this end, the various forms of intervention are briefly described below, based on the simplifying assumption that state interventions in social circumstances are structured to achieve typical outcomes, that is, that the variety of claimed or actual social policy objectives can be reduced to a reasonably small number of categorical effects. Four types of intended social policy outcomes can be distinguished:

1. Improvement of a people's *legal status*, i.e. of socially recognized rights to participation in social resources and opportunities as previously expressed in basic constitutional rights or legal entitlements. An additional prerequisite for the social realization of these rights is that they are respected in practice in the process of status allocation by third parties.

2. The increase in *resources* available to people who are socially and economically disadvantaged. Resources (especially time, money and property) are basically freely available means of meeting needs but are nevertheless usually scarce. All forms of social participation make use of certain resources, which may lead to problems of scarcity.

3. Improvement in people's *environmental opportunities*. A prerequisite for social participation is a supply of participatory opportunities (e.g. social services), which can be accessed according to status, resources and powers. Opportunities, as opposed to resources, are elements of the social, spatial and material environment that are not freely available to individuals. They only become available under the conditions imposed by third parties (for example entry restrictions, ability to pay, deserts, behavioural compliance).

4. Improvement of people's *capabilities for action*. Competences such as education, health, knowledge and skills are prerequisites for the capacity and willingness (normative orientation, readiness to perform or specific motivations) to act. They count as necessary preconditions for social activity.

The systematization in figure 6.1 is based on the previously mentioned principle of inclusion as the functional equivalent of the older form of elementary solidarity. It is easy to show that there are four distinct preconditions for participation in the typical modern forms of satisfying needs, articulating interests, and cultural orientation. To the extent that opportunities for self-subsistence have declined and people have become

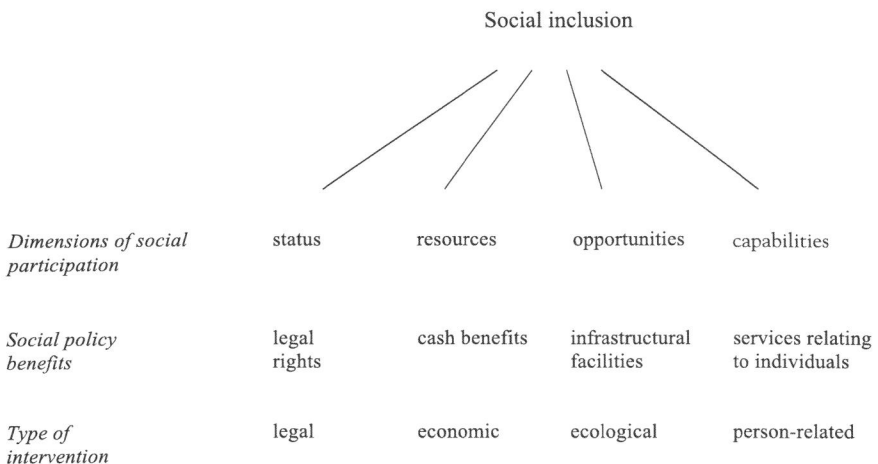

Social inclusion

Dimensions of social participation	status	resources	opportunities	capabilities
Social policy benefits	legal rights	cash benefits	infrastructural facilities	services relating to individuals
Type of intervention	legal	economic	ecological	person-related

Figure 6.1. Social Participation and Social Policy Intervention

dependent upon the processes of market supply and public provision, and on the essential services provided by organized entities that exceed the capacity of individuals to comprehend or influence them, the realization of inclusion demands the definition and protection of individuals' specific rights vis-à-vis such organizations. Furthermore, real inclusion requires the availability of appropriate opportunities or possibilities for action in the accessible environment, the capability for action and disposable cash resources, at least in the sphere of market provision but also indirectly for most other forms of participation.

These four preconditions for social inclusion can be substituted to only a limited degree. For instance, a person with an above-average income could compensate for a lack of operative skills by hiring advisers, lawyers or the like, or could afford to travel further to access a service. Or legal status or access to free legal advice could be so improved that people with fewer capabilities are not so disadvantaged. But as consumer protection demonstrates, such compensatory strategies are strictly limited, and people with greater capabilities often use the compensatory facilities intended for those with less. Basically, these four distinct necessary conditions for social participation can generate sufficient conditions for social inclusion only when working together in combination. There are thus four categorical aspects of personal circumstances of life that can now be discussed in terms of the various distinct fields such as work, housing, health, education, social security and so on.

Forms of Intervention

This typology of conditions for social participation is not, however, sufficient to characterize the forms of intervention, because it focuses only on the potential effects and not on the intervention itself, which represents a process of multilevel measures. It is therefore necessary to determine whether the typology is analytically appropriate for categorizing social policy measures. If it proves feasible to allocate the majority of these measures specifically to one of these four types of effect, then this would offer a heuristically fruitful simplification from which to start to characterize various forms of intervention and examine their ways in which they work, as briefly follows.

Legal Intervention: Measures for Improving the Legal Status of Individuals and Groups

The grant of legal protection (as for instance in the case of female and child labour) and the codification of individual, and later collective, labour law represent the oldest form of social policy intervention. Even today the codification of legal relationships – for instance the tightening of consumer protection, the introduction of a legal right to social assistance or to freedom of information, the modification of parents' rights of maintenance, or tenancy law – still constitute an important form of social policy intervention.

The statutory form of intervention is not to be confused with the state's use of law as a general means of regulation. The constitutional rule of law demands that each and every form of state intervention be embodied in statute. However, the vast majority of all legal norms relevant to social policy do not directly affect the legal status of those to whom social policy measures are addressed. Only those modifications of law that aim to enhance the legal status of the weaker partner in a legal relationship can be classified as legal forms of intervention in social policy.

While inequalities in power in early capitalism predominantly lay in the distribution of wealth, or of poverty, the power inequality under late capitalist welfare state conditions is essentially based on organizational status. The individual person must typically confront corporations – in other words, one side of the legal relationship is occupied by single individuals and the other by organizations characterized by a division of labour, such as business enterprises, insurance companies, hospitals, social services or their legal representatives. The principle of formal organization clearly distinguishes between agencies and clients. What seems to emerge from this process is the typical disparity in interactive style between organizations and individuals that Coleman (1974: 92) reduced to a pithy statement: 'Persons give preferential treatment to other persons, and corporative actors give preferential treatment to other corporative actors.' Thus the procedural rights of those affected and the judicial review of administrative decisions are clearly key outcome factors in social policy. What is of interest here is not the content of the legal relationship (e.g. a pension rise would be functionally classified as an economic measure), but rather the fact of the legal right itself (in this instance as distinct from either a claim to social assistance or to charity).

Legal interventions in the field of social policy are essentially not different from those in other fields. The study of the conditions for effective legal protection can thus start with juridical research into legal facts and the sociology of law.

To speak of legal intervention in the sense given here presupposes the grant of defined legal rights to individuals, specifically against those who have defined legal duties. But not all actual social circumstances can be equally subject to legal standardization. In each case where the actual situational link is constitutive for the success of acts and decisions, that is, where it depends on the specific circumstances, then forms of legal regulation based on generalization fail (Pankoke 1977). Within the sphere of social policy this particularly applies to personal services, where legal regulation often simply muddles through by granting discretionary powers or using vague legal terminology.

The effectiveness of this form of intervention rests on two conditions. The first is the creation and dissemination of a corresponding awareness of legal rights. In this context it is to be expected that outside the ambit of professional jurisprudence the diffusion of even the most elementary ideas of legal relationships requires long-lasting stability of the rules. This is already the case in organizational contexts (e.g. staff in business, administration and social services who are not legally trained), but applies even more strongly to all those who potentially could assert claims based on the rights granted to them. It can thus be assumed that the more widespread the applicable legal relationships are in a specific social context, and the greater the communication density is within this social context, then the more likely it is that a public awareness of the rule of law will be formed. Because legal knowledge depends to a considerable extent on education and occupation (cf. Grunow, Hegner and Kaufmann 1978: 95ff.), one may deduce that legal interventions whose success is based on the initiative of the beneficiary become effective only very slowly. This also means that frequent modifications of statute can undermine public respect for the rule of law and therefore reduce effectiveness (cf. Kaufmann 1985).

Second, because this kind of intervention often occurs in direct conflicts of interest where it is improbable that the more powerful interest would accept modifications without objection, compliance with the set standards cannot by any means be taken for granted. Opposition to such standards may be anticipated on the part of socially stronger interests, while socially weaker groups by definition lack relative power, and thus the problem becomes one of norm enforcement. Solutions in such instances are types of public monitoring and forms of collective or organizational management, as well as the provision of a range of legal advice and advocacy services for the beneficiaries of the standards.

In general, basic control mechanisms are probably the most effective – that is to say, institutional arrangements encouraging the acceptance of standards in direct interaction with the beneficiaries of a standard (for instance works councils). Although the judicial bureaucracy and regulatory authorities can quickly become overstretched by an increase in conflict-laden legal situations, they nevertheless constitute the core of the legal form of intervention. Public agencies supervising social policy regulations are far better developed than their independent or private counterparts. For instance, the establishment of works councils (in England) and administrative controls on protective rules in industry (in Germany) count among the oldest institutions for control and represent a fundamental precondition for making protection at work more effective (Windhoff-Héritier et al. 1990).

Typically, one must rely on controls at a number of levels; judicial controls are only effective to the extent that preceding control processes are appropriately selective. Account must also be taken of the facts that the beneficiaries of the standards (and often those to whom they are addressed as well) are rarely legal experts, their views about standards vary, and their grasp of reality is not juridically informed. Raising the legal profile of social relations can often damage continued interaction and may give rise to dysfunctional side effects in situations where normal control modes are social, as in families, in neighbourly tenancy relationships, in small businesses and in personal social services.[5]

Legal interventions can be highly generalized, making them eminently suitable as instruments of overall state intervention. As long as state authorities are not directly affected by the duties, the public costs are relatively small, comprising mainly the costs of regulation and legal administration. On the other hand, legal interventions often entail third-party costs, involving conflict between opposing entrenched interests and systematic infringement of standards. As far as legal relations between third parties are concerned, access to legal protection and remedy should be decentralized in the interests of the legal protection of socially powerless groups of individuals. The organizational problems of implementation appear relatively slight: the central problem is the enforcement or acceptance of measures, both by the beneficiaries (knowledge, capacity to act) and the responsible agencies (opposing interests).

Economic Intervention: Measures to Improve the Income Conditions of Individuals and Groups

Individuals' economic situation – their ability to meet their immediate or prospective material living needs – represents a core aspect of their life situation. Under the conditions of the private capitalist economic system, a person's economic circumstances are largely dependent upon regular income payments. Measures have long been in place to ensure an income to individuals lacking an income from work or property. While the agencies of legal intervention are necessarily invested with sovereign and therefore government powers, this applies only partially to economic forms of intervention. In democratic constitutional states, for instance, raising taxes and public income (such as social insurance contributions) obviously requires a basis in law, and statutory means are employed to enforce payment in the more or less predictable occurrence of resistance to taxation. In the administration of economic interventions, however, a division of responsibilities can be seen between state and other agencies. In Germany, for instance, employers are directly involved in collecting such income taxes as social security contributions, and representatives of both the employers and employees jointly manage the centralized social security agencies responsible for income maintenance and redistribution. However, this fundamental concept in German social insurance has become increasingly hollowed-out in recent decades by direct state interventions aimed at financial equalization, based on the idea of a 'unified social budget'. This tendency is increasingly apparent in the corresponding statistical activities (see chapter 7). The development of economic forms of intervention originated with poverty relief and private or mutual insurance. The increasing influence of the state is theoretically anchored in Keynesian economic theory arguing for redistribution to stabilize private consumption.

Although, in macroeconomic terms, transfers in kind (e.g. social services free of charge) could also be considered a form of income redistribution, they fall outside the category of economic intervention in the sense of this discussion. They can instead be better categorized as an ecological form of invention (see below), because in-kind 'real' transfers are determined completely differently from income transfers, both in terms of their production and their acceptability or effectiveness. From the perspective of those affected, they are not perceived as components of income but are allocated to other aspects of an individual's life situation. Thus the public measures counted as economic forms of intervention are those that influence the life situation of the population in the form of an immediately experienced modification of disposable income, in particular cash benefits or modifications of the taxation system. These measures can be described as social policy to the extent that they result in an improvement in the economic situation of economically disadvantaged groups of people. While recently introduced instruments concerning income redistribution (such as new legal rights to income benefits or new grounds for tax deductions) can all be analytically classified as legal forms of intervention, modifications in the size of payments or of taxes and contributions can be classified as economic interventions.

The following discussion concerning the operation of economic intervention emphasizes the chief intended social policy outcome, and therefore stresses the supply side of provision. From this perspective, the main constraint on this form of intervention is funding. Increases in income benefits are necessarily dependent on increased charges or even expenditure cuts elsewhere in the public purse. This means that the effectiveness of economic intervention, in the sense of a net redistribution effect, largely depends on the selectivity of the complex legal regulations of duties to contribute and rights to benefit. Such regulations have long been a staple of empirical economic research. The stability of monetary value is also highly important, because the higher the inflation rate, the greater the probability of negative distributional consequences for weaker sections of the population.

In each individual case, the implementation of economic intervention is relatively simple. If documentary evidence can prove entitlement to claim, the administration can be centralized. Benefit uptake is high – in other words it can be assumed that, on the whole, eligible claimants will assert their rights if they are aware of them. This in turn demonstrates the advantages of the highly flexible communication medium 'money', which by virtue of its abstractness is particularly well suited to generalized measures. Because money can cover all kinds of needs, it can be taken for granted that everybody appreciates its usefulness.

That said, these circumstances can simultaneously also create specific problems if the aim of economic intervention is not simply the modification of disposable income but also the attempt to achieve specific outcomes using cash benefits for those purposes. Increasing the selectivity of cash benefits, for instance to secure a minimum income or to calculate rent allowances, demands considerable factual inquiry and, as a rule, the consideration of a variety of different circumstances of life. Even approximately achieving the intended selectivity in these cases requires both a substantial increase in administrative effort and decentralization.

The full realization of legal economic rights is more likely if the factual criteria by which they are measured are (1) simple and comprehensible to all, (2) generally known and (3) non-discriminatory in nature. Conversely, if the legal criteria for granting a benefit become more complicated, and the criteria for entitlement to claim become more specific, then it is unlikely that a wider understanding of the eligibility criteria for claiming will emerge. Moreover, it is clear that increasing differentiation in the claim criteria simultaneously makes administrative decision-making more complex, meaning that a disproportionate emphasis is put on the direct interactive processes between those entitled to claim and the staff of the benefit agency. It is therefore questionable to what extent an increase in the selectivity of economic interventions can actually lead to an improvement in effectiveness, that is, in the distributional effects and the fight against poverty. This is because it must be anticipated that socially disadvantaged people will show greater reluctance to deal with authorities, and that when they do they are comparatively less skilled in their contacts with them (Grunow and Hegner 1979).

A particular limit on the effectiveness of economic interventions is manifest when cash benefits target specific forms of behaviour. Even in the case of earmarked benefits such as rent allowances, the effects of incentives to modify behaviour are questionable. The economic form of intervention acts best when it can be assumed that the preferences of the benefit holders are reasonable, and when market forces can guarantee the required supply of goods and services. To this extent, income redistribution is a form of social intervention that ideally matches the idea of the social market economy.

Ecological Intervention: Measures to Improve Opportunity Structures for Individuals and Groups

While legal and economic forms of intervention cover what may be called the traditional aspects of governmental social policy, two other forms of intervention first emerged after 1960 as forms of deliberate political intervention. As subject matter this chiefly concerns the aspects of welfare state activities that the European Commission called 'Services of General Interest in Europe'.[6] In terms of social policy they chiefly cover educational and health services, employment agencies, youth and old people's centres, and social housing, but also environmental policies such as those concerning recreation areas or public transportation services.

The services at issue are normally provided locally, and depending on a country's political structure and division of government responsibilities, their operative agencies may either be the central state, the federal states or other intermediate bodies, or lastly local authorities or non-public agencies. Facilities such as these have long been in existence, but perceiving them as a political responsibility has taken place only slowly. Public responsibility becomes operative mainly if the costs of the provisions are born entirely or at least in part by public budgets.

Viewed from a social policy intervention perspective, this extensive and multifarious complex of measures displays two specific characteristics in particular:

1. The measures concern locationally fixed provisions whose services are based on direct contact with the service recipient. The spatial tie is a result of features of both the supply and the demand side. Typically the facilities are buildings, and the service recipients are themselves bound to a locality, simply because of the fact that even in the motorized age most people remain rooted where they live. The services to be accessed are not randomly moveable, because they either come in the form of spatial provisions to be physically

accessed by the individuals themselves (e.g. parks, sports facilities, language laboratories) or take the form of personal social services as opposed to money and goods. In order to reach the recipients and be effective, they have to be on offer in the immediate or nearby surroundings, depending on the mobility of the recipients.[7] This aspect suggests the necessary social policy measures in this field can be considered under the heading of environmental design (cf. Kaufmann and Schäfer 1977).

2. However, a purely ecological perspective on the personal social service sector would appear to be reductive. A spatially nearby supply source is patently no guarantee of achieving the intended social policy effects (Gartner and Riessman 1974). In this case, rather, the decisive factor is the communication between the facility's staff and its clientele, that is, when the provision of the service occurs through direct interpersonal contact or is at least constructively based on it. It is therefore not sufficient only to make the necessary facilities and staff available. Instead, the desired objective can only be achieved by ensuring a specific quality of service in addition. The second aspect of this problem will be discussed below under the heading of person-related intervention.

The effectiveness of ecological interventions depends on how far the facilities created and the services offered actually penetrate the life situation of their target groups by being freely available on demand. In the case of less mobile underprivileged population groups, spatial proximity would appear to be a necessary, albeit not sufficient, precondition (Göschel et al. 1979).

Ecological interventions would appear most justifiable when it can be presumed that mere market regulation of the supply of these specific services would result in spatial and/or social disparities in provision, and that there is a public interest in a greater or more equal level of provision. Market regulation seems problematic in this case because in supply terms, the goods are largely immoveable (and partly indivisible), and because in demand terms the service recipients are insufficiently ready or able to pay cost-covering prices. But disparities in provision are equally likely to arise in local authority production (as a result of differences in the financial positions of the local authorities) and in non-profit-distributing or charitable production (as a result of a lack of coordination between the various agencies). These disparities prompt state attempts to exert an influence over the supply by means of planning, financial allocations and, where necessary, the imposition of obligations and regulatory measures.

Here the type and scope of state intervention raises considerably more complex problems than do the cases of legal and economic forms of intervention (Franz 1991). In this case it is vitally important to examine the provision of services from a multistage perspective, and to ensure that governmental and non-governmental agencies act in unison. The transmission processes vary between different stages of implementing service provision, and effects are therefore more contingent. Statutory bases and financial allocations still play a central role, but they do not have an impact on the final outcome, since it depends (or at least should depend) to a far greater extent on identifying the particular opportunities for targeting services at very specific needs.

In theorizing the problems that arise in this case, we are in essence dealing with the question of how the state can exert any influence at all on the structure of the material and social environment of its citizens. If, in keeping with the general approach, theorists choose to restrict themselves simply to an analysis of the shortest possible chains of effects, then state intervention first takes place through the planning of spatial functions (regional planning). This form of spatial planning is then carried on at a local authority level, leading to spatial differentiations that decisively affect the quality of the population's habitat (housing and its surroundings) (Strohmeier and Matthiessen 1992). Technical planning (such as planning for potential hospital capacity, for services for old people or for youth welfare services) occurs in parallel to spatial planning, so planning powers are variably distributed between and within local authorities. Understandably, the respective potential agencies themselves have considerable interest in the use of planning powers as well as in their ability to influence planning decisions. The first decisive transmission process lies at the level of planning, where the relative power of the individual service providers is also determined.

In no other form of intervention is the self-interest of the social service agency tied to the process of service provision to such an extent as in the area of ecological intervention. What is invariably at stake is not merely the service itself, but simultaneously the scope of the powers of the specific competing agencies. It therefore follows that the degree of centralization and decentralization of responsibilities is a key issue both for politics and for social science. The real difficulty here lies in achieving a proper ratio between the centralization and decentralization of responsibilities in terms of each of the relevant necessary levels of service provision. If the responsibilities are clearly delineated and correspond to each other, then implementation within the framework of the available means would appear to be more or less unproblematic. The real bottleneck is the cooperation required between the state authorities and the intermediary authorities. Sometimes, at any rate in Germany, the prevailing political system means that the state's ability to assert itself against the intermediary authorities is extremely limited (Wirth 1991a). However, in terms of services this limitation of the state's ability to exert its will may also have positive aspects, because the intermediate authorities are presumably much closer to the locality and its population and know the particular local conditions and problems better than the central authorities do (Kaufmann 1979; Wirth 1991b).

Disadvantaged groups' use of available opportunities presents a second constraint on the effectiveness of ecological forms of intervention. There are many kinds of disadvantage, and they affect various aspects of life. Low income is generally not a primary cause in these cases, although it often correlates with above-average levels of deprivation (Hauser, Cremer-Schäfer and Nouvertné 1981). There are some grounds for believing that people's access to the services of environmentally related facilities does not by any means correspond to the breadth of their problems, but that instead the patterns we observe occur from the use of particular forms of selectivity. While this problem has gone largely unremarked in the case of self-service facilities, there is considerable evidence of problems in the personal social services.

The problem of restricted access can be broken down into four stages (based on Wirth 1982):

1. The basic likelihood of a demand for social services arising seems to depend on the extent to which the various different population groups are vulnerable to deprivation, on the individual ability to act, and on their access to the necessary resources (knowledge and money, but particularly time).

2. The experience of need is not identical with the articulation of a specific demand in the decision to make use of a service. When a problem first occurs, the individual is often not yet aware of the available provisions. This necessitates a search, which in turn involves certain costs – psychological, temporal and often also financial. Whether a specific demand for service is made depends on the one hand on the subjective feelings of being weighed down by the problem or complaint, and on the other on the perceived relevance, availability and accessibility of the corresponding facilities.

3. If the facility is not self-service, an individual's request for provision is decided only by first passing through an application stage in which the scope and selectivity of the relevant facilities plays a decisive role. Social services develop characteristic admissions strategies, in which the vested interests of the staff or the facilities can

sometimes be of considerable importance. In such situations, simpler cases are often given preferential treatment over more difficult ones. This creaming effect increases the facility's success rate and thereby boosts its legitimacy. Thus the harder cases often remain excluded.

4. Once the application has been accepted, then the actual use of the service usually takes place over a period of time as a process of interaction between the recipient and the facility's staff, who typically provide services involving either protection and care, therapy and education, or advisory services (Schulze and Wirth 1996). Usage as a single event occurs only in marginal cases; rather, service usage tends to depend far more on the continuous involvement of the user with the facility's staff, and on the motivation this needs. Thus the experience of tangible effects depends on interpersonal processes. How these in turn can be influenced is the subject of the following form of intervention.

Personal Intervention: Measures to Improve the Ability and Willingness to Act of Individuals and Groups

It has already been noted that social participation is based not only on the ability to act, but equally on the willingness to act. There is considerable public interest, both at the level of values as well as of action, in increasing the ability to act of everyone in society, though of course only to the extent that the abilities are socially desirable. Some measures such as general education and the health system aim to raise or revive general abilities, even if the misdirection of some efforts is unavoidable: a well-educated and healthy criminal may be harder to detect.

The majority of measures, however, target specific abilities such as vocational education and training, or information and advice about particular subjects and problems. A measure's substance is already implicit in the type of provision because some socio-cultural aspects are reinforced while others are disregarded. This may to some extent also apply to general education, for instance when decisions are made on the curriculum.

In the sense intended here, interventions directed at individuals can be addressed straight at groups whose capacity to act is identified as restricted: in a general sense, groups such as children, young people or members of marginalized groups, or more specifically groups such as handicapped traffic users, uninformed taxpayers, helpless parents or people suffering specific disabilities. The typical aim of social policy measures in such instances is to raise the ability to act through efforts in education, advice and information, or rehabilitation. The objective is to increase people's participation opportunities by making existing aspects of the social culture available to them in ways that add to their competences.[8]

However, person-centred interventions can similarly be directed at third parties professionally involved with disadvantaged groups, as in the case of vocational training and professional development for occupations engaged in, for example, education, health care, and professional advice or assistance. It could also include public measures to sensitize the general public to particular groups with problems, such as those exemplified in recent international initiatives under the heading 'year of …' (women, the child, the disabled, and so on). The common factor in all these measures is that they aim at realizing or reinforcing the supply of sociocultural facilities to individuals, to influence the processes of social learning in terms of content. This is in itself a multistage process, but as in legal and economic types of intervention, the necessary transmission processes basically resemble each other closely: they always involve the development of capabilities by facilitating people's ability to combine knowledge and motivation. Learning processes like these are generally based on interpersonal communications.

By what means can the state affect these kinds of social learning processes?[9] It is no mere coincidence that educational interventions are highly controversial politically. The reservations refer to both values and effectiveness. To the extent that the desired objectives lie in changing the recipient's personal characteristics, such as consciousness – awareness of problems and abilities – the question therefore arises who in a pluralist society should have the right to determine these orientations, and in particular how far such powers should be delegated to the state itself. In recent times it has become noticeable that direct attempts at political intervention are made under the banner of educational aims, as in campaigns for health awareness, traffic safety or consumer awareness.[10] Information in the age of mass media can in principle be centrally controlled, although when measured in the context of today's generally accepted theory of multistage communication its actual effectiveness is considered very limited. Information can be forgotten again and is of very little behavioural relevance if social communication processes do not reinforce it; meanwhile, although social communications can have a reinforcing effect, they can equally reinterpret or dilute content. This fact alone makes state influence in social learning processes highly fortuitous, meaning that the potential for directly controlling learning content by means of state measures is probably very limited.

Indirect measures would thus seem to offer greater success, especially measures aimed at the qualification and potential professionalization of staff working in the social services and/or the development of standards for adequate action.[11] It remains contentious how far the development of educational programmes can successfully drive learning processes.

In any case, it is certain that the state's potential impact in this field is not only controversial but can be controlled only to a limited extent. The impact of interventional and situational factors is so considerable here that even evaluation studies offer few generalizable findings. Nevertheless, this fact does not give state authorities insight into the inevitable limits on their acts but instead often leads to increased attempts to exercise control, which may simply prove counterproductive. At all events, it is axiomatic that client motivation or willingness to cooperate is crucial to the success of a measure (Schulze and Wirth 1996). It must constantly be reiterated in this connection that tendencies towards (over-) regulation, bureaucratization and sometimes even professionalization may have the side effect of compromising the clients' willingness to cooperate, and possibilities are sought to institutionalize the various kinds of individual or collective self-help as more effective kinds of social interaction for increasing the capacity to act (Badura and von Ferber 1981).

These points of view have by no means been exhausted, and doubtless also appear topical today in the opinion that increasing the power of self-help might lead to an expected reduction in the costs of the personal social services. To avoid this argument being hijacked as legitimating the dismantling of social services, it is essential to examine and explain the conditions for the effectiveness of person-related interventions more thoroughly. This necessarily involves paying attention to what conditions not only social learning but also the motivation of the service provider's staff. Even if the effectiveness of person-related interventions is hard to quantify, the impressive achievements of all modern educational systems still give grounds for believing that the state's potential in educational intervention is not as limited as current assessments often assert.[12] But it is also important to keep in mind that educational interventions rely particularly on supplementary social provisions such as the family or social networks. The question of the potential collaboration of the state, intermediate institutions and collective forms of self-help has proved to have many aspects.

Conclusion

The aim of this chapter was to develop analytical categories that can be used to classify social policy measures according to their kinds of operation. Figure 6.2 summarizes the results and shows the categories employed above in tabular form.

	Legal intervention	Economic intervention	Ecological intervention	Person-related intervention
I Types of effect	Influences the legal status in social relations via the regulation and protection of legal relations	Influences the structure of disposable household resources via the inter-personal redistribution of primary income	Influences the distribution of spatially fixed participatory opportunities via the planning of spatial functions and the creation of infrastructure	Influences the transfer of bio-physical or socio-cultural capabilities to individuals; determines the content of educational or therapeutic processes
II Generic measures	Creates bodies for supervision and jurisdiction; granting of protective, participatory, claimant, and appeal rights, as well as participatory obligations in procedural rules.	Taxes and charges; transfer payments; tax allowances	Regional and town planning; social planning; public housing construction; financing of offices and staff	Professionalisation; curricula; supply of education, advice, information; rehabilitation, therapy; support of self-help activities
III Main targeted social policy outcomes	Reinforcing the legal position of socially disadvantaged groups and individuals in terms of opportunities for inclusion	Increasing the disposable income of groups and individuals with insufficient private income	Improving access opportunities and the quality of environments relevant to the life situation of individuals and families	Increasing individuals' abilities to act in pursuit of legitimate participatory opportunities
IV Agency	The state by necessity and definition	State or quasi-autonomous state organisations; partly collective self management	Combination of state and intermediate bodies	State, intermediate bodies, collective self help
V Chief problems of realisation	Understanding of the law and statute: compliance with standards and rules	Financing	Inter-organisational coordination; access	Efficient inter-personal communication
VI Regulation by general rules	High	High	Low	Low
VII Public costs	Low	High	High, depending on distribution	Variable
VIII Potential for efficient governmental implementation	Central-local, moderately difficult	Central, easy	Central-local, moderately difficult	Localised, difficult
IX Acceptance	Dependent on interests and abilities	Generally unproblematic; selective when targeted	Selective and variable	Uncontrollable and contested

Figure 6.2. Forms of Intervention

There are already many typologies of political intervention (see Kaufmann and Rosewitz 1983), but they make use of very different definitions of the concept of intervention, and the systems they embody are correspondingly heterogeneous. It was therefore essential to develop the basis of this typology in the first part of this chapter and to discuss it in detail in the second part. It exhibits similarities to the typologies of F. Scharpf[13] and R. Mayntz,[14] in that (by contrast with most other classification attempts) they place more emphasis on the analytical aspects than on the object- or institution-related or mixed analytical and institutional aspects.

The typology proposed above attempts to maintain a consistent connection between state measures and intended outcomes – to allow the discovery of the most clearly distinct types, corresponding to various conditions and regularities, that focus on the normative idea of raising social participation. As distinct from the attempted general systematization of government actions in Scharpf and Mayntz's typologies, the typology above is explicitly one of social policy. That means it starts by treating the level of policy outcomes seriously, in the sense that the declared general aim of social policies is to improve the basic well-being of all members of a political commonwealth. This well-being is revealed here in terms of the conditions for social participation or inclusion. As can be seen, a plausible connection exists between the policy measures used and characteristic outcomes, which (and this is the gist of the argument) need to complement each other in order to secure the desired effects.

Notes

1. This switch in perspective results from the transformation of working-class political objectives into welfare state ones. See chapter 4.
2. Article 22 of the United Nations Universal Declaration of Human Rights. For details see chapter 4.
3. The individualization of welfare is not merely a result of the normative individualism of Western capitalist societies but is also rooted in an analysis of the evolutionary conditions of modern societies. See introduction.
4. The description 'collective implication' is deliberately used here instead of 'collective benefits' in order to avoid an economistic or utilitarian reduction of the problem.
5. For the doctor-patient relationship see Kaufmann (1984a). A more detailed discussion of the legal form of intervention can be found in numerous papers in Grimm and Maihofer (1988).
6. European Commission: DOC/00/25.
7. Under some conditions these facilities can be made moveable by means of travelling services, but this possibility is far too seldom used. The possibilities offered by multimedia networking will undoubtedly become more important in the future.

8. One could therefore more precisely call it 'educational intervention', but this might be misinterpreted as meaning only what is done by educational institutions. What matters is that the services, whether pedagogic, therapeutic or informative inputs, mean 'work on people' so that the clients are co-producers of the output (Gartner and Riessman 1974; Wirth 1991b).

9. Literature discussing the regulatory theory perspective focused upon here is rare. See for instance Corwin 1973; Kogan 1978; Luhmann and Schorr 1979; Cerych and Sabatier 1986.

10. Mayntz (1980: 6) refers in this context to 'persuasive programmes'. See Dahme and Grunow (1983).

11. On the significance of such measures for the reform of primary schools or kindergartens, see the case study by Domscheit and Kühn (1984).

12. Scandinavia is considerably more successful in its educational policies than Germany is, as shown for instance in the PISA studies.

13. Scharpf, Reissert and Schnabel (1976: 15) distinguish between four types of state intervention instruments to steer economic and social processes: (1) direct behavioural steering by means of compulsory orders and prohibitions sanctioned by legal power; (2) indirect behavioural steering by means of positive and negative incentives, for instance subventions and taxes; (3) indirect behavioural steering by means of the prior provision of infrastucture; (4) direct provision of services by the state.

14. Mayntz (1980: 5–6) distinguishes between five regulatory types: (1) regulation by law; (2) incentives and financial transfers; (3) public construction of infrastructure and technical services; (4) information and persuasion campaigns; (5) the establishment of procedural standards.

Chapter 7

FIRST-ORDER AND SECOND-ORDER SOCIAL POLICIES

A large part of the recent literature on comparative welfare state research tries to explain the similarities and differences in institutional development in different countries from the perspective of how they came to be as they are. Thus from a functional perspective the focus is on the significance of the common challenges of industrialization and urbanization (a seminal work is Rimlinger 1971), the conflict theory view stresses analysis of political power relationships (seminally Esping-Andersen 1985), and in institutional terms the focus is on the implications of earlier social policy decisions for the further development of the system (seminally Evans, Rueschemeyer and Skocpol 1985; Rieger 1992). In these ways, social policy's past stands as an arguable way of understanding its present form. By contrast, a second strand in the discussion examines current social policy primarily in terms of perspectives on the future, in general diagnosing problematic trends that call welfare state achievements up to now into question and are expected to lead to a 'crisis of the welfare state' (seminal works are Offe 1972; 1984; Habermas 1985). While the 'genetic' perspective treats the social- or welfare state as a historical fact, crisis-oriented theories view it as transitory. Both perspectives tend to underplay the inherent dynamic of the development of the welfare state.

It was this inherent dynamic, seen as a theoretically important feature of welfare state development, to which Hans F. Zacher, the author of a juridical constitutional theory of the German social state, first drew attention:

Insofar as the social state *averts want*, this is only fully apparent when want or the danger of want is actually experienced. So if the social state system avoids want in the long term from representing any threat, the perceptible satisfactions decline.... To the extent that the social state aims for *equality*, then if the people and the situation are too unequal, if the readiness for equality is too limited, if the conviction of the legitimacy of individual interests is too great and the patience to put up with the interests of 'the other' is too limited, equality itself cannot bring about satisfaction. To put it negatively, social policy in modern society can never remain static, without ceasing to integrate society. More positively, the social state means permanent development – or rather more soberly, it is permanent change. Its very being is *processual* (Zacher 1978: 75; emphasis in original).

This chapter enlarges on these ideas, focusing particularly on the institutionalization of social policy. The processual aspects of welfare state developments consist chiefly of the multiplication, intensification and extension of social policy interventions, whose consequences can only partially be foreseen. These interventions are manifest not only in legislation and its implementation, but simultaneously in the creation of organizations that, through specialization in their ascribed functions, develop a particular body of skills and professionalism, consequently shaping a style of relationship with their clients and their clients' responses to it. The more the scope of social policy interventions expands, the more likely it becomes that the spheres of influence of a variety of different social policy organizations will interact, which may lead to further unpredictable consequences.

As a result of its expansion, existing social policy has feedback effects on political processes. The state's managerial capacity faces novel demands that have little to do with the original problems to which those measures were addressed. The political treatment of the problems following social policy interventions are in their turn described as social policy, and not infrequently even as 'social reform', but they have a different character since this is a matter of *second-order social policy*. And it is remarkable that these second-order social problems today occupy politicians far more than the social problems originally emphasized by the first-order social policy. The distinction between these two types of social policy will be analysed in what follows.

A Critical Analysis of 'the Social State'

The concept of 'the social state' is already a crude simplification, namely in four respects:

1. The responsibility for social affairs is merely one among many essential characteristics of statehood in the Federal Republic of Germany (and elsewhere). The state's role is never exhausted in the social sphere, however broadly one interprets this concept. What in the Anglophone countries is known as 'the welfare state' refers only to a limited set of state institutions and does not refer to a constitutional responsibility. It would be more accurate to distinguish between the constitutionally accepted welfare responsibilities of the collective political entity (the social or welfare 'state') on the one hand and their institutional realization (the social or welfare 'sector') on the other.

2. In the sense of Hegel's distinction between state and civil society, which is fundamental in any German discussion, social policy's role is to mediate between both spheres (see chapter 2). The social tasks of the state are realized through their effects on structured social conditions, that is, also through the impact of civil society. Every discursive consideration of the social or welfare state must therefore take the relationship between state and civil society as its subject, and not simply the activities of the state (see chapter 6).

3. This relationship between state and civil society itself varies between countries. In international comparisons, the characteristic differences between welfare states can be seen both in terms of the legitimizing norms and views of the state, and in respect of the institutional arrangements of political, economic and social conditions. The development of the welfare state is carried out within the framework of national traditions, and its pioneers not infrequently develop their own ideologies (see chapter 9).

4. Even within a national tradition, the relationship between state and civil society remains historically variable. This is as true for the legitimization of state activities as it is for institutional arrangements and making changes in them. In any case, these variations are not arbitrary; in most countries a high degree of path dependency of institutional development is commonly discernible. Previous decisions about the forms of state intervention mould later developments in clearly recognizable forms. Fundamental changes in direction are extremely rare. When certain institutional solutions appear to need reform, the options for change are to a considerable extent determined by the existing methods and the organizational arrangements associated with them (Döhler and Manow 1995: 157ff.).

The following observations stand in the context of a historical understanding of the development of the welfare state. It is a constitutive element of a particular form of modernization, one that is clearly distinguished from the liberal model of progress led by the dominance of market forces as well as from the socialist model of state-planned economic and social development (see introduction). The substantive characteristic of the form of the welfare state that follows is an essentially complementary yet strained relationship between regulation by markets in the realm of production on the one hand, and a state-regulated sphere of labour relations, income distribution and the production of essential services on the other. The issue is a complex interaction of state, economy and social structure within whose framework even private welfare interests become objects of political responsibility (see chapter 8). Fundamental to this is thus the tension between the inherent dynamic of the competitive private-capital mode of production and the institutional inertia of the welfare sector's long existent arrangements. This tension is a constitutive factor in all nation states developing as welfare states. One of the basic hopes promoted by the evolution of the social or welfare state is that politics, through the rule of law, can succeed in protecting the individual against the unforeseeable consequences of the competitive dynamic of the economy, which itself pays no regard to the social repercussions of the 'process of creative destruction' (J.A. Schumpeter) that it releases. However, this protection itself cannot remain static, because the state's provisions, especially the social security system, are for their part dependent on economic developments. The processual nature of the social state is thus not just a matter of rising expectations, as the previous quotation from Zacher suggested, but also above all a consequence of changing problems and the institutional 'reforms' that follow.

First-order Social Policy Interventions

The agenda of the state's responsibility for the well-being of its members is not the invention of either the social democratic or the Christian social movement; rather, it is as old as the very idea of the state. The responsibility of the prince ruling the early modern state included 'the safety, the well-being and the happiness' of his subjects, to be realized through the medium of 'good policy' (Preu 1983; on its practice, see Dorwart 1971). Behind this stands the Aristotelian political idea of a self-evident synergy between individual and collective welfare, conceptualized as *eudaemonia*: whoever acts well furthers the common good. The difference between the public and the private spheres and the contingent relations between good intentions and beneficent acts was not yet apparent here.

Adam Smith, too, stood in the Aristotelian tradition of a 'science for the statesman and legislator' (Winch 1984) when he recommended that the monarch concede to his subjects the freedom to pursue their own interests. By contrast, Wilhelm von Humboldt, following Kant, opposed individual well-being as a state objective and recommended that the state's role should be confined to the goal of security (Humboldt 1982).

It is evident that these liberal ideas were never really followed on the European continent. They found their historical realization in the Anglo-Saxon countries in which the conditions for the development of a strong concept of the state were never present. Nevertheless, even on the continent the principles of economic liberty were asserted in establishing industrialization. Thus, as structures grew, a richly antagonistic confrontation developed here between 'the state' and 'civil society', though not in terms of the association and competition of equal property-owning citizens, as the liberals had hoped, but of the class differences between bourgeois property owners and proletarians without property. The theoretical programme for 'social policy' that arose in the mid nineteenth century was therefore concerned with negotiating this class conflict (chapter 2). By contrast, state practice confined itself mainly to selective measures to deal with conspicuous harm and need.

Industrial workers' protection offers a clear example. In the nineteenth century, free-market doctrines gradually took root in the German states, to the extent that state regulation of economic life became confined only to essentially justified cases. From then on, problems had to become very pressing before government would take measures to protect workers. As in Britain, in Germany it was initially the suffering caused by child labour that led to state intervention in free labour market contracts (Windhoff-Héritier et al. 1990: 15ff.). The forerunner was Prussia in 1839, prohibiting the employment of children under the age of nine years, confining the working hours of young people between nine and sixteen to ten hours a day, imposing rest periods, and forbidding work at night and on Sunday.[1] However, it soon became apparent that it was not enough to regulate child labour by prohibition; supplementary intervention was also needed to supervise the standards set. Since the introduction of timesheets and the recommendation for voluntary local inspection were hardly ever observed, Prussia founded the Institute of Factory Inspectors (1853) to supervise compliance with the higher standards introduced in the meantime. But this supervision of industry was only carried out sporadically. More than half a century passed before the permanent institutional form of state supervision of industry in Germany was fully developed in 1891, then also covering adult workers' conditions and those of women in particular. This example allows the process of the extension and intensification of social policy interventions to be seen very clearly. In retrospect, the development of industrial working standards can be seen as an absolutely single-minded process of solving a social problem that was an integral part of factory labour – a prototype of a regulative first-order social policy. The goal orientation of this process seems, however, to have been much less apparent to its contemporaries.

A comparison with Britain shows that these developments were not inevitable but reflected the German centralized state perspective. It is true that the national factory inspectorate was first introduced in Britain, but employers there succeeded in restricting the disciplinary powers of the inspectorate and delaying the implementation of the extended safety regulations for so long that the trades unions recognized workers' protection as their own duty. As a result, industrial health and safety at work increasingly became matters for collective agreements (Windhoff-Héritier et al. 1990: 43ff.).

A second, related example in this field – namely, the way industrial injuries were dealt with – points to the relationship between first- and second-order social policy. The juridical status of employers' obligations in civil law varied from country to country. In France, for instance, the courts took a broad view of the principle of employers' liability, such that injured workers were awarded considerable damages (Ewald 1986), and the situation was similar in Britain (Koch 1992: 32ff.). In Germany, by contrast, such strong emphasis was placed on the claimant's duty to prove the employer's liability that most injured claimants did not succeed in establishing that the employer had caused the actual injury incurred, and thus their claims were dismissed. 'Law and legal protection were so patently out of step here that injured workers' weak legal standing became one of the most important arguments in favour of a reform of legal liability' (Ogorek 1975: 97).

Despite numerous strikes against dangerously unhealthy working conditions, Bismarck firmly opposed all initiatives for strengthening labour protection and factory inspection, lest they hamper the sensitive growth of German industry. Instead, he favoured a social insurance solution, the industrial injuries insurance scheme (1884). What developed as a result were employers' liability insurance associations (*Berufsgenossenschaften*), managed by the employers themselves, as more or less effective agents also of accident prevention. The fact that different insurance associations were set up for each branch of industry was seen as a positive advantage because the causes of so many industrial accidents are specific to their industries, and in this way specialized knowledge of particular occupational dangers could be developed. The 1884 statute empowered the insurance associations to lay down accident prevention regulations and to supervise their performance.

At first, highly variable use was made of these powers to act, mainly for reasons of economy in order to keep insurance premiums low. Industrial injuries insurance was amended in 1900 to make the accident prevention regulations compulsory, so that from then on, alongside the administrative supervision of industries through factory inspectors (*Gewerbeaufsicht*), the industrial insurance associations became responsible for preventing accidents. As a result, 'two separate institutions created for different purposes and entirely independent of each other, each with their own regulatory responsibilities, were working within practically the same field of obligations' (Windhoff-Héritier et al. 1990: 26). Thus two social policy interventions, originally completely distinct from each other, which overlapped in their effects, gave rise to new problems of coordination between the supervision arrangements of public administration and the industrial associations' accident prevention arrangements. In what follows, the growing features of nascent welfare state development exemplified here will be expressed in a more generalized form.

Phases of Social Policy Intervention

What can be described overall as welfare state development consists, on closer sight, of a multiplicity of almost entirely unrelated processes of institutional formation and evolution. Their interconnectedness becomes recognized only gradually, and the extent to which new organizations and institutional arrangements are created to cope with the complexities of multifarious interventions depends on political and administrative interpretation. Solutions to social problems differ in quite specific ways between one country and another, in spite of the obvious similarities of the challenges arising from industrialization and urbanization. In particular, the countries that pioneered social policy developed their own characteristic styles, though something similar would probably be found in any other country closely studied. Both the causes and justifications for state action, as well as the relations between state and civil activity in dealing with problems, are influenced by the national circumstances of the time, as are of course the kinds of organization selected (see Kaufmann 2003c; also chapter 9).

Social policy is an aspect of national interior policy and therefore plays a part in the political decision-making process through specific power relations and structures. Social politics decisions are complex processes that generally end in compromise, more or less reflecting the various interests taking part in the decision.[2] Factors that accordingly have great significance for the actual direction of institutional development include the structure of the state, the degree of local autonomy, the relations between church(es) and state, the types of relation between employers and employees, and political cleavages, as well as the way in which the representation of private interests is publicly institutionalized. Besides all these common structural aspects of political systems one might also expect the independent effect of particular fundamental social policy decisions (path dependency).

In the following section, national differences will be taken for granted because in spite of them, the aim is to typify characteristic stages of institutional developments in social policy.

[a] In general, primary social policy interventions start from specific publicly debated and then politicized problematic situations. The form of intervention taken depends on which definition of the problem is adopted by the public and in the political arena, on the intervention methods available to the state at the time and also on pre-governmental experience of attempts to solve the problem by local authorities, business enterprises or voluntary organizations, for instance. The potential for so implementing social policy interventions, or from another angle the evolutionary success of the institutional decisions chosen, seems to increase in direct proportion to the regard paid to 'elective affinities', that is, to 'parallels, homologues or analogies between the institutional structures in social fields' and the political intervention (Rieger 1992: 57).[3] State regulation is thus often linked to previously existent non-governmental patterns for solving problems. It is far easier to strengthen them by state intervention than to supersede them by new patterns.

[b] Once particular institutional methods have been adopted in policymaking (the responsibilities legally defined and agents equipped with authority and resources), these methods operate – if they are not obviously unfit for purpose – as precedents for the intensification of social policy interventions. The most important forms of intervention are as follows:
   • *Intensification of regulatory detail and cost control.* Most commonly, where previous problem-solving methods have been ineffective, attempts are made to raise the efficiency of the measures used through supplementary standardization. In this case state intervention can take the form of promotion and support to primary non-governmental methods, but of course it chiefly happens where the state directly institutionalizes new methods.
   • *The transfer of existing patterns of regulation to new target groups.* For instance, intervention to protect young people in factory labour was extended to women, then to factory workers in general, and finally to all employed persons in selected industries.

- *Differentiation of problematic conditions and models for solutions*, together with the development of complementary models. Thus, for example, the Bismarckian invalidity insurance system only later differentiated 'age' as a separate insurance status from that of 'invalidity'. Similarly, the prohibition of child labour only became effective through the complementary introduction of universal compulsory school attendance.
- *Creation of additional levels of management in public administration*, such as differentiation of government departmental functions, development of supervisory authorities, the creation of hierarchies and centralization as the expression of the state's evolving managerial responsibility.
- *Juridification of the relevant regulations* through the concession of the right of appeal to those affected and the extension of jurisdiction.[4]

[c] As a result of the intensification of continued state intervention in a specified field of social problems it is likely a more or less complex system of measures will evolve, for which the state may bear responsibility and which it may control but does not necessarily implement. The agents that are created or regulated by such a system, especially collective agents in the form of organizations, gradually develop their own interests, which then increasingly influence the further development of the institutional system. This may come about through their expertise as well as through the growth of their collective power. These interests, directly related to the structural forms of the nascent social policy provisions, have considerable impact on the persistence of national peculiarities of social policy evolution. It is common for actors with similar interests to form federations that parallel the organizational structure of the measures and their political management, and together with these and outside experts (e.g. in universities) form 'policy communities' with different forms of expertise. The convergence of approaches taken by such networks significantly influences the further development of any specified system.

[d] The intensification of interventions in a specified problem field must be distinguished from the accumulation of interventions. As was shown in the case of labour protection in the context of industrial inspection, and prevention in the context of injuries insurance, problems that were defined in their own terms may at first lead to more or less discrete solutions, but as the scope of their applicability expands, their consequences begin to overlap with the patterns of response to other problems. A classical example is

the 'interlocking of social services' that was first studied by Gerhard Mackenroth (1954). There are many interactions between, for instance, sickness insurance, invalidity insurance and, most recently, personal care insurance, just as there are between educational, youth and family policy. And currently the interactions between employment activation measures and social assistance are widely debated in Germany and elsewhere. The interactions between their effects are largely unclear; nevertheless many assumptions are made about such connections, and these assumptions affect the definition of the problem adopted by the political decision-makers.

[e] From a financial perspective, the intensification and accumulation of interventions lead to a continually growing demand for the expansion of social budgets that tend to consume an even larger share of public resources and, together with other effects, to rising state expenditure. This inherent tendency towards rising expenditure for social purposes derives from the interaction of three principal factors:

- the growth of service demands, for instance for higher benefit levels (transfer ratio);
- the expansion of the groups of those entitled to services (eligibility ratio);
- demographic changes that alter the relationship between age groups and thus also between those who pay most of the taxes and contributions and those who receive the services (the demographic or dependency ratio).[5]

Second-order Social Policy

Now I will examine these developments from the perspective of a distinction between first- and second-order social policy. Self-evidently, the state's primary interventions belong exclusively in the sphere of first-order social policy. Dominating the circumstances in which policies emerge are the political pressures arising from moral convictions and/or crises in society. The problems to which politics responds with new measures are those plainly defined as social, for example basic necessities for those concerned or a deficit in social integration, though this concept generally remains ambiguous.[6]

The measures categorized here under the heading of intensification of social policy interventions also belong to the context of first-order social policy. They focus on the goal of primary intervention or a broader definition of the problem within the ambit of the primary problem. By contrast with primary interventions, the setting of precedents in the shaping of further measures has to be taken into account from the outset. In these circumstances, the knowledge and skills of practitioners (e.g. factory inspectors, health officers, insurance experts and so on) gradually grows, so that their practical experience of the consequences of intervention supplements politicians' expectations about the potential effects of the measures.

The creation of additional levels of management and the concession of judicial oversight leads into the grey zone between first- and second-order social policy. On one side lie the examples of making appropriate measures effective; on the other side the complexity of the intervening structures increases, thereby creating a new dynamic whose management comprises the actual object of second-order social policy. The quantitative expansion of interventions changes into the quality of the growing internal structures and the conflicts associated with them.

The systematic inherent dynamic becomes evident as soon as the social policy interventions bring about the reactive formation of interests. A brief example is the evolution of statutory health insurance in the German Reich. The introduction of statutory health insurance for the workers within the framework of the Bismarckian social reforms (1883) incorporated the old sickness funds, which in general paid cash benefits but covered medical treatment only as an exception. The new legislation obliged the sickness insurance agents (*Krankenkassen*) to guarantee free medical treatment. Only the autonomous management bodies of the individual sickness funds could determine what this covered in practice. During the last decades of the nineteenth century, the supply of doctors increased greatly, and thus competition between them grew. As a result most doctors could not earn a living from private practice alone and welcomed the additional demand from social sickness insurance, even though the conditions of service and the scales of fees were unilaterally imposed and only meagre fees were paid. Many doctors perceived this situation as humiliating on both financial and status grounds, and it led to the foundation in 1900 of a kind of doctors' trade union (the Leipzig Society, nowadays known as the Hartmann League) to strengthen the power of the doctors in negotiations with the sickness funds.[7]

As a reaction to the success of this organization, the sickness funds themselves soon combined into various federations according to their political orientations. The unified structure of the doctors' association continued to oppose the fragmented insurance federations and, helped by a threatened general strike and government mediation, the so-called Berlin Agreement was reached in 1913 between the doctors' associations and the insurance federations regulating localized bargaining systems among doctors and sickness funds. This marked the beginnings of corporatist regulation of German health services under government supervision, a key characteristic of its management style up to modern times (Döhler and Manow-Borgwardt 1992a, 1992b). This example also illustrates the nature of second-order social policy. The conflicts over the insurance offices' restrictions on doctors' professional independence and over fees for insured patients' treatment were certainly a consequence of the creation of the insurance offices, but their settlement was only indirectly concerned with patients' interests. The central issue was the coordination of interests between the doctors' associations and the insurance funds, which came about only through government arbitration and subsequent state legislation.

With the expansion of residential care and hospital modernization through state funding, the costs of the health services grew rapidly in the 1970s. Driven by the dramatic description of a 'health care cost explosion', political thought gradually turned towards targeted cost reductions in health services and to the adjustment of fees to the incomes of the sickness funds and away from the quantity of the services delivered. Since the founding in 1977 of a representative body for almost all interests in health policies (*Konzertierte Aktion im Gesundheitswesen*) strengthened by an expert advisory committee (*Sachverständigenrat*), the idea has become ever stronger that it is the state's role to create incentives, through appropriate institutions, that encourage the agents of the health services to act in the spirit of the system's aim – high-quality, inexpensive care of sick people. The underlying political intention is not primarily to benefit the sick but to manage a complex system of care for the sick as a whole, chiefly from the perspective of cost control (Kaufmann 1999).

The characteristics of second-order social policy become even clearer when the focus is not just on one specific institutional part of the social welfare sector but on the interconnection between its various institutional parts. Initially this interconnection grows gradually and at a variety of levels. At the basic level, the practical interdependences sketched above lie chiefly between various operational fields that require clarification, demarcation of powers and, not infrequently, coordinating measures. What is particularly influential is government departmental reorganization and the grouping of departmental responsibilities for several fields into a single ministry that then often carries the label 'social' in its title. However, in most countries the overall field of welfare state policies has now become so complex that several government ministries continue to be responsible.

Growing importance is attributed to comprehensive approaches to organizational order, increasingly influenced by substantial contributions from a range of sciences. A notable first example is the German project to codify statutory law on social insurance and related services into a single Code of Social Legislation. Even if this process drags on and the potential for common regulations is repeatedly constrained by circumstances and interests, the development of social law in the interplay between what can be legislated and social jurisprudence is itself a significant process in facilitating the autonomy of the social sphere, and thus an element of second-order social policy.

The integration of all the social cash benefits into one unified, computerized system, as now exists in most countries, is no less successful. The systematic statistical compilation of social expenditure has already resulted in this field of government action being symbolized as a unity, and by now the level of social protection has become a standard measure in comparisons over time and between countries. Such unified measures easily acquire a polemical character, especially in the face of the growing tensions between economic and social policy. It is no longer a matter of this or that social service or benefit being judged in terms of its goal orientation, efficiency or effectiveness; instead 'the welfare state' is treated as a single entity in an undifferentiated attack on the totality of the cost of all social services in cash or kind as represented in the social budget.

Conclusion

The idea of 'the welfare state as a process' (H.F. Zacher) introduces, into scholarly ways of examining social policy, a dynamic perspective that has been made explicit here from the perspective of the development of social policy institutions. Two types of dynamic have been distinguished. The first type consists of the tension between social policy goals and the actual effects of social policy interventions. The second type of dynamic follows from the increasingly systematic character of the institutional and organizational problems resulting from social policy interventions. The concepts of first-order and second-order social policy allow differentiation of the ways in which policy deals with these two types of dynamic.

When the achievable effects of social policy interventions persist in failing to meet the expectations of their initiators and also of the public, or even when it is just the success itself of particular interventions that suggests extension into related problem areas, political pressure arises to intensify the social policy interventions. Insofar as problematic conditions, and the ways they are normatively judged as impinging on particular situations, shape the criteria of political decision-making,[8] first-order social policy is applicable. This is social policy in the original sense of a morally justified activity, one that began in the first half of the nineteenth century with simple case-by-case interventions and was then intensified through collective learning processes and expanded into ever-broader problem areas. The claim of solving moral problems of a social kind by political means even today conditions the normative character of the concept of social policy, as well as related concepts.

Where, by contrast, the talk nowadays is of cost-cutting, savings packages or the rationalization of the welfare state, experience shows that in the power struggle over the distribution of what are considered to be the required budget cuts, it is often precisely those in greatest need who are among the losers. It may then be appropriate to speak of 'unsocial social policy' – a paradox from which common usage recoils, referring instead to 'attacks on the welfare state', 'downsizing' and similar terms, while those who promote such measures prefer to use formulas like 'reconstructing the welfare state' or 'social reform'. Neither type of phrasing expresses what the issues are in fact all about.

Apart from the introduction of personal care insurance (probably the last major example of first-order social policy for a long time), social policy in Germany since the middle of the 1970s has not primarily concerned itself with how to deal with social problems but with how to deal with the governance of the apparatus or structures of intervention, and the same applies to other welfare states. Though the organizational structures of intervention were first created to ameliorate social problems, they have today acquired an institutional importance of their own, one that generally has little to do with the original reasons why the problems came to political notice. Social policy is no longer a matter of intervention in social conditions for the benefit of those in need or the powerless, but is instead about guaranteeing and managing institutionalized systems, especially the structures of negotiated earnings, of income insurance and for the production of personal services. Though such regulations are justified even on the grounds that they serve the maintenance and efficiency of a system in view of its declared social goal, this defensive excuse remains common, and it does not affect the definitions of the problem in political action. The question is rather, for instance, one of constraining expenditure, of modifying the competences and incentive structures of particular collective actors, or of changes in the rules for calculating and financing the services supplied. Recently it has even been a matter of the relative importance of particular modes of governance such as hierarchies, the market or negotiating systems. The context of such proposals and decisions is no longer decided on the basis of the urgency of social needs but by the requirements of each individual system's management or the distributive interests of the major actors involved. This is what is meant by the concept of second-order social policy suggested here.

With growth in the importance of second-order social policy, the functions of research change, which applies to all the social sciences concerned. At the forefront stands the investigation of the interactions between different social policy measures and of their institutional and administrative management.[9] This suggests that cooperation between the representatives of the different disciplines would be productive to the extent that they treat each other's perspectives seriously – in other words, that they understand that each perspective can shed a complementary light on the common subject matter.

Notes

1. The Prussian regulations were based on the British Factory Act of 1833, an early example of cross-national learning in social policy. Other German states only very gradually adopted the Prussian initiative.
2. The relation between groups of actors and processes of institutionalization in social policy has been clarified by Rieger (1992: 36ff.).
3. Thus, for example, the introduction of compulsory sickness insurance in the German Reich (1883) was significantly facilitated by the statutory incorporation of the existing sickness insurance funds into the new system, so that new insurance organizations (*Allgemeine Ortskrankenkassen*) had only to be created for those groups not previously insured (Frerich and Frey 1996: vol. 1, 97ff).
4. Special courts for adjudicating disputes between employers and workers were first introduced in Germany in 1890. The Federal Republic of Germany nowadays divides and operates labour jurisdiction and social jurisdiction separately at three levels: local authority, Land and the federal level.
5. On the influence of these various components on the long-term growth in social service expenditures, see OECD (1985).
6. Thus on the one hand Bismarck introduced social insurance in order to relieve local Poor Law authorities, while on the other hand he wanted to complement the repressive 'socialist law' and win the workers over to the newly created German Reich.
7. On the weak position of the medical profession around 1900, and on the medical context of the earlier sickness funds, see Tennstedt (1977: 77ff.). Mayntz and Rosewitz (1988: 117ff.) offer a sociological analysis of the institutional development of German health services.
8. Which is not to deny that even in the sphere of first-order social policy the power and interest perspectives of the political actors do play a substantial role.
9. Though the concept of intervention is perfectly viable in analysing first-order social policy (see chapter 6), it is not sufficiently sophisticated for the analysis of second-order social policy. In that context discussion is therefore chiefly about regulation, management or governance and not about intervention (see chapter 14).

Part III

THEORY OF AND FOR THE WELFARE STATE

Chapter 8

THE STATE AND
THE PRODUCTION OF WELFARE

This chapter outlines a theoretical perspective that takes the normative claims made for the welfare state seriously. 'The welfare state is the institutional outcome of the assumption by a society of legal, and therefore formal and explicit, responsibility for the basic well-being of all of its members. Such a state emerges when a society or its decision-making groups become convinced that the welfare of the individual … is too important to be left to custom or to informal arrangements and private understandings, and is therefore a concern of government' (Girvetz 1968: 512). It is thus public responsibility for the welfare of the members of the community that constitutes the normative core of the welfare state.

The idea of the state as the centralized power for the regulation of social development has remained foreign to the Anglo-Saxon tradition, while on the continent its roots stretch back to the pre-liberal age. This factor similarly determines the differences in the basic conceptions of law (see introduction). The ambivalence of the concept of the welfare state does not rest simply on contrasts in political attitudes, but equally on these fundamental structural differences. The idea of the welfare *state* implies an idea of the state as a constitutionally organized network of political institutions, invested with the ability to influence the process of the production of welfare along institutional guidelines. Obviously social policy measures are not necessarily successful in terms of particular set goals, but the idea of the welfare state presupposes the ability of politics, the administration and the judicature to learn to find ever better solutions to social problems in an incremental way (Kaufmann 1991b).

Since the beginnings of social policy, and again at times of increasing fiscal stringency, questionable side effects of social policy interventions and sharper conflicts over distribution, there has been argument over whether and how the state is capable of satisfying these political demands. The historical outlines of the discourse of the welfare state will be outlined first, followed by a specification of the comparative problems of welfare production from which the implications for understanding the state will then be derived. What is proposed is neither a liberal laissez-faire nor voluntaristic interventionism, but instead an organizational policy perspective illuminated by control theory that sees the market, the state, the sphere of intermediaries and private households as different and virtually complementary ways of achieving the functions of welfare production.

Welfare: The Political Discourse

'Welfare' is a key political concept in the European political tradition, whose origins lie in the numinous layers of the Roman cult of the goddess Salus (Rassem 1992). Three ideas have been interwoven in the term welfare from time immemorial: (1) welfare concerns the community as a whole, (2) the provision of welfare is a duty of the rulers, (3) the welfare of the whole is expressed in the welfare of the individual who 'gets along well', living happily and thriving. In modern terms welfare therefore essentially means the political task of establishing or maintaining social relations within which individual and common benefits do not diverge but reinforce each other synergistically.

Aristotle developed the idea that the *eudaemonia* of the individual household and the *polis* are mutually dependent. Political theory based on Aristotle hence saw no contradiction between individual and collective interests. This welfare formula remained self-evident until the mid-eighteenth century, not merely as political rhetoric but also as the predominant political theory.

It was only with the liberal critique of the absolutist welfare state, and the debacle of the French revolutionary 'welfare committee' leading to the Terror of 1793, that the desire awakened for a more complex social theory, one that allowed reconciliation between the postulate of individual civil liberties and the necessity of maintaining domestic order and national independence, but without expecting the same ethics of either. The liberal idea of the constitutional state based on and restricted by law and the separation of public and private spheres initially represented a seemingly practicable solution. The institutional autonomy of political power, with its emphasis on the goals of domestic order and external security, went along with an explicit renunciation of all welfare aims, which were declared to be 'private matters'. Henceforth politics and ethics, legality and morality, went their own ways. While every individual was accorded the right to pursue his or her own happiness, the question of 'the good life' now had to be excluded from political discourse.

This also limited the meaning of the idea of welfare. From now on welfare was reduced to private happiness and even, from an economic perspective, down to the opportunity of satisfying individual needs regardless of any collective value: 'Quantity of pleasure being equal, pushpin is as good as poetry' (Jeremy Bentham). But even precisely this was understood as an element of the general good. In terms of the classic idea of welfare, guaranteeing the right of every individual to pursue his or her own happiness had to be described as the welfare programme of the liberal state.

But whence did liberal political theory derive its conviction that this individualist programme of the pursuit of happiness promoted not only individual but also collective benefit? A plausible answer is offered above all by Adam Smith's idea of a competitive market led by an 'invisible hand', by contrast with the visible hand of the sovereign. The increasing autonomy of the economy and of the science of economics led to an ideological and political utilization of Smith's ideas, in the sense that a generalized market model was offered as the answer to the synergetic demands of welfare production; Smith himself, however, advocated a considerably broader understanding of the conditions for social welfare (see Kaufmann and Krüsselberg 1984). Market economics replaced the moral economy of reciprocity with a far more complex mechanism, generalized through money and with flexible prices as a response to supply and demand driven by impersonal exchange.

The complete depoliticization of the discourse on welfare thus depends on three mutually supportive arguments:

1. All people define the criteria of their own welfare for themselves and accordingly determine the priorities of their needs; consumer sovereignty becomes an expression of the welfare value of 'freedom'.
2. The state's relinquishment of any form of economic regulation fosters competition, which in turn leads to supply becoming more efficiently responsive to demand.
3. Because in principle only that for which there is a demand is produced, and because precisely this demand depends on the individual's positive evaluations, the growth of the social product becomes in itself an indicator of welfare development.

This welfare model met with opposition even at the level of economics, expressed first by Sismondi (1819), who argued that in the first place growth in the social product does not automatically lead to optimum distribution. Second, the capital intensification of production displaces labour, for whose subsequent livelihood the capitalist no longer has to pay. The abandonment of the old social assistance obligations allowed the ancillary costs of these increases in productivity to be externalized (see chapter 1). This economic tendency was amplified in practice by the social imbalance of power.

As opposed to Marx and Engels, who derived a theory of the collapse of capitalism from these arguments and accorded the state no compensatory powers to intervene, the nineteenth-century social reformers seized on Sismondi's idea to call on the state itself to resolve the exacerbation of pauperization resulting from industrialization. To the extent that the welfare problem is simply conceived as a problem of distribution – as reflected in political rhetoric to the present day – the discourse nevertheless remains trapped in an individualistic and economistic reduction of the problem that appears almost entirely insoluble. In functionally differentiated societies, as Luhmann (1985b) astutely demonstrated, there are no longer any consensual distributional norms on which the state can base distributional intervention policies. Pure distributional problems are zero-sum games. The Pareto optimum relates merely to the functional, not the interpersonal, distribution of income. Because of its multidimensionality in conflicts over distribution, the premise of justice or fairness is helpful only in borderline cases of life-threatening poverty or a generally accepted higher standard of basic well-being. Only a static model permits the argument that the greatest possible equality in the distribution of goods equates with the optimal production of welfare. As soon as the variability and controllability of the level of production is included in the equation – and this is precisely the strength of classical economics – static distributional norms lose their significance. No consensual principle of political action can be deduced from weighing up sectional interests, but only the conclusion that right is on the side of the many and mighty. And it would be even more unrealistic to determine the common good as the sum of individual interests.

Admittedly the nineteenth-century social reformers developed more sophisticated arguments, framing the benefits and necessity of state intervention not solely in terms of fairness or distribution but also in terms that today could be described as functionally rational. The original idea developed in a number of stages, above all in the work of Lorenz von Stein (see chapter 2). He posited that the state, which at the constitutional level protected the conditions of rising social diversity, should work at the governmental level to counteract the emergence of classes and thus create the social prerequisites for the realization of freedom for everyone. This suggests an evolutionary formula implying the ability to increase intervention by the state and self-regulation by society *simultaneously*. This is precisely what is meant by mediation between state and civil society (see Pankoke 1970: 167ff.), once the distinction between them has become an established fact. The state becomes guarantor of an indirect exchange that distinguishes between the vital interests of both the opposing parties while simultaneously blocking the potential for inflicting reciprocal damage. It is precisely this role that offers both parties insight into the complementary nature of their interests and the advantages of the direct exchange of wages for work.

Even if Stein's scheme failed to provide an entirely convincing answer to the problem of how the state was to occupy a position that was both sufficiently independent of class interests and capable of taking these selfsame class interests into account, it nevertheless already contains a clear expression of a core functional element of the welfare state: the pacification of class conflict. This occurs through the political creation of institutional arrangements that guarantee on the one hand the existence of the private capitalist system and on the other the prospects of workers' rights to self-organization, safeguards against exploitation, and income support in case of loss of employment.

In England at around the same period, J.S. Mill (1861) developed principles of representational democracy that can be considered the appropriate institutional structure for the representation of interests in the welfare state (see chapter 1). Nevertheless, to set it up and accept the decisions that arise presupposes a common normative consensus whose significance for welfare state development was first noted by Eduard Heimann (1929), namely that social ideals drawing on Christian and Enlightenment values were shared by both bourgeoisie and workers. Indeed, the working classes legitimized their demands for freedom and equality by basing them on bourgeois values. Following Marshall (1950), the underlying idea in this consensus can be characterized as the generalization of civil, political and social rights for everyone, a process described in Parsons' and Luhmann's social theories as inclusion. From this perspective the welfare state appears as guarantor of basically equal participation in political decisionmaking and guardian of rights to protection, income and social services, precisely what are understood as expressions of political fairness. Here we encounter the second element of the functional rationality of the welfare state: insofar as the benefits provided are seen as manifestations of a fair and well-regulated political system, they are conducive not only to individual welfare but also to citizens' political loyalty, and to preventing more radical or totalitarian movements.

The welfare state's political credibility does not, however, explain why state social policy has proved to be not only economically sustainable (in spite of business complaints ever since the first restrictions on child labour) but even economically advantageous (see Alber 2001: 69ff.). Even when there are no direct causal linkages and cost benefit analysis is scarcely practicable, it can nevertheless be credibly shown that increases in labour productivity during the evolution of the welfare state are in part attributable to social policy measures. This is most clearly shown in the long-term increase in real wages despite the continuous reduction in annual working hours. The increase in labour skills, more rational use of labour and, not least, the scope for pushing less productive workers into the social security system, all promote shock-free technical and economic change and thus arouse little opposition. Even if social benefits at first appear simply as a cost factor on the balance sheet, closer examination shows that both their individual and collective advantages mean more and better use of human capital as well as a reduction or balancing of negative external effects of economic processes. Thus a third functionally rational aspect of welfare state development is exposed, which helps to explain its acceptability to the business economy.

These three effects of welfare state policies – pacification of class antagonisms, inclusion and increased political loyalty, and support for labour productivity – are complementary, and together explain their collective advantages.[1] It is highly unlikely that industrialization and democratization could have led European societies in the aftermath of feudalism to have evolved so stably without this mediating process of the development of the welfare state.

Welfare: the Economic Discourse

The concept of welfare in classical economics assumes that the only effective form of welfare production is the exchange of goods and services in the market between autonomous producers and consumers. The dynamic of the division of labour, accumulation, competition and innovation should lead to an increase in the quantity and quality of goods produced, which become cheaper in relation to the working time spent, which therefore enables average real wages to continue to rise. In the process, the degree of individually realizable welfare is defined as proportional to the available individual income, which in turn can be generated by the availability of different factors of production – land, capital, labour, knowledge.

Early liberals hoped for a civil society of self-sufficient producers in which employed work was, as a rule, meant to be no more than a transitional stage of life. Instead (as Marx pointedly showed, following Sismondi), the abolition of feudal ties resulted in a growing concentration and capital intensification of production and a continuing redundancy of less productive workers or those whose health had been ruined by working conditions; it thus led to the exclusion of large sections of the population from participation in the economic process in their own right. It took almost a century for the whole of Europe to realize that this form of impoverishment was neither self-inflicted nor adequately treatable with mere alms.

Seen in economic terms, two lines of argument in particular led to the legitimation of what has since become the secondary income distribution, institutionalized in state policy. On the one hand it became clear that market prices do not necessarily reflect all the costs of the production process, and that, on the contrary, additional social costs can be incurred that do not enter into the calculations of individual economic actors or, therefore, into price-setting. Social costs include, for instance, damage to health caused by working conditions, or damage to the natural environment by the toxic side effects of production, but they also include the costs of constructing transport networks, which are borne by the state with the aim of promoting individual mobility (Kapp and Vilmar 1972). Thus the older social security systems based on employment contracts, which were generally financed mainly by employers, could be legitimized as a compensation for the externalization of labour reproduction costs.

A second legitimization strategy is based on the perspective introduced by Keynes, according to which income redistribution from the producing to the non-producing part of the population stabilizes the demand for consumer goods and therefore the business cycle. However, because of the persistently unstable balance between consumption, savings and investments, it still remains a matter of dispute what the necessary or beneficial extent of such redistribution should be. Whatever the detailed rationale, state-regulated secondary income distribution may mean redistributing opportunities to satisfy needs and thereby a biased alignment of individual welfare levels, but it does not involve abandoning the idea of welfare production exclusively through the market. Thus even in terms of economic policy it is fundamentally consistent with price regulation by the market.

However, this becomes problematic in the case of personal services as provided by health, education and other social service authorities, which in recent decades have increasingly become the focus of welfare state activity. These are regulated, financed and often administered by the state, but they cannot be treated as public goods in the strict sense (e.g. national or domestic security) because the goods are divisible and the exclusion of particular consumers is perfectly feasible. There is thus no technical necessity for state regulation as in the case of pure public goods. Public intervention in personal social services is usually justified by the collective benefits of individual consumption of these goods on the assumption that use generates positive external effects (merits), which is why they are described as merit goods.[2] An obvious example is educational expenditure on skills and qualifications, but the same could be said of all social services aimed at contributing to the maintenance or improvement of working abilities – which at an aggregate level means human capital. They are both in the interest of the individual (or at least of every individual willing to work), and they promote for instance the international competitiveness of a national economy. We owe the first systematic discussion of the state's responsibility for developing the 'forces of production' to F. List (1841) (see chapter 1). Personal social services additionally require joint production of outcomes by professionals with clients and demand standards of effectiveness that differ from those of the production of goods.

The study and analysis of positive and negative externalities has become a central theme in welfare economics (a seminal work is Baumol 1965: 24ff.). In sociological terms, the expression 'external effect' is important because it refers to an issue that the theory of functional differentiation formulates in more generalized terms, especially in its autopoietic version (Luhmann 1984: 242ff.). This says that the differentiation and autonomy of a system's particular functional areas is regularly accompanied by a heightened selectivity of relevant contextual connections but coupled at the same time with increased indifference to other effects of action. These actions may be positive or negative, but in either case an actor subject to a system's assumptions does not take them into account in cost-benefit considerations. As de Swaan (1988) demonstrated in an important study of welfare state development, it was chiefly the negative external effects of the neglect of particular sections of the population that repeatedly led to the extension of social provisions and to new collective solutions to typical problems of individual welfare.

In terms of the idea of a generalized welfare balance (which is not based on the perspective of individual social subsystems, but rather on an overall perspective incorporating the interests of all as far as possible), externalities or side effects are as significant as the intended impact of social services. An overarching perspective like this is nevertheless confronted by characteristic difficulties, or can even be said to embody a paradoxical claim, just as a Copernican locus seems impossible outside the differentiated social subsystem and therefore beyond a specified perspective. The solution to the problem can only be sought in a theoretical mediation between the subsystem's achievements, including also the private household.

Welfare as a Synergetic Relationship between Individual and Collective Benefits

It is now high time to ask whether any kind of constructive response to understanding the welfare state can be expected at all from discussing welfare discourses. Is 'welfare' an empty formula subject to arbitrary political interpretation and aimed at distracting attention from the contingent nature of historical development? In the case in question, I take the view that value concepts, particularly those with a millenarian tradition, contain historically discoverable information that also characterizes their current cultural meaning (see Kaufmann 1973: 28ff.).

The following ideas of welfare are particularly common: (1) welfare as individual welfare or well-being, (2) welfare as the equivalent of charity, (3) welfare as the provisions or function of the social services, (4) welfare as prosperity and (5) welfare as an expression of the 'good shape' of a society. These simple and noncontradictory ideas are interpretable as elements of a more complex concept of welfare embracing not only individual and intermediate aspects but the whole of a political society. In the spirit of the preceding ideas, welfare can be defined as the value for open communication concerning the mediation between particular life situations or lifestyles and a community's current state or future prospects.

By contrast with older social forms, the focal point of a particular lifestyle is nowadays considered to be the individual and no longer the household or kinship relations. It is therefore logical that individual welfare has become the normative frame of reference for the problem of welfare in political and economic rhetoric. But at the same time this stance seems to lead to a dead end, since whatever 'individual welfare' is understood to mean, the locus of human well-being lies in each human being's experienced cognitive world, which is not directly accessible. All real experience is bound up in our corporeality and can be communicated only in a highly selective and abstract manner. What we call reality is composed at best of collectively typified experiences, which at best form the material of open communication.

The claim to contribute to human welfare through state provisions is therefore paradoxical. How can third parties decide what serves an individual's welfare, when we have to assume that what constitutes individual well-being remains inaccessible, not merely for structural or accidental reasons but in principle? It is for precisely this reason that the liberal economic concept of welfare (each individual manifests their priorities of need through their demands, and therefore the best measure of welfare is their satisfaction) gains plausibility. Every public attempt to control the production of welfare must therefore justify itself.

The decisive question is, however, whether political discourse about individual welfare is necessarily dependent on the subjective judgements of those affected by the policy measures, and if so, to what extent. Since in any case people can communicate only about collectively typified experiences, under conditions of democracy the plausibility and resonance of public argument about individual welfare seem a thoroughly utilizable information medium. It may well be that these typifications are highly (and thus one-sidedly) influenced by the power to define them, held by collective actors and professionals in particular, but this does not exclude the possibility of taking precisely this factor as the starting point for a critical understanding of the problem of individual welfare.

The reasons given above for welfare state interventions do not refer to individual welfare but rather to systemic effects asserted to be in the collective or public interest. This without question presupposes the philanthropic intentions of the social policy measures – their utility to individuals. In principle this argument is as one-sided as the preference theory basis for public goods, but in reverse. The latter legitimizes state decisions about allocation for the production of public goods by referring to individual needs for these goods, which have to be publicly financed through compulsory contributions simply because of the indivisibility of their benefits and the advantages of free rider behaviour that this conditions. But what here appears as the indivisibility of benefits is a systemic effect to be distinguished from appropriable individual benefits, as seen in the case of merit goods. Collective benefits as systemic effects and individual effects must now be treated as belonging to two distinct spheres; they cannot simply be offset or even reduced to each other.

Only on the basis of this explicit distinction can one specify the starting question about the welfare theory. The issue is how to locate the conditions for the production of individual welfare in relation to the conditions for collective welfare production, which are themselves graded: that is, they must be understood as having varying effects at different levels of social reality.

Before tackling the many-layered problematics that this implies, the basic issue is illustrated in figure 8.1.

    a. Generally approved social conditions can be characterized by institutional features under which each participant's pursuit of particu-

Particular interests = System rationality	+	—
+	(a) synergy	(b) exploitation
—	(c) tragedy of the com- mons; free-rider sit- uation	(d) social disorganisation

Figure 8.1. Particular Interests and Systems Rationality

lar interests results in predominantly positive external effects. This pursuit of particular interests can therefore also improve the system's conditions in basic ways that benefit all the participants. This 'Aristotelian' example of synergy can nevertheless be considered a priori to be ensured by nothing more than an implied intended aim or 'invisible hand', whereas to establish or guarantee it is far more of an analytical and practical problem.

b. What often occur in practice are constellations in which a synergetic relationship between the pursuit of particular interests and system effects benefits only a minority of the participants, who behave parasitically in relation to the majority. In this situation the system structures act in ways that exclude wide sections of the population from access to some of the system's achievements, even as they sustain an imbalance of power facilitating the exploitation of the underprivileged. This is what Marx famously meant when he interpreted the history of the world as the history of class struggle.

c. Even if 'collective self-damaging behaviour by the pursuit of one's own advantage' (Jöhr 1976) is familiar from premodern times as the 'tragedy of the commons', the situation becomes typical in modern times only when individualization and demands for freedom force the abandonment of any overall control over individual actions. In this case the selfish pursuit of individual interests may generate what independent criteria would judge as mainly negative external effects when the system lacks the power to prevent over-exploitation of its resources, or to requisition the necessary equivalents (E. Ostrom 1990). To the extent that such abuses remain marginal to the system's ability to work, the phenomenon is generally described as a free-rider situation.

d. Last, the case of social disorganization needs to be considered because it has once again become a possibility since the collapse of the structures of socialist and colonial rule. This occurs when, for domestic or international reasons, institutions' ability to perform falls below the minimum necessary for the stabilization of expectations and the generation of conformity to custom. In these circumstances, the participants' erratic behaviour will predictably lead to a progressive disorganization of the system and a reduction in the sum of potential individual benefits as well.

In addition to these four cases, a fifth is conceivable, namely that of *no association* between the pursuit of particular interests and system rationality. Here each dimension is defined independently of the other, which obviously simplifies political discourse very greatly because it means that the pursuit of individual interests in our individualistic culture emerges as legitimate per se. This idea is probably an illusion arising from the positive external effects of economic, political and social developments in Europe so far outweighing the negative ones. But contrary to liberal notions, this is not a natural condition but instead the outcome of historical conjunctions and institutional progress. The narrower the scope for distribution becomes, the more likely become attempts at exploitation (e.g. cuts in services for the socially disadvantaged) or free riding (e.g. tax evasion, illicit employment or fraudulent claims for social benefits).

The increasingly shrill demands for reform of the welfare state are too sweeping to be instructive, especially if they focus on cost-cutting alone. It undeniably has to be limited in some respects, but the boundaries of redistribution remain contentious and depend on the strength of value orientations as well as of particular interests. It is empirically doubtful whether the effectiveness and efficiency of a national economy are in fact primarily dependent on the scale and distribution of the share devoted to social services (see Scharpf and Schmidt 2000; Pfaller, Gough and Therborn 1991).

The Production of Welfare as a Multilayered Problem

The widespread tendency in economics to equate 'economic man' with the social individual is a simplification akin to that of the French Revolution's declaration of the individual's direct relationship with the state, that is, the abolition of all intermediary bodies. Though the character of the intermediary bodies abhorred by the French Revolution has undoubtedly changed in the course of modernization, their significance to individual and collective welfare has not diminished at all, but has become more diverse. Nevertheless, both of these individualistic ways of thinking have remained characteristic in economic and political welfare discourses.

The increasing complexity of modern societies is based in essence on two evolutionary achievements. First is the differentiation and institutionalized autonomy of the higher spheres of meaning: religion, politics, science, the economy, the law. These can be understood as functional systems characterized by specific values or codes, styles of interaction and organizational forms (see introduction). Second is the emergence of modern configurations of formal organizations with sharply delineated external boundaries and internal functional structures, based on the temporary and non-exclusive membership of individuals (Thompson 1967; Scott 1992).

The development of the welfare state cuts across the differentiation of the higher spheres of meaning. Employment protection and social security organizations crossed the boundaries between politics and the economy; educational and health service systems became autonomous under the influence of politics and science, running parallel to the declining influence of religion; and lastly the differentiation of social relief organizations occurred at the boundary between politics and religion. At the same time, a process of institutional specialization and a development of more or less autonomous organizations took place, whose achievement still remains to be explained fully because it took place in the contested boundary between social functional systems. For this reason, the development of the characteristic system structures of the welfare state cannot be adequately described by structural separation and functional differentiation theory. If we accept the idea that social policy should mediate between the rationalities of society's different functional systems, then it is immediately obvious precisely why it is so difficult to identify a coherent welfare state rationality. In this context it is more productive to adopt Elmar Rieger's suggestion that the successful institutional development of social policy's autonomy depends on 'elective affinities', that is, on 'internal parallels, homologies or analogies between the institutional structures of social fields' (Rieger 1992a: 57). The perspective of a growth of institutional autonomy in the contested borderland between the state on the one side and the agents of the other social spheres of meaning on the other corresponds precisely to the idea of the mediation between state and civil society that marked the earliest concept of social policy (see chapter 2). To describe the process from the perspective of functional differentiation, it must be borne in mind that we are dealing with a second-order differentiation arising from conflict-laden disputes at the boundaries between first-order differentiations.

This reveals that the one-sided allocation of social policy arrangements to the state, which is implicit in the concept 'welfare state', obscures the real issue. It would be more practical to distinguish analytically between the state or government on the one hand and the welfare sector on the other, with the latter subsuming all the state-controlled social service fields that affect people's living conditions and thus their individual welfare.[3] The enormous increase in individual welfare in Europe during the last 150 years is a consequence of institutional developments whose circumstances and ramifications have not yet been thought through very systematically. The concept of welfare production is introduced to crystallize the issues. It emphasizes that the extent of individual welfare is always the result of actions that must be examined in terms of both their operation (process benefits) and their outcomes (output benefits). The actions are not simply those of individuals pursuing their own well-being but exist in a variety of institutional contexts and involve large numbers of people and often organizations as well. Thus welfare production is a process that can be sociologically constructed at a number of levels simultaneously, involving the state, the productive economy, the voluntary welfare sector and private households, all at the same time.

While individual welfare in pre-industrial societies generally depended on a single social context, the household, today's individual welfare depends on social participation in a variety of social contexts belonging to different spheres of meaning, which requires the individual to possess a high degree of self-judgement, flexibility and ability to make choices.[4] In an examination of recent debates about the nature of individual (hence human) needs, the degree of social consensus is surprisingly high. This can clearly be seen, for example, in the systematization of quality of life indicators, where despite differences in detail the sets bear strong similarities in international comparison (see Zapf 1972). Closer examination reveals that in essence they reflect the range of social provisions in all relevant areas of life as institutionalized in society: the family, work, social security, education, health, public safety, the administration of justice, politics, culture, religion. The consensus also holds for the list of human rights, as for instance laid out in the United Nations Universal Declaration of Human Rights, the European Convention on Human Rights, or the Council of Europe's Social Charter. Thus there is a wide range of collective images of individual welfare from which the welfare state programme can similarly be broadly constructed.

If one interprets these images as collectively shared ideas of 'the good life', then three substantial sets of meanings emerge: (1) civil rights and liberties as the entitlement to opportunities for freedom of organization and action, (2) rights to participate in collective decision-making processes and (3) social rights as the entitlement to participate in the services provided by public welfare-producing services. This is also how the United Nations Universal Declaration of Human Rights is structured (see chapter 4); T.H. Marshall's theory of citizenship is based on this distinction as well. Hence these rights can be assumed to be the critical dimensions of inclusion.

While all this forms the normative framework, it does not constitute the social reality of welfare production. The latter takes place in specific given forms at various levels of social structure and will be analysed here as distinct individual, interactive, organizational and institutional levels of welfare production.

At the *individual level*, welfare production is the outcome of interplay between personal action and opportunity structures, that is, from the use made of concrete life opportunities. Disparities in individual levels of welfare are conditioned by both subjective mindsets and abilities, and by spatial and personal opportunity structures, but above all by the degree of fit between personal dispositions and the options that are structurally opened up. The decisive conditions of life for individual welfare production do not depend on the options seen from the external observer's perspective, but on subjectively perceived life opportunities.

The degree to which differences arise between these two conditions is basically determined at the *interactive level*. Welfare-sector services thus enter an individual's life, and his or her own welfare production, only to the degree that they are triggered by interactions generally initiated by those affected as claimants, clients, patients and so on. Exceptions such as compulsory schooling or intrusive forms of personal help confirm this rule. Social services distinguish themselves from other production processes by the necessary inclusion of the consumer in the production process, or to be more precise, consumers become co-producers (Gartner and Riessman 1974). This is obvious in all kinds of personal social services whose effectiveness evolves as a direct result of their use, at the point where the outcome benefits depend directly on the process benefits. However, this also applies, mutatis mutandis, to access to financial services or gaining legal aid, where similarly the responsible organizations only act upon application. It is thus no exaggeration to claim that the individual welfare effects of social policy are determined at the interactive level, which nevertheless is itself largely devoid of any direct political influence.

This is a consequence of the multilevel character of public service provisions. On the whole it is organized local facilities that determine the extent and content of the interactively accessible services. Social service *organizations* take decisions based on assumptions that derive in essence from statutory obligations but in practice are mainly defined by supra-local regulatory organizations or groups of organizations. Both the local social service providers and the supra-local regulatory bodies can be of a governmental, intermediary (public or self-governing) or private (corporate) nature, the legal forms varying between states and between service sectors. What is decisive is that a hierarchical relationship between superiors and subordinates can be seen in various different organizational patterns. This leads to the level of the organizational and inter-organizational implementation of policy programmes. As the findings of implementation research have demonstrated (Mayntz 1980, 1983), this is a clearly defined level of public welfare production, one that can be considered analogous to the operational and entrepreneurial levels in the private economy. It cannot by any means be taken for granted that organized welfare facilities are sufficiently responsive to the needs of their clients. Instead, they and their staff develop characteristic forms of self-interested discrimination, which shapes interactive claim behaviour (see Kaufmann 1980; Schulze and Wirth 1996).

Finally, an *institutional level* of welfare production must be distinguished, at which the social service programme is defined and the basic rules of organized provision of services are determined. Only at this level does the state's influence become the decisive factor, in that social services usually have a statutory basis and are financed either through compulsory contributions or from the public budget. It would nevertheless be wrong to attribute unlimited discretionary powers to the state at this level. As already outlined above, social policy institutions usually emerge on the continuously contested boundaries between primary functional systems. The forms of institutional autonomy are therefore generally associated with limitations on the state's power to regulate them. The types of participation offered to typical organizations in each area of social functioning (e.g. unions, associations, churches) depend on the concrete situation, as do the ways in which the organized interests of the autonomous sectors come into play. It seems to be increasingly common, not only in Germany but also in other states, for institutional arrangements to be formed on the basis of ever greater self-government by the institutionally autonomous fields. The introduction of elements of market regulation is the most prominent but not the sole example. This is an expression of a changing self-understanding of the state, to which I shall return at the end of the chapter.

Family, Social Networks and Human Capital

Together with Montesquieu, with whom Durkheim engaged during the formative period of his thought, it is Hegel who must be considered the founding father of the functional differentiation theory of society. He not only set out the difference between state and civil society but also distinguished both of them from the family as the third form of the 'objective spirit' (Hegel 1821). Outside of France (where, particularly under the influence of F. Le Play, the constitutive significance of the family for the overall social context was addressed early on), the international theory and practice of social policy has only recently rediscovered the family (Esping-Andersen 2002), and accordingly the family enters neither political nor economic welfare discourses. But if one takes seriously the idea that the political welfare problem lies centrally in guaranteeing a synergetic relation between individual and collective welfare production, then the family, as a social function system and as a meaningful form of social interaction, cannot be disregarded.

From the perspective of social theory the family may appear to be a functional system, but it differs from all others (Kaufmann 1994). Its macrosystemic character is not mediated through organizational structures, but instead links society-wide institutionalized meanings directly with the interactive level of small groups and social networks. Whereas the other social subsystems constitute themselves in public, the family is the institutional locus of privacy. Throughout society, the family exclusively discharges an institutionalized function that justifies it being considered a social function system, namely, the combination of procreation and primary socialization. Not until the twentieth century did the separate complex of normative values around 'responsible parenthood' emerge, with high levels of obligation.[5] The increasing obligations of parenthood stand in stark contrast to the currently observable tendency towards deinstitutionalization of the dimension of partnership in families. Families are responsible for ensuring a new generation of personnel for all the other social subsystems. They reproduce the human resources of them, and the performance of all the social subsystems is highly dependent on the quality of the new recruits. The significance of primary socialization for later development has been very recently underscored by findings in brain research that have established a causal correlation between the extent of nerve linkages and the amount of attention experienced during the initial months of life. Moreover, family households and their networks, as well as serving the regeneration of human capital, are also a locus of mutual aid and social recognition (Kaufmann 1990/1995: 34ff.).

Whereas the quantity of offspring depends solely on family performance, their quality today is a function of the highly contingent combination of various different functional systems, such as family, education, mass communication and so on. The critical influences on this process are rooted in primary relations, which, though not determined at the level of the subsystem, generally convey the meanings of these subsystems selectively.

Obviously the quantity and quality of an individual's offspring are key features of the theoretical combination of personal and collective welfare (see chapter 12). This factor affects each and every social subsystem, and simultaneously extends beyond them. No subsystem can monopolize its offspring for itself in a society based on principles of freedom, and even traditional ties such as a profession or a belief system are today increasingly losing their significance. There is scarcely any potential for specific recruitment any longer; instead, all social organizations are non-specifically reliant on the size and quality of the upcoming generation (including immigration when necessary).

To a limited extent, the economy has already responded to this issue with the premise of an increase in and improved utilization of human capital. But the problem is one of recruiting not simply for the economy but also for politics, sciences, religion and the family, as well as for secondary differentiated service sectors. To express this factor more broadly, the term 'human assets' has been put forward, fruitfully linking the micro-perspective (individual abilities as resources) with the macro-perspective (assets as the sum of human abilities). In this way human economic assets as the aggregate of abilities mobilized for wage labour are distinguished from human life resources as the aggregate of the competences required for non-economic roles such as parent or citizen.[6]

The human assets of a society are therefore constituted by the aggregate abilities or even capabilities[7] of its members insofar as they contribute in the context of overall social performance as mediated by interaction with the organizations of the various social function systems. Inasmuch as the development of each individual's abilities depends on his or her participation in different functional areas (output benefits) and thereby also aims to expand them further (process benefits), the cumulative reciprocal interdependency this reveals would clearly equate to the idea of synergy. The services of almost all social policy organizations contribute to the production, maintenance or renewal of human assets. The concept can be operationalized in these contexts and thus represents a useful criterion for the proposed complex concept of welfare (see chapter 12).

The introduction of an asset theory perspective into the welfare discourse, as occurred first in the (German) Commission for the *Fifth Report on the Family* (Bundesministerium für Familie und Senioren 1994), results in several reorientations:

1. It frees the welfare discourse from a consumer-centred perspective and puts it into a production-oriented one. Personal welfare is less a function of disposable income and more a function of the capacity to mobilize resources. The development and maintenance of capabilities naturally depends on an appropriate inflow of resources,

but this constitutes merely the prerequisite and not the meaning of personal welfare.[8]

2. If personal welfare is determined by the factor of capability, it loses its solipsist associations, and it becomes clear that people's welfare remains dependent on constant interaction with their fellow human beings, which by no means precludes the pursuit of personal interests.[9]

3. By this means the collective welfare discourse is clearly distinguished from the distribution discourse that social policy practice generally tends to identify with. The distribution discourse is predicated on a zero-sum game, whereas the welfare theory perspective adopted here tries to argue that it is possible *to increase both individual and collective welfare* simultaneously.

4. It complements political and economic perspectives on the problem of welfare production with a sociological perspective emphasizing the constitutive importance of the services arising in the framework of primary relations to personal welfare.[10] One of the characteristics of these services is their general association not only with outcome benefits but also with *process benefits,* exemplified as social recognition, learning, the development of abilities and the like. Other process benefits of participation in activities in other social areas, which hitherto have been discussed chiefly in terms of their outcome benefits, are similarly demonstrable, for instance increasing qualifications through professional experience.

If welfare production is taken to be all those activities that contribute to the maintenance and development of human assets, then a normative criterion is achieved that has the potential to attract a wide degree of support, irrespective of market prices and political preferences. It particularly excludes as undesirable all those activities that are commonly understood as detrimental to the maintenance and development of human assets, such as health-damaging forms of consumption and production, environmental damage, social exclusion and so on. However, many activities may doubtless be judged either especially useful or particularly damaging depending on circumstance, and on these it would be hard to achieve consensus, for instance on the effects of drugs or watching television. Ambivalence results from many complex situations.

Forms of Welfare Production

A broader concept of welfare like this seems well suited to achieve better comparative evaluations of different forms of welfare production, without being vulnerable to discipline-specific or ideological distortions. The various attempts at social accounting (see Stone and Stone 1959; Juster and Land 1981, Stahmer 2002) undoubtedly represent the most systematic advance in this direction. Building on this concept, Zapf (1984) distinguishes between four types of welfare production underpinning particular forms of distribution and mechanisms for decision-making:

1. Market-mediated welfare production by profit-seeking businesses. This is the most widely recognized form of producing goods and services. It is regulated by supply and demand, and if sufficient competition exists among producers it can be expected to provide the consumer with an advantageous choice.

2. Politically regulated welfare production taking place directly at the point where state-dependent organizations (e.g. agencies, local authorities or public facilities) provide citizens with services that are useful to them. The management of supply in such instances is primarily hierarchical and, in theory, based on elaborate planning. The influence of clients or consumers on the service providers is largely confined to the interactive level and is mainly modest. Bureaucratic controls are least responsive. Improvements in social services can at best be expected from staff qualification; indirect control may be exercised through mass media or elected representatives. When private enterprises or non-profit organizations provide services, there may be also an indirect state influence through statutory regulations and their implementation (e.g. work protection, consumer protection, price controls, supervisory bodies).

3. Associational welfare production. This heading subsumes numerous activities of the so-called third or non-profit sector, ranging from elementary forms of collective self-help to voluntary associations, and on to highly organized, corporately managed supply systems. The original management mode is solidarity, facilitated by common values and interests (e.g. unions, consumer associations) or altruism (e.g. charities). If organizations like these are successful and expand, for instance at a national level, then federal associations arise with complex forms of organization, potentially raising effectiveness through staff qualification; however, incorporation and bureaucratization can lead to increasing division between the organization itself and its grass-roots members. The interaction of associations normally takes the form of bargaining.

4. Household welfare production. Occurring within and among private households, this is the form of welfare production whose significance is most undervalued. According to data in the German Federal Statistical Office's time budget studies, including the value

of household production at even a modest price would increase the social product by an estimated 42 per cent (Blanke, Ehling and Schwarz 1996: 6–7). At least a third of welfare production still takes place on a non-monetary basis within the framework of family or voluntary commitments. The mode of coordination is largely solidaristic, and these activities remain informal in character. The process benefits largely outweigh the outcome benefits.

On the Role of the State

In the light of the dominant political debates, one might suppose that the state's primary responsibility in terms of welfare is to organize the redistribution of income and to produce social services. Every increase in social services is seen as social progress, and all cuts as a setback. Even critics of the welfare state see the chief irritant as the scale of its costs. As opposed to this one-dimensional, mainly economic perspective, this book attempts to develop a more complex sociological argument. The functional differentiation of society and the individual's liberation from the comprehensive control of corporate society lead at the same time to differentiation of the idea of welfare. Individual welfare, the collective welfare of certain groups, and public welfare nowadays depend in part on differing circumstances. The synergy between individual, collective and public welfare is no longer self-evident.

What sort of welfare does the state have to provide? The state cannot provide directly for the individual well-being of its citizens. The structures of organized societies have, as a rule, become far too complex for direct policy interventions in citizens' lives to be successful. Nobody could today imagine a government leader or head of state throwing banknotes or pieces of gold like a Roman emperor to the needy masses in order to appease them. The particular way in which the state influences the lives of its citizens takes the form of law. For this reason the specific duty of the welfare state can be described as the safeguarding of economic, cultural and social rights as the basis of social inclusion.

This does not necessarily require social services to implement these rights, financed from the state budget by means of taxes or provided by state agencies, as is commonly the case in Scandinavia. A wide variety of institutional arrangements, including semi-autonomous or private organizations, also provide social services, although always within a framework of state guidelines and regulations.

The state's responsibility for welfare applies not only to the social inclusion of individuals but also to economic prosperity and internal peace, and thus to maintaining the democratically legitimated order. From an analytical perspective, the state's welfare responsibility should address the problem of synergy between individual, collective and public welfare. Conflict over distribution should not be addressed at the same level as the fundamentals of social order. Long-term, widespread unemployment or prolonged periods of population shrinkage due to low fertility rates are as much indicators of a breakdown in social organization as are inflation, a spike in crime or high rates of social conflict. The state's responsibility for economic prosperity and domestic harmony often clashes with the interests of important social groups, and with the demand for more individual welfare. In this context, a core task of the state is to defuse such conflicts by managing the institutional conditions of welfare production intelligently.

Even if it is internationally acknowledged in today's world that the state is fundamentally responsible for the well-being of all its citizens, as is the case in most highly developed Western nations, the various patterns of different national starting points and their institutional internal dynamics have resulted in the development of highly disparate arrangements of welfare production in different countries. Until recent years, however, these particular national traditions led their own existence. This also applied to the social sciences, which similarly took account of developments abroad in only limited and disparaging ways. Only in recent decades has the number of international comparative studies on aspects of welfare state development expanded enough to allow generalized statements about 'the' welfare state to reflect more than simply the idiosyncrasies of separate traditions.[11] The discussion here will avoid such categorizations. Rather, it remains to examine the hypothesis that the welfare sector's rising costs and management problems generate similar problematic pressures in all welfare states. They may at first lead to different outcomes depending on their institutional complexities, but these are subject to identifiable optimization conditions.

The welfare state has developed both at the level of state measures and consequent services, and at the level of ideas legitimizing and interpreting the state and its tasks. In this process, social policy measures are initially seen as an interference or intervention, that is, as an external intrusion into the context of an already constituted system (see chapter 6). This implies the liberal assumption of an autonomous market system or a civil society essentially independent of the state, and as long as state measures remained characteristically limited, as was generally the case for early social policy, this perspective was entirely appropriate. But the history of social policy consists of the advancing spread and intensification of those state interventions that proved to be reasonably successful. This boosted organizational development in every nation, in terms of both the direct service providers and those who develop a vested interest in the services. This has led to the creation of facilities, authorities, self-governed enterprises and associations with more or less specialization in particular fields of social service provision.

The forms taken by the concrete institutionalization and functional differentiation of specific welfare sectors seem to be highly contingent on national circumstances, such as the structure of the nation state, the degree of local authority autonomy, the relationship between church and state, the character of labour relations and the ways in which private-interest lobbies are publicly recognized. Further, in most countries the original institutional decisions have demonstrably developed their own dynamic or path dependency. Whatever the precise detail of the composition of these structures, a multiplicity of agencies and interest groups has emerged whose relationships may be described as inter-organizational networks. Their functional specialization results in typical policy fields with various constellations of actors. In Germany, for example, one can distinguish between policy fields focused on social insurance (with the marked involvement of business and trades unions), on health policy (under the strong influence of the producer associations), on social help services (strongly influenced by local authorities and voluntary welfare bodies), or on educational policy (under the strong influence of the Länder and teachers' associations).

In the period of welfare-state expansion after the Second World War, the optimistic belief in social planning led directly to the conclusion that the failure of the market must indicate the state's ability to solve threatening problems in appropriate ways. The oft-cited 'crisis of the welfare state' since the mid 1970s relates not simply to the increasingly obvious limits to the redistribution of primary income, but also to rising doubt that state authorities have a general ability to solve social problems. The critical discussions about economization, juridification, bureaucratization, professionalization and centralization in social policy led to two things – to a rediscovery of the potential for self-help as an aspect of welfare production within and outside the family unit, and to demands for a 'new subsidiarity' (Heinze 1986) and to a 'welfare pluralism' (Evers and Olk 1996), in contradistinction to demands for blanket regulation by the welfare state. Zapf's (1984) distinction between four types of welfare production, quoted above, is also relevant in this context, although this typology suggests an autonomy and functional equivalence of the four types that does not exist. Rather, the contributions of the various factors apply to welfare production at different levels of social development. The state's input concerns the institutional basis of the various social service systems and the assurance of social inclusion through the grant and implementation of social rights. The production of specific goods and services based on the division of labour occurs either through private-sector providers or welfare-sector organizations, which themselves may be either public or private. Lastly and crucially, the satisfaction of individual needs generally arises in the context of households and networks, which are themselves crucial to the welfare effects of the available goods and services.

According to neoliberal *Ordnungstheorie* (a specialized form of German institutional analysis), fully operative competition is nowadays no longer the outcome of an organic development process but results from state arrangements. That is, the state has a duty to ensure the institutional conditions within which the market economy can function, and to that extent the market economy depends on state interventions. Similarly, the creation of institutional conditions for a functional social service system in the welfare sector is a problem of regulation, in which competition is only one of many potential ways of organizing behaviour institutionally. This is shown in figure 8.2, which illustrates the chief types of institutional coordination discussed in the literature, together with their specific characteristics: hierarchy, market, solidarity, professionalism and corporatism.[12] As this synopsis shows, the conditions of efficient coordination, namely the linking of guidance, control and feedback, are very specific to each type, as well as are the typical failures. Thus each type has its own strengths and weaknesses. Though it would certainly be too optimistic to suggest that the a priori choice of a particular type of coordination could solve practical problems of coordination, these analytical distinctions may help to raise awareness of the specific causes of success and failure in real situations.

Naturally the empirically observable institutional arrangements of welfare production do not as a rule correspond to pure types but represent hybrid forms that can themselves be better analysed in turn on the basis of this typology. Scharpf (1993: 29) concludes that 'the combined effects of different coordination procedures are on the whole more advantageous than the effects of single coordination mechanisms'. Nevertheless, this presupposes the use of intelligent combinations.

The provision of social services is not a sovereign task that the state is unable to delegate. Detailed state regulation often proves to be counterproductive, especially for personal social services, because it is incompatible with professional and solidary forms of coordination. Debates over privatization and deregulation hinge on the fact that statute law has a limited ability to regulate social service production processes in detail (Kaufmann 1988b). In this field, the task of state regulation is chiefly constitutive: to set up collective agents with specific rights and obligations capable of providing the necessary services. This depends inter alia on secure

Type of Coordination	Dominant Form of Communication	Guidance (standard setting)	Control (providing conformity)	Motives for compliance	Feedback (evaluation of results)	Typical Failures
Hierarchy	norms, orders	planning	dominance	fear	no spontaneous, directive assessment	not responsive, repressive
Market	money, exchange	demand	prices, competition	interest	gains and losses	external effects, inconsiderate to non-monetary needs
Solidarity	everyday language, sympathy	shared values and defined situations, consensus	social control	commitment, trust, approval	informal evaluation by sense of propriety, talk, voice	group egotism, resistance to chance
Professionalism (expert-systems)	knowledge, debate	scientific standards, consultation	instruction, reputation	status, influence	evaluation research, discussion of experiences	overspecialization, esotericism
Corporatism (bargaining systems)	multidimensional bargaining	procedure, agreement	mutual dependence, threat of exit	cost of exit	habituation, sedimentation, voice	ruthlessness against third parties

Figure 8.2. Pure Forms of Institutional Coordination
Source: Kaufmann (1991c: 228) revised.

sources of funding, which can hardly afford to forgo the use of compulsion, namely obligatory contributions or taxes. Although it is in principle possible to finance the services through direct fees for service, this would exclude those most in need as well as those who do not care about the utility of the service; for instance immigrants with different cultural backgrounds may not be interested in sending their children to national kindergardens or schools. The inclusion of everyone necessitates forms of funding that are independent of the economic situation of those targeted. So alongside the statutory regulation of services, securing finance remains a non-delegable task of government.

If one accepts the idea that the provision of social services is not an essential task of public services, then one has to add that it is by no means self-evident that private enterprises, voluntary charitable agencies or public organizations can meet the needs of their clients in ways that are impartial and flexibly adapted to the range of their capabilities. It is, however, precisely these requirements that crucially determine not only personal welfare but also, indirectly, collective welfare effects. The state's guarantee of social inclusion is not only a matter of granting and ensuring social rights. Additional potential state influences include promoting the process of professionalization and professional regulation, for example by promoting qualification and certifying services. Moreover, it is a public task to extend rights of representation to the clientele in the procedural system. This might also include the creation of inspection and participation rights (e.g. rights to information, means of appeal, certificates of entitlement) at the level of provider facilities. However, these kinds of institutional measures can only facilitate what is an inherently precarious relationship between formal systems and lived experience; they cannot ensure it in individual cases.

Meanwhile, one cannot disregard the fact that all the institutions in the welfare sector and their services are in competition with each other for limited funding resources, whose distribution essentially depends on governmental decisions. At a time of stagnating economic growth, the expenditure dynamics of each individual system lead to pressure for increases in either contributions or budget subsidies, neither of which can be tackled without resort to imposing some sort of ceiling on spending. Depending on institutional realities, however, these attempts to reduce costs can have disparate management effects. For this reason, there is a growing push to strengthen the potential for self-regulation in each field of the social services, aiming at better coordination of cost-cutting measures that are fair, effective and efficient, as exemplified by the German statutory pension scheme (Mayntz 1987; Leisering 1992). This tendency is even more clearly evident in German health care, where the cost-cutting policy begun in 1977 has involved continuous experimentation with institutional reforms aimed at ensuring a revenue-oriented spending policy without any noticeable deterioration in the quality of health care. Increasing the effect of professional and organizational regulation was particularly emphasized in this instance (see Mayntz 1990; Döhler and Manow-Borgwardt 1992b).[13]

Even if this kind of solution is particularly applicable to the German welfare sector because of its pronounced corporatist elements, the underlying idea can nevertheless be generalized: the basic role of the state in welfare production lies in safeguarding social rights and creating and financing functional structures for service provision whose internal dynamics can be used to build up the potential for self-regulation. This generates an innovative state obligation no longer based solely on the duty to maintain the rule of law or safeguard the individual welfare of its citizens, but also on ensuring the harm-free interaction of the inherent dynamic of the various social function systems (Willke 1992; see also chapter 14). Such prospective state action could be described as 'regulatory duties' that no longer envisage the relations between the state and other social function spheres as given, but rather as something to be reflexively designed and continually modernized by means of political decision-making. Following the ideas outlined above, the criterion for this type of reflexive design would be the potential for expanding, in parallel, the competence of the state to regulate and of system-specific self-management, so as to further synergetic relations between the conditions of individual and collective welfare production.

Notes

1. Further arguments can be found in the introduction.
2. The concept of merit goods or needs, based on the work of the economist Richard Musgrave (1959), has been subject to different interpretations in the literature (see summary in K. Schmidt [1964] and Head [1969]). Interpretations in economics generally draw less on the meaning of externalities and more on the distortion of individual preferences. This distortion is usually ascribed either to limited information about the benefits of particular goods or to irrationality, for example in the presumed preference for short-term as opposed to long-term benefits. It is probably more realistic to base consumption of merit goods on public judgements about collective benefits or on system benefit. The construct 'real preferences', from which Head also argues, assumes that the 'correct' demand for a product corresponds directly to that which maximizes the collective benefits. This seems (like Adam Smith's 'invisible hand' previously) like a teleological postulate, which in the sociology of religion would be

treated as a secular belief in providence, and scientifically as a petitio principii (on Smith see Kittsteiner 1984). The argument based on preference theory follows de facto from the premise of methodological individualism, which this author considers incapable of explaining complex social issues.

3. This distinction specifies the problem in relation to social policy organizations. However, the state's influence on social relations affects a far wider range, for instance science policy or the promotion of large-scale technical systems. Here the growth of institutional autonomy is also observable in the borderland of the political system on the one side and the scientific respectively economic system on the other. The political science problem of control concerns precisely the problem of the state's power to intervene in these institutionally independent borderlands (developed with the help of the state itself), which can be described by the common term 'public sector'. See Mayntz et al. (1988) and Kaufmann (1991b), summarized by Ulrich (1994).

4. The individual's subjective satisfaction of these self-directive facilities seems possible only on the basis of self-assurance or a developed sense of identity (for the first systematic appraisal see Krappmann [1988]; see also chapter 5). This aspect of the problem has been omitted here.

5. This explains, among other factors, why the restraint on procreation is becoming a problem for the demographic equilibrium in many European countries.

6. Often a broader term of capital is used for the aspect under consideration, for instance by F. List (1841), who wanted to link the economic theory of value to a theory of productive forces. Bourdieu's (1970) distinction between economic, cultural and social capital, and the concept of social capital introduced into the U.S. discussion by Coleman (1988) similarly address related topics. Amartya Sen's (1985, 2001) category of capabilities also points to similar ideas. The basis of the asset theory discourse was first formulated by Krüsselberg (1977).

7. We use the term 'abilities' to denote specific features of the human capacity to act, whereas 'capability' – following Sen (1985) – refers to this same capacity to act in a given situation.

8. In a pragmatic sense, health as a core aspect of welfare, for example, means the feeling and experience of being able to cope physically and mentally with everyday duties and opportunities. But even this presupposes appropriate abilities that may themselves become impaired by illness.

9. The essential prerequisites for personal well-being include the experience of attention and recognition from others, and the ability to sympathize with the fate of others (Smith 1759). Primary relationships within and beyond the private household therefore represent core human social capital (Coleman 1988).

10. These services have stimulated increasing interest recently, including empirical research (Heinze and Offe 1990; Hochschild 1997), together with the increasing importance of time budgeting research.

11. See especially Ashford (1986); de Swaan (1988); Esping-Andersen (1990); Rieger (1992a); Scharpf and Schmidt (2000); Kaufmann (2003c).

12. Taken from Kaufmann (1991c: 228) and expanded in the dimension 'motives for compliance'. The original inspiration for this type of examination is found in Dahl and Lindblom (1976). For the context of its origins see Kaufmann (1991a).

13. More recent reforms in the German pension and health care systems have abandoned the enhancement of self-regulation and have reverted to direct governmental interventions.

Chapter 9

NATIONAL WELFARE STATE TRADITIONS AND THE EUROPEAN SOCIAL MODEL

The Idea of a European Social Model and the Three Levels of Change in the Welfare State in Europe

The term 'European social model' was first heard at the European level around 1990 and was soon in common use. The 2004 yearbook of the Wissenschaftszentrum Berlin (Social Science Research Centre, Berlin) was entitled *The European Social Model: Towards a Trans-National Welfare State*, placing the concept in the immediate context of the process of European integration (Kaelble and Schmid 2004). The term can thus have two meanings: either the features characteristic of welfare production that are common to European states, or the as-yet unrealized programmatic peculiarities of welfare production in a future European context. As propaganda, the term implies that the future European social model will have the same common features of today's European states' social models.

The first thing to say about the 'European social model' usage is that in retrospect, such a entity has never existed, or only analytically.[1] The national welfare states did not emerge as variants of a European social model but were instead the outcome of disparate national developments that may, however, be seen as showing some signs of convergence, particularly intensifying since 1990 under EU influence. How far European states exhibit common characteristics that distinguish them from other parts of the modernized world, and what these are, is a rather recent question, answered differently in different parts of the world. For example, Kaelble's account (2004) emphasizes particularities and transnational convergence but systematically ignores non-European British Commonwealth countries, which by comparison with the U.S. could well be described as welfare states in a European sense. New Zealand, for example, introduced an extensive social security system and national health service as early as 1937, well before the Beveridge Report and its selective implementation after the Second World War.

The rhetoric of a European social model becomes more credible if it is regarded as a discourse within the framework of the search for a European identity. The search for identity inherently suggests links between past, present and future, and thus the quest for a European social model operates as historical reconstruction in terms of an imagined future. While such identity constructs tend to suppress the factor of change, social science analysis must determine more precisely what is meant by the current state of 'the European welfare state', characterized as it is by profound change at both national and transnational levels. What remains the same? What has changed? And within what frame of reference should these questions be answered?

The frame of reference of the European social model clearly does not refer to President Charles de Gaulle's description of Europe as stretching 'from the Atlantic to the Urals', but primarily instead to those northern and western European states that, following the economic upturn after the Second World War, both wanted and could afford to construct comprehensive systems of social security and social services to cover more or less the entire population, in other words a state-regulated welfare sector. With the exception of Switzerland and Norway, these European welfare states have combined in the European Union and have also increasingly offered membership to states whose resources were insufficient for the creation of comparable welfare sectors. European socialist states to the east also implemented wide-ranging provisions for the welfare of the whole population, though they were based on other methods such as guaranteed employment, occupational social welfare and price controls (Tomka 2004). Since 1990 these countries have been busy restructuring their economies at grass-roots levels.[2] The EU's guiding principles have become more important to them since their accession to the EU, but at the same time the low levels of wages and job security in the new member states have made them highly competitive as locations for investment, especially for neighbouring EU states such as Germany, Austria and the Scandinavian countries.

In analytical terms the transformation of the European welfare state can mean three things:

a) Transformation of the self-image of the developed European welfare states and in their institutional provisions for welfare production;
b) Transformation in the relations between EU members in terms of issues concerning the welfare state, particularly following the latest round of enlargement;
c) Transformation of the historically developed national provisions for welfare production through increasing EU influence at the supervisory level.

National Traditions[3]

I now turn to explaining what distinguishes the models of welfare of the two typical examples of socialism and capitalism – the Soviet Union and the United States of America – from those of representative European welfare states. This concerns the common features and differences of the historically developed European social model compared with those of the USSR and U.S. The emphasis here, unlike in comparative welfare research, is not primarily on the common characteristics of and differences between institutions of welfare production, but rather on the underlying, age-old institutional and cultural differences that characterize the structural foundations of each of the welfare models and circumscribe the argumentative scope of the political discussion. This primarily concerns political and administrative arrangements in relation to social forces and consequent differences in the priority given to different forms of welfare production. At the same time it also concerns the cultural principles of the relations between individual and collective outcomes, between 'state' and '(civil) society'.

The assumptions touched on here are important factors in the high path-dependency of social policy developments, constantly emphasized in cross-national comparative literature. As argued in the second part of this chapter, the tendency towards crisis in the welfare sectors of European states, manifested in such measures as benefit cuts, seem so far to have called the legitimacy of political institutions into question as little as it has questioned the general principles of the welfare state. Moreover, the level of national development nevertheless continues to determine the scope for redistribution and social services, and thus also the details of different nations' political and welfare cultures. The EU has become decisively influential only in the fields of occupational welfare, above all in employment protection and occupational health. Other fields remain subject to case-by-case amendment in the light of judgements by the European Court of Justice, and by voluntary administrative adjustments in the framework of the Open Method of Coordination.

Even though Robert Owen first articulated the idea of international responsibility for welfare in the face of the inhuman consequences of industrialization in 1818, the measures and justifications for improvement of the social conditions of the working class developed exclusively at national level. At the international level there was no discussion of a more comprehensive political responsibility for the welfare of the entire global population before 1944, and at national levels any such thinking remained exceptional (see chapter 4).

The Soviet Union

The first comprehensive social policy programme, formulated by Vladimir I. Lenin at the 6th All-Russian Conference in Prague (1910), was largely embodied in legislation following the Bolshevik seizure of power.

> By a decree of October 31, 1918, social insurance, or, as it was now called, social security … was extended to cover all those who were gainfully employed, as long as they were not employing hired labor. This included wage and salary earners as well as self-employed peasants, artisans, and others, and the members of their families. The covered risks included all major contingencies of life. There was protection in cash and in kind in case of illness, permanent disability, unemployment, old age, and the loss of breadwinner. There were also maternity benefits and burial grants. Cash benefits and pensions were egalitarian; they were geared to the average wage in a locality instead of to the previous earnings of the beneficiary. The main source of financing was employer contributions. This program of universal and comprehensive protection was consistent with the universal duty to work that had been decreed in 1918 and became embodied in the Bolshevik Labour Code of 1919. An individual was either working or incapable of work and, therefore, was entitled to support. (Rimlinger 1971: 260)

Despite the law remaining little more than paper because of the subsequent collapse of the economic system, it gives an insight into the basic concept of socialist welfare politics. Its underlying ideas can be summarized as follows:

1. The conflict of interests between the individual and society is neutralized by the abolition of capitalism and the introduction of a so-

cialist economy. A socialist society is a harmonious society without internal conflicts.

2. The obligation to work therefore does not depend on coercion but reflects the natural need of the human conscious of the community's care for his welfare. This is what the wide-ranging programme of social security was meant to embody.

3. In accordance with the principle of reciprocity there is thus a legal entitlement to social services corresponding to the obligation to work.

4. The standard of living safeguarded by work or social security provisions improves the workers' living conditions in ways that motivate higher productivity, thus setting a process of economic growth in train that leads to further increases.

The social question is thus considered to be fundamentally resolved by the introduction of socialism. Socialism aims to create the material prerequisites for a transformation of the workers' motivation and behaviour and the emergence of a 'new man' (Rimlinger 1971: 252–257; Madison 1968: 25–30).

Admittedly, the right to work subsequently evolved more and more into a basically obligatory duty to work, coercible even as far as the forced labour of the Gulags. The possibility and necessity of very high employment rates depended not least on the slow rate of increases in labour productivity. The right to social security was confined essentially to those willing and able to work, and above all during the Stalin era was patterned very selectively to reward increased productivity. Those who were inherently unfit for work were largely ignored by policy, in the luckiest cases remaining in family care. In this way the system as a whole was given a highly 'productivist' orientation, though without becoming genuinely productive. Even when dependence on market-driven capitalist exploitative conditions was abolished, the coercion in the planned economy to which the population had to submit for the sake of its livelihood did not diminish, and the privileges became even more selective. The primary cause of this, however, was not the economic system but chiefly the centralized exercise of power by the Central Committee of the Communist Party, which allowed neither market nor cooperative forms of welfare production and gave very little support to family forms of welfare production. At the centre of the system stood welfare production in the context of the economic enterprise.

Even if the subsequent history of Soviet social policy, with its permanent underfunding and political instrumentality, has created an entirely different picture from that of the original Leninist programme, the original policy aims explain why comprehensive state planning for welfare has often been condemned in the West as socialist or communist. Characteristically, in the run-up to the UN's General Declaration of Human Rights the Soviet Union supported the inclusion of social, economic and cultural rights but opposed the inclusion of liberal civil rights.

The United States of America

While in Russia's case the unbroken tradition of centralized rule since the time of the Tsars characterized and affected the historical conditions for modernization, the historical conditions for modernization in the U.S. were almost diametrically the opposite. The conditions in the American case were characterized by the myths of liberty and of the western 'frontier' – the secular experience of almost unlimited opportunities for all who had the courage to set off in pursuit of new ventures. There was neither a previous history of traditional rule, nor of the absolutist state; instead the United States itself emerged in the very process of modernization. Indeed, in many ways it arguably constituted the experimental field and pioneer country of the developments that drove European modernization. As Alexis de Tocqueville had emphasized previously, the U.S. political self-image envisions the construction of political order from below upwards and the principle of self-government involving all citizens. Even today, the belief in the superior capacities and adaptability of decentralized and fragmented power structures represents a key factor in the 'American creed' (V. Ostrom 1991). The U.S. is the only great territory on earth in which capitalist principles have been able to develop with minimal political constraint.

The U.S. does have a welfare sector, albeit a comparatively fragmented one, but it is not a social or welfare state. As a country it has no comprehension of public responsibility for the basic aspects of well-being for all citizens, and its political system is based on principles that have little in common with European concepts of the state. Three of the most prominent social science experts on American social policy commented:

> The United States has no comprehensive 'welfare state' in the European sense. Instead it has developed a disjointed patchwork of programs bifurcated into two tiers. In the realm of social transfers, the upper tier is 'social security'. Since the 1950s, this portion of public social provision has been politically protected by a strong bureaucracy and a broad base of public support made possible by its relatively universal scope. In contrast, the lower tier of social transfers includes programs grouped under the rubric of 'welfare', programs that have been far less popular and much more vulnerable to political counter-pressures than those considered part of the 'social security' system. (Weir, Orloff and Skocpol 1988a: 422f.)

The cultural background of these institutionalized arrangements, which reinforce social inequality and a tendency to exclude further segments of the population from economic progress, is the conviction that a lack of economic and social success are personal failings, a conviction fed on Calvinistic predestination and social Darwinian survival of the fittest. This belief in the legitimacy of very serious social inequalities (extending to the death of homeless people in public places) constitutes a crucial difference from European welfare states characterized by Catholicism or Lutheranism.

The greatest difference, however, lies in the concept of the state. Even if the U.S. as an economic and political superpower today plays first fiddle in the concert of states and its international capacity to act and military efficiency are awe-inspiring, nevertheless its domestic political structures have never had much in common with the uniformity observable in most European democracies. In spite of their similar political structures, conditions in the fifty states of the union are far more different from one another than in other federally constituted nations, and this applies particularly to the focus on welfare policy.

From the very outset the union of the United States was characterized by tension between the Federalists (proponents of a stronger union) and the Anti-Federalists (defenders of the greatest degree of individual state sovereignty),[4] and this tension affects U.S. social policy to the present day. Federal state powers do not stem from the constitution but derive from Supreme Court rulings responding to particular political initiatives. The general American mistrust of 'big government'[5] is based both on individual state interests and on the absence of central government power, but at heart it derives from American traditions of liberty.

Common-law traditions give both the U.S. and the U.K. a fundamentally different legal culture and thus a different meaning of political rule compared to that of continental European countries founded on Roman law (Dyson 1980, see also introduction). In the latter, the state itself is the embodiment of a unitary legal and political social order, which through the self-limitation of the constitutional state and the accompanying emancipation of civil society is clearly divided into two spheres dominated by the differing legal principles of public and of private law. By contrast, the Anglo-Saxon concept of government understands government as a function of civil society. This is rooted in the ancient Aristotelian term 'polity', while the distinction between state and civil society was principally developed by Hegel (see chapter 2). In addition, Calvinist origins in the U.S. legitimized a democratic conception of the polity.

These diverse concepts of government functions similarly correspond to differing administrative traditions. In Anglo-Saxon regions administration remained an honorary matter for wealthy citizens well into the nineteenth century, while on the continent the idea of professional public servants, and therefore a unified civil service, took shape much earlier – in the sixteenth century in Sweden under the Vasa dynasty, in the second half of the seventeenth century in France under the Finance Minister J.-B. Colbert and in Prussia under the Great Elector Friedrich Wilhelm. While a unified civil service eventually emerged in the U.K. during the Victorian era, the U.S. has so far failed to develop a coherent administrative culture. Despite this, a number of highly professionalized and relatively politically independent specialized administrations have evolved there, the Social Security Administration among them. However, the term 'social security' covers a much narrower range of social risks in the the U.S. (old age, disability, surviving dependants) than in Europe, and a structural similarity to European welfare states exists only in this respect.

The normative assumptions of the American model of welfare can be summarized roughly as follows:

1. Individual liberty is the foundation of coexistence in society. Every individual is the author of his or her own fortune and must as a rule bear the consequences of his or her own decisions.
2. The polity is democratically constituted from below. The individual states are free to regulate their own internal order and generally concede wide-ranging autonomy to local communities. The central state level is assigned powers only by law or the Supreme Court, and thus in the field of social policy there are endless conflicts over competences.
3. At the heart of the American idea of welfare lie education and free access to the labour market.[6]
4. Belief is widespread that maximizing competition produces the greatest possible progress, and that progress over time cures all ills.
5. Toleration of social inequalities is high and limited only by the moral imperative to ensure everyone's physical survival. It is not individual position in the production process (class) that forms the structural basis of social inequality, but belonging to different ethnic groups (race).

The market and the family constitute the primary forms of welfare production in the U.S., but equally no hindrance is given to other forms of association. Nevertheless, policy measures for social protection have so far lacked any cultural legitimacy, which explains why the U.S. continues to refuse to sign the UN International Covenant on Economic, Social and Cultural Rights. As opposed to many other countries that ratified and observed the international agreement without hesitation, in the U.S. law plays a strong role as a unifying force, and maintaining this force is far more the task of the courts than of public administration.

If one starts not from individual institutions but the overall context of institutional forms of welfare production and their legitimation, then the USSR and the U.S. appear to offer contrasting models to European welfare states.[7] While in the Soviet Union a centralized system tried to control all forms of welfare production politically, in the U.S. fundamental reservations about state control (particularly central state control) of welfare production relegate the latter to the 'anarchic' guidance of markets and powerful private organizations.

Great Britain, Sweden, France and Germany

Set against this background, the common features of Western European welfare states become more obvious, but there are characteristic differences within Western Europe as well. A brief comparative sketch of four welfare states in representative European nations demonstrates this. Following Esping-Andersen's typology (1990), as a welfare state the United Kingdom can be considered liberal, Sweden social-democratic and France and Germany conservative, though subsequent critiques have questioned the similarity between France and Germany (Kersbergen 1995).

All four states can look back on a long tradition of centralist monarchical rule that was nevertheless held in check by decentralized political forces. Although it took Germany until 1870 to become a unified empire and it retains a federal structure to the present (formally at least), nevertheless its predecessor states such as Prussia, Saxony and Bavaria themselves possessed well-developed bureaucratic state systems. By contrast with the United States, Europe as a whole can be said to have had a far better experience of public administration, and consequently there is far less basic mistrust of social policy interventions legitimized by welfare aims.[8]

While French and German civil society first emerged as a consequence of constitutional self-restriction by the hitherto absolutist state, in Britain the balance of power between the monarchy and the nobility, established after the high Middle Ages, resulted in a gradual extension of the range of groups represented in parliament, which led to a gradual diminishment of class distinction between the nobility and the bourgeoisie. The right to vote was substantially expanded in 1832, and in 1867 the franchise was extended to the majority of male industrial workers. As in many other countries, voting rights grew into universal suffrage, including women, after the First World War. In Sweden, a precarious balance of power between the king and the four estates similarly developed relatively early, and constitutional reform and democratization took place without any significant conflict over the constitution. However, while Britain became the birthplace and stronghold of liberalism and developed public service functions very slowly, Sweden experienced scarcely any liberal revolution, and tensions between the professionally competent state and the comparatively homogeneous civil society remained minimal. Sweden to that extent resembles Germany, where economic liberalism was subordinated to the Prussian nationalist movement and a distinctive state ideology developed. Finally France, the land of the 'Great Revolution', has never been able to overcome the division between 'left' and 'right' (in whatever terminology the parties clothed themselves) that the French Revolution created, and for that reason its underlying political composition is the most conflict-ridden of the four countries compared here. Faced with the power of conservative paternalism, women in France did not obtain the right to vote until 1946. These developments contrast strongly with the 'democracy from below' model in the U.S.

In terms of administrative development, Great Britain stood in contrast to the continent. Apart from the fiscal bureaucracy, the emphasis was not on the royal court, and to the extent that there was administration at all it was done by decentralized local government. A specialized civil service only gradually emerged during the nineteenth century, where at the local level the guardians of the new differentiated Poor Law (poor relief and health) initiated developments themselves (Fry 1979: 154–157). The emergent social policies thus played a leading role in the development of administration, and the professionalization and bureaucratization of administration affecting local government first took place in the twentieth century. During this process, relations between the central state and local government were liable to repeated shifts, particularly over local boundaries and social reforms. However, even though the trend was towards stronger decentralization, the power to take final decisions remained centralized. There was no autonomy at the local level such as in Germany and even more so in Sweden.

The *United Kingdom* is the country in which the fundamentals of liberalism found their most concrete practical expression, and where they most deeply influenced economics, politics and poor relief in the nineteenth century. Inspired by the spirit of Jeremy Bentham (see chapter 1), the sixteenth-century Elizabethan Poor Laws were reformed in 1834 and radicalized in terms of greater social control of the 'able-bodied poor'. Conflict over these Poor Laws made *the poverty question* the dominant theme of social policy debate until well into the twentieth century. The hegemonic liberal principles formed an ongoing obstruction to demands for political intervention to resolve contemporary social problems. Every attempt to justify state interference had first to contend with the slogan 'government shall not interfere', but as the Liberals were displaced by the Labour Party in the twentieth century, the idea of managing social conditions similarly became legitimate in principle in Britain. The Beveridge Report of 1942 became a blueprint for social reform for the post-war era even outside the United Kingdom.

The *Scandinavian countries* experienced a tradition of social assistance reaching back to before the Christian era, which in a variety of ways ultimately progressed to universal social security systems. By comparison with the other three states under consideration, very little effort was made to hinder the workers' own political and industrial organization. In Denmark as early as 1899, following violent industrial conflict, the leading employers' associations and trade unions signed the so-called September Agreement, which included recognition of the unions' and employers' joint involvement in plant management and pay questions, and envisioned arbitration to deal with conflict. This agreement represents the earliest example of a corporatist compromise, which would point the way to welfare state developments in other countries. A similar agreement was concluded in 1938 at Saltsjöbaden in Sweden; as a consequence, virtually all major issues of labour relations were subject to a staged wage settlement system instead of employment or occupational law. In addition to the workers' movement, the farmers' and peasants' movement and the women's movement quickly became influential, and these various social movements converged in the *demand for equality*, which was to become the central theme of social policy struggle in Sweden.

Before industrialization began seriously, Prussia and other German states too managed poverty in a more or less humane manner, so that *Germany* never experienced the kind of political conflict surrounding the poverty question in Britain. Instead, the central topic of argument in the German Reich after its creation in 1870 was *the workers' question*. The social insurance system set up by Bismarck (1883/1889) was aimed at industrial workers, as was the labour protection legislation under Kaiser Wilhelm II. When other social groups subsequently became the focus of state social policy, a variety of distinct institutions were set up for them. Even after the Second World War, social security was revived in Federal Germany along occupational lines (civil servants, waged workers, salaried employees, the self-employed), whereas the Beveridge Plan's proposals for universal social insurance never entered practical politics in spite of academic debate about them.

In *France* the virulent antagonism between largely authoritarian entrepreneurs and generally radical trade unions barred both corporatist compromises and the emergence of a stable system of social insurance until after the Second World War. The chiefly middle-class governments began to adopt greater responsibility for welfare only as a result of the 1968 May Revolution, and to replace unsuccessful corporatism with state management. For that reason, the central concern of French social policy was not the problem of workers or of poverty (for which the Catholic Church long remained responsible), but instead the problem of *the family*. The birth rate in France had begun to decline markedly around 1830, so that by the end of the nineteenth century nationalist anxieties about a predicted depopulation were being expressed. In parallel with these concerns a social movement emerged, inspired by Christian values and agitating for family interests. These developments made family policy the only field in which the ideas of anticlerical nationalism and Catholic conservatism converged (Schultheis 1988). The *Code de la Famille*, passed shortly before the Second World War, formed the foundation for comprehensive national family policies introduced after 1945, which also had some success in demographic terms. However, numerous special provisions for particular organized interests split up the unified system of *Sécurité Sociale* planned after the Second World War, and it suffered from continuing funding problems. Pressing social problems, particularly in poverty policy, still remain to be properly resolved.

In spite of these differences (and many others that could be added by including more countries), the common features of the European model of the welfare state can be outlined in contrast with those of the U.S. and USSR:

1. A long-lasting tension existed between political focal points (mainly monarchical, aiming to centralize powers) and the political forces aiming to limit these centralizing powers (the churches, aristocracy, landowners, self-governing cities). This tension moulded the establishment of constitutional and increasingly representative democracies in the nationalist era.
2. Constitutional restrictions on the state affected both the political rights and the civil liberties of citizens, contributing to the evolution of a private capitalist market economy in principle free of political interference, while also advancing a pluralistic civil society.[9]
3. Normative traditions of poverty relief and criticisms of the rich, already to be found in antique Judaism, were further refined in Christianity, to the effect that respect and aid were due not only to members of one's own folk but basically to any person in need. This moral intuition first shaped poor relief by the church and later its secular counterparts, and has inspired social movements of various

political orientations to the present day, often in the name of the same ideas of equality and justice stretching back into antiquity.[10]

4. On the basis of these circumstances, social policy in Europe developed as the legislators' morally legitimized intervention in fundamentally adaptable economic and social relations, namely as mediation between state and civil society.

5. Political responsibility for meeting the requirements of individual and collective welfare – the practical forms of which remain politically contested – is ascribed to the state. The central feature of European social order has become the establishment of a social security system covering all recognized social risks and all residents, funded by taxation or compulsory contributions, as well as an educational system regulated by the state.

6. To the extent that any common idea of progress can be ascribed to European societies, it is based on the concept of collaboration between the state and the market economy, together with the negotiation of organized interests within the framework of representative democracy. By contrast with both USSR and the U.S., no clear priority is given to any particular form of welfare production; instead, belief in welfare pluralism is growing.

The So-called Crisis of the Welfare State

Since the 1980s, the developed European welfare states have faced growing programmatic and fiscal problems, primarily triggered by changes in the monetary order and changes in the terms of trade. This subject is seldom addressed in discussions about the crisis of the welfare state.

The post–Second World War stage of construction of the European welfare states took place under the international currency regime agreed at Bretton Woods in 1944, driven by the U.S. dollar, which was the sole currency tied to the price of gold. At the time, European currencies were pegged to a fixed dollar rate based on pre-war circumstances (the Deutschmark, e.g., was set at a value of DM 4 to $1). Upon Europe's economic recovery, European currencies became undervalued, contributing to post-war economic growth and full employment, and so to the scope for redistribution that eased system building in the welfare states. The Bretton Woods monetary system collapsed in 1973, and Europe's competitive advantage over the U.S. waned. The oil price crises of 1973–74 and 1979–81 worsened this situation, setting off the first serious economic crisis since the Second World War and seriously slowing down European national economic growth rates.

The first references to the 'crisis of the welfare state' date to this point. Between 1963 and 1973 global industrial production had risen by 7 per cent per year, whereas between 1973 and 1982 it grew by only 2.5 per cent; after 1995 growth in Germany eventually fell to only 1 per cent. The return of unemployment caused by these falling growth rates has since then posed the greatest challenge to the developed welfare states. The international deregulation of financial markets after 1985 made national borders irrelevant to capital transactions, resulting in a significant reduction in economic autonomy. The merging of various European states into the eurozone can be understood as a defensive alliance against the globalization of financial markets and the speculative attacks it facilitated on some currencies. The EU's fiscal policy targets now operate far more directly to restrict expansion of social security provisions than do international monetary relations. At the same time the euro has advanced to a position of equal power with the dollar in the world monetary system, which benefits the long-term stability of European national economies.

Social policy's service capacities have become circumscribed not only by unemployment but also, from a demographic perspective, by an increasingly ageing population and its disproportionate increase in cost-intensive demands by clients of the welfare state. However, the decline in birth rates poses an even more serious problem and the consequent reduction in human capital or human assets (see chapter 12) poses an even more serious problem. In the case of the former West Germany, the reproduction rate fell by a third between 1970 and 2000, which is equivalent to an estimated investment gap, in terms of human assets, of around €2,500 billion (Kaufmann 2005: 77ff.). These missing human assets are the basic reason for the dire long-term prognoses for the German social insurance system. The sharp decline in birth rates set in later in southern and eastern Europe, but will in time have equally profound effects. Over the long term other countries in western and northern Europe are in a somewhat better position than Germany – France especially, because it dealt with demographic developments politically at an early stage.

In the end, all the European welfare states are affected by change in the overall political and ideological climate. The collapse of the Eastern bloc made the previous social concerns of owners of capital and their political exponents redundant in terms of power relations, and gave renewed impetus to neo-liberal and globalization discourses. As a result, it is no longer enough to claim that the welfare state represents a 'third way' under the slogan 'neither capitalism nor socialism'. What is needed instead is substantial debate about the value and utility of welfare state arrangements so as to challenge the claims of neo-liberalism.

Cross-national comparative studies have shown that welfare states have reacted to these challenges in very different ways and with varying degrees of success (Scharpf and Schmidt 2000; Huber and Stephens 2001). These differences are explained by identifiable institutional as well as political and cultural variations, although they defy reduction to simplistic regularities and connections. Nevertheless, these observations merit greater consideration in the course of the attempt to think through a contextual theory of the welfare state.

In Europe, distinct national patterns of welfare state development are more obvious than are cross-national similarities. Despite facing similar challenges (democratization, industrialization, urbanization), social problems were identified in different ways from country to country, and the political priorities and institutional solutions vary accordingly. By comparison with developments in the rule of law, democracy and the market economy, institutional developments in the sphere of state regulation of the conditions of production, social security and social services seem to be more internationally contingent. Assumptions about national traditions, that is, path-dependent developments dominantly influenced by national peculiarities, would appear to offer a more plausible explanation for developments so far than do explanations based on abstract approaches such as functionalism or conflict theory. Welfare-state typologies themselves explain nothing but instead at best offer generalized descriptions of similar national patterns.

Comparative national case studies offer a better understanding of welfare state developments than does the typological approach, at least in my view (Kaufmann 2003c: 16ff.). For example, as shown above, each of the four European countries examined can be seen to have a particular key problem explicable in terms of understanding social policy priorities and the peculiarities of institutional developments. In Great Britain this key problem was the fight against poverty, in Germany the resolution of the workers' question, in Sweden the establishment of equality and in France the reinforcement of the family. These differing key problems structured social policy development in the nineteenth century and first half of the twentieth century; in other words, welfare state reforms remained coloured by these national problems even after the Second World War. Admittedly, institutional expansion caused a degree of convergence between European welfare states, in that the field of social insurance addressed roughly similar risks and state-regulated systems of health and education as well as other forms of publicly regulated personal social services were established. Nevertheless, the definition of risks, the thrust of the services and above all their organization and institutional arrangements remained very diverse.

Moreover, prior assumptions about social policy have scarcely converged in the various states. Germany and France, for instance, continue to regard educational policy as separate from social policy, while in the Anglo-Saxon and Scandinavian regions (as well as in the U.S.) it is seen as a core element of social policy. Equally, employment policies treated as important in Germany and Sweden have for separate reasons remained marginal in France and Great Britain. However, differences in political assumptions about the state, law and society are even more profound. In the case of the U.K., the term 'state' is treated internally as inappropriate for the purpose of describing the political system; the term used instead is 'government', which does not include the judiciary. While the idea of regulating social development by legal means is characteristic of continental states historically based on Roman law, in Anglo-Saxon countries the idea has hardly developed. The basic concept of society is most antagonistic in France and most harmonious in Sweden. All these characteristics can be explained in terms of historical development. One could even describe basic ideas of the nature of the welfare state in terms of differing cosmologies. Above all, it is basic assumptions about the right ordering of society that diverge, even if under the influence of European unification some convergence can be seen in the field of social policy institutions.

Reflections on the Theoretical Concept of the Welfare State

These various prior assumptions present considerable challenges to a theoretical engagement with questions about the welfare state. What social policy constituents do the European states have in common? There may be conceptual agreement that the common features include the rule of law, democracy, the market economy and the provision of welfare. However, while well-developed and internationally accepted major disciplines cover the rule of law (jurisprudence), democracy (political science) and the market economy (economics), which legitimize the aims of their institutionalized complexes and offer problem-oriented interpretations, there is no equivalent major discipline, or even a theoretical consensus, in respect of the provision of welfare. The welfare state thus suffers from a deficit of reflexivity (Kaube 2003).

The 'welfare state' can be interpreted as both a descriptive and a normative term. Descriptive interpretations of the provision of welfare are nowadays chiefly based on international standards and statistical conventions, which almost by default fix the focus on the social security system because it counts as the core feature of the welfare state, it is sufficiently well recorded in statistics and the relevant facilities are also internationally connected. From a more detached perspective, however, the social security system is only one partial aspect of distributive social policy: proper study of the distributive policy would also have to include the existing fiscal system. The social policies of production – that is, employment protection, wage and tariff policies, workers' participation and labour market policies – are rarely if ever included in international comparisons. Similarly, the social policies of reproduction – such as family, education, housing and health policies, together with social services for the young, the disabled and the old – are largely excluded from international comparisons (see chapter 10).

To arrive at a non-partisan and cross-nationally credible normative definition of what the welfare state is about, it would be advisable to start from the international developments that led to the founding of the United Nations and its programmes of civil, political and social human rights. On this basis, a politically constituted community can qualify as a welfare state if it guarantees to all its citizens not only civil and political rights but rights of social participation as well. This approach would also seem acceptable in that the transition from social policy concepts of specific interventions to welfare state concepts of universal provision can clearly be deduced from international developments (see chapter 4). Moreover, in the interim there is a series of international agreements that operationalize the scope of the guarantee of social rights.

A review of international literature shows that works dealing with the welfare state in conceptual terms and not only in terms of institutions are dominated by national and ideologically biased preconceptions. These are best dealt with systematically by means of assumptions in social theory. For example, a social theory approach is found in the concept of inclusion used by Talcott Parsons and Niklas Luhmann, which, taken together with the earlier work by T.H. Marshall (1964) can easily be related to the doctrine of human rights. Despite this, the concept of inclusion by no means exhausts the theoretical interpretations of welfare state development in terms of differentiation and modernization (Huf 1998; Leisering 2004a). In the international literature it is chiefly Göran Therborn (1995) who attempted to combine modernization theory and social state theory (see introduction), while my view is that most other authors remained too closely engaged with institutional welfare state development.

A foundation in social theory is indispensable for a theory of the welfare state, but it is not sufficient. It initially serves to emphasize that the evolution of the welfare state is a reaction against modern forms of functional social differentiation, and it is therefore essential to examine closely the interplay between the central features of society – the interaction between politics, the market economy, civil forms of association and households or families. To arrive at an internationally acceptable theory of the welfare state demands a sociological foundation and an interdisciplinary orientation.

In theorizing the transformation of the European welfare state, it would be expedient to start neither from a historical-geographical space (Europe) nor a politically value-laden concept (the welfare state) but instead postulate a comparative problem overarching the different forms of society, within whose frame the transformation of the European welfare state can be reconceptualized in the threefold sense introduced above. I describe this problem of conceptual relations as welfare production so that the perspective is also compatible with economic considerations. Welfare production is a concept covering all activities that are considered useful to third parties. The problem of the social or welfare state thus refers to the state's role in respect of the entire process of welfare production in the context it defines (see chapter 8).

Welfare production typically occurs within the framework of institutional contexts, which stabilize participants' expectations of the direct or indirect beneficial reciprocity of transactions and thereby reinforce participants' willingness to take part in such transactions. Established discourses refer to the four institutional contexts of market, state, (incorporated) association and family or household, for each of which differing production methods and regulatory conditions can be formulated (Kaufmann 1991c). At first sight, differences in national welfare production arrangements are identifiable in terms of the relations or importance of the features subsumed by any one of these four institutional contexts. Changes over time may be explained by changes in circumstances or importance. In Sweden, for instance, centralized state welfare production was formerly dominant, but more recently greater freedom has been given to associative forms of welfare production. In the U.K., market elements are introduced in a traditional public system. By contrast, in Germany welfare production by the strongly incorporated forms of association has changed remarkably little until now in spite of reunification and growing fiscal pressure.

The European Union and the Transformation of the Welfare State

How have the connections between the European states in the EU and its most recent expansion affected the transformation of the welfare state?

Compared with the rule of law and the market economy, the EU influence on the sphere of the welfare state has so far remained modest.

In terms of regulation, Brussels's role has remained limited to work and health protection and gender equality (Schulte 2004). Like the fundamentals of democracy, the principles of income distribution continue to appear as core competences for national domestic politics, in relation to which the surrender of national sovereignty would seem neither necessary on the grounds of EU integration nor desirable for social policy. The social services, however, are so marked by historical peculiarities and so immediately affect people's everyday lives that harmonization across the EU would have to expect considerable resistance. This means that democracy and welfare provision have become institutional core areas of national political cohesion. Nevertheless, the pursuit of welfare-state goals remains constrained by the market economy's readiness to invest and its rules of efficiency, the deregulation of which has always been a key aim of European integration. This process of integration has given new impetus to the tension between market and state that has always been a constitutive factor in the politics of the welfare state.

So-called globalization imposes increasing restrictions on welfare state developments, especially in terms of the almost unimpeded cross-national mobility of finance capital and the internationalization of competition to attract local investment. Furthermore, globalization generally reinforces opportunities for multinational businesses, especially financial service providers and other large economic agents. But these developments also profit international associations of states, non-governmental organizations, cross-national movements, migrant networks and criminal syndicates.

In terms of welfare state development, European integration has had an ambivalent effect, especially with the creation of the eurozone. On the one hand it reinforces the principles of the political guarantee of social rights and cushions the shock of intercontinental competition for local investment and the power of currency speculation.[11] On the other hand, it promotes internal competition to attract local investment, as well as the internal mobility of goods, capital, services and persons, so that wage rates (including overheads) and the levels of social protection and taxation become factors in business decisions on locating inside the EU. This is detrimental only to countries with higher wages and stricter social protection when these factors are not linked with higher productivity and other positional advantages such as legal security and reliability. The accession of countries with low wage levels and looser social protection does not affect competition (the wage-dumping thesis) in general terms but only in specific industries and activities. Countries with high wages and stricter social security provisions are confronting new forms of structural economic change and the demands of accelerated technical and social innovations. This can become a serious challenge to those segments of the population and groups negatively affected by the changes, such as specific industries and trades unions. In the same way, cumbersome political decision-making systems like Germany's also experience the complex challenges of international competition.

The European states have dealt in various ways with the pressure of internal EU (and in some sectors also intercontinental) competition between business locations. So far national paradigms of welfare provision show few signs of change, but a shift in emphasis is observable, for instance from protective to active social policies. Emerging problems are tackled in terms of established patterns, even leading to institutional restructuring and service cuts, which reveal divisions between discourses of welfare state responsibilities. In countries where contributions from business finance a large part of the services, the welfare state tends to be seen as a locational disadvantage, a tendency particularly prevalent in Germany, where reunification costs and adverse demographic projections lead to particularly marked increases in labour overhead costs. These factors also damage opportunities for economic growth in Germany, so changes in welfare state funding patterns cannot be expected to produce an employment miracle. German demographic problems derive largely from limitations on household production that have so far been more adversely affected by statutory distributive systems, compared to most other European states (Künzler 2002).

In most countries the fiscal crisis has led to service cuts that in some cases could lead to reductions in the existing welfare standards; however, where they have been legally sanctioned they have not faced lasting opposition so far. This has not called either the political institutions or principles of welfare provision into question, although in the latter case the details are disputed. There have been no sustained changes at either institutional or principled levels, and certainly no transformations of the 'European social model'. However, as the central features of social policy have remained a national preserve, social standards in the economically less developed EU countries cannot be expected to reach those of their richer and more developed neighbours quickly.

At the EU level, growing attempts to enlarge social policy influence since Maastricht II have led to clashes between different national ideas of welfare. Regulatory powers have so far been confined to fields associated with production, where the orientation towards best practice has succeeded in averting a race to the bottom (Majone 1993). In the field of social security since the Rome treaties, there has been pressure for cross-national coordination of services concerned with migrant labour. Following the principle that migrant employees should not be more disadvantaged than they were in their country of origin, but also in view of European Court of Justice rulings favouring integration, there has been some tendency to balance provisions upwards. The Open Method of Coordination, introduced since Lisbon in 2000, focuses on best practice and thus points towards social policy goals designed to raise average levels of social protection in the EU. Attempts of this kind are of course often opposed by business interests (a conflict already familiar at the national level) and have to be argued out, chiefly in the European Council.

Contrary to widespread fears, then, European integration has not led to erosion of welfare state arrangements at the level of member states, even if it has tipped the balance in favour of economic versus social policy considerations. As in the past, the nation state remains the decisive level for the configuration of most social policy provisions, albeit under the increasing discursive pressure of international comparisons. The internal dynamics of nation states still seem to dominate welfare state development, and any convergence that emerges is accepted simply as a latent outcome. Thus the idea of the welfare state in Europe is changing at several levels simultaneously, and these changes do not necessarily all run in the same direction. There are some signs that the consequences of deregulation at the national level are partially compensated by adjustments at the European level.

The growing powers of action at the European level contrast with tendencies towards deregulation at the global level. It is improbable that binding regulations with protective and redistributive effects can be achieved at a global economic level. The efforts of the International Labour Organization have had very variable success from country to country (Senti 2002). The international implementation of minimum protection standards for child labour in developing countries really represents the most pressing challenge for global social policy. How far these can be achieved depends not only on economic and social progress in the regions concerned, but also on cultural premises. Changing the mindset of the political actors to delegitimize grave social discrimination, or so that they recognize particular situations as abuses or as social problems, is the first step to overcoming the problem through social policies – and that presupposes the necessary moral standards.

Conclusions

Referring back to the three different questions raised in the introduction, the following conclusions can be drawn:

1. The national identity of the developed European welfare states has changed remarkably little over the last few decades, but nevertheless a trend of convergence can be detected. As regards modes of welfare production, priorities have tended to level out towards a kind of welfare pluralism. In addition, the EU's attempts at coordination and those between national social administrations have resulted in pragmatic harmonizations.

2. In terms of social policy, little has changed so far in the relations between older Western European and the more recent Eastern European members of the EU, other than technical assistance. Occupational social policy played a major role in the former Eastern bloc countries, which proved to be unsustainable after the introduction of market economy conditions (Götting 1998). Social policy does not rank high among political priorities in most of these countries. In the long term, however, the norms and practices of the EU will become established there as well, insofar as economic progress succeeds, though without forgetting the socialist past (Aidukaite 2004).

3. The greatest pressure towards change comes from the EU's growing regulatory powers, and especially from the rulings of the European Court of Justice. They have a greater effect on methods of operation than on institutional peculiarities or national identities. The European Charter contains a number of statements of values that may be read as commitments to welfare state responsibilities, but it nevertheless contains no coherent list of economic, social or cultural rights.

Notes

1. 'There is much that EU-countries share but certainly not a European social model.... Ironically the attempts by welfare state researchers to reduce the complexity of welfare statism in Europe has led to the opposite' (Lamping 2009).
2. A summary description of the welfare sectors of all twenty-five EU members can be found in Schubert, Hegelich and Bazant (2008).
3. This section is a brief synopsis of the results of an international comparative study of the programmatic aspects of four European welfare states, the U.S. and the Soviet Union (Kaufmann 2003c; English translation 2012). For the institutional developments and sources of information refer to the original.
4. Note that the terminology is the opposite of conventional European usage.
5. The argument is not about a 'strong' or 'weak' state, but concerns the purview of the nation state's authority. Within the sphere of its responsibilities (e.g. police or taxes) effective administrative practice is widely approved, including practices that at times appear intrusive to Europeans.

6. The origins of U.S. social security stem from provisions for American Civil War veterans. The growing clientelism of these provisions later contributed to the distrust of centralized state social policy. See Skocpol (1992: 102–151).

7. These social ideas can be described using the categories 'socialism' and 'capitalism', but in my view the latter have become so stereotyped that the words should be avoided in scientific terminology.

8. Empirical studies of population attitudes to public administration show distinct national differences, although the dominant attitude is one of ambivalence. Apart from the theme of excessive bureaucratization there are hardly any radical patterns of criticism of public administration.

9. The semantics of these relationships, in other words the ruling ideas of government, vary greatly. The most thought-through idea is the so-called 'Ordoliberal' model of a social market economy, which sees the state's responsibility as the regulation of economic conditions on the basis of a market economy based on competition. For the various interpretations see Manow (2001) and Kaufmann (2003b: 129ff.)

10. See Gestrich, Raphael and Uerlings (2009). In my view the 'culture of welfare' perspective is of great importance (Kaufmann 1991d). Western Europe was shaped by Catholicism, the High Church and the Lutheran Reformation, that is, by hierarchically organized denominations (see chapter 3). By contrast, the Calvinism that shaped the U.S. was founded on the idea of the covenant between God and Israel (e.g. the Mayflower Compact), and thus on a model of human equality. Orthodox Christianity lacks any impetus towards practical engagement to benefit the poor. The idea of universal social policy is even more precarious under the cultural conditions of East Asia: see Rieger and Leibfried (2004).

11. The most recent crisis in the international financial system has not in principle called this statement into question. Without the euro, distortions caused by the financial crisis would certainly endanger the stability of the European states far more.

Chapter 10

TOWARDS A THEORY
OF THE WELFARE STATE

The word 'theory' has a wide range of meanings, from trivial inductive generalization up to the highest vision of God or the universe. In any event it concerns the systematic ordering of concepts in the light of an overarching idea or a delimited field of experience. The aim of this book is to enquire into something between an overarching idea and a field of experience. What is commonly called the welfare state is both, a collective idea of the 'good life' and a set of institutions legitimized by concern for the welfare of the members of a political commonwealth. Though comparative research on the welfare state has become widespread, there is little discussion about what it means precisely. As we have seen in the last chapter, different national traditions of thought focus on different issues. This book hopes to develop a more complex frame of reference for a scientific reformulation of the welfare state issues debated internationally.

There is plenty of evidence of the 'uncertainty over exactly what it is what the welfare state (and its cognate terms) connotes' (C. Pierson and Leimgruber 2010: 33). This uncertainty is not only about the institutional definition but also about the basic approach to the empirical object. The 'nature of the animal' remains unknown, and most of the literature on the welfare state treats it as known or beyond discussion. An exception is the widely debated approach of Gösta Esping-Andersen, which distinguishes between *Three Worlds of Welfare Capitalism* (1990). This book brought about real progress in understanding welfare states, and not just for its threefold typology, which can already be found in seminal terms in Richard Titmuss's work. What is path-breaking about this book is that it tries to describe the animal itself, not in generic terms but in terms of three typical species. Its thrust consists of going beyond mere description of aspects of the welfare state to a consistently explanatory approach to the connections between the structures and legitimizations of liberal, conservative and social-democratic welfare capitalism, and its impact on social structure and individual welfare. Moreover, Esping-Andersen does not speak of the 'welfare state' as a generic name but of 'welfare capitalism', and thus does not focus primarily on the welfare sector but on the societal configuration of politics, economics and social structure in relation to social policies. This approach in terms of a politico-sociological theory has hardly been accepted by the research community, which instead criticized the details of the approach very thoroughly.

Although the present book follows a different approach grounded more in history and sociology, it relates to a similar level of analysis. It tries to relate cultural backgrounds and structural transformations of society to welfare politics, the emergence of a welfare sector and its impact on the life situation of individuals as well as on social structure. The present chapter gives a broad overview of issues concerning the analysis and the current political debate about the welfare state. More specific concepts for a political theory of welfare production are discussed in chapters 6–8 and 11–14.

Starting Points for a General Idea of the Welfare State

What we generally term the welfare state refers not only to the state but also, as mid-nineteenth-century German social scientists expressed it precisely, to civil society. In about 1850 the 'mediation' between the private sphere of the market economy and the public sphere of government under law was described as *Sozialpolitik*, a term that can be translated into English as either 'social policy' or 'social politics'. In the German context, the main concern of social politics was the political and social integration of the emergent working classes into the newly constituted German Reich. The British and Scandinavian traditions long lacked a comprehensive concept for developing policies for labour protection, social security and social services. The term welfare state was introduced in Scandinavia in the 1930s, but only after the Second World War did it gain broad currency in Great Britain, where it applies less to social politics than to social policies.

Political theories start with the state and economic theories start with the (market) economy; thus each approach has a one-sided view of the specific characteristics of social welfare. However, not even the social scientists' metaphors of 'mediation' or 'mixture' can serve as keys for solving the problem since they do not recognize or reveal the reasons for the inadequacy of the mere separation of the spheres of the rule of law – enforced by compulsion – and the free-market economy. As is well known, these reasons, thematized under the term 'the social question', originally referred to the pauperism of the transitional period and later to the problematic situation of workers in general. Legally (e.g. in terms of the right to vote and the right of free association) as well as economically (in terms of poverty and precarious employment), workers were excluded from the status of both citizen and property-owning bourgeois. The abolition of feudal ties had given workers legal and contractual rights but not the opportunity to own the means of production that were considered a prerequisite of bourgeois society. From the outset of industrialization, it was not implausible that with the necessary diligence one could save enough money to go into business for oneself. Even economic liberalism recognized a 'right to work' for independent workers; no one was to be excluded from a trade by guild or state restrictions. However, Karl Marx showed in his analysis of capitalism that the competitive mechanism had an intrinsic tendency to the 'centralisation of capital' and hence to big business, so that the wage-dependent employment of workers without property was not only a stage of life (youth) as the artisanship model suggested, but a class condition lasting for life. At the same time, Lorenz von Stein (1964, 1850) developed the idea of state mediation in the conflict between the classes of proprietors and workers. This involved the protection of private property but also conferred rights on workers for their education and protection (see chapter 2).

At stake was not only the situation of the individual worker, but also that of his family. This aspect was neglected in the German discussion but from an early stage, influenced by Frederic Le Play, became the centre of the discussion in France, where Christian entrepreneurs experimented with family wages. As long as child labour was not forbidden, family income at least tended to match family size. However, the ban on child labour and the introduction of universal compulsory education deprived parents of their children's working capacity, putting children exclusively on the debit side of the family budget.

English liberals had grounds for opposing the ban on child labour based on the systematic economic policy principle 'government shall not interfere', since every state intervention results in new problems and political demands. However, the moral objections to child labour practices uncovered by commissions of inquiry proved more compelling than such liberal ideological convictions, even in England (see Frazer 1984: 11 ff.). In France and Prussia, this argument was supplemented early on by nationalist political justifications such as the weakening of military power, which were also brought to bear in Great Britain during the Boer War. Today, demographic arguments and especially arguments based on the theory of human capital emphasize the family's indispensable reproductive services to society (Myrdal and Myrdal 1934; O'Neill 1994; Esping-Andersen 2002, Kaufmann 1990, 2005).

Thus, two starting points are identified for the development of a general conception of social welfare – the first concerns social rights and the second, societal reproduction.

First, as early as 1949, T.H. Marshall designated social rights as a systematic supplement to the civil and political rights accompanying citizenship (Marshall 1964). Like political rights, these are not defensive rights against state intervention but participatory rights; they refer to participation in social life. That makes these rights ambivalent for systematic economic policy, since they can be guaranteed only by state intervention in economic and social relationships, which the liberal credo would exclude. Expanding on T.H. Marshall, Talcott Parsons and Niklas Luhmann coined the term 'inclusion' to underscore the characteristic of welfare-state responsibility. For Parsons (1971), inclusion means the recognition of a person as a member of a societal community, that is, it is primarily a moral state of affairs with legal consequences. Luhmann, by contrast, defines the term functionally: 'The principle of inclusion replaces that of solidarity based on belonging to one and only one group'. (Luhmann 1980: 30)

The requirement of inclusion is here clearly applied to societal modernization, meaning the abolition of feudal bonds (see introduction). This allowed for personal freedom but at the same time abolished the previously existing rights to protection and participation. At the same time, modernization means that social functions performed by the system's differentiated parts become routine, and their services indispensable, as a rule, for the lives of individuals. Political and social rights are supposed to ensure that individuals get the opportunity to participate in the different realms of life. Here, the social rights refer first to the protection of wages and of working conditions, then to financial transfers to secure existence where other income is insufficient, and finally to personal health, education and social services.

The second starting point is the problem of societal reproduction. To the extent that human life proceeds in the form of a delimited, imagined collective whose participants recognize each other as members, a basic solidarity can be assumed. The recognition of 'people like myself' is the foundation of all social life—which, of course, does not rule out systems of social ranking or multiple memberships. The normative implications of such basic solidarity are culture-bound and also depend on existing network structures. For the idea of the social welfare state, the politically constituted society of the nation state appears to be the relevant reference point for now. In Europe, the recognition of the right to life for every human being can be assumed to be culturally normative,[1] but the recognition of full membership rights in the sense of the quality of citizenship always remains tied to specific preconditions that also mark the boundary of the collective. Each collective needs to gain new members; in the case of states, this can proceed only through biological reproduction and education or through the assimilation of immigrants. Since there are limits to the latter, not only the state but also all societal system parts depend quantitatively and qualitatively on the services of families to guarantee their recruiting potential. These services must be systematically included in any theory of the welfare state.

Finally, a theory of the welfare state must assume political power and legislation as a systematic reference point in the construction and maintenance of social solidarity. This assumption has lost some of its obviousness under the influence of so-called globalization. I shall address the problems this raises later and start here by clarifying the necessity (and the limits of the necessity) of state responsibility for social welfare.

The Production of Welfare as a General Reference Point

Family services are mobilized neither by the mechanism of trade nor by coercion. Instead they are motivated by a mixture of emotional bonds and considerations of expediency, as well as by moral and (in the case of conflict) legal obligations. As a rule, family services are carried out within a common household but can also go beyond a single household, for example in assisting relatives. Political and economic theories presuppose these generally unpaid family services as given, but the more affluent a society becomes, that is, the higher the opportunity costs of family services become, the more difficult it is to take them for granted. In reaction to egalitarian Napoleonic inheritance law, the French started having fewer children in the nineteenth century, and in the twentieth century birth control became widespread. Within the three years after 1989, the birth rate in the territory of the former East Germany fell by half, showing that today the population of a country is able to adjust its reproductive behavior rapidly and significantly to changes in its living conditions. The introduction of nursing care insurance in the Federal Republic of Germany in 1994 is another indication that family services may no longer be taken for granted.

Despite the displacement of self-sufficiency by market-mediated production and consumption, the private household has not become a mere unit of consumption, as posited by economic theory (Teichert 1993). Here, economic theory goes astray because it regards 'one who raises pigs … as a productive member, and one who raises people as an unproductive member of society' (List 1928). The services the modern family household characteristically provides no longer concern the production of goods but rather personal services, in particular education, care, counsel and assistance, as well as emotional support. Additionally, monetary and commodity transfers still take place within households and within kinship relations going beyond individual households.

Social services have developed essentially as a supplement and partial substitute for these family services. Systems of social security and the service organizations of the educational, health and social spheres have supplanted very few market-mediated services; rather, they provide, in an organized and professional form, services previously performed in rudimentary or undifferentiated form in the framework of private households. As an international comparison shows, these transfer and service systems often arose as collective self-help institutions (e.g. friendly societies) on the one hand or, on the other, in the context of private and church charity (schools for the poor, hospitals) or service institutions (private schools, private practices and clinics). State interventions then extended them by categories or universally, in which process different countries exhibited substantial differences in the degree of state control of these institutions.

What is today generally termed the welfare state, meaning all the institutions of social security and the publicly financed social services, does not necessarily appear to be a state institution like the police and courts: the degree of state control over such institutions is historically contingent. A more neutral term such as 'social welfare sector' is therefore preferable, because the kind and extent of these services is for the most part independent of the degree of their control by the state. This change of name allows for a more precise terminology in several ways.

First, the term must bring to mind all social welfare services – market-mediated, non-profit and state, as well as unpaid services performed in kinship or other social networks. This enables us to conceive of them all from a common perspective. To this end, we follow Zapf (1984) in suggesting the term 'welfare production' (see chapter 8). This encompasses all individual services that arise through transferable sources, regardless of who performs them.

The sum of these welfare-producing services is substantially greater than the gross national product, since it includes more than paid services. A representative time-budget survey by the German Federal Statistical Office found the annual volume of paid and unpaid work in Germany in 1992 to be composed of 60 billion hours of paid work (36%), 10 billion hours of transportation (6%), and 95.5 billion hours of unpaid work (58%). Unpaid work included the time for household production, network assistance and volunteer activities. 'In a macro-economically reasonable estimation, unpaid work in what was already the Federal Republic of Germany before unification had a value of 1,125 billion DM in 1992. This is only 9% less than the total of all the gross wages and salaries in the West German economy, the entire (that is paid and unpaid) economic production is thus 42% higher than the gross domestic product.' Using other methods of evaluation, 'the value of unpaid work could be even twice as high' (Blanke, Ehling and Schwarz 1996).

This view of welfare production is heuristically fertile in two ways. First, it allows the thematization of sectoral shifts in welfare production, whether in regard to the relationship between paid and unpaid work or in regard to the relationship between market-controlled, associative and state-controlled forms of service production. If, as can be assumed, the market and state sectors have expanded at the expense of household and network production, the consequence is that the actual gain in welfare due to economic expansion is much lower than the official economic growth rates. As in the case of environmental consumption, here, too, we have to consider social costs when household services are commodified, for instance, losses of transaction utilities from emotional relationships. If the services of households and networks are taken into account, the welfare balance sheet for overall economic development is substantially less favourable than the official economic figures show.

Second, the perspective of welfare production allows us to incorporate the highly diverse forms of industrial relations into the framework of a theory of the welfare state.[2] The influence of law and government ranges from nearly full abstention (as in Great Britain until Margaret Thatcher) to the regulation of bargaining systems (as e.g. in the Federal Republic of Germany) to tripartite corporatistic wage policy arrangements (e.g. in the Netherlands and Sweden), to minimum wage legislation (e.g. in France). The determination of wages is of course a central element in the distribution of gains in productivity and thus of shares in the national product and the distribution of welfare. The fact that state intervention here assumes manifold forms and degrees within the political arrangements of welfare states renders industrial relations hard to localize from a state-centred perspective. However, they fit easily in a more comprehensive framework of welfare production.

The Social Welfare Sector

In the relationship between market-controlled and non-market-controlled production, only the services of the social welfare sector are of interest in our context. To begin with we note that, for historical and systematic reasons, this sector is neither a part of the genuine state nor of the genuine market sector. It contains two functional segments – fiscal redistribution and public or non-profit services – that directly aim to improve living conditions. Income redistribution as such is only indirectly related to the idea of welfare production, since it does not actually produce anything. Public and non-profit services may be differentiated in the provision of infrastructure and of personal social services. We focus our attention on personal services as they represent by far the most expensive services in the public welfare sector and partially substitute for unpaid forms of welfare production.

Personal Services

Personal services lack the specific qualities typical of commodities as emphasized by economic theory: they are mobile only to a limited degree, they cannot be stored and they generally depend on the active cooperation of their 'consumers', which is why everyday language calls them clients, students or patients instead (Gartner and Riessman 1974). The limits to the rationalization of personal services are thus very narrow, and the scope for increases in profits due to growth in the size of operations (economies of scale) also remains modest. The distinction between production costs and transaction costs becomes irrelevant, at least at the level of interactive services. Product quality cannot be standardized but remains dependent on the interaction of the persons involved in the individual case. All this is true for paid and unpaid services alike. The transition is typically fluid, as shown for example by reimbursements for volunteer workers or by social insurance payments for family members providing care.

There is thus much evidence that the conventional distinctions made by economics in this field lack any substance. The characteristic of this field is the proximity between the formal and the informal economy. Whether the formal or the informal economy is more advantageous is a matter of perspective: should we rely on differentiated professional services or on 'lay' or, perhaps more precisely, 'amateurish' provision of these services (parents, caring spouses or relatives being amateurs in the original sense of the word)? It is also the case for self-help groups and many associations that the aims officially pursued are embedded in broader social relationships, so that here the participants often receive not only instrumental assistance but also emotional support, which in some circumstances can combine to pursue common interests vis-à-vis third parties. In the 1980s in Germany, the number of psychosocial and health self-help groups alone was estimated at 45,000 (Hondrich and Koch-Arzberger 1992).

Seen from an economic perspective, the distinction between 'utility of transactions' themselves and the 'utility of results' seems helpful. Market theory recognizes only the utility of results: all things that are traded on markets are results of production processes, which turn into consumer or investment goods through third-party use.[3] In personal services, however, production and consumption become inseparable; the utility evolves in the interactive process between the professional and the client, and it cannot be distinguished from the interaction between the participants. This becomes especially clear in consulting processes but is also true for pedagogical and most therapeutic processes: only to the degree that the process itself is experienced as useful (that is, that transaction use arises) can utilities can be expected to go beyond the interactive process. Interest in the utility of results generally dominates in paid service production, but in unpaid services interest in the necessary interaction (the utility of the transaction itself) is often in the foreground (for example, in families or self-help groups).

Paid personal services thus stand in a close complementary or substitutive relationship to informal forms of welfare production (Evers and Olk 1996). This warrants particular attention to differences in quality and to unquantifiable positive and negative side effects that cannot be adequately controlled with the help of legal norms or economic incentives. The participants' personal motives and competencies play a central role here. From the perspective of institutional theory, it is foreseeable that the formation of a common ethos, whether professional, company, group, or family, is of central importance.

To summarize, the field of personal services is substantially larger and more influential for lasting welfare production than is generally supposed (Anheier and Seibel 1990). Welfare state debates mostly address not the overall field but only a variable section of it, one not subject to sufficient investigation in terms of the tension between market and state, whether in regard to efficiency or to ethics. Here, qualitative aspects that have to do with the mutual responsibility of the participants play a central role.

Thus, quite apart from state or market coordination, we can speak here of 'co-ordination by solidarity' (Hegner 1991, see chapter 13).

The special character of social services has also been recognized in the theory of public goods. Here we deal with justifying state interventions, although the services in question do not match the defining characteristics of 'pure' public goods; instead the problem is treated under the term 'merit good'. In principle, the market could control the supply of these services. Under the sole influence of market prices, however, demand would likely be much lower, especially from the lower-income sections of the population. This expectation becomes all the more plausible the more the relative price of personal services rises in relation to the price of goods, as is the tendency owing to services' lower potential for rationalization as the productivity of the manufacture of goods rises.

From the perspective of liberal economic theory, this problem of inadequate demand should not be solved by subsidizing providers or through the public provision of services. If a solution is considered necessary at all, it is seen in income transfers to those with lower incomes, or in benefits in kind. The leading argument for public provision relies on 'distorted preferences', that is, the idea that state interventions are necessary because recipients underestimate the long-term utility of such services and give priority to short-term over long-term needs. However, the distorted preferences argument cannot by itself explain why there should be any intervention in consumer sovereignty. Additional evaluations of the side effects of the neglected need to use these services are required, evaluations transcending the stereotypical actor's horizon of experience. Here, reference is often made to a public interest, for example with regard to the education of future generations (the formation of human capital) or to the avoidance of severe disease and early invalidity, that is, to the expectation of higher costs that would otherwise have to be borne by the general public or by an insurance community. Whether and how such a public interest can be justified is one of the most controversial issues between proponents and critics of the welfare state. Market control can solve only the problem of the allocation of resources, not that of appropriate distribution of goods. Pareto optimality is compatible with extremely variable patterns of distribution of income and goods. The special quality of personal social services has been analyzed also in chapter 6 under the headlines of ecological and personal intervention.

Income Redistribution

Political debate and comparative scientific inquiry about the welfare state do not focus on non-cash benefits and services, but on income subsidies.

However, the priority given to services in kind or to cash transfers differs substantially among welfare states. The Scandinavian states emphasize investment in social services, whereas Germany emphasizes income redistribution.

So-called secondary income distribution is carried out by siphoning off income-dependent levies from primary income; this includes social insurance contributions in addition to direct and indirect taxes. Again, there are substantial international differences in how the social welfare sector is financed. In Sweden, for example, the social budget was until very recently financed almost exclusively by general taxes and to some extent by employers' contributions. On the continent, the social insurance principle prevails, whereby the burden is normally shared among the insured and their employers. The redistributive effect from the rich to the poor is normally stronger when financing occurs through taxes rather than contributions. However, the effect also depends upon the nature of the taxes and the way in which tax laws are implemented.

In German social insurance, for example, pensions paid to the insured individual are based on the amount of contributions previously paid (equivalency principle) and there is no guarantee of a minimum benefit. An international comparison clearly reveals the low weight of need in the assigning of income transfers in the German social insurance system; for example, payments are not related to family status. Accordingly, contribution-financed payments are essentially limited to redistribution between various phases of life or between generations (horizontal redistribution); redistribution between differing abilities to pay or differing degrees of need (vertical redistribution) takes place almost exclusively through tax-financed payments (for example, child benefits, housing subsidies, social assistance). One would expect such a system to produce rather high levels of income inequality, but this seems not to be the case, which points to higher pre–welfare state income equality. Calculations of the Gini Index for standardized household incomes show that, compared to other EU members in 1993, Germany's was the second lowest value. Only Denmark had a more egalitarian income structure (Alber 1998). The interaction of corporate wage policies, tax policy and social redistribution may explain this counter-intuitive effect. The power of trade unions, alongside cultural factors fostering equality, makes wage differentials in Germany rather restricted and income tax rather progressive.[4]

Functionally, social insurance essentially replaces feudal, guild and kinship obligations of solidarity. In pre-industrial times, the essential economic rights of disposal were based on land; as a result, communities at risk depended primarily on the ground rules of the local agrarian system and on land ownership. The disappearance of the feudal system and the privatization of land destroyed this basis of social security, and with the spread of dependent wage labour, the 'free' labour contract prevailed over the patriarchal operating principle. 'Free' contracts expressed not only the freedom of the parties to contract, but also the separation of the work relationship from all other considerations. The principle of 'wages for work' considers neither the state of health nor the family obligations of the worker (see introduction).

The wide variety of organized aid funds in the second half of the nineteenth century was a first attempt, on a money-economy basis, to offer protection against the risks of life now separated from working life, and to form new communities of solidarity. In some countries the state stepped in to protect and subsidize these funds. Contribution-financed social insurance schemes – which, with the exception of Bismarck's earlier workers' insurance, were established in the twentieth century – followed a distinct but similar principle. An alternative can be seen in the tax-financed, exclusively needs-oriented 'people's pension', which was first introduced in Sweden in 1913 to replace the earlier poor relief and has moulded basic old-age security in the Scandinavian states to this day. In 1948, Switzerland introduced an interesting mixed model of needs-oriented but contribution-financed basic security with substantial vertical redistribution; in the wide range of middle incomes the principle of equivalency of contributions and pensions is preserved, while the higher contributions of the wealthy compensate for the otherwise inadequate coverage among those with low incomes.

Along with insuring against income losses due to invalidity and old age, the second problem labour contracts fail to consider is how to finance raising the next generation. This problem was first recognized in France, where experiments with family wages had failed. Regional trans-company family benefit funds were subsequently established, and today, in generalized form, they provide the organizational core structure of the French system of social security. In Germany, the problem of equalizing family burdens as a task for the 'social state' remained a neglected aspect of social policy until the late 1980s; since then, the Supreme Court has ruled repeatedly in favour of family needs. In many European countries there is still little concern about family policy, but the needs-oriented systems of protection against poverty (e.g. in Great Britain) or the concern for gender equality (e.g. in Sweden) may provide equivalents.

A third complex of problems in income security lies in the temporary loss of income among adults due to sickness or unemployment. The situations in question here are less clearly defined than age, invalidity and parenthood, and they are more dependent on the behaviour of the risk-bearer, that is, they are more exposed to 'moral hazard'. At the same time, they are more closely related to the employment relationship and the labour market; indeed, they are greatly influenced by general economic development and by the situation of companies. Here, a multilayered area of overlap between economic and social policy is apparent; but its organization is particularly controversial and thus attracts the most attention in political and economic debates. Most economists' objections to social policy's productivity-inhibiting incentive structures refer to this field alone, although it is small in relation to the entirety of all social welfare measures.

Worker Protection and Industrial Relations

Mostly absent from the international debate is a third aspect of the development of welfare states, the regulation of industrial work, meaning occupational health and safety, the labour contract and the occupational rights of workers. Together with poverty, this was the first field of state intervention for the sake of social welfare, but it developed quite unevenly among nations.

The forerunner of industrialization was Great Britain, which abolished laws forbidding trades union organization as early as 1824; the right to strike was achieved there by 1875. Male workers were granted the franchise between 1867 and 1884. The workers' movement thus developed gradually and experienced the strength of self-help by creating trades unions, friendly societies, cooperatives for various purposes, and eventually its own Labour Party. In the industries employing mainly male workers, labour conditions became regulated through bargaining within local trade boards composed of representatives of employers and workers in a defined trade. Labour legislation remained restricted to child and female labour, and wages were considered to be exclusively a matter of private bargaining. Until the 1980s, the dominant employment pattern remained clearly outside state regulation. Even judicial control remained weak. The same non-intervention pattern developed in the United States, although the labour movement succeeded only temporarily, and only to a limited extent in certain spheres, in gaining strength against the much more ruthless behaviour of American employers. Problems of unemployment were not defined in either country as a collective issue of public concern but remained a problem to be solved solely at the level of business.

In Scandinavia, similarly, industrial relations developed without strong state support. National associations of trades unions and employers formed as early as 1900, and their bargaining patterns set the example for the evolving regulation of labour and wages. Problems of unemployment became defined primarily as a structural problem requiring public intervention. Labour market policies were considered an integral part of welfare policies.

In Germany, by contrast, labour legislation was a dominant issue of social politics from the start. Bismarck was opposed to the regulation of labour as an imposition on industry, which became a lasting political conflict until the First World War and again during the Weimar Republic. Under the pressures of industrial conflicts, the determination of wages also came under public influence. The workers' question (*Arbeiterfrage*) remained the focus of social policy until legislation in the 1950s eliminated the remaining differences between industrial workers and other employees and secured the right to co-determination in industry. The emergence of state regulation of labour and occasionally also wages became central to the development of the German social state, as it also did in most other continental nations. Labour market policies are less developed than in Scandinavia, although some public responsibility for full employment is acknowledged.

This begins to explain why the international concept of the welfare state does not necessarily include the regulation of labour, although it is seen as indispensable from a continental European perspective. Also from the theoretical perspective of welfare production presented above, labour regulation needs to be included. If one sees state intervention as only one route among many in the development of welfare production, than nothing prevents the inclusion of Anglo-Saxon and Scandinavian models of labour regulation through industrial relations in this analytical framework. Labour market and full employment policies affect both working and living conditions of welfare, so it seems reasonable to include them, although they belong more to the realm of economic than of social policy.

Political Arrangements of Social Welfare

It should by now be clear that a theory of the welfare state needs to be more complex than the debate between proponents of liberal 'faith in the market' and the 'believers in the state', both of whom consider themselves socially responsible, allows. The question of income redistribution, central to current disputes, is also only part of the complex issues related to the welfare state. Now it is time to define the welfare state more precisely in terms of the role of the state as well as in terms of criteria for judging redistributive processes. At the same time it must be clear in what respects welfare states differ from other political arrangements of social welfare, such as liberal welfare capitalism or socialist modes of welfare production.

In German constitutional law, Article 20.I of the *Grundgesetz* (Basic Law) defines the German republic as a *sozialer Rechtsstaat*, a social state under the rule of law. This formula is anything but clear, but what has prevailed is the interpretation that the state has a responsibility towards the weak to 'effect their sharing in the economic goods in accordance with the principles of justice and with the goal of ensuring a life with human dignity for everyone' (Zacher 1987/1993: 16). This formula accords with the social-ethical postulate of a common responsibility for the guarantee of equal rights for all, and also fits with the sociological derivation of the inclusion principle as sketched above. According to another classic formulation, the goal of the social state is to guarantee the 'social preconditions for the realization of constitutional freedom' (Böckenförde 1976a: 238) – this version is more closely related to a liberal understanding of the constitution. Similarly in the English-speaking world, according to Girvetz (1968), 'The welfare state is the institutional outcome of a society's assumption of legal and therefore formal and explicit responsibility for the basic well-being of all of its members. Such a state emerges when a society or its decision-making groups become convinced that the welfare of the individual is too important to be left to custom or to informal arrangements and private understandings and is therefore a concern of government.' At the level of international developments, the Council of Europe's Social Charter (1961), the UN International Covenant on Economic, Social and Cultural Rights (1976) and similar EU standards define the goals of public welfare developments.

The formulation of this political, or even constitutional, commitment to individual welfare still says nothing about the methods to be used in its pursuit, or about the extent of direct state intervention; it is in these areas that disagreement often ensues. In the following, I suggest an interpretation of the welfare state that remains as open as possible with regard to different solutions.

Despite differences in detail, certain features shared by all welfare states distinguish them as an independent and modern form of society apart from the liberal type of society approached in the United States of America and from the socialistic type of society in the former Eastern European bloc. The defining properties are (cf. Kaufmann 1997a: 27ff.):

(a) In the sphere of *production*, private property and the entrepreneurial freedom of disposal are preserved. However, these freedoms are limited by the recognized rights of employees and their public protection. The types of limitations that dominate – state bans, tort law, procedural rules, and systems of supervision and negotiation – vary among national welfare states. They differ, moreover, to the extent that they regulate issues of the labour market and promote full employment.

(b) In the sphere of *distribution*, in accordance with the principles of a market economy, primary income distribution is exclusively oriented towards payment for production. The price of labour is determined not only by individual but also by collective bargaining. There is no 'social wage' as in the socialist system. Instead, the primary distribution of incomes is corrected with secondary income distribution based on legislation. This secondary income distribution directly or indirectly ensures a minimum subsistence to those who have no income from capital or labour. National social welfare states differ in the methods of financing these income transfers through taxes or contributions, as well as in the system of entitlements and the organization of the system of social security.

(c) In the sphere of *reproduction*, the services of private households are supplemented and supported by publicly regulated and subsidized or entirely publicly financed services of education, health and social aid. National welfare states differ in the proportions of state, community, private non-profit and business responsibility for the institutions providing services, as well as in the kind and extent of their state financing and legal control.

Of course there are strong links between these three dimensions at the level of individual welfare, and some effects are, in part, mutually substitutive. Others impinge on the welfare production of households, families or networks, which, as we have seen, remain a major form of welfare production.

Seen historically, welfare state development depends on a compromise between employer and union interests, which in many countries has found expression in explicit agreements between employers' associations and unions, often after vehement labour disputes.[5] Seen functionally, welfare states try to combine the advantages of the liberal entrepreneurial economic system with those of more egalitarian access to the economic, social and cultural resources.

The political arrangement of social welfare, which we call the welfare state, differs from the liberal type of welfare capitalism (with the latter's fundamental separation between the state and the market economy) in the former's higher degree of legitimate state intervention; the state is recognized, and so, in principle, is its ability to increase welfare by public intervention. In the paramount 'liberal' case of the United States, the differences from the Western European pattern are essentially due to the weaker idea of the state and the more radical individualism of American culture, which ideas of Roman law and Western metaphysical thought have influenced less. Moreover, it is mostly race and not class that matters in the politics of social inequality in the U.S,[6] where substantial differences in social protection exist between regions and states. Some states, such as Wisconsin, pioneered social policies under European influence. However, the decisions of the Supreme Court worked against most federal interventions. Until now, the United States of America and South Africa are the only developed countries that have not signed the UN International Covenant on Economic, Social and Cultural Rights.[7]

The welfare state differs from the socialistic type of society in its guarantee of the independence of the entrepreneurial function and in the separation of primary and secondary income distribution. Principles of need affect only the secondary income distribution, whereas the primary distribution of incomes is determined by the price of the utility. This links to the underlying difference between these two economic systems. The socialist economy is considered as dominated by a political planning system in which decisions about the distribution of incomes go hand in hand with decisions on the allocation of resources.[8] In welfare states, on the contrary, allocative decisions are free, while the distribution of the resulting incomes is influenced by collective bargaining, taxation and social policies.

Compared to the imaginary pure liberal and socialist forms, the social welfare state form is less elegant, more tension-laden, and also more complex. It proceeds from the idea that it is possible simultaneously to increase individual freedom and collective provisions, that is, the coexistence of the capacities for simultaneous state intervention and spontaneous self-direction. Here, the market and the state are not seen as opposites but as complementary principles of control based on different logics. Freedom is not regarded as a pre-constitutional condition (John Locke), but as the result of political processes forming a constitution and thus institutional givens, which also influence the distribution of opportunities to act.

Sociologically, the hypothesis that political intervention and social self-direction can be increased simultaneously is best specified by relying on a theory of social differentiation of functions. In modernization, societal contexts became differentiated into functionally oriented subsystems that complement each other in their efficient one-sidedness and also provide checks on each other. The development of the market economy and the rise of the modern state are understood as processes of functional differentiation and growing institutional autonomy whereby these two partial systems of society specialize in different problem areas, develop their own institutional patterns and, with the help of their respectively appropriate sciences, their own different logics (see introduction). The tension between the economic sciences on the one hand and the legal and social sciences on the other underscores precisely this real tension in modern societies, a tension that became constitutive with functional differentiation. This tension manifests itself in the rise of 'social problems' and cannot be fundamentally dissolved. Thus the tension between the dynamics of the economic system and the demands of the social welfare system is a constitutive feature of welfare states. It is a permanent challenge for politics to achieve repeated synergies between economic and social policies.

The need to mobilize the state to address problems stemming from the independence of the economic system, problems that resulted from the spread of private property and the institutionalization of economic freedoms, seemed obvious in Europe. Here, in contrast to the United States, the development of the state historically preceded liberalization, and the problems of intensified competition could not be ameliorated by territorial expansion. This mobilization occurred in both paternalistic and democratic states in reaction to similar socio-economic challenges. The development of the welfare state is an essential outcome of the processing of problems that derive from the mutual structural independence of the market economy and the state. Thus the welfare state does not follow a unified logic but instead strives towards a synthesis of differing political, economic, and ethical-social logics. This is why it is typically interdisciplinary and cannot be adequately understood from the viewpoint of a single discipline.

One should therefore speak of a political arrangement of social welfare that takes the form of a welfare state wherever an independent political system is legitimized to react with continuing legal and organizational interventions to the undesired consequences of unfettered competition within the independent economic system. Problematic effects emerge mainly in the working and living conditions of individuals and their families. As a result of these interventions, a social welfare sector arises, controlled by state regulation. In this context, the central political task consists of guiding and moulding the interaction of the four areas – state, economy, social welfare sector and households/families – towards as synergetic (mutually fostering) a relationship as possible (chapter 8).

Is There a Crisis of the Welfare State?

Immediately after the 1973 oil crisis, which ended 'the short dream of everlasting prosperity' (Lutz 1984), a discussion began in the social sciences about the 'crisis of the welfare state'. This discussion has now lasted for more than thirty years and is still going on. The most important diagnoses of the crisis can be typified as follows.

(a) *Fiscal crisis*. The expansion of social expenditure after the Second World War was furthered by a historically unique phase of economic growth, which is petering out as the scope for distribution has been massively reduced. Postponing outstanding distributive conflicts by increasing the governmental debt leads to inflationary pressures, and since the liberalization of financial markets and the intensification of competition between international locations, national freedom of action in labour policy and social policy has been limited. The financial constraints welfare states now face assume various forms depending on the institutional structure of the country's social sectors, but all welfare states face the task of restoring the lost synergy between economic and social policy. To this end, limitations in social services and a restrained wage policy have been proposed.

(b) *Demographically induced crisis*. Throughout Europe, the declining birth rate that has continued throughout the twentieth century with only temporary reversals is leading to a long-term shift in the population's age distribution, enhanced by growing longevity. As a result of welfare-state interventions and of retirement, occupational activity is increasingly concentrated in the age group of 20- to 60-year-olds. This makes social policy dependent on demographic development, which has become one of the most important determinants of the extent of income redistribution. Supported by long-term falls in mortality, especially among the elderly in recent times, in coming decades the share of the retired generations will increase disproportionately at the expense of the occupationally active generations. Most welfare states leave the support of the succeeding generation to families but have widely collectivized the support of the older generation. This not only provides a continued incentive to limit births but also increasingly burdens the systems of social security for age and ill health, thus further intensifying the problems of distribution.

(c) *Crisis of control*. Various arguments support the suspicion that the state is no longer able to make efficient social policy decisions to maintain the prerequisites for a successful arrangement of welfare production. Thus, the 'entitlement society' thesis proposes that democratic systems have a tendency to overextend social expenditures because all parties believe they can gain votes through 'social good deeds'. Marxist theoreticians see in the intensification of distribution conflicts a re-eruption of the basic antagonism between capital and labour. Liberal critics point to undesirable side effects of social welfare state development, effects the political system cannot master, namely a weakening of the work ethic as well as erosion of the family's potential for self-help. They also lament the expenses and inefficiency of administratively controlled services. Critics from the field of political science fear that democratic institutions will be overburdened with demands for decisions ('crisis of governability') or overruled by corporatistic bargaining. In addition, critics from sociology point to the lack of quality and effectiveness in legally and bureaucratically controlled service production.

(d) *Crisis of trust*. Proponents of social services for individual recipients have always underscored their public or collective merits along with their utility. Social policy itself therefore has macroeconomic value, for instance in increasing labour productivity or in stabilizing macroeconomic demand (Vobruba 1989). Its pacifying and socially integrating value is emphasized above all: social policy ameliorates class conflicts and contributes to a just social order, thus increasing the legitimacy of the connection between the state and the market economy. The social welfare state has released 'utopian energies' of hope for a just social order, but these are becoming exhausted under the impact of intensified distributive conflicts (Habermas 1985). Worsened perspectives for the future, especially with regard to security in old age, have led to a loss of trust in state security systems and hence to a loss of solidarity on the part of the younger generations. Disappointed expectations could thus produce mistrust, instead of trust in the problem-solving capacities of politics, and contribute to social disintegration.

Especially taken together, the arguments sketched here suggest a scenario of the collapse of the welfare state – a collapse, however, that has not actually occurred anywhere yet. Financial difficulties and distributive conflicts have increased everywhere, but most welfare states have evinced no substantial signs of political disintegration; even political movements (for example, tax protests) have remained too marginal even to cast doubt on existing constellations of parties. All empirical studies show that the populations have high regard for the central institutions of the social welfare sector as well as a willingness to accept restrictions in their services or increases in contributions in order to ensure these institutions' ability to function. Apparently the institutional integrity of the social welfare sector's institutions is not yet threatened by financial difficulties and cuts in services alone. No self-fuelling process of mutually exacerbating crisis scenarios has begun.

In strongly developed welfare states like Denmark, Sweden and the Netherlands, reforms aimed at reducing services show that the 'welfare state compromise' between employers and unions can also prove itself politically. In Germany, the 'posturing' of representatives of employers' associations and trades unions should not be taken at face value. Nevertheless, before the 1998 parliamentary elections a backlog of overdue reforms had accumulated, not only in the field of laws concerned with social services but also with regard to the financing framework and the clear division of tasks among the federal, state and community levels. Overall, substantial conflicts of interest exist, but there is no sign that these cannot be resolved within the framework of the constitutionally provided political processes.[9]

Despite a wide variety of rhetorics of crisis, there cannot be serious talk of any lasting economic danger to the welfare state arrangement.[10] So far, the conflict between optimal allocation and equalizing distribution, as formulated in economic theory, has not been evident over a long period. Societies organized on democratic and market-economy lines are highly flexible, allowing them to adjust to various institutional solutions to the distribution problem (see Scharpf and Schmidt 2000). Structurally, the distribution conflict is a characteristic of all political arrangements of social welfare; the welfare state should not be confused with a 'land of milk and honey'. Between the end of the Second World War and the 1980s, the development of the welfare state led primarily to an equalization of income and supply conditions, but more recent developments have tended to restore greater socio-economic inequality.

Globalization

The diagnoses of the crisis of the social welfare state have recently received new nourishment from the debate on globalization. In this connection, four different but mutually reinforcing developments have to be distinguished.

1. *Internationalization.* This has to do with the increasing importance of border-crossing transactions. Thus the economy is internationalized by the rising proportion of imports and exports, the population is internationalized by the increased proportion of foreign migrants, public opinion is internationalized under the influence of foreign mass media, and so on.

2. *Globalization* in the narrower sense can be understood as the world moving closer together, operationally and cognitively. This happens on the basis of worldwide technical and institutional standardization. Thanks to technological progress, international agreements and political liberalization, the worldwide networking of information and transportation has decreased transmission times and reduced the importance of spatial distance, so that local events are perceived and become effective worldwide with less and less delay. For the first time in history, routine intercontinental cooperation is emerging – along with conflict situations including environmental problems, human rights conflicts and the international confrontation between wealth and poverty.

3. *Transnationalization.* Increasingly, emerging institutional structures and collective actors transcend national legal systems and thus can no longer be controlled by nation states. This development is especially marked in the field of large firms that merge into multinational corporations and seek optimal combinations of business locations. The emergence of transnational economic relations, especially in the currency and financial markets, clearly reduces the scope for autonomous policy in the respective nation states. This must be distinguished from explicit renunciations of sovereign rights in the context of multilateral agreements in international law, such as the creation and intensification of the European Union or the GATT and WTO agreements. The latter create transnational regimes that typically remain limited to specific functional areas; unlike nation states, these regimes cannot claim any fundamental comprehensive responsibility as the nation state can.

4. *Globalism.* In the sphere of collective cultural representations of the world as a unity of fate, thought and action gain growing credit. The first pictures of the earth as seen from the moon became an icon of the new conscience. The Internet has become an infrastructure for free access to worldwide communication, and social movements such as Attac focus increasingly on matters of global significance. The emergence of the universal ethos of human rights is the moral expression of an emerging solidarity of mankind.

These developments, which have accelerated in recent decades, become problematical against the backdrop of the still prevailing consciousness of sovereign nation-statehood. Under the influences sketched above, the idea of the nation state as a self-governing (democratic) community of shared fate and of responsibility, solidified through the combination of common sociocultural (national) and political (state) characteristics, is becoming less and less realistic. More and more clearly, the various sectors of human coexistence are gaining different spatial and social ranges; in reality, and increasingly in consciousness, they are less and less exclusively bound to the limits of the nation state (Hurrelmann et al. 2008).

Consequences for the Welfare State

In several ways, these developments pose several far-reaching challenges to nation states' responsibility for social welfare:

(a) Since the mobility of capital is much greater than that of labour, liberalization of the commodity and financial markets entails a shift in power relations in favour of capital. This development is further supported by the collapse of socialism. The tension between the dynamics of the rapidly expanding international financial markets and the attempts of individual states to conduct economic and monetary policy in their own interests have also increased capital owners' preference for liquidity; falling interest rates have intensified this still further. Capital has become more site-sensitive and responds more rapidly than before to fiscal burdens, be they taxes or social contributions. This has often thrown existing modes of financing the social sector into question.

(b) Public debt is increasingly less able to ease financial pressure in the social sector, because the inflationary tendencies that public debt unleashes induce the international financial and currency markets to lower the external value of a currency or to raise interest rates. Intensification of internal distributional conflicts is typically unavoidable as a consequence. Conflicts arise, first, over the relationship between the employed and those dependent on transfer income, and second, over the relationship between various groups of transfer recipients, for example pensioners, families, the unemployed and the handicapped. Public arguments leading to consensus are especially lacking in the second type of conflict, because the various forms of social need must be weighed against each other.

(c) As the degree to which the individual groups (e.g. the self-employed, civil servants) are able to escape from redistributive pressure grows, a decrease of solidarity can be expected (see chapter 13). This is also expressed in the deteriorating power of employers' associations and unions to keep and discipline their members and thus in the loss of the binding power of collective bargaining agreements for complete sectors or the economy as a whole. The decreasing power of the nation state favours the revival of regional interests. All these developments concern not simply an individualization of interests, but rather a pluralization of horizons of solidarity. It is becoming clear that the concentration of all collective interests into only the solidarity horizon of the nation state is a historical exception of the last century and a half. However, the ideas of the welfare state that have prevailed until now assume precisely this unified national horizon of solidarity. To the degree that the latter dwindles, cognitive and normative reorientations become necessary; these have already begun here and there but have not yet led to clearly recognizable new structures. In the context of these processes of reorientation, the importance of the nation state is not simply eroded; rather, it becomes focused on a few fundamental decisions.

There is no visible legitimate alternative to the democratic formation of will in the form of state legislation, by means of which rights and duties are defined and the communities of solidarity are constituted. However, these relatively unwieldy procedures are no longer well suited to address the growing complexity of the real situations and the dynamics they later produce. In particular, the processes of European unification will probably involve extremely far-reaching political restructuring that, to increase problem-solving capacity, will end in a separation of the responsibilities and powers of various levels of political decision-making (Leibfried and Zürn 2005). From the perspective of functional efficiency one could argue that regulations in the realm of market-oriented production should operate at the European level, income redistribution at the national level, and regulation of personal services at a regional or local level (see chapter 8). Accordingly, it appears quite conceivable that the facilities of the social sector, too, will fall more clearly under the jurisdiction of various political decision-making levels and that the extent of the state's central regulating activity will be reduced. Thus the nation state's freedom to structure will be limited, but it will not be lost, as is often claimed.

A predictable consequence of European unification is increasing competition over business locations between regions and communities. However, we need not expect these processes of competition to involve prices alone and thus be explicable through conventional economic analysis. On the contrary, immaterial site factors will gain in importance; these include not only such aspects of the quality of life as culture and natural surroundings, but also social peace, infrastructure, the quality of human capital and the security obtained through a well-functioning legal system. Welfare production remains a multidimensional process that will still be controlled by policy, economic decisions, solidarity and associations. Political communities will fare better or worse than others in finding synergetic solutions for economic attractiveness and generalized qualities of life.

For this reason, the components of the existing arrangements of social welfare will not evaporate under the pressure of transnationalization but merely re-order themselves (Leibfried and Pierson 1995). Growth of fiscal and social welfare is contained by the processes of globalization, at least in states with an especially high level of welfare and security. Increasing international competition will probably lead to more equalization of the average level of welfare in wider contexts – for example, continental or intercontinental contexts – while the level of security of the currently leading social welfare states will suffer at least relative losses (P. Pierson 1998). From the perspective of universal ethics, however, these developments must be welcome even if they are painful for the populations or population sections affected. In this context one has to expect an intensification of distributional conflicts and an increase in social inequality, both at the level of interpersonal patterns of distribution and at the regional level. These two dimensions of inequality, however, remain contingent. The degree of interpersonal redistribution is more dependent on cultural and political factors than on economic ones.

It would be short-sighted to turn the growing opportunities for reduced solidarity into an argument for the legitimacy of greater inequalities, for legitimacy cannot be merely a question of power relations (Habermas 1992). Rather, the fear that the welfare concern of politics fosters paralysis – as expressed by economic liberals – is arguably losing importance as the balance of power tips from politics to the markets. The danger of the foreseeable future no longer appears to be political but economic overconfidence.[11] Politics still faces great disappointments. It will have to learn to make decisions suitable to meet the future under more difficult conditions than any since the Second World War. Politics of the future will resemble the attempt to steer a sailboat dependent on fair winds more than the command of a steamer dependent on the power of its own engine.[12] It is the task of social science to redefine and to explore empirically the boundaries between the dynamics of markets and their social consequences in a multi-tiered political system.

Notes

1. The development of the doctrine of human rights has evident sources in the teachings of the Christian gospel and its impact on European history; see chapter 3. For the different development of social policies in the Confucian context see Rieger and Leibfried (1999).
2. This idea is not new. It was Richard Titmuss who, under the title 'The Social Division of Welfare' (1958), introduced the differentiation of institutional welfare into social services, fiscal welfare and occupational welfare, which approximates the differentiation discussed in the next section.
3. Consequently Adam Smith considered most services, including government, as nonproductive (see Smith 1979: vol. 2, 3).
4. Pension reform and tax policies as well as labour market policies in the first decade of the twenty-first century suggest a reversal of this trend, i.e. growing income inequality. It remains to be seen how strong the overall statistical effect of these changes in legislation will become.
5. The earliest of these agreements was the September Agreement in Denmark (1900); other important agreements were the Stinnes Legien Agreement (1918) at the start of the Weimar Republic, the Swiss Metal Industry Agreement (1937), and the Swedish Saltsjöbaden Agreement (1938). The French Accord de Matignon (1936) failed, whereas the Accords de Grenelle (1968) still contribute to pacifying class conflict, which in French history was more bitter than anywhere else in the West. In recent times the Akkoord van Wassenaar (1982) has built foundations for quite successful revisions of welfare politics in the Netherlands.
6. Substantial overviews of the American politics of welfare can be found in Weir, Orloff and Skocpol (1988b) and in Noble (1997).
7. For the history of this covenant and the withdrawal of the United States, see Köhler (1987: 924ff.).
8. For descriptions of the economic and the social welfare system of the USSR, see Madison (1968), Osborn (1970) and Lane (1985).
9. Events since this was written confirm this assessment.
10. This is also the conclusion of most serious inquiries into the question, see e.g. Pfaller, Gough and Therborn (1991); Esping-Andersen (1996); P. Pierson (1996); Alber (1998).
11. This guess was impressively confirmed by the crisis in the financial markets in 2008.
12. On naval metaphors of polities and politics see Leibfried (2009).

Part IV

The Future of
the Welfare State

Chapter 11

THE WELFARE STATE'S ACHIEVEMENTS AND CONTINUING PROBLEMS

This account of the welfare state's evolution so far presents it mainly as a success story – in striking contrast to the many criticisms and fears expressed about it. These have been increasing since around 1975, roughly the time of the first oil crisis and the end of the Bretton Woods international exchange system dominated by the U.S. dollar. These last chapters examine the principal challenges facing the welfare state: not only changes in economic structure, demographic shifts, globalization and regulatory issues around the mixed economy of welfare, but also the cultural and scientific challenge of dealing with the growing complexity of demands for welfare policies. This chapter starts by summarizing the basis of the welfare state's achievements and then shows why further success cannot be expected from a mere continuation of the hitherto state-centralized arrangements for welfare production. Beyond the perspective of redistribution, new perspectives on equity emerge that need to be integrated in order to understand the challenges of the future.

Conditions for the Success of Welfare State Provisions

To what can one ascribe the historic achievements of the development of the European welfare state, whose provisions are also being increasingly adopted by rapidly growing economies even outside Europe? Generally speaking, only individual factors are identified, which on their own cannot explain such a fundamental and long-lasting transformation of society as the development of the European welfare state. It is precisely the interaction of political, economic, cultural and social consequences that account for the welfare state's evolutionary advantage.

The chief consequence of state guarantees of social rights is the secure inclusion of wider sections of the population in all the principal services society offers. It means universalizing the right to access to all the important opportunities for social life. It is widely assumed that this corresponds to the basic moral intuitions of modern diversified societies and thus contributes to citizens' basic loyalty to their commonwealth. This assumption would not be sustainable, however, if the promotion of individual welfare did not in general contribute to the functioning of the economy, the polity and the family under the conditions of rapid social change.

Economic Benefits

While the market production of welfare depends on the participation of paid labour and the availability of capital, and the results are distributed solely in relation to the scarcity of the factors of production, intervention by social policies aims to guarantee access to the means of existence even for those who for a variety of reasons do not contribute to paid work or are restricted in their ability to do so (e.g. because of age, disability, parenthood, or limited skills or inappropriate qualifications). Beyond that, it aims at development (through educational provision) or renewal (by health services) of competences that can be productively exploited.

The welfare sector's services functionally complement those of the market economy. They depend on the market system's productive abilities, since welfare benefits are chiefly financed from its output through taxes and contributions. However, the social services contribute significantly to the productive efficiency of the market economy by improving the creation of human capital, protecting the labour force against premature exhaustion, promoting readiness to work and maintaining or even raising labour productivity. This is particularly true of the roles of the education and health services, as well as labour market policies and safety at work, but it also applies to family and housing policy because families are the principal investors in human capital. It is even the case for pensions policy, since security in old age should not be underestimated as a motive force for the employed workforce. Social policy thus has an economic value, but one that is apparent only from the perspective of the national economy – not of business, since social policy either hinders or compensates for the negative externalities of the private capitalist mode of production. At the same time, and through family and educational policy in particular, it stabilizes the formation of human assets as a precondition of both private and social productivity (see chapter 12). In addition to its significance for the performance of the national economy in the long term, social policy also has an economic function through its effect on the stabilization of demand, though this is a question of the degree of social redistribution, an argument used chiefly by the employees' side and thus valid only with qualifications.

The profitability of the social welfare sector for the national economy does not exclude the possibility that from a microeconomic perspective the burdens of social expenditure may be seen as disadvantageous. A majority of social policy interventions are legitimated in terms of being public goods; they are system-rational and in that sense are in the interest of all, but because of their intrinsic qualities the costs and benefits cannot be clearly balanced against each other. However, this applies to only a small part of all public goods in the strict sense, that is, to those services that, because of characteristics such as the indivisibility of their production or consumption, can only be produced by the state. More common are the so-called merit goods, whose production or consumption gives rise to external benefits that derive simply from their utility to individual consumers. The classic example is the formation of human assets: the utility of education lies not only in what pupils find interesting or worthwhile to learn in school, but in the qualifications they will come to value and on which the national economy depends.

The concept of merit goods, originally described by the scholar of public finance Richard A. Musgrave (1959), has developed in disparate ways. Economists such as Head (1969) trace the meritorious character of the goods back to invalid individual preferences. From the perspective here, however, the decisive issue is the relevance of externalities, that is to say, the effects of economic goods on other social sectors, as mediated by the individual who benefits or suffers from them. So negative externalities (such as premature exhaustion of the workers) are tackled by social policy measures, and conditions and competences are promoted to create system-rational collective benefits in addition to individual benefits (see chapter 8). And in a further sense the added benefits also derive from the consequences of the welfare state's political, cultural and social arrangements, which will be discussed below.

A rather indirect but plausible connection seems to exist between the extent of social protection and the openness of national economies in the process of globalization (Rieger and Leibfried 2001). Whereas in the United States the external threats to profits and employment are countered by demands and measures for economic protection, Europe's economies opt more for open markets as they depend substantially on external markets for their growth. Social protection then operates to absorb risk for those who find themselves among the losers from international competition.

Political Benefits

The contemporaries of great social reforms were impressed above all by their political value. Most great social reforms arose from highly stressed situations seized as challenges by political actors. Thus the earliest welfare statist legislation, the English Poor Laws (1597 and 1601) of Queen Elizabeth I, was a constructive response to the problem of vagabond beggars who had been treated as a plague throughout Europe since the late Middle Ages, and whom the rulers of the time tried to control, chiefly by repressive measures.[1] The Bismarckian social insurance legislation of 1881–1889 complemented the (anti-)Socialist Law of 1878, aiming 'to instil, even in the unpropertied classes of the population who are at present the most numerous and lest educated, the perception … that the State is not only a necessary but also a benevolent institution'.[2]

The conciliatory (because socially integrative) aspect of welfare statist development becomes more apparent in the historical agreement between the employers' organizations and the trades unions that in many countries underpinned the 'compromise over the welfare state'. Thus in Denmark in September 1899, the recently established national associations of both sides united in an agreement after the longest and most bitter labour conflict in Danish history. This agreement stipulated mutual recognition of partnership in wage negotiations, the regulation of strikes and lockouts, and a fundamental obligation to negotiate peacefully. On the one hand, the unions acknowledged employers' right to manage business and the division of labour, and accepted the duty of influencing their members in the spirit of increasing labour discipline. On the other hand, the employers were required to abandon the pressure of piecework rates and to reinstate all employees in their previous positions after strikes. Plant disputes were to be subject to conciliation, and to arbitration in the event of crisis. The ordinary judicial system was declared competent to adjudicate breaches of the agreement. In particular, it was also agreed that individual unions or employers could not withdraw from their obligations under the agreement by resigning from the national federations (Hepple 1986: 383ff.). The Danish government immediately endorsed this so-called September Agreement, many of its clauses were later absorbed into legislation.

Similar arrangements were agreed in Sweden (in 1906 and then in the Saltsjöbaden Agreement of 1938) and in Switzerland (the peace agreement in the metals and horological industries, 1937). In Germany, the Stinnes-Legien Agreement of 1918, an important prerequisite for the Weimar Constitution, failed under the pressure of the adverse events of the time. The wage agreements and joint negotiation laws, and the acknowledgement in principle of the 'social market economy' by the trades unions in the 1950s, can nevertheless be seen as aspects of a 'compromise over the welfare state' (Kaufmann 1998: 90ff.). The Atlantic Charter of 1941, which Roosevelt and Churchill proclaimed at the time of the Axis powers' principal war achievements, must also be noted – along with its consequences (chapter 4). It was meant to strengthen people's will to resist by shaping hopes for a peaceful post-war social order under the Allies' rule.

German scholarship about social policy placed great emphasis on its socially integrative significance, following the seminal ideas of Lorenz von Stein. According to the Marxist interpretation, the ruling classes used social policy to induce the loyalty of the masses, a motive nowadays often described as Bonapartist.[3] But democratic majorities, too, produced and drove forward social policies as the expression of a pacification of class conflicts, and it was by no means only left-wing majorities that brought about welfare statist developments, since in many countries Christian-Social movements became decisive, negating the fundamental character of class conflict (Kersbergen 1995). Whatever inevitable reservations must be expressed about individual motives, it is clear that the pacification of industrial conditions and the expansion of the social sector are in fact closely related to political stability, as the social developments of the last fifty years have shown. The trades unions succeeded in contributing significantly to the occupational and political discipline of wide sections of the population, on whose allegiance the problem-free functioning of the existing system depends. In most countries they have not used their powers in a spirit of opposition to economic expansion, but rather more significantly they have taught employees to accept each further change in working conditions, something productivity-oriented economic modernization cannot avoid. This is not to assert any cause-and-effect relationship; rather, the composition of the welfare state as an effective market economy, political democracy and evolving social policy and/or expanded social sector represents a specific type of emergent society, the preconditions of whose stability deserve more detailed examination.

Cultural Significance

The model of a community that offers its citizens guarantees of freedom, equality under the law and solidarity through the interaction of market economy and the social state has developed only at the level of Western European societies whose culture was patterned on Christianity and the Enlightenment. This model did not, however, exist at the beginning of the welfare state's evolution, but grew considerably following the first national measures to protect children working in factories. The practical results of the state's almost wholly piecemeal interventions gave legitimacy to further state interventions. Despite this, the pragmatic use of piecemeal measures lacking any principled value-oriented basis was not enough to give any particular direction to welfare statist developments. Considerations of potential benefits naturally also played some role in social reform, but their results were not always immediately apparent, and short-term considerations not infrequently led to repressive measures. Most social reformers drew chiefly on moral convictions, and the dominant legitimation remained moralistic as a rule. The source of these efforts to protect the weak and ensure the minimum conditions of existence for all (to name only two core moral forces driving social policy) lay in the Western tradition of Christian and humanitarian beliefs (see chapter 3).

Eduard Heimann was foremost in emphasizing the key significance of the 'common ideal' held by two social classes: the bourgeoisie and the working class. Christian beliefs and the memory of more 'communal' ways of living acted as powerful correctives to Enlightenment individualism. 'Liberalism surmounts itself by means of the social movement growing on its own soil' (Heimann 1929/1980: 140). It was this shared value orientation – or, more precisely, the occidental ideas of justice – that gave social policy its thematic direction and made social reform ready for agreement in principle, regardless of all contrary interests. Where such levelling ideas of equity did not apply (for instance in U.S. culture, characterized by beliefs blending predestination with social Darwinism), public concern for the welfare of all citizens only evolved rather later and in a relatively rudimentary manner. The ideal of a welfare state thus became a constitutive element of the underlying normative consensus of European countries, which is also apparent in the guarantee of cultural and social rights by constitutions and international treaties.

Social Significance

It is striking that the conceptual history of the word 'social' is closely tied up with the development of the welfare state (see chapter 2). The word 'social' was used quite early in contradistinction to 'political' or even to 'economic', and invariably contained a double meaning of both description and prescription, which is also characteristic of the concept of 'order'. A 'social' order is, in terms of interpersonal relations, a harmonious one; it implies agreement and satisfaction. Insofar as 'social' has developed as a critical concept, it refers chiefly to the moral and communicative deficits of the new industrial and financial economy, to its calculating nature, its anonymity and its 'non-humanity'. 'System integration' and 'social integration' increasingly diverge and justify this by reference to the conditions for their maintenance.[4] Consequently, social policy is typically torn between the demands of system integration and social integration, a tension expressed for instance in the growing criticism of its juridification or bureaucratization (already Achinger 1958).

From the perspective of social theory, the particular significance of social policy lies in its implications for maintaining the reproduction and regeneration of human resources required by the various parts of the social system (see chapter 12). The working of all parts depends on the ability and intentions of the individuals who interact under the leading assumptions of different partial systems and who maintain their particular effectiveness. The social distress of early industrialization consisted precisely in the fact that for the mass of the population, the conditions of housing, income and disposable time did not allow for family life. This aspect of the social question was articulated mainly in France and thus lastingly affected the form of French social policy (Schultheis 1988). Social policy's multifaceted contributions to the reproduction and regeneration of human resources range from personal social services to education, family and housing policy to social security policies, since the availability of income even in the event of inability to work is a basic precondition for any kind of household management. In the past, the effectiveness of social policy depended on the assumed normality of family roles legitimating women's duties as unpaid housework and child-rearing. The development of human resources depends not only on family conditions and educational provisions, but also on a wide range of voluntary associations that are often identified as an independent sector of welfare production (see chapter 8).

Summary

To summarize this section, the welfare state's evolutionary advantages can be explained by the interaction of economic, political, cultural and social forces, which mutually reinforce and stabilize each other. These can be typified briefly as follows:

1. From the point of view of culture, social policy contributes to ensuring generalized reciprocity, meaning a social system perceived as

basically fair and just, and thereby enhances the legitimacy of the current relations between state and society.

2. From a political perspective, social policy has pacifying effects in that it reduces class conflict and generally transforms antagonistic interests into more productive modes of conflict resolution.

3. An economic viewpoint is that social policy enhances human capital formation, develops working capacities and contributes to raising labour productivity.

4. From a social perspective, social policy guarantees the social conditions of welfare production by stabilizing the sphere of private life in which the various aspects of society responsible for the reproduction and regeneration of human resources are located.

The decisive test of this argument is the *synergy* and *mutual complementarity* of these effects. Successful social policy interventions do not affect only one part of the social system; rather, in the light of the functional differentiation of modern societies, they are *multifunctional*. This follows not least from social policy's direct effects on the population's level of living, which for its part maintains the range of interactions with the organizations and operations of society's various parts. Its evolutionary advantage and thereby its position in social theory lie precisely in the fact that it compensates for the negative effects of processes that nowadays are summarized under the heading of modernization, without calling into question the structural differentiation connected with these processes.

This analysis has focused solely on social policy's generally positively evaluated effects and tried to elaborate their interactions, in order to emphasize the centrality of welfare statist development for modern social transformation. In the context of welfare statist development, these were and are usually discussed under the heading of industrialization. But industrialization was only the first stage of the modernization process, which today continues in the transition to a 'post-industrial' or 'service' or 'knowledge' economy. A key driving force of the continuing process is, by contrast, the growing structural independence of the sections of the social system that social theory interprets as functionally specialized. This 'disembedding' (A. Giddens) of organized social systems and their allocation to particular conceptual fields, such as the economy, politics, religion, science or mass communications, releases internal dynamics that distance their interactive communications from their original lifeworld aims (Schimank 2007; see also introduction). Thereby the social system's parts simultaneously gain particular capabilities but also a particular irresponsibility towards their environment, one that affects the lives of individuals playing their various roles. This internally dynamic systemic autonomy (which, with respect to the economic system, Karl Marx was the first to analyse critically, in his *Critique of Political Economy*) is not, however, held up by social policy measures. Even when these aim and operate as correctives, particularly to the consequences of economic dynamics, they may also release internal forces of their own in the form of competition for power, as a tendency to cost expansion, or in resistance to change and in the declining 'social' efficiency of services.

The Maturation of Welfare State Systems

The idea that the welfare state has reached its limits and that the expansion of social services cannot go further is increasingly, though reluctantly, accepted even by champions of the welfare state project. The proportion of GDP devoted to expenditure on social protection, the so-called social benefit quota, has grown considerably in the post-war period. A variety of theoretical explanations have been offered for this expansion, as well as for the growth of the public sector by comparison with the whole of the private market sector (Hood 1994). I shall forgo debate over highly abstract explanatory models and stick instead to the observable fact that in most countries since the 1970s, government attempts to restrain social expenditure have intensified. In particular, broadening the spectrum of social services by creating new social programmes or expanding existing ones has become markedly less common. Notwithstanding this political reluctance, and despite renewed attempts to cut costs or even reduce services, efforts so far to reduce the share taken by social expenditure have enjoyed little success (P. Pierson 1994). The inevitable assumption, then, is that there are inherent reasons why these programmes lead to increasingly disproportionate cost expansion that can only be brought under limited control by cost-cutting measures.

The sociological significance of these facts is discernible in three explanatory patterns:

1. The first explanation assumes that the development of the welfare state represents a particular historical phase leading to the creation of important social policy programmes that appear to resolve problems and diminish the scale of unresolved social problems. The pressure of social problems is reduced or hidden within others that are not seen as falling within the ambit of the welfare sector – within environmental problems, for instance. *Growth to Limits*, the title of the most ambitious comparative project of welfare state research

(Flora 1986), can serve as a catchphrase to interpret this 'optimistic' position.

2. A second position, often conceptualized as advancing the Marxist theory of crisis, assumes a crisis of the welfare state. This position ascribes the welfare state's success not simply to the actual social services but rather to the nature of its programme to create a society 'free from fear and want' (F.D. Roosevelt). The more it appears that the welfare state is incapable of overcoming the capitalistic character of the economy and itself depends on capitalist accumulation, and the less that the hopes raised for well-being, justice and security for all can be satisfied, the greater its loss of legitimacy. With the 'exhaustion of its utopian energy' the welfare state loses its political function of establishing loyalty and solidarity and thus its indispensable political support; that is, the 'critical' position (e.g. Habermas 1985).

3. A third interpretation recently gaining in influence sees the welfare state as a mainly successful solution to the problems of their time, but one whose effectiveness is declining because of further events occurring in the course of time, some independently and some as the consequence of welfare state developments. The institutional forms of the social sector were consequently the solutions to the social problems of particular periods, but they cannot be seen as applicable for all time, and the 'ageing' of welfare state provisions has to be taken into account (Jessop 1994). This historically aware position is considerably more complex by comparison with the other two positions, but in my view it is more appropriate for better understanding current difficulties and the need for change in the nature of the social state.

The following section briefly sketches the principal changes in order to question the problem-solving effectiveness of welfare state provisions so far.

Industrial Manufacture's Loss of Significance and Service Production's Gain

Jean Fourastié (1949) developed a theory of continued structural change of the employed population that depends on two explanatory factors: rising labour productivity on one side, and the saturation of demand for goods on the other. Before industrialization, about 80 per cent of the labour force were employed in the primary sector (agriculture, raw materials), but industrialization brought increasing opportunities for work in the secondary sector, as well as growth in productivity, which reacted with the primary sector, where demand became more and more saturated. With the transition to mass production and its increased automatization, labour became increasingly displaced by capital in the secondary sector, a development already foreseen by Marx. As demand for industrial production approached its limits, especially after the Second World War, employment increasingly shifted to the sphere of services. To the extent that the development of the welfare state's provisions led to the expansion of person-centred services such as education, health and personal social services, it itself contributed forcefully to this shift.

The societal policy implications of this drive towards a tertiary economy have received insufficient attention so far.[5] They express themselves first in changes in the nature of work and growing demand for workers' skills and qualifications. The dominance of large-scale manufacture predicted by Marx was shown not to be history's last word.[6] Instead, the importance of the industrial labour force is declining both quantitatively and politically. Workers in the newly developing service occupations have a more limited class consciousness and are harder for trade unions to organize. The classic coalition between social democracy and the trades unions thus lost significance, just as did the religious social influences that had hitherto stabilized the conservative political parties. The professionalization and individualization of occupational aspirations connected with the trend towards a tertiary economy do not call into question the need for social security, but rather the standard uniform provision typical of existing state social programmes. Increased demand for qualifications raises employers' interests in highly motivated, flexible and dependable workers, tied to their employment by higher-than-negotiated wage rates and fringe benefits. This reduces the importance of state social provisions for this section of the labour force on which the rest of the population increasingly depends.

A further consequence of the tertiary sector's growth is the growing importance of female labour force participation. In agriculture and manual crafts women were predominantly occupied as family members helping their fathers and husbands. Women's employment in industry and service occupations remained concentrated mainly in the period before marriage. The expansion of office occupations and personal services, combined with women's growing educational participation, widened their occupational perspectives and led to long-term attitudinal change – the combination of family care and paid work has increasingly become the ideal for women's careers.

Finally, reference must be made to an indirect consequence of the sector-specific differences in productivity growth. By comparison with the primary and secondary sector, services become increasingly more expensive as pressures for rationalization become stronger, since they cannot be correspondingly rationalized. This is particularly the case for the skilled personal social services that dominate the social sector. Human interactions set strict limits to the scope for their technical rationalization, resulting in an unavoidable tendency towards cost increases in the spheres of education, health and social welfare services, at any rate as long as considerable deterioration in service quality is not acceptable. It is no accident that these spheres are increasingly financed by public money and subject to public regulation, even if in principle private market provision were possible. Without public regulation, for example in the framework of compulsory insurance, large sections of the population would be excluded from these services because they were unable to pay for them.

Growing International Entanglement

The nineteenth-century economy was a national economy. Overseas trade was mainly carried out in the context of colonial rule, and even between the rich nations trade in goods remained limited. Not until decolonization after the Second World War and the liberalization of international trade was the global market formed; that is, intercontinental trade lost its political boundaries and became focused on market conditions alone. The international integration of flows of capital and goods (and also of services such as tourism and electronic data communication) has intensified greatly in recent decades, and this development is likely to accelerate further. To the extent that the most developed economies suffer from competitive pressure from nations with cheap labour, which is increasingly the case owing to the industrialization of the developing nations and the collapse of the Iron Curtain, the economies of the welfare states are under growing pressure to make structural changes. Traditional branches of production lose their importance and have to be superseded by new lines. This gives rise to a displacement of job profiles in the labour force; the proportion of jobs demanding high qualifications increases, while at the same time less skilled jobs are reduced. International competition thus accelerates the trend towards the tertiary economy and simultaneously, if structural change is not successful, threatens a country's level of employment.

In the long run, national economic policy's growing dependence on developments in the international currency and capital markets is even more influential. Since the 1980s, the proliferation of links between financial organizations operating internationally has circumvented the regulatory capacities of capital markets, and in addition, state regulation of capital transfers has been abolished in many countries. Investment decisions in one country nowadays no longer depend only on internal tax and liquidity conditions but also on investment opportunities elsewhere. Since investment decisions are based on profit expectations, an investment for which funds are available will be made only if no higher returns can be expected from the international money or capital markets. This is why national Keynesian economic policies aimed at full employment are no longer generally effective (Scharpf 1987).

In almost all the countries in which welfare statist development has taken place, it has led to an increase in the importance of the national or central government, and in Europe nationalism dominated political developments from the beginning of the nineteenth century to the second half of the twentieth. With the formation of larger political units following European integration and comparable regional associations in other parts of the world, and also as a result of the growing interweaving of global markets referred to above, nation states have lost the ability to control the conditions of their own economic development autonomously. Moreover, sub-national (regional) units' interest in their own economic development is growing. Thus the level of the national state's management suffers from competition at both the supranational and lower levels. This does not necessarily result in a reduction of social services, but it is obvious that the influence of the sociopolitical coalitions is decreasing, whereas liberal economic influences have increased at the transnational levels of the European Union and the World Trade Organization. Thus the national state as a welfare state is even more strongly driven to react against the liberalized regional or even global economic tendencies it cannot control. The structural conditions for the pursuit of coherent welfare state policies have worsened. The mobility of capital and the private wealth of rich individuals have risen. The state's ability to impose levies on incomes in the form of taxes or contributions is restricted by the growing mobility of capital, and perhaps also because of rising tax resistance and evasion.

Changes in Gender Roles and the Break-up of the Welfare State's 'Silent Reserve Army'

Domestic enterprises dominated pre-industrial economies, generally in the context of the wide-ranging rule of the male head of household over wife and children as well as servants. Not until the legal reforms in the wake of the French Revolution were other household members accorded a civil status in their own right, which coincided with the first effects of early industrialization facilitating a wider range of occupations beyond the domestic sphere. The dissolution of the domestic economy, together with the civil conception of marriage as a legal association between two equal partners nevertheless distinguished by sex into 'different beings', led to the role model of 'married housewife', one that was typical of family law in the civil codes of the nineteenth and early twentieth centuries. This complementary allocation of male roles to occupational career and the public sphere, and female roles to domesticity and the private sphere, appeared almost as social progress, to the extent that it tended to free women in the lower social classes from the demanding and often humiliating double burden of gainful employment and housework. This gender-related division of labour also contributed to stabilizing the family and improving the socialization of the younger generation. Among male workers it became a matter of pride to earn enough so that their wives would no longer have to go out to work. At the same time, it meant the codification of gender distinctions as unequal social relationships, and thus the exclusion of women from rapidly evolving spheres of modern life.

Evolving social policy consolidated the housewife role as the typical normal form of female existence, particularly in Germany. Statutory sickness insurance treated the married woman as covered by her husband's income-related contributions. Even the 1957 pension reforms took for granted the retention of an unrestricted widows' pension, modelled on the public employees' scheme, which presupposed the non-employment of wives. A universal child benefit was introduced by the National Socialist government on primarily demographic grounds, and for that reason it was abolished by the Allied occupation powers. When a child benefit of DM 25 per month for the third and each subsequent child was introduced on a federal basis in 1954, it was based on the assumption that a male wage was sufficient to keep a family with two children. Bringing up the next generation was self-evidently the task of the family, or more precisely the mother, who for this reason was to be released from paid work. The earlier welfare state provisions thus depended on particular assumptions about normality, such as men's permanent employment, possibly together with sporadic employment by women, the normality for both sexes of marriage and family, and a division of labour within the family on the housewife model.[7]

What may have passed as progress in the nineteenth century became, in the context of rising living standards after the Second World War, a handicap on the unfolding of women's emancipation. In the last sixty years, women have won enormous increases in educational and occupational opportunities and prospects, and thus in independent living. Elisabeth Beck-Gernsheim (1983) succinctly described the change in attitudes associated with this as 'from being there for others to having a right to a bit of life of one's own'.

Between 1970 and 1990 in the Federal Republic of Germany, for example, the proportion of married women aged 30–34 in employment rose from 39 per cent to 58 per cent, while that of women aged 45–49 rose from 41 per cent to 61 per cent, and the trend continues upwards (Klauder 1992: 437). However, only one third of all mothers of two or more children are in employment, since considerable obstacles remain as in the past, such as a shortage of child care and after-school facilities. Germany ranked at the extreme end of the EU scale on this specific aspect of family policy, along with Greece, Italy and Portugal (Kaufmann 1993: 151ff.). At the cross-national comparative level, Germany belonged (together with Ireland and the Netherlands) among those countries whose social policy provisions have until recently treated women to a considerable extent as committed to family care and dependent on their husbands. Newer and more comprehensive research at the OECD level confirms that only Japan and Luxembourg are less modernized in their gender relations, and that family policies in Germany are shaped to inhibit mothers' participation in the workforce (Künzler 2002: 270, 280).

In the face of this tension between desire and reality, it is not surprising that the proportion of women remaining permanently childless in Germany has grown rapidly (see chapter 12). Women seem increasingly less prepared to be the welfare state's silent reserve army and to put up with the disadvantages of parental responsibility on their own. As Künzler's study shows, there is a general correlation between lower fertility and the dominance of traditional patterns in gender roles, as well as with inhibitory and inactive family policies (Künzler 2002: 285).

The growing independence of women also affects the decline in marriage and the increase in divorce. This goes together with a pluralization of lifestyles, of which three kinds may be distinguished: child-oriented forms, partner-oriented forms and living on one's own (Kaufmann 1990/1995: 148ff.). In many circles the institution of marriage has lost its binding nature and hence is often strategically chosen or rejected in the light of its legal effects. Thus the norms of labour and civil law influence the private circumstances of life far more than previously, and often in ways unintended by legislators and indeed in opposition to the aims of statute.

How Far is the Welfare State Author of its Own Problems?

It is clear that the changes referred to above did not develop independently of the circumstances in which the welfare state developed, but the connection as a whole is nevertheless a strictly indirect one. The changes affect even countries that did not pursue the welfare state project. Here, the question must remain open whether and how far they have coped with these changes better or worse than the mature welfare states have done. The capabilities of governments and the conditions for forming national consensus are probably far more influential in coping with the challenges of social change than are the peculiarities of the regime of welfare production.

Given the developments sketched, it is likely harder to pursue welfare policies today than it was in the first few decades after the Second World War, but they do not yet show any essential need for abolition or adaptation. The fact that demonstrably there are financial limits to the expansion of the social sector is not in itself a symptom of crisis in the welfare state. The limitless nature of compensation needs may seem plausible (Luhmann 1981a), but empirical research shows that the population as a whole has a generally realistic and moderate approach to the welfare state.[8] Because the costs of the social sector are mainly financed by taxes and contributions to the national budget, the available resources are structurally dependent on the workings of the economy. This dependency is structured in various ways in different countries, depending on their financial regimes, but they are ineluctable. Some countries try to gain more room for manoeuvre by raising borrowing and increasing the public debt, but even these tactics run up against ever stricter limits, chiefly under the pressure of reduced economic growth and EU fiscal rules. In addition, much evidence indicates that inflation burdens the socially weakest most, so even from a social policy perspective the idea of solving public expenditure problems with inflation has to be treated with reserve.

As several studies at different points in time have shown, there is no systematic relationship between the levels of social expenditure and of national debt. Obviously some countries manage to balance their national economies even in spite of conspicuous social provisions, treating increases in social expenditure as merely one factor among others.

A somewhat outdated but comprehensive attempt, through cross-national comparative research, to analyse welfare statist development has come to the even more far-reaching conclusion that what economists in particular have proclaimed as the contradictions between employment security and labour productivity, between social expenditure and capital investment, and between income levelling and economic growth, cannot be demonstrated empirically. In practice it appears to be the case that strongly corporatist countries with high levels of social expenditure are also generally also more economically successful.[9] The relative level of social expenditure (the social quota) is primarily dependent on the attained affluence level. If the analysis is confined to economies with relatively similar affluence levels, the key explanatory variables appear to be the maturity of the social welfare system and the proportion of elderly in the population. Neither dominant political tendencies nor the structure of prevailing political systems seem to have any lasting influence (Wilensky 1985: 6ff.).

Later research, however, suggests that in recent times national economies with highly developed market-oriented approaches are better able to combat rising unemployment in the current context of growing global influences. A complex comparison of national ranking shows that between 1980 and 1991, the most economically successful countries were those with the most developed welfare systems. However, deterioration is noticeable as of 1991, particularly among the Nordic states, since the types of active labour-market policy used until then were clearly no longer effective in slowing the growth of unemployment, and public expenditure levels reached critical heights. Even so, these studies clarify that the relative levels of public expenditure and also of taxes and contributions have only a relatively limited influence on economic success, in the same way as national debt levels. The greatest impact is ascribed to social and fiscal stability, followed by the degree of activity of labour market policy, particularly in raising qualification levels; even economic growth exceeds fiscal factors in influence (Schröder and van Suntum 1996).

The most comprehensive study of the politics of adjustment in OECD countries from 1970 to 1997 came to the following conclusion:

> In short, the policy legacies that advanced welfare states are carrying forward from the defining choices of the early postwar period – which, in turn, were often path-dependent extrapolations from structural features that had already been in place at the end of nineteenth century – have come to have much greater importance for their international economic viability than was the case a few decades ago. While it is true … that the size of the welfare state as such, or the overall tax burden, has no negative impact on economic performance, international competitiveness or employment levels, it is equally true that the specific shape of national welfare-state institutions and programs, and in particular the different ways in which the welfare state is paid for, have greatly gained in economic importance. At the same time, however, the fact that these characteristics have an effect on international economic competitiveness adds to the difficulties which national reform efforts must overcome. (Scharpf and Schmidt 2000: 329f.)

In sum, there is no general answer to the question of how far welfare states create their own problems. The institutional choices made by particular welfare states may be better or worse adapted to the perceived long-term challenges of globalization or demographic change, and Germany seems to be among those that are confronted with particular handicaps. Given the evidence that large majorities of the populations of most nations choose 'their' welfare system, one may expect that the internal tensions will nevertheless be managed on the institutional basis of the existing systems.

The evolution of social services and the extent of social redistribution result from the complex interaction of demographic, economic, political and cultural factors. In that process, the expansion of social expenditure is held within bounds by competition between the variety of government responsibilities on the one hand and between the private and public sectors on the other. In that context it must be noted that some sectors of the welfare system have powerful inherent tendencies towards growth, though possibly for diverse reasons. In the case of the income maintenance system, the most significant inherent factor driving up costs is increases in the number of eligible claimants such as pensioners or the unemployed. In the personal social services the chief cause is a relative rise in the cost of providing services, which to the extent that they depend on staffing are liable to strict rationalization limits. What almost inevitably follows is an intensification of conflicts over distribution, not simply between the beneficiaries of the primary and secondary government redistributions of income, but between the producers and consumers dependent on the secondary distribution. Still, this should not be seen as symptomatic of a welfare state crisis, even if frustrations arise that may be reflected in growing dissatisfaction with some particular public form of welfare production. Conflicts over distribution are not symptoms of crisis but constituent aspects of social policy.

The critical problem fields of welfare statist development become apparent only where structural characteristics of the welfare state's existing provisions call into question either their own effectiveness or the potential for development in other social fields. Two problematic fields will be examined in greater detail below. One is the problem of the so-called intergenerational contract that arises from demographic trends (chapter 12); the other is that of the labour market and globalization. In both fields it can be shown that the problems are to some extent homemade, that is, they can be seen as consequences of welfare state development (see chapter 13). In both cases a consequence is an increase in the sections of the population who depend on the secondary income redistribution, in other words a discrepant quantitative relationship between those who pay for the welfare state and those who benefit from it. This gives rise to an intensification of the underlying distributive conflict between producers and non-producers, which is also exacerbated by the overarching trends outlined above.

In addition to these manifest challenges, the welfare state also faces further and more hidden challenges. Apparently the limits of intervention by the welfare state are not simply financial, as the dominant elitist and bureaucratic mode of intervention has itself often reached the limits of its effectiveness. Thus the public methods of finance and distribution lead smoothly to changes in motivation and behaviour directly contradicting the original purposes of political intervention. As a result, new kinds of 'statehood' are increasingly being promoted, responding in different ways to the various distinct social dynamics and attempting to direct them in accordance with overarching objectives (Leisering 2007b; see also chapter 14). Finally, increasingly constrained public finances and future demographic scenarios pose further political and cultural challenges hitherto unforeseen by the welfare state project. Perceptions of justice in the social state are in flux.

The Resurgence of the Problem of Social Justice

The movement towards the social state is a political creation that has always brought together morality, economy and administration by means of law. The influence of manifestly moral arguments has always fluctuated considerably according to place, time and the cultural context. In the sense of the distinction between first- and second-order social policy (see chapter 7), the moral aspects evidently play a greater role in the definition of social problems and calls for solutions to them (first-order social policy) than they do in the arguments about the structure and coordination of already established social administration (second-order social policy). Moral arguments gain their persuasive powers from simple notions, perceiving social problems as uncomplicated but severe offences against norms and values. The more complex the problems appear to be, the harder it is to find a simple moral standard by which to judge them.

In view of the complexity of the social state's current problems, it may almost be surprising that since around 1990, cultural discourses of the social state have been increasingly momentous (Oorschot, Opielka and Pfau-Effinger 2008a), and in the last decade the discourse of social justice has gained currency (Miller 1999; Leisering 2004b; Brettschneider 2007). However, Parsons (1971) has previously suggested that social development is secured through the interaction of increasing differentiation, growing inclusion and normatively through the generalization of values. The rise of highly generalized concepts like 'security' (see chapter 5), 'solidarity' (see chapter 13) and 'justice' or 'equity' to become the welfare state's core ideas is the expression of this development.

The historical evidence shows 'justice' as a central theme in Judeo-Christian culture in interpreting a 'just' and 'proper' human social life. From Plato to Thomas Aquinas, justice was counted as a virtue of life in both the domestic sphere (*oikos*) and the public one (*polis*). Its basis and scope equally included religious, political, judicial and ethical elements; thus justice applied to the previously scarcely differentiated totality of interpersonal relations. The virtue of giving each what is due to them was intellectually embedded in the ethos of the public sphere (*polis*) and for its part needed no further justification.

During the transition to modernity, the continental European ideas of justice (chiefly German in origin) diverged from those of the Anglo-Saxons. For the state-centred continental societies, Kant's distinction between religion, morals and law was authoritative; hence the discourse of justice focused increasingly on the sphere of law and thus directly on the political sphere. Justice became a regulatory idea in the legal as opposed to the moral order. This last point has not become irrelevant to the issue of justice, however, since experiences of inequity are sustained by deeply embedded cultural and social moral assumptions (Moore 1978).

At the heart of the post-Kantian debate lies the problem of political justice, meaning the question of a generally acceptable political order, that is, institutional justice. In his standard work on the subject, Otfried Höffe (1987: 469ff.) positions the state's social responsibility functionally as 'a condition for the realization of equity', showing that in the absence of certain social statist elements the fundamental freedoms cannot achieve a proper historical realization. 'After functional legitimation the social state is a strategy for political equity' – in other words, it is not the topic of a specific idea of social justice.

Empirical rationalism rules in the Anglo-Saxon countries, for which justice cannot have any moral content beyond utilitarian principles. Here, justice is generally reduced to a matter of due process; practical demands in the name of justice or equity are seen as ideological. Only in recent decades have distinct discourses of justice been treated seriously, largely as the result of the work of John Rawls (1999, 2001) and subsequent debate. These discourses converge with those in Europe in the attempt to find a basis for a simultaneously just and practicable social order.[10] They focus more specifically on the character of institutional order and on the basis of its juridical authority. The appeal to certain principles of justice depends not only on their normative content but invariably on the institutional context of the claims and its social functions (Walzer 1983).

The enlargement of the perspective of justice from the level of individual action (virtue) to that of institutions is a consequence of the temporal character of modern consciousness and the treatment of 'the future' as a topic for argument, especially conspicuous in the demands for the sustainability of institutional provisions. This also applies to the welfare sector, particularly where it is affected by demographic change. In place of the traditional conflict between capital and labour, which has become almost ritualized, come problems of distribution between current and future generations: 'generational equity' (see Hauser 2007; also chapter 12).

In current German discussion of justice in the social state, the political debate must be distinguished from the scholarly debate. As before, the political debate revolves around distributional equity, even where new concepts such as 'generational equity' or 'justice for families' appear. In the scholarly debate it is plain that efforts are going beyond the established perspective of distributive justice, because its concretizations remain inevitably partisan: they assume a zero-sum game in which what one person or group deserves has to be taken away from others. In the face of increasingly powerful competition and unfavourable demographic projections, no significant growth in per capita income in Germany can be relied on in the foreseeable future. Discourses of distributive justice are hardly helpful for the resulting predictable conflicts over the distribution of the national product, since at issue are not only the traditional viewpoints of those who pay and those who benefit but, in view of generational equity, additional criteria of equity in life chances (in favour of the next generation) and justice for acquired rights (e.g. in favour of pensioners) (Kaufmann 2008). In view of this multidimensional complex of antagonistic claims, a general solution remains elusive.

Leisering has distinguished what he calls 'four paradigms of social justice' in German social policy discourse: 'entitlement equity, contributory equity; productive equity and participatory equity' (2004b: 33).

'Productive equity' embraces all the discourses that lay emphasis on the essential synergy between economic and social policy, seeking solutions 'which create middle and long-term utility, maximizing everyone's welfare' (see Jessop 2002). Care of the dependent population is no longer central; the core aim is instead the promotion of the productive population (Kersting 2003; Vobruba 2003). Social investment and economic growth count for more than consumption and a fair distribution of income (Priddat 2003), even though widespread assertions of a general antithesis or trade-off between these dimensions cannot be demonstrated either empirically or theoretically (Clarke 1995). Latterly the role of human capital or human resources in the economy and society has become central to this discourse.

The concept of 'participatory equity' originated in the sphere of religious social ethics and refers to the postulate of inclusion or the practical realization of civil, political and social rights in the spirit of the UDHR, or more vividly in Göran Therborn's phrase, 'rights to act, membership and entitlements' (Therborn 1995: 85ff.). The social state's criterion of success then becomes not the degree of redistribution brought about by the state, but the degree to which the guarantee of freedom of action, participation and protection against life's risks is offered to all sections of the population (Nullmeier 2003).

Like entitlement equity and contributory equity, the latter two discourses of justice also stand in tension with one another, but not to the extent of consequently totally excluding each other. From some points of view they complement each other, since 'at the heart of productive equity stands ... the aim of the long-term protection of the international competitiveness of the national economy. The idea of the social state does not derive in the first place from individual rights but rather from considerations of public benefit and of systematic functional necessity' (Brettschneider 2007: 369). This therefore risks pushing the individual's rights and entitlements into the background in favour of collective judgements about public benefit. The postulate of participatory equity can act as a counterweight to this risk. What is common to both criteria of equity is that neither emphasizes individual problems as the criteria of distributive justice do; however, their yardstick of equity is measured against complex institutional relationships. As is argued throughout this book, the basic argument for the welfare state (or its 'logic') is the synergy of individual and collective welfare. Discourses that eliminate one of the two dimensions remain below the standard needed to cope intellectually with actual and predictable challenges.

Notes

1. Marx gave a striking illustration of this repression (*Capital*, Book 1, in the chapter on the so-called Primitive Accumulation). Recent scholarship approaches the question from the broader perspective of social discipline (Sachße and Tennstedt 1986).
2. Quoted from the introduction to the Sickness Insurance Law of 1883 (Schiekel 1955: 9).
3. This refers to French emperor Napoleon III, who had tried to 'embourgeoisify' the working class by means of social measures even before Bismarck. For a systematic analysis see Narr and Offe (1975).
4. This diagnosis is central to Habermas's thesis of an 'inner colonization', as a result of which 'the subsystems economy and state become even more complex following capitalist growth, and penetrate even more deeply into the symbolic reproduction of the "Lifeworld"' (Habermas 1981: vol. 1, 539).
5. Lasting attempts have been made by Bell (1973) and Gartner and Riessman (1974).

6. In this connection Jessop (1994: 59ff.) refers to the transition from a Fordist to a post-Fordist mode of production (referring to mass production methods, first introduced by Henry Ford into the motor industry), which depended on continuous technological innovation and growing organizational flexibility. But in my view the increased importance of service production (and thus the related changes in organizational demands) is the central social policy trend in economic development.

7. The emancipation of women began in the Nordic countries, particularly in Sweden, as early as the nineteenth century (Kolberg 1991; Kulawik 1999).

8. To be more precise, attitudes mainly relate to the existing situation, and further wide-ranging demands are called for only by minorities, while large majorities oppose any reduction in services. For Germany, see Roller (1992); Ullrich (1996, 2000).

9. Wilensky (1985: 41ff.); see also Scharpf (1987); Pfaller, Gough and Therborn (1991); Scharpf and Schmidt (2000).

10. For an overview on the issue of economic redistribution see Kirchgässner (1995).

Chapter 12

HUMAN ASSETS AND DEMOGRAPHIC CHALLENGES TO THE WELFARE STATE

Whoever has once looked through 'demographic spectacles' knows the extent to which everything is interlinked: social policy and education, urban development and family policy, civil education and integration. And he knows how important it is to connect thought and action.
— Horst Köhler, President of the Federal Republic of Germany, 2 April 2009

The growth in the numbers and abilities of society's newly added members is obviously a key aspect of the theoretical connection between individual and collective welfare. No social subsystem in a society founded on liberal principles can claim sole rights over its younger generation, and even family, occupational and religious traditions lose their significance. There are scarcely any specific recruitment forces, so instead all social institutions depend loosely on the abilities of the next generation and hence on the particular contributions of the family and educational systems. A society's human assets consist of the sum of the abilities of its members to the extent that – mediated through interaction with society's various functional systems – they are actively realized in the context of a commonwealth.

In this chapter I shall sketch the origins of the idea of human assets and related concepts, and then delineate the term more precisely to discuss the problem of its operationalization and measurement. The final section discusses the value of the concept for understanding the welfare state's current problems.

Origins

The social economist Hans-Günter Krüsselberg introduced the concept of human assets (*Humanvermögen*, see Krüsselberg 1977) into German social policy debate in the context of a memorable session of the 1976 Bielefeld Conference of the German Sociological Association that marked the beginnings of systematic sociological consideration of social policy in Germany (see von Ferber and Kaufmann 1977). In the course of this session, Krüsselberg revived an idea first formulated by Friedrich List, namely that human welfare rests less on actual production of values and more on the 'productive forces' that enable this production (List 1927/1837, 1928/1841; see also chapter 1).

List's formulation emphasized an economy's productive circumstances, or to express it in today's terms, its locational advantages, which List saw as dependent basically on four sets of factors: (1) natural conditions such as climate, soil fertility, mineral resources and potential mobility (e.g. navigable rivers or impassable mountains); (2) the institutional framework of the entrepreneurial economy (i.e. the achieved levels of culture, regulation and organization); (3) the population's abilities; (4) the level of technological development of a national economy. In terms of this discussion we are concerned only with the third complex, namely, the numbers and abilities of the population of a nation, the entirety of which List refers to as the 'national productive forces'. In formulating his idea List criticized the tendency of classic economics to reduce a population's abilities and achievements simply to wage labour, arguing instead that a people's productive forces cannot be reduced to their market value, but in fact include intellectual activity, personal services and also household production.

Krüsselberg adopted a further element in the term 'human assets' from Kenneth Boulding (1971): 'For him the welfare of a person depends to a far greater extent on the requisites for action available to him as "stocks" (an inventory variable), ... and less on his income or even his consumption, which represent "flows", in other words momentums required to maintain or expand stock variables or the requisites for action' (Krüsselberg 1977: 237). Thus human assets mean both the stock of personal resources (e.g. education, work and life experience, motivational structures) and their potential to generate advantages for third parties, generally by means of role-related application of abilities. While the macroeconomic aspect is dominant for List, Boulding's view is based on microeconomic observations. Nevertheless, at heart the two are sides of the same coin as conveyed in the German term *Humanvermögen* and the English terms human capital or human assets (or human resources in a general sense), inasmuch as assets can be understood in the sense of both individual and collective abilities.

Related ideas can be found in Amartya Sen's notion of capabilities (Sen 1982, 1985; Osmani 2009). Sen criticizes utilitarianism for its too-restrictive concept of utility and postulates 'well-being' as the appropriate dimension for evaluating individual outcomes. Whereas utility refers mainly to the value of single commodities, well-being refers to the situation of the individual. Thus Sen's focus is not on the utility of commodities as such but on their potential use for the individual in terms of his dimensions of 'functioning'. It is not commodities at all but advantages and capabilities that are central, that is, the specific set of resources and opportunities open to an individual in a given situation. Sen's concept of capability is broader than the concept of human assets, insofar it comprises not only personal abilities but commodities as well as opportunities. It is parent to the concept of *Lebenslage* ('life circumstances') in Weisser's sense (1956: 635), namely, the 'scope that people's external circumstances offer for meeting their basic wants, as determined by unhindered and thorough contemplation of the meaning of their lives' (see chapter 6).

In Germany the term human assets was introduced to public debate in the government's *Fifth Family Report* (1994):

> The term human assets describes on the one hand the totality of the abilities of all of society's members – young and old; children, parents and grandparents; the sick, the disabled and those in good health. On the other hand the term is intended in an individualised and personal sense to describe the individual's action potential, that is, everything that enables a person to move freely within our complex world and to engage with it. (Bundesministerium für Familie und Senioren 1994: 28)

The analytical difference from the economic term human capital becomes particularly clear in this quotation. The focus is not merely on economically realizable skills or their paid application, but rather on all the abilities needed for living in contemporary society:

> The development of human assets includes, above all, imparting the capacity to tackle everyday life, that is, the creation of positive attitudes and values in the world of interpersonal relationships. What is needed is both the formation of social life skills (vital assets) as well as the promotion

of the ability to solve specialised social challenges in an economic society based on the division of labour, that is, the development of specialised skills (occupational assets). (Bundesministerium für Familie und Senioren 1994: 28.)

The term is therefore based on a comprehensive social, rather than a reductionist economic, idea of individual welfare. It is moreover grounded in the social theory of functionally differentiated subsystems on whose benefits absolutely everyone is directly or indirectly dependent (see introduction). To the extent that they are able, individuals are active as members in the organizations that offer such services, and they make their contribution at that point. In economic terms, most people are simultaneously both producers (agents producing gains for third parties) and consumers of the benefits produced by third parties. By contrast with prevalent economic ideas, however, the human asset perspective does not rely simply on paid work but instead also includes unpaid work, especially that undertaken by family members or in the context of circles of friends, neighbourhoods, clubs, political parties and so on. It also includes the educational achievements of students engaged in contributing to building up their own human assets.

The history of the only slightly older American term 'human capital' shows that it too originally possessed a meaning extending beyond the boundaries of the modern market economy.[1] Theodore W. Schultz introduced the phrase in his presidential address to the American Economic Association (Schultz 1961). In his Nobel Prize speech in 1979, he explained that the economics of poor people in the Third World could not be understood in terms of the classic factors of production: 'While land *per se* is not the critical factor in being poor, the human agent is: investment in improving population quality can significantly enhance the economic prospects. Child care, home and work experience, the acquisition of information and skills through schooling, and other investments in health and schooling can improve population quality' (Schultz 1981: 7). The presidential address of 1961 triggered intensive debate about the concept.[2] A complementary perspective was developed by Gary S. Becker, whose contribution was to enable the application of economic rational choice theory to the analysis of non-market exchange processes as well, for example within the family (summarized in Becker 1991). The role of the family in the creation of human capital was itself developed early on in this context (Schultz 1974).

In the process of developing and operationalizing the concept further, however, human capital at the microeconomic level became increasingly associated with achieved educational levels and only with consequent short- or long-term earnings, in other words, with cash returns to private and public expenditure on education. At the macroeconomic level the concept profited from the critique of neoclassical growth theory and its revision. Whereas neoclassical growth theory explains economic growth in terms of exogenous factors (technical progress, population growth, the development of new territories), more recent growth theories are based on endogenous growth tendencies largely explained by the accumulation of human and intellectual capital (Romer 1994). Similarly, the relationship between human capital creation and economic growth can be demonstrated empirically if it is adequately operationalized (Schütt 2003).

It is essential to distinguish the two new forms of capital from each other. 'Human capital is *human,* in other words has a finite lifespan and is tied to people' (Homburg 1995: 345), and it is therefore inherently non-tradable.[3] By contrast, intellectual capital is typically tied to forms of organization, meaning that it is acquired by individuals, if not by personal study then through their inclusion in organizations. Intellectual capital is – as far as it can be documented – tradable and in principle imperishable, but nevertheless risks losing value through advances in knowledge. Both forms of capital are the outcome of accumulation processes, the costs of which have to be accounted for as investments.

Human Capital and Human Assets, Social Capital and Social Assets

The institutional and contextual foundations of economic behaviour have been rediscovered in recent economic approaches, though without reference to Friedrich List. Thus Clar, Doré and Mohr distinguish between human capital, intellectual capital and social capital. Human capital means precisely 'the productive potential of a population as represented by educated and educationally receptive individuals. It is a mass embodied in individuals, the value of which can change over time and also depending on transformations in the environment of human capital deployment.' By contrast, intellectual capital is 'impersonal economically relevant knowledge' as generally accessible in libraries, databanks and the like, or available within organizations as a specific resource ('organizational knowledge') (Clar, Doré and Mohr 1997: vi–vii). Mohr (1997: 97) describes social capital as 'common basic values, traditional rules, binding norms, mutual trust, interpersonal networks, social peace, orientation towards the common good, social and political commitment at all levels', and as 'not only an important precondition for a functioning democracy, but equally for an efficient economy'.

In this approach, the term social capital subsumes sociologically hetero-geneous factors, namely institutional conditions, structures of interaction and individual orientations and forms of action. In economic terms these factors all share the common characteristic of contributing to smooth economic processes, as allocated to the category of reductions in transac-tion costs. A clarifying distinction between social assets and moral assets was introduced by Habisch (1997), based on Lindbeck (1995), where so-cial assets are understood in Putnam's sense (1995) as network relations or as extended structures of social communication. Moral capital or moral assets, on the other hand, mean collectively binding norms and values, infringements of which incur psychological costs. The creation and de-struction of moral assets are long-term sociocultural processes stretching over generations, whose thrust, Habisch argues, is determined by endur-ing incentive structures or their transformation.

The semantics of non-material capitals has in the meantime become diverse. Bourdieu's approach has been particularly influential, starting with a study in education that distinguished between cultural and social capital (Bourdieu 1973). However, in Bourdieu's sociological work 'capi-tal' is turned into a metaphorical term and lacks any relation to economic processes. Cultural capital and social capital are understood as individual resources, not as characteristics of social relations, leaving them close to our concept of human assets. The previous distinction between human capital, social capital and intellectual capital is more selective.

Despite the international spread of the term human capital, *human as-sets* would seem more appropriate for the case in point, for three reasons. First, it is preferable for the sake of semantic precision: in accounting terms, assets describe an enterprise's available resources, whereas capital describes its liabilities. Clearly the aspects at issue here are relevant in terms of resources and not liabilities. Second, instead of speaking about the ability or capacity to act, reference can be made to action-specific assets, so that the term assets can be used for both the micro-theoretical description of individual abilities as well as the macro-theoretical descrip-tion of the sum of all the abilities in a population (Krüsselberg 2002: 95). Third, above all this relabeling aims to avoid the economic reductionism of human capital theory, in that social progress depends not merely on a qualified workforce or enlightened consumers, but equally on responsible parents, participating citizens and active members of civil society. These contributions are just as important to the welfare state as are quantifiable economic factors.

This distinction becomes clearer if the economy as the institutional locus of financial transactions is distinct from the perspective of economics
as a scientific discipline. As shown chiefly by Gary S. Becker, the analytical
instruments of economics can indeed be applied to non-economic social
relationships such as family or social exchange processes, and following
James Coleman, rational choice theory has also become established in sociology. However, the concept of capital has a precise meaning only in
terms of economic returns, which for Schultz are strictly limited to 'sources
of income streams'.[4] The concept of human capital should therefore be
used only in the restricted sense of the *economic* use of human abilities.

The topic here, however, is a sociological theory of the welfare state
that aims to address the interaction between different social spheres, not
simply to describe an external effect of the economic system, but *to express
the reciprocal dependency of the economy, family, associations and policies in
terms of individual and collective welfare*. Hence, following Zapf (1984), the
concept of welfare production comes into use, thus distinguishing between the market economy, household, social and welfare state production (see chapter 8).

The distinction between occupational assets and vital assets quoted
above is an attempt to give more precision to the expanded scope of the
term human assets in relation to the term human capital. However, this
distinction fails to reflect reality precisely, because it is natural that so-
called life skills (such as a responsible lifestyle, tolerance or long-term
planning) are also useful in economic activities, and equally because
transfers occur between specialized skills and everyday life. The accumulation of human assets in family, school and other social relations is an
integral process that occurs independently of its potential or actual application, or of its remunerative potential. A procedural objective of the
welfare state is to facilitate the interaction between restrictive specialized
agencies and subjective states of mind.[5]

It must nevertheless be said that the sociological concept of human
assets also concerns factors addressed by the economic concept of human
capital, in that both approaches deal with the scale of stocks understood
as the accumulated results of investment processes. Similarly, the use of
the term social assets is preferable to the term social capital. In general,
stable social relations interest participants chiefly in terms of their procedural benefits, that is, the advantages of participating and trusting in
the relationship itself. An economically beneficial result, for instance the
smooth completion of business between two mutually trusting people, is
often merely a by-product. This does not exclude the possibility that enterprises cultivate social relations between cooperating partners precisely
in order to achieve this side effect.

The Measurement of Human Assets[6]

The operationalization of human assets starts from the idea that human abilities and skills develop in the interplay of the maturing of endogenous factors (especially the brain) and engagement with exogenous influences and opportunities through learning, a process commonly described as socialization. Though the adult individual continues to accumulate experiences and abilities and hence human assets, this learning normally results as a side effect of other activities. The most important and most expensive loci for learning are within adolescent individuals, hence involving the family and the educational system. Consequently these two areas are the focus of attempts to arrive at a satisfactory estimate of the scale of human asset building processes.[7] Admittedly, this is not yet a very satisfactory approach, since it fails to take account of either the growth in human assets through adult learning or the loss of acquired abilities through illness, unemployment and ageing, among other influences.

Human assets can be estimated in a variety of ways, but of interest here are only those methods that include unpaid activities. The ideas of Richard Stone, developed in the first half of the 1970s for the United Nations in connection with the development of a universal system of social and demographic statistics (see United Nations 1975; Stahmer 2002), offer the most comprehensive theoretical basis for this approach. The system is concerned not with goods but with individuals as statistical units, and it is therefore appropriate for stimulating specific calculations.

Socialization processes require time, on the part of both the learners and their close people. Because the greater part of this time use is not paid, it is appropriate to calculate individual human asset building in terms of time units, to start with. The best basis for these calculations is time budget studies such as those first undertaken in Germany on a representative sample basis by the Federal Office of Statistics in 1991/92 and repeated in 2001/02. The question that then arises is exactly which activities should be labelled as contributing to human asset building. Only after it is answered can the second step be undertaken – estimating the time expenditure for economic purposes – which raises the further question about the most appropriate standard of estimation.

Seen from this perspective, the human assets of an aggregate such as a welfare state or a national economy can be defined as the sum of the time and money costs that are typically important for a growing individual's life and learning. This expenditure can be seen as an *investment*, even if in microeconomic terms it appears initially as consumption. It can therefore be assumed that, as a rule, these expenditures serve to further the development of abilities that in the given context can give rise to paid or unpaid benefits, contributing in other words not only to individual but also collective welfare.[8] Calculating the scale of investment on the basis of expenditure is also common in the macroeconomic calculation of human capital, although the theoretical concept requires it to be calculated by means of net values.

As far as family expenditure is concerned, Heinz Lampert calculated the cash expenditure as well as the time spent (valued as the net wage rates for housework) for various family types, on the basis of the first time budget study carried out by the German Federal Office of Statistics mentioned above at 1992 prices. For the first eighteen years of life alone, Lampert estimated a total average value of DM 306,000 per child for the reference year 1983 (Lampert 1996: 30ff., 307ff.). Projected to the entire population aged 15–60 in 1991 (as a proxy for the working population) in the former West Germany, he calculated the total value for the human assets created by families at DM 12.7 million millions (henceforth termed a billion in accordance with European continental usage versus a trillion in U.S. and other Anglo-Saxon contexts), which corresponded approximately to the gross fixed capital assets of the entire German economy in the same year. Lampert's calculation derives from simple addition of the parental household's expenses in time and money during the first eighteen years of life and does not take account of either the growth or decline occurring in the course of adult life. To this extent his method is consistent with the dominant tendency in empirical human capital research, which simply calculates aggregate gross costs.

The public expenditure involved in raising the next generation is not included in Lampert's calculations,[9] which according to Ewerhart's calculations (see below) can be put at DM 8.1 billion at a similar point in time (Ewerhart 2001: 3). Although Lampert's and Ewerhart's figures are undoubtedly rough estimates, it nevertheless appears that the stock of human capital in the German Federal Republic was approximately two thirds larger than that of real capital. Despite this, the national income and expenditure accounts contain no references to human assets: their asset calculations are confined to the balance of investments in real capital.

It is true that economic models include all educational expenditure that consists of paid work – the services of educational institutions as well as paid private work, although that may not be included if undertaken in the informal economy. However, depending on the types of funding, these factors are treated as state or private consumption and not as investment in future human assets. The extensive sphere of unpaid private household production, particularly upbringing by family members, is in fact entirely excluded from common statistical models. In this way, a central activity crucial for the future of society is only taken into account to the extent that it relates to the purchase of commodities or consumer durables such as clothing or computer equipment for children. What is similarly omitted is children's work in learning, which ranks beside the work of teachers as an essential precondition for young people's later educational achievements.

For decades experts have criticized national accounting methods for focusing exclusively on those economic activities that are paid in cash. Labour markets, product markets and financial markets remain at the forefront of public and political attention, while unpaid activities and physical flows without monetary values (such as environmental costs) remain nebulous. One outcome of this argument since the 1980s has been the development of subsidiary economic accounting models.

To illustrate private household production over a decade, two comparable satellite models have been developed in Germany based on the representative sample time budget surveys of 1991/92 and 2001/02 (see Statistisches Bundesamt 1995, 2004; Blanke, Ehling and Schwarz 1996; Schäfer 2004). The main focus of these models was time use specifications for the entire spectrum of daily household activities. Where the activities met the 'third-party criterion' (meaning that they could have been carried out by a paid third party), the time usage was additionally evaluated in cash terms. This also applied to childcare. Personal participation in the educational system counted as individual activity that was not accorded a monetary value. In spite of these qualifications, these satellite models represent an important milestone in calculating human assets. They enable a comprehensive documentation of family production for the coming generation for the first time, as well as time use assessment of schoolchildren's own educational production. Nevertheless, these factors still continue to be treated as consumption and not as investment for the future.[10]

At the end of the 1990s, Stahmer and Ewerhart began to construct a further satellite model for education and to bring their results into a closer structural relationship with data in the national accounts (Stahmer, Ewerhart and Herrchen 2003; Ewerhart 2001, 2002, 2003). In keeping with the concept of human assets, educational production was not treated as direct consumption but as investment that initially accumulated in educational assets for later use. To achieve it, the learning and teaching durations of a variety of educational careers were calculated and then amortized progressively through the period of use of the acquired knowledge. In a second stage of the calculations, the estimated times used were allocated monetary values (using statistics of educational costs) to allow the calculation of educational assets in cash terms. This complex mathematical model enabled the comprehensive estimation of the educational share of human assets for the first time. Subsequently, family care provision was brought into the estimates.

In the definition chosen by Stahmer et al. human assets include not only school education but also family care provision. The first step towards linking these two important components was undertaken by the Federal Office of Statistics in a study titled *Time for Children* (Stahmer, Mecke and Herrchen 2002). The study estimated time and costs for the care and education of children and young people according to family types. For the first time, at least the growth in human assets could be estimated comprehensively. The material results are sobering. In his estimate for the growth in educational assets for 1990, Ewerhart (2001: 32) concluded that only some 5 per cent of educational expenditure contributed to increasing human assets as new investment, while 95 per cent served to cover demographically determined replacement needs.[11] Other studies have corroborated these findings of stagnation in the growth of human capital in Germany (Plünnecke und Seyda 2004: 131ff.). While it may be true that demographic decline in future generations will be roughly compensated for by higher average qualifications, this would still fail to stimulate further economic growth.

Human Assets and the Welfare State

Statistical evidence functions as a premise for policy decisions much as existing laws do: by defining the situation within which decisions have to be made. Starting with population censuses and tax lists, rulers have tried for centuries to form a statistical picture of the military and economic strengths of their subjects. Today, national income accounts constitute the most important statistical instrument in the art of government. They combine a range of statistical data series into a standardized mathematical model based on internationally agreed conventions, which can therefore be used for international comparisons. They facilitate a sophisticated image of economic interactions, to the extent that these can be quantitatively ascertained through cash-based transactions, and serve to assess the consequences of alternative financial, economic and social policy decisions. Human capital, however, is systematically excluded from these calculations, despite it being perhaps the most important source of national prosperity.

This also has practical consequences. Until recently, the low birth rates in Germany (and elsewhere) were largely ignored. Even a German parliamentary commission charged with enquiry into demographic change, which met over three legislative periods from 1992 to 2002, concerned itself almost exclusively with the social insurance problems of senior citizens. That demographic change is less a question of excess ageing than of inadequate rejuvenation is an idea that has only recently and slowly entered public consciousness. German politics has consistently failed to appreciate the need to ensure generational renewal both quantitatively and qualitatively. As the former Finnish Prime Minister Paavo Lipponen appositely noted:

> The connection between investment in education and a healthy national economy is often ignored by the neo-liberals in their calls for ever lower taxation, ever less public spending and ever less state. But sound education prevents social exclusion. By this means expensive education and integration measures are avoided that later become necessary to compensate for insufficient school education. (Lipponen 2005)

It is noticeable that in international comparison Germany generally lags behind in terms of recognizing the rights of children (Therborn 1993). While in the United States education policy is acknowledged as the most sustainable form of social policy (Heidenheimer 1981), in Germany education policy is not even recognized as a component of social policy. This was explicable as long as social policy was seen as only the federal responsibility for social insurance policy, but it has long been apparent that even in traditional German terms, the federal Länder and the local authorities also carry responsibility for social policy. In this sense, in spite of the Länder's primary responsibility, the exclusion of education policy is no longer justifiable. Rather, from the perspective of ensuring generational renewal, an integrated approach to family, youth and education policy is in fact indispensable (Kaufmann 2005: 173ff.). From a welfare state perspective, the education system has the characteristics of social investment (Allmendinger and Leibfried 2002; Gottschall 2004).

The concept of human assets can be seen as the key to at least three problems currently facing the welfare state:

1. Demographic change is foremost, and population statistics paint a pessimistic picture of the future. For over thirty years, on average only two thirds of the number of children required for population stability in the long term are born in Germany. As of 2000, the generations born after the dramatic drop in birth rates (1966–1975) entered optimal childbearing age, meaning that even if the number of children per woman remains constant, the birth rate will still fall further. At the same time, average life expectancy is increasing, but less in childhood and youth than in old age. A disproportionate increase in individuals reaching advanced old age can be predicted

(Kaufmann 2005: 38ff.). The threatening character of this scenario is also fed by particular stereotypes of old age. However, if instead of counting heads among this ageing population one calculated the human assets those heads contain, especially in the light of educational expansion and opportunities for lifelong learning in recent years, then the scope for policy opportunities becomes apparent in ways that purely demographic descriptions fail to suggest.

2. The most serious aspect of demographic change is the predictable reduction in the working population, which in the future will have to bear the costs of ever-increasing numbers of older citizens. For many years continuing immigration was recommended to compensate, but considering migration flows into and out of Germany in terms of not just demographic but human asset factors, it seems that the hopes of relief through a positive immigration balance are receding. By comparison with Switzerland, for instance, Germany has so far failed either to attract larger numbers of highly qualified individuals or to make it attractive for them to remain. It is generally the case that the welfare balance of immigration is positive only when such individuals decide to settle (Sinn et al. 2001). Even then, the problem arises of the second and third generations, whose socialization and integration proceeds unfavourably by comparison with the native generation (Kaufmann 2005: 177ff.). From the perspective of human asset theory, the prospects for the labour market, and thus for economic growth, are therefore even less promising than from a demographic viewpoint.

3. It is thus not surprising that the human asset perspective offers legitimation to a paradigm shift in social policy that is often recognized but interpreted in a variety of ways.[12] Priorities have clearly shifted away from social insurance policy towards educational, women's and family policy (Esping-Andersen et al. 2002; Bleses and Seeleib-Kaiser 2004). Conflicts over distribution have moved away from relations between capital and labour towards intergenerational relations (Leisering 2003). What is perhaps most fundamental is that political interests have shifted from questions of distribution to questions of productivity (Evers 2008).

Even if the concept of human assets (or the better known concept of human capital) is still rarely used in this context, it can credibly be argued to offer analytical structure. Social policy based solely on redistribution has shown itself to be an over-simplified model. It fails to do justice to the challenges posed by inevitable economic transformations, especially when in social equity terms it is no longer at all clear at whose cost and to whose advantage such redistribution should take place. The criteria of distributive justice have become more complex and increasingly conflict with other criteria of equity (see chapter 11).

The heuristic value of the concept of human assets is revealed by its applicability in two directions: the performance of the welfare state depends on economic strength, and the reproduction of human assets similarly depends on the performance of the welfare state. On the one hand, the sum of human abilities embodied in the individuals constituting a commonwealth is its principal resource and the fundamental basis of its future viability, together with the integrity and flexibility of its institutions. This fact was recognized early on by List, and although his observation found little resonance at the time, its relevance was conspicuously demonstrated in the reconstruction of Germany after the Second World War. The additional factors List named (natural resources and the level of technological development) may be more attractive from the perspective of the short-term interests of the economy, but they carry less weight in the longer term. Seen in economic terms, the value of human capital exceeds that of real capital, and it appears that the importance of human skills continues to increase in the transition to a knowledge-based society. Nevertheless, national economic productivity remains a key constraint on the expansion of the scope for political and thus also social policy action.

On the other hand, most social policy institutions contribute to the sustainable regeneration or reproduction of human assets. Cash benefits stabilize household income in periods of reduced wage income, while the benefits in kind of health care or adult education services support the regeneration of impaired work capacity. Above all, however, the welfare state's goal of securing future generational growth appears to have two principal dimensions: first, to compensate for the disadvantages suffered by families, especially those with many children, in an economic system dominated by economic achievement principles; and second, to train the already less populous next generation so that their increased qualifications may at least partially counterbalance their reduced numbers (Kaufmann 2007). This necessitates compensatory support for children from socially deprived backgrounds and the children of immigrants.

It is not simply a country's economic strength that depends on the extent and quality of the human assets of parents and other key carers, but also the vitality of that country's political institutions and its free associations, not least the willingness to rear new generations and impart cultural heritage in the forms of knowledge and moral values.

The concept of human assets is appropriate for returning the anthropological dimension to ideas of the welfare state, as it has been marginalized in recent social theory, especially Luhmann's. Although the concept of inclusion postulates the role of the welfare state as ensuring, in an increasingly individualized society, people's inclusion in all the differentiated contexts of action relevant to their lives, this remains a strictly formal definition. Admittedly its substance can be concretized in the doctrine of economic, social and cultural human rights, but this serves only to make the problem a normative one. The concept of human assets addresses the issue of the guarantee of inclusion (in the sense of giving all members of a community the greatest possible opportunities for life and development) being not only normatively desirable but also collectively advantageous in practice. A community's human assets result from its members' extent, characteristics and capacities of generating benefit for third parties. Even highly organized modern societies depend on the abilities and motivation of a sufficient number of individuals for their achievements, although they have become almost incapable of debating the subject collectively. This is precisely the issue to which the concept of human assets can contribute.

The concept can prove helpful in both academic and policy terms, revealing that the distinction between human assets and human capital is conceptual and not substantive. The existing scientific work of defining and measuring human capital statistically is unquestionably useful, though incomplete. The predictable dwindling of human assets in coming decades represents one of the greatest challenges to economic and social policy. From a welfare state perspective it is therefore essential to fight for the inclusion of human capital in the national income accounts. Its exclusion serves to focus political decisions on short-term rather than long-term economic considerations. Because national income accounts form a central database for preparing policy decisions, the only way to give sufficient weight to demographic aspects of socio-economic developments in economic, social and financial policies is to suitably show changes in human capital in a satellite system closely tied to the core national income accounts. In policy debates this would help to ensure proper recognition of the role of support for the next generation and of lifelong learning.

Notes

1. Apart from Friedrich List, the forerunners of human capital theory above all also include Rudolf Goldscheid (1908), rescued from obscurity by Exner (2004).
2. See *Journal of Political Economy* 70 (1962), Supplement.
3. Exceptions are slave-owning societies and football transfer markets.

4. 'This concept treats all sources of income streams as forms of capital. These sources include not only such material forms as natural resources and reproducible producer and consumer goods and commodities, but also such human forms as the inherited and acquired abilities of producers and consumers' (Schultz 1968: 278).

5. I previously attempted to illustrate this task through the concept of responsiveness; see Kaufmann (1980).

6. This section, which draws on an earlier paper by Kaufmann and Stahmer (2007), contains substantial ideas and formulations by Carsten Stahmer, to whom I am grateful for permission to publish them here.

7. Moreover, the costs of raising a child actually include the complex of health services, as well as expenditure on public youth services, which are far from insignificant. The only German study to include these components (Wissenschaftlicher Beirat für Familienfragen 1979) concluded that 87 per cent of the public services in kind provided to families or children fell under the heading of education. It follows that the omission of health provision and youth services makes little difference in the scale of the estimates.

8. Immigration and emigration have not yet been taken into account at the aggregate level.

9. With the exception of direct support for families via transfer payments or tax allowances. If these are included in the calculation, then Lampert's estimate of family expenditure is reduced from a gross figure of DM 12.7 billion gross to a net figure of DM 10.8 billion.

10. The German Institute for Labour Market and Occupational Research has followed a different approach to the national education accounts based on status rankings in the educational system and statistics of their staffing (Tessaring 1986).

11. See also the corresponding time series of human assets from 1990 to 1999 in Ewerhart (2003).

12. Leibfried and Mau (2008) now offer a comprehensive overview of the discussion.

Chapter 13

SOLIDARITY AND REDISTRIBUTION UNDER THE PRESSURE OF INTERNATIONAL COMPETITION

Posing the Problem

Michael Schumacher does it. And Boris Becker has done it. Countless rich people avoid the demands of the tax authorities at home by moving their tax-liable domicile abroad. Everyone knows that. But when the head of a south German milk factory announced he would move his domicile to Switzerland to avoid German inheritance tax, Federal Chancellor Schröder had had enough – he publicly accused the maker of Müller dairy products and others like him of a lack of patriotism. That released a rumble of muttering and indignant complaints.

The many ambivalences the question raises call for sociological analysis. I shall concentrate on one aspect that can be best illustrated by Hirschman's distinction between 'exit' and 'voice' (Hirschman 1970). Most leavers exit silently with more or less bad consciences, but Mr Theo Müller by contrast announced his departure and thereby openly chose the strategy of 'voice' – of protest.[1] Public protest is a more powerful political challenge than is silent exit, which is why it made such an impact on the chancellor. The impact is evident in his appeal to patriotism, the most sacred belief of the nation state.

This story reveals a distinction – solidarity and redistribution find their place in different spheres of real life, and not just in theory. Tax exiles do not explain why they evade state responsibilities, let alone declare them; what matters to them is concrete conditions and their fiscal consequences, and neither are usually publicized. By contrast, solidarity's social context is symbolic, by no means only at the level of the mass media but equally in relations between individuals. As a rule, solidary behaviour is acknowledged and given credit by third parties. Those who pass judgement on solidarity or its absence do so in debating terms, making use of or appealing to concepts drawing on common values such as morality, belonging, approval and disapproval, trust or social control. Discourses like these will be characterized as *solidaristic semantics*. Solidarity is conceptualized primarily from the perspective of the observer of the act; it is not inherent to the act itself, even if the concept refers to social links deeply anchored in daily life. To describe this, I shall use the term *solidary relationships*.

Redistribution by the welfare state seems, at any rate from the perspective of the social democratic paradigm, to be a matter of bringing profit under the fiscal control of the state. This power is currently declining, chiefly because of the growing global mobility of capital and people. In democratically constituted states, the state's fiscal control depends on popular consent and practical everyday loyalty, whose legitimation often refers back to solidaristic semantics (about patriotism in this account), so that solidarity becomes seen as the legitimating foundation of state redistribution. The language of solidarity is addressed to the members of a social group, the nation state in this instance, to justify the duty or imposition of disadvantage on the individual in the interests of all members, taking account of the greater good of the majority. Does this reasoning still carry any weight in the age of globalization?

The problem is even more complex than this. It is not just a matter of the imposition and justification of solidary behaviour. Rather, modern nation states of the European kind do not in practice derive their legitimation solely from their function of forming and ensuring normative order under the rule of law, but equally from their social and cultural function of protecting the weak, covering everyone's basic risks and promoting individual and social development. Through its social institutions the nation state constitutes the practical forms of mutual interdependence and collective advantage that can operate only to the extent that the overwhelming majority of citizens (and those in equivalent positions) loyally carry out the associated duties. We can therefore denote these as solidary relationships.

This discussion is less concerned with answering the thematic question of the possibility of solidarity beyond the nation state than with examining the problem underlying it. Obviously the greater intensity of

international competition puts pressure on the parameters of solidary relationships formed by the welfare state. How is this pressure expressed
precisely, and how can the consequent problems be interpreted in terms
of solidarity theory? I shall start by laying out an idea of solidarity, following with a sketch of some of globalization's implications for political
theory. The two perspectives will then be brought to bear on the problem
of redistribution by the welfare state.

Solidarity as a Sociological Concept

Solidarity as a concept played almost no part in German sociology until
modern times; only then did the German workers' movement, and especially the SPD (the German Social Democratic Party) after 1945, embla-
zon this concept on their banners. The term originated in France in the
1840s among Saint-Simon's followers and was subsequently introduced
to the sociological vocabulary, chiefly by Comte and Durkheim (Wildt
1996). Following its French origin, Catholic social thought also adopted
the concept at an early stage (Große Kracht 2003). Since the political
overtones are declining the word seems open to scientific interpretations,
even in German, as recent publications show (Hondrich and Arzberger
1992; Gabriel, Herlth and Strohmeier 1997; Bayertz 1998, Brunkhorst
2002, Beckert et al. 2004). Dominant among them are philosophical attempts to explain the concept in the sense of normative obligations, but
in this discussion I shall concentrate on a sociological perspective that,
following Max Weber, also treats normative discourse as observable social
fact.

A common thread in recent sociological thought on solidarity is that
the concept is particularly suited to the description or analysis of modern
circumstances. This offers an antithesis to the school of Durkheim and
structural-functionalism, but also to German discourses of 'community
and society' in the wake of Ferdinand Tönnies (1963/1887). The older
theories postulate solidarity (or community) as a characteristic property
of pre-modern societies, and its functional equivalents are sought – sometimes nostalgically, sometimes analytically –in modern social relationships, for instance relating to integration or attachment. Now, by contrast,
solidarity is postulated as a problem or as a specific phenomenon of modernity, as a response to the demands of individualistic social theories and
highly individualized social relationships (Elkana et al. 2002). Taking up
an idea of Jan Assmann,[2] one might speak of a Rousseauian differentiation between true and false interpersonal relations, which engenders the
question of social order.[3] The concept of 'solidarité' inherits Rousseau's

emphasis on 'the social', and at the same time realistically emphasizes the problem of integrating a society composed of individuals and not of, for instance, estates (Donzelot 1984).

Earlier social theory treated the concept of solidarity as the 'social bond' in a general sense. This viewed the inescapable interconnectedness of humans from the perspective of their equality, to wit sometimes in a normative appellative sense and sometimes in an analytical descriptive one. More recent social theory assumes that modern complex societies are held together by many different kinds of social bonds, dominated by the politico-legal and the utilitarian economic forms. Solidarity and similar terms appear by contrast to denote the residue of miscellaneous forms of bonding, though only a positive definition can be heuristically rewarding.

In short, solidarity can be understood sociologically as a typical kind of coordinated action that subordinates the pursuit of individual interests to collective interests (Kaufmann 1984b, 2002b: 37–49). In games theory it refers to the choice of cooperative tactics, and in a theory of public goods to avoiding the pursuit of individual advantage at the expense of others (to abstain from free-riding). At the level of solidaristic semantics, four underlying types can be distinguished on the basis of their increasing moral demands:

1. Loyalty, for example voluntary fulfilment of duties even if no sanctions against non-fulfilment are expected;
2. Extended reciprocity, for example acting in ones long-term rather than short-term interests, expecting reciprocal action from third parties;
3. Collective orientation, such as orientation towards collective goals or interests over and above legal obligations;
4. Altruism, value-based action even in the absence of reciprocity.

As to such discourses grounding the claim to solidarity as these, clearly if they are to have relevance to action, they must embody two constitutive elements: (1) the (implicit or explicit) call on particular value-orientations assumed to be commonly shared; and (2) the precept of particular definitions of the actual situation that suggest the necessity of solaridaristic behaviour. Their relevance to action remains weak if they do not chime with concrete expectations (e.g. paying charity) or support for groups (such as Amnesty International). The example of democratization in South Korea shows that even under current conditions, normative value-orientations, the creation of solidarity and the mobilization of feelings can all lead to historic upheavals (Kern 2005).

Calls for solidarity may certainly bring about behavioural conse-quences, especially when they are transmitted via those who for this pur-pose are 'significant others' (in G.H. Mead's sense). Neither fear of state sanctions nor concern for material rewards can ensure solidary behaviour, but it can instead be secured by custom and tradition as well as by the sense of sympathetic care and need for recognition or (particularly in the circumstances of the modern individual) the need for self-affirmation and self-respect. In pre-modern contexts solidary action would be subsumed under Weberian traditional or affective action, but in modern contexts by contrast it would embrace affective or value-oriented action. Thus con-cludes the view from the micro-perspective.

The macro-perspective raises the question how such explanations can reasonably be put forward for the long run. This becomes much easier the more obvious the mutual interdependence of the participants is, which is why solidary behaviour in small-scale, manageable contexts makes far more sense than it does in large-scale, anonymous contexts such as wel-fare states. However, as Prisching put it, 'The welfare state is the mod-ern collective institutionalization of solidarity' (2003: 179; see also Tragl 2000). The real challenge posed to a theory of solidarity lies precisely in the clarification of the wide-ranging forms of solidarity, such as also are implicit in the proposition of transnational solidarities.

As a rule, small-scale solidarities live in the practical mundane defini-tions of the situation. Even small communities are not ruled so much by solidarity as by strife, jealousy and hate, though indifferent everyday habits generally prevail. Solidarity is usually apparent here in the reality of affective behaviour, for instance in rituals but also through collective dangers or blows of fate. What solidary discourses express is apparent to participants, at least in principle, and is also often called for by infor-mal sanctions. Solidary discourses tend to become explicit, if at all, only in anonymous social contexts relevant to action. Solidarity as a problem emerges from the diversification of life contexts resulting from structural social differentiation and the 'structural constraint to self-constraint' (Elias 1994, see introduction). Value-oriented arguments such as are widespread in the context of current solidary semantics implicitly take the anonymity of the social context for granted and try to gloss over ano-nymity through institutional provisions and normative justifications.

The democratic constitutional state represents by far the most effec-tive institutionalization of wide-ranging solidarity. It manages 'to offer a symbolic bond constituting a framework of belonging to everyone, within which they can locate their status as well as their fundamental mutual rights and duties' (Frankenberg 1997: 77). Significantly, at the same time the solidarity of the constitutional state manages this with a minimum of commonly held value-orientations, drawing largely on mutual recognition, by citizens with a variety of interests and ideals, of the principle of the peaceful and procedurally correct settlement of disputes and the acceptance of statutory solutions. Thus democracy mediates between disparate groups and interests in civil society and the necessity of authorized governance. Indeed, functioning democracies have hitherto always been able to support themselves by means of additional symbolic and cultural commonalities.

The call to collective identity may conceal the anonymity of the social context, but it does not render it ineffective. Solidary constructs do not need to correspond precisely to actual interdependencies. State legislation and the market economy are much more effective ways of creating complex interactions. While economic conditions are rather more resistant to the implementation of solidarity because they not only emphasize self-interest but also legitimate it, there is a certain affinity between state legislation and solidary obligations: morality and justice conflict only in certain circumstances, and they are distinguished chiefly by how far their authority is recognized and what kinds of sanction are associated with their non-observance.

The State and Globalization

The growing irrelevance of national boundaries is the most immediate challenge to the national identity of the state, at both the political and the scholarly level. With regard to what is known as globalization, four mutually reinforcing trends are apparent: (1) Internationalization as the intensification of cross-border transactions of goods, capital, people and ideas; (2) Globalization in the narrower sense of the emergence and acceleration of worldwide communication networks and the intensification of exchanges between various regions of the world; (3) Transnational processes of the formation of institutions and collective actors largely independent of national legal regulation; and (4) The evolution of a global consciousness and the arrangements to serve it; that is, the reflexive and increasing strategic interaction with growing worldwide interdependence. (see chapter 10).

Closed borders operate as obstructions to interdependence. The conventional identity of the nation state implies not only sovereignty but also autonomy. It can essentially do whatever it wants, and thus the political decision-makers can also essentially decide what they want, at least to the extent that the current constitutional order allows. This principle of the sovereign state, as formulated by Jean Bodin and Giovanni Botero, has stood in conflict with the universalistic tradition of Christianity and later of the liberal enlightenment, as is evident in the dual formulation of human and civil rights in the framework of the French revolutionary constitutions. Institutional developments and the globalization discourse tend to resolve this tension in favour of a 'world society'. But the growth of global interdependence does not bring with it any genuine realization of the universalistic normative models of freedom, equality and solidarity. 'Reason is wrecked on the forms of globalisation' (Richter 1992: 242). World economic integration seems to threaten the social integration of nations (Rodrik 1997); at any rate, no functional equivalents of the role of citizen are so far recognizable at the transnational level to enable system integration and social integration to combine with one another (Brunkhorst 2002). If worldwide governmental systems could be established, they could take the form of political networks specializing in particular problem areas (Reinicke 1998).

Trade goods, capital, ideas and people make up the principal elements of cross-border traffic, and controlling it in various ways has become the object of a number of national and international policy fields. The creation of worldwide technological infrastructures and the accompanying acceleration of all sorts of transactions are a necessary but not sufficient condition for its noticeable internationalization, since the lowering of trade barriers, the creation and stabilization of international financial markets, and the free exchange of ideas and people were and are the subject matter of explicit political decisions. This internationalization of cross-border traffic is chiefly a matter of multilateral national renunciations of what previously were national control powers, for instance within the framework of GATT, the WTO or the Schengen Agreement, but it is most developed under the auspices of the European Union.

European unification represents an ambivalent process in relation to globalization. On the one hand, its present institutional form involves it in most ongoing deregulation of national borders (Zürn 1996; Hurrelmann et al. 2008). The precedence of EU law makes for an increasing convergence of national law, and with the creation of a common currency a unified economic space is in theory very close to being achieved. National economic, fiscal and social policies are therefore subject to translocal competition, which the expansion to the east is likely to intensify. In that sense, much of the pressure ascribed to globalization is more immediately occasioned by Europeanization.

But on the other hand, European unification itself has evolved in reaction to worldwide tendencies towards globalization. Common foreign trade and foreign exchange policies assume certain protective functions overall probably better than do the corresponding policies at the national level (Kaufmann 2000a). These considerations should act as a warning against assuming that globalization is fated to make economic regulation by the state obsolete. Even when one takes account of the parochialism of all political prediction, it remains unlikely that, in the face of the alleged imperatives of globalization, states would of their own accord give up their autonomy or even their sovereignty if such renunciations did not also offer them the expectation of concrete advantage.[4]

However, because these judgement situations typically underestimate the consequential problems, advantages thereby appear exaggerated and disillusionment inevitably follows.[5] It is not just the social sciences that are concerned about the significance of such consequential problems. It prompts the question whether, and under what conditions, state institutions can still carry out functions that are being made more difficult by the elimination of national borders – to be precise, redistribution legitimated by the welfare state. A scenario is conceivable in which repeated political failure to meet the demands of complex decision-making has so dissipated the loyalty of the citizen that that state can no longer fulfil even its basic functions. If respect for law fails over a wide front, it could allow the emergence of the kind of political and social disintegration that is nowadays seen in some parts of the Third World and the former Soviet Union.

Democratically constituted polities have nevertheless so far shown a remarkable robustness from this point of view. Wherever largely democratic conditions have once become embedded (and even this was lacking in the Weimar Republic), very few dictatorships or civil wars have emerged without external influences. In Europe especially, the institutions of the nation state today appear less endangered than does their self-image as autonomous powers. The EU both destabilizes and stabilizes the national context equally. Demands on the political sphere are increasing. The 'limits on the efficacy of the state' (Wilhelm von Humboldt) become more apparent, and voluntaristic policies lose their credibility. Policy now seems less a matter of the forceful pursuit of politically declared goals than one of crisis management and the art of the possible. Or to use a navigational metaphor, one should imagine the state as less a motorboat than a sailing vessel. Politics must learn to use its own resources in the light of external conditions. The weighing up of the external and internal requirements of any policy is of course not a fundamentally new problem, but without doubt it is becoming both harder and more complicated.

The Welfare State and Redistribution

What effect do these developments have on the welfare state's particular problem of redistribution, that is, on the role of the state in relation to the distribution of the social product? The relevant institutions that do this vary from one country to another, and similarly the cosmologies of the welfare state differ in the complex of legitimations they offer for state intervention in productive and distributive processes (see chapter 9).

In Germany, a perspective of (income) distribution policy dominates the understanding of social policy and the social state more than it does in most other welfare states. It is not the social services or employment policy that prevails in social policy debates but social security policy. That is a calamitous constraint on how the social state is understood.

By contrast, the ideas about welfare state theory presented here are based on the postulate of a synergic relationship between economic and social policy. The key condition for welfare state policies is the achievement of an approximate balance between the demands of economic policy on the one hand (especially economic growth and financial stability) and social policy's requirements on the other – in particular, the guarantee of minimum social participation in life's various spheres, and in addition greater social equality according to a country's ruling ideas of justice. The idea of an equilibrium between economic and social policies is admittedly still too vague. But by contrast with neo-liberal claims, it must be said that there is no necessary contradiction between economic and social policy, and that in fact many social policies have economic value and in certain circumstances can add to a country's competitive strength.

This is shown by the classic example of the protection of the workers, where the improvement of working conditions generally led to a rise in labour productivity; such measures also seem to profit business. It is no accident that employment and health protection are the two spheres of social policy for which standards are set at the European level. And contrary to many fears, there has been no 'race to the bottom' and the most developed countries have not seen their standards undercut. Rather, the European standards have been developed by experts in terms of 'best practice' and then accepted politically, so that in several instances the hitherto ruling standards have been exceeded (see Majone 1993).

Education policy – which international usage groups under the heading of social policy, though this has not been the custom in Germany – also offers direct economic benefits. However, the socio-economic benefits deriving from the formation of human capital, to which family policy also contributes, do not necessarily equate to business advantage. What complicates the matter in Germany is that significant responsibilities are located not at the federal level but with the Länder. The recent impact of emerging European standards remains to be seen.

Employment policies represent a major field in which economic and social policy overlap. The extent of employment, represented as the proportion of employed people in the total population (and not just the proportion of those who are unemployed, which is heavily dependent on the definition used) is perhaps the most important indicator of successful synergy between economic and social policy. The lower the employment rate, the lower (other things being equal) the economy's potential for growth, and with it the possibility of increasing welfare through redistribution. The European level also tries to exercise an influence here.

By contrast, the most politically contested sphere of social policy, that is, income distribution, has most strongly remained a national domain. At the European level, distributive policies concentrate on regional development, which at best results in indirect effects on personal income distribution through labour market policies. However, the states themselves have not given up direct responsibility for distributive policy decisions. This matter concerns the very same ground on which a country's peculiarities of social structure and culture are most directly engaged.

Political argument usually deals with redistribution by the welfare state from either a fiscal or funding perspective, or it is seen as an aspect of benefits and the impact of redistribution. Social science sees the subject as constituting an inherent relationship: in essence, only what has been produced can be divided, and thus an income redistribution to raise welfare levels steadily is achievable only to the extent that it does not restrain long-term economic growth. Both unemployment and inflation are symptoms of a disturbed relationship between economic growth and redistribution, and the alleged conflict between economic and social policy often focuses on this topic. But it is wrong to suggest there is a zero-sum game between economic growth and redistribution, as empirical analysis has shown. The trade-off between the degree of state-induced redistribution and economic growth is generally subject to far more conditional reservations. For example, the large-scale study by Fritz Scharpf and Vivien Schmidt (2000) shows a wide range of employment levels even within the EU, which the authors ascribe to different institutional conditions and ruling assumptions about the transformation from housework to paid employment.

State intervention in the distribution of incomes essentially takes place in three ways:

1. By sovereign right of taxation and allocation of fiscally collected resources;
2. By setting up and structuring social security schemes financed through contributions;
3. By indirectly influencing the primary income distribution, particularly through policies promoting trade and industry, the labour market and the rules of wage policies.

This raises the question to what extent the state's choice of activities in this field is constrained by growing international competition. As suggested above, freely chosen policy options are limited, but the pursuit of political advantages and internal configurations is not, as long as majorities can be found in favour of them.

It is no accident that the metaphor of 'local competition' (which is in fact a translocal competition) has been thrust into the foreground of political discourse. States remain enclosed spaces with unified legal systems, specific civil and administrative traditions, and their own characteristic institutional ways of solving problems. The average citizen relies on them, and it would hardly occur to him or her to pursue an international strategy in order to optimize his or her range of options in life. But the potential for such international strategies for organizing individual lives is growing at a breathtaking rate, especially for those who can afford the appropriate advice and a range of choices. And where attractive employment opportunities are wanting, as in large parts of the new German Federal Länder or EU member states, the average citizen may decide to move to a better location. Migration within Europe is now chiefly motivated by economic reasons.

Even more striking is the local competition at the level of the business enterprise, in connection with investment and thus job creation. The economic attraction of a region does not follow only from the balance of such direct factors as market proximity, production costs and tax levels, but also from indirect factors such as legal security, quality of life, labour qualifications and other 'soft' factors such as popular attitudes or the flexibility of the government bureaucracy. Empirical studies so far have concluded that tax levels on their own are only subordinate variables in decisions on location, though in conjunction with other variables they may become highly influential (Calzonetti and Walker 1991; Kirchgässner and Feld 2001).

Redistribution and the Problem of Solidarity

In almost all welfare states, the noticeable cuts in resources for statutory social services in recent years have led to political debate over the level and standards of social services and remedies for the financial constraints. But the proposed solutions diverge very widely, and serious civil unrest, let alone instances of political disintegration, has failed to materialize (Clayton and Pontusson 1998; Scharpf and Schmidt 2000; Siegel 2002). This is evidence of both the robustness of democratic legitimation and the nation state's continuing possession of the autonomous power to take action at its own level.[6]

Conflicts over social policy distributive arrangements are where the problem of solidarity is most directly addressed. Limited economic growth and rising competition restrict the scope for redistribution, particularly in respect of further burdens on business. Conflicts over distribution there-fore increasingly seem to be displaced into the social sector itself and are less concerned with relations between the economic and social sectors. Decisions have to be taken on prioritizing the maintenance and support of the welfare state's very diverse clientele. Why do most citizens con-tinue to remain loyal in spite of increasing opportunities for escape?

To start with, the welfare states' provisions enjoy solid support from the population in spite of increasing neo-liberal attacks (see for Germany Andreß, Heien and Hofäcker 2001; Roller 1992). Even cuts in services have not yet produced lasting polarizations in the population. Alongside the underlying democratic legitimation, another important reason for valuing the welfare state relates to the concept of the social contract, which underpins the entire process of redistribution in society. The idea of a contract is of course being used metaphorically here, just as Rousseau used it. It suggests ideas of distributive justice and their rationale embod-ied in social legislation, that is, the implicit morality of institutionalized distributive arrangements that are justified by a variety of solidaristic ar-guments. The pressure of globalization is seen as so unspecific, if it is seen at all, that arguments critical of globalization have hardly any resonance, by contrast with those of environmental protection. Is this just a case of 'false consciousness'?

Despite the broader horizon beyond national boundaries that this sug-gests, the question remains how far it is in fact the forces for Europe-anization or even globalization that have put pressure on solidarity and redistribution in the welfare state. I tend to the view that, at least in Germany, much greater significance should be attached to completely dif-ferent factors.

The trigger of the social budget's financial problems, and also of the trend towards inflation of employment costs, was primarily the reunifi-cation of the two German states and their unstable financial basis. As far as can be established, it seems Germany's performance on relevant socio-economic dimensions fell, chiefly in the 1990s. At any rate, these unique political developments happened against the background of long-term change with adverse prospects. This was particularly compounded by demographic trends that have recently risen to public consciousness. Since the mid 1970s, the demographic replacement rate has been running at only about two thirds, leading to critical demographic differences between the generations and the outlook for their welfare. Immigration, which is often hailed as the solution to the demographic problem, can relieve it to only a limited extent and brings its own problems with it. But even the inherent dynamic of the existing social systems leads to rising social expenditures, so that hope for further social advance is followed by the disillusionment that 'with renewed strength returns the experience of scarcity, inequality and the vicissitudes of fate to public consciousness' (Leisering 1997: 271–272). Furthermore, increasing awareness of threats to 'the rights of future generations' lends debates about the welfare state and the discourse of solidarity a new temporal dimension, cutting right across conventional argument about distributive policies. Undeniably, in Germany the time is ripe for the negotiation of new normative orientations and social policy priorities – which will, however, drive scarcely organized constellations of interests into confrontation, and suggest different conclusions according to different criteria of fairness (Kaufmann 2008, see also chapter 11). That handicaps the adoption of unequivocal frontline positions and conflict over fundamental issues.

There are in sum many internal reasons for questioning conventional welfare-state arrangements which have not directly to do with the growing competition between localities or nations. These reasons challenge the legitimacy of the welfare state's solidary relationships as little as the pressures of globalization do. However, the problems they cause burden the quality of a location.. To that extent, the way that politics addresses these problems is also significant for international competitiveness. Conversely, the increase in local competition is a factor that limits the ability of capital and labour to cope with redistributive impositions. In the face of the superior mobility of capital, the trades unions will have to accustom themselves to the notion that restrained wage demands are furthering growth more than destroying social benefits, and that wage restraint also tames the expansion of social costs. Whereas in the past the conventional social policy discourse was usually able to refer to social norms and argument to counter the demands of the economy, the conflict over distribution is now increasingly being displaced to the relationship between the welfare state's various clienteles. In other words, priorities must increasingly be implanted in the social sector, encouraging a new kind of normative argument. A rebirth of solidaristic discourses that appeal to the existing common ground of those sharing the same national fate, or to the responsibility for certain socially weak groups, would therefore not be surprising (Leisering 2002). Moralistic debate is the unavoidable price of modern anonymous conflicts (Höffe 1995).

Conclusion

The current experience of pluralization of the structure of opportunities as well as loyalties calls into question the nation states' customary demands for exclusive loyalty. Admittedly, a symbolization of national citizenship still generally rules intact in Europe, one that the inhabitants of the continent can identify with and that immigrants do not question in principle. But national identity is losing its exclusive claims in public consciousness. This is owed less to a lack of solidarity than to a diversification of the horizons of solidarity, which interfere with conventional understandings of the state and enable inhabitants to take account of a range of identities and thus legitimate the adoption of diverse strategies for action.

The traditional redistributive model of the welfare state is voluntaristic and premised on the assumption that cross-border transactions of goods, capital and people can be controlled. This assumption has lost its validity. Thus even the welfare state's distributive arrangements become liable to competition between localities. This does not, however, point to the inevitability of a 'race to the bottom'. Stability can itself be a local advantage in international competition. The variety of practices among European welfare states shows that a wide range of strategies can be pursued very successfully (Obinger et al. 2010).

Germany is currently in an especially uncomfortable situation because the problems of the new federal Länder and the intensifying drop in the birth rate, which are particular handicaps as against the other European member states, endanger the synergy between economic and social policy in particular ways. However, politicians' calls for patriotism – for a particularly demanding kind of national solidarity – have no effect in these complex situations. 'The moral consensus of a free state is not something mysteriously prior to or above politics: it is the activity (the civilizing activity) of politics itself' (Crick 1962: 24).

Notes

1. See the interview with Theo Müller, 'Money Is Better Tended by Better Bankers' (*Frankfurter Allgemeine Zeitung*, 16 February 2004, 6).
2. According to Assmann (2003), the 'Mosaic Distinction' is the difference between true and false religion, parallel to the Parmenidean Distinction between true and false knowledge. The evolutionary significance of these distinctions is that they be-

gin to allow 'religion' and 'knowledge' to be differentiated as discrete problems in the diffuse social contexts of archaic societies. Invariably reflexively constituted, differences thereafter gain a momentum of their own.

3. Rousseau did not merely introduce the term 'social' to the theory of human coexistence but was above all the first to diagnose the existing conditions as false and the individual as alienated from his true nature, and to postulate the social contract as the basis for a total integration of the person suffering from the alienation of his identity (see particularly Jonas 1976: vol. 1, 53–63). The sphere of 'the social' was not constituted as distinct from that of 'the political' until after Rousseau, and from that grew the problem of its transformation into 'social policy' (see chapter 2).

4. In addition, one aspect of current developments, particularly in technology, is that the opportunities for evading state control are increasing. As a result, the costs of supervision are rising and its undesired side effects are also increasing. This would also constitute a strong reason for deregulation or reregulation on a broader scale.

5. Wahl (2003) sets out the consequences for public law in Germany; see also Zürn (1996).

6. This is again proven by the reaction of different members of the EU in the face of the crisis of the world's financial system in 2008/09 and even in the aftermath crisis of some members of the euro-zone.

Chapter 14

WHAT COMES AFTER THE CLASSIC WELFARE STATE?

This concluding chapter was, in its original form, the introductory chapter of the final report on the responsibilities of the state (*Staatsaufgaben*) by an international and interdisciplinary research group of lawyers, political scientists, economists and sociologists at the Centre for Interdisciplinary Research (ZiF) of the University of Bielefeld (Grimm 1994b). It combines traditional ideas of the state with new perspectives the group developed to understand the actual challenges faced by political systems. It supplements this volume with some basic considerations of political theory to complement the dominant sociological perspective. The second part of the chapter offers some afterthoughts to the book as a whole, as a kind of bookend to the introduction.

All human order is symbolically mediated. People orient their expectations, their mutual relations and their actions to both intangible representations and significant signals discernible to the senses. We can only speak of 'order' as coherent representation to the extent that speech reliably refers to tangible contexts. Cultural and social development as the idea of a targeted process (even if no individual intended it to be) can be understood, in the context of current sociological ideas about modern societies, as a growing complexity of the symbolic reference system, as the enlargement of the scope of interdependent social relations and as the progressive differentiation and specialization of behavioural systems.

The creation and development of modern states plays a key role in this process. The state itself is a particular representation of an ordered system, and it simultaneously acts as a guarantor of social order. The idea of the state is not, however, immutable; its interpretation varies in place and time, as do its consequential effects. Discourses that relate meaning and effect to each other often refer to the state having aims, functions or responsibilities. Four levels of statehood or stages of state development can be distinguished, characterized by the dominance of differing state responsibilities in understandings of state actions, namely (1) the policing state, (2) the constitutional or legal state, (3) the welfare state, and (4) the system-regulating state. These will be interpreted by reference to the idea of cultural and social development noted above.

The Responsibility of the State as a Problem of State Theory

The modern concept of the state differs from other ideas of politically ordered structures chiefly in the idea of the unity of its organizing principles. It is therefore of no consequence whether the antique *polis* constitution or the Roman imperial order were based on similar unitary ideas, or whether 'the ancient idea of the unity of the state ... the immortal ideal of the Roman Empire with its fixed organisation, concentrating on state power' (Jellinek 1900/1966: 317) represents a retrospective, but nevertheless historically powerful idealization. Whatever the case, the social system of the Middle Ages, insofar as it was politically and legally codified, was far removed from this unity. On the one hand larger empires remained constantly unstable and mostly short-lived, and on the other neither the origins nor the practices of the Middle Ages expressed any unified form of law. The coexistence of popular law and sovereign law, of ecclesiastical and secular law – and their differentiation into forms of feudal, seigniorial, mercantile and municipal law – shaped social relations in the Middle Ages (Berman 1983).

This social order, marked by its heterogeneous legal systems and by the spatial incoherence of its dominions, gave way only very gradually to the idea of the modern state. The latter is characterized in spatial terms by the unity of its territory (including its inhabitants – hence 'national population'), in social terms by the unity of its governing organization and in cultural terms by the unity of its legal system. These three conceptual aspects of the idea of the state became increasingly interlinked in the historical development of political organization, but the wider realization of these ideals occurred only through codification by constitutional nation states in the nineteenth century. The preceding form of the absolutist state had failed to unify the continuing regional and local legal systems (see Oestreich 1969).

Thus the state, as the historically realized type of territorial entity constituted by unified law and unified administration, could only be first achieved as a constitutional state, one in which a self-controlling political entity, self-limiting by the division of powers, entirely renounced any claims to regulate *all* social relations (Jellinek 1900/1966: 326). While in the absolutist conception of the state the entity was conceived as the unity of state and society, historically this was achievable only to the extent that the actual political order was not seen as a totality but as a self-bounded unity that coexisted with others, often described as social corporations or civil society. Only when the systemic idea of the unitary state was separated from the idea of an all-encompassing regime could it be established historically. European absolutism did not turn into despotism – not only because of the princes' limited powers but also because the circumscriptions of this power were themselves the outcome of competing authorities and legal systems. The unity of state order therefore had to be acquired by liberating the non-political domains through constitutional liberties.

As the limits of not only the state's actual sovereignty but even of the model of the state regime itself became apparent, and as the boundaries of state power became part of the concept of the state itself, the urgent question arose of what the object of state power ought to be and what should, by contrast, be autonomous or belong to other social systems. This may be described as the question of the responsibility or role of the state. It is sometimes discussed under the heading of the purposes or functions of the state, but these terms have too many extraneous meanings. The term 'purposes or aims of the state' (*Staatszwecke*) implies a teleology whose justification becomes ever less convincing. The term state functions is ambiguous, and is usually understood as being restricted to partial functions of statehood (e.g. legislative, executive, judicial), or instead confined to certain state activities in some broader social context excluding the activities for the citizens or other sectional subsystems in society. Hence the term 'responsibility' or 'role of the state' seems more appropriate, as its everyday meaning suggests the question of what the state should do, without any essentialist connotations. State roles or responsibilities can be assigned, stipulated or deduced inductively. For this reason, and though discourses on the role or responsibilities of the state may range very widely, it seems almost impossible to say anything sensible about the modern state without implicitly or explicitly taking a stance on the question of its responsibilities.

Discourses on the role of the state can be arranged according to a variety of perspectives. In the present context, the only relevant aspects are those that relate to theories of the state – those that do not arbitrarily demand or deny the state something but do so only in respect of a specific concept of the state. These kinds of discourses demonstrably possess a characteristic dual structure, in that they regularly contain statements about both the responsibilities and the (at least potential) effectiveness of the state. A premise of the rationale of this kind of discourse is that nothing is demanded of the state that (from the proponent's perspective) it is inherently incapable of supplying. If for example, following Aristotle, the objectives of the state are understood to be 'the goal of the prevailing political community', this is predicated on the assumption that the latter does not prescribe an irrational intention, one that is unrealizable in principle. And where the essential role of the state is extrapolated from what it actually does, it confirms this dual structure in itself. Thus for instance Heller identifies the 'function of the state' with 'the autonomous organisation and activation of regional social cooperation, based on the historical necessity of a common *status vivendi* for all conflicting interests, within a territory that encompasses them all' (Heller 1970: 203). In this case the 'imminent essential function of the state' (ibid.) is based on the ideal type of democratic state method of operation and its postulated capacity to mediate between conflicting interests.

Juridical discourses on state objectives aim to resolve the state's legitimation problem at a stroke. 'The practical significance of recognising the state's aims consists, however, in that thereby it consummates the necessary psychological and ethical justification of the state' (Jellinek 1900/1966: 236). For that reason certain state objectives are conceptually transcendent, although this does not exclude the possibility of specifying further, historically variable state roles. This, too, is characteristic of all logical system rationales: the purposive nature of the state justifies its responsibility for order, and the goal lies precisely in producing just that order. As soon as political order is no longer conceived of as the expression of divine providence, or at least of divine authority or other ordained norms (such as customary or natural laws), its justification (insofar as it rests upon necessity) is inherently circular.

The theories of the purpose of the state, 'in the eighteenth century the linchpin of general constitutional law and political science, the reason and boundary for all state power [have] today sunk into insignificance' (Preu 1983: 9). Instead they seems to have been supplanted by a concept of the state that renounces any ultimate extra-constitutional justifications, and that bases the state's legitimation on the fact of the constitution and its provisions.

The theoretical critique and the collapse of the theory of state purposes must [nevertheless] not lead to the conclusion that in the sphere of political systems a focus on function is inappropriate or has lost its significance.... They simply mean that the political system is no longer defined in terms of socially predetermined goals, accepted as being true (and therefore invariant), but has instead become autonomous in determining its objectives. Not only law but equally the functional tasks of the political system's roles, have become in this sense activised: they are determined by programmatic decisions which have to be made within the political system itself. (Luhmann 1968: 71)

This means that what is taken to be the state's role or responsibilities can no longer be derived from the referential framework of state theory, but choices about the role have in essence become matters of political process. Naturally, the state's role has in fact invariably been manifested in political decisions, in other words, always come into being as the power holders' planned arrangements. What is new, however, is that these plans can no longer be opposed by any inherent criteria beyond those set by constitutional limits. Consequently, the state's responsibilities are those programmes that parliament and government implement lawfully.

Against this background, the question arises whether the substance and limits of state action have become a matter of mere political decision. Modern constitutions not only comprise jurisdictional rules and codes of practice but also regularly set both limits to state action (especially in the form of the rules protecting individual freedoms) and increasingly positive declarations about the state's objectives. Nevertheless, constitutions can be radically amended, and their regulations generally allow plenty of latitude to politics. One must ask if there are any impartial criteria by which to evaluate proposals for extending or reducing the scope of the state, independent of vested interests or party-political or ideological preferences.

Four Discourses and their Backgrounds in Social Theory

An examination of the history of the discourses about state roles – the theoretical and political arguments about what the state should or should not do – shows that not only a variety of political tendencies are identifiable, but also particular key periods in which certain problems were salient. It may be conjectured that this focus of discourses on specific issues relates to real problems in the development of state and society, so that the sequence reflects changes in relations between state and society at the same time. The following section tries to correlate these discourses with the problems that underlay them, and to interpret them in a sequential model based on a reconstruction of the continental European development of the state.

The Policing State

The first stage of the development of the state in Europe, roughly from the sixteenth to the eighteenth century, consisted of constituting statehood itself as the consolidation of autonomous rule over a defined territory. The decisive characteristics of this phase are the centralization of the instruments of power and their legitimation, differentiation between the power holders' domestic and national finances, and the emergence of state administration organized according to functions. Thus this is primarily a matter of the legitimation, concentration and organization of forms of government, uniformly institutionalized, ruling over a demarcated territory and completely distinct from the person of a prince or other potentates.

Similarly, discourses on state purposes at these times largely served to legitimate rule by the state. Hence they served to clarify why unitary territorial rule was necessary and what it consisted of. Preu (1983) gives a comprehensive overview of these discourses, in which the terms *gute Polizey* (roughly, good polity) and *Staatszwecke* (state purposes) are of central significance.[1] In this context the term 'polity' comprises both the state's functional 'policies' aspect and the administrative forms of their implementation, the 'policing' aspect. The functions of the state are thus derived from its purposes or legitimated by them. The dominant agenda concepts in the discourse of the state's functions are security, welfare, utility and happiness. These concepts are not distinguished in any precise sense but instead serve, depending on commentator, to legitimate various state purposes. What is typical of these discourses is the sweeping or even sole authority of the state, which stands not only as the guarantor of universal welfare but also as the mediator of the individual's well-being. But equally typically in these discourses, the idea of a potential contradiction between individual and collective welfare and utility is lacking, not just in the literature of practice-relevant treatises on government and the civil service but even in the rational-law justification for the state. In keeping with Aristotelian tradition, the state is understood as society politically composed, which constitutes itself through this process of composition.

Among the agenda concepts mentioned above, security holds a key position because it most directly refers to the obvious capacities of the emergent state. The concept originally acted as a corollary to the concept of peace, which in the late Middle Ages meant chiefly the protection of regional transport against attacks on life and property. As territorial rule became consolidated, a distinction grew between external (defensive) and domestic (protective) security. Since the time of Hobbes and Pufendorf, security 'has become a key concept in the role of the state. It is understood not merely as safeguarding existence but as the basis for a comfortable, unburdened, satisfying life' (Conze 1984: 845). Nevertheless, the typical eighteenth-century formula 'common welfare and security' reveals the dominant intention 'that the state was to be regarded not only as a protective power but also as bestowing welfare and happiness by means of well-ordered "polity"' (Conze 1984: 846).

The prominence of the concept of security in the discourse of the state's role during this period represents a retrospective choice. The idea of a specific state objective crystallized only gradually in the concept of public safety, which, being analytically distinct from welfare objectives, was hence posed against them. In this way 'public security' came to mean not only security as the state's protection of life and property at home and abroad, but also its maintenance of the rule of law and its derivation, private law. The idea of public security thus implied the creation of a condition of mutual reliability between people in which the 'double contingency of the process of interaction' (T. Parsons) that accompanies human 'freedom' was overruled, or at least brought under control (Kaufmann 1973: 56). The specific state role at issue here concerns the formulation and protection of a system of civil rights and the constitution of bourgeois or civil society, which itself depends upon principles of private law and the scope of individual action. Under authoritarian rule, however, the protection of private rights exists between individuals but not yet vis-à-vis the state itself. This was precisely the problem that led to a radical change in the discourse about the role of the state.

The Constitutional or Legal State

To the extent that the authoritarian state (which includes not only the varieties of European absolutism but also the republican *ancien régimes* of the Netherlands, Italy and Switzerland) consolidated itself and assumed protection of the growing market economy, its security objectives came to be taken for granted but its welfare objectives became questionable. This reorientation was triggered by the institutional success of constitutional political theory in the U.S. Constitution. Constitutional theory had its origins in England, where early limits on royal rule inhibited the emergence of an absolutist conception of the state and instead furthered the breakthrough of ideas of individual civil rights and liberties and the right of resistance.

In German-speaking countries, the new state discourse was given direction by Kant:

> The saying *salus publica suprema civitatis lex est* remains undiminished in its worth and authority; but the public well-being that must be first taken into account is precisely the lawful constitution which secures everyone his freedom by laws, whereby each remains at liberty to seek his happiness in whatever way seems best to him, provided he does not infringe upon that universal freedom in conformity with law and hence upon the right of other fellow subjects. (Kant 1997/1793: 297)

At around the same time, the question of the state's role was formulated even more precisely by Wilhelm von Humboldt in a work with the significant title 'Proposals for an Attempt to Define the Limits of the Powers of the State' (translated as *The Sphere and Duties of Government*). He not only distinguished the duties of security and welfare (dismissing the latter) but also reduced security 'as the proper object of state power' to 'the assurance of lawful freedom' (von Humboldt 1982/1792: 115, 118) or the protection of private law. Nevertheless, in this most radical liberal theory of the limits of the state, the problem of the structural characteristics and boundaries of 'the state' and 'civil society' remain remarkably unclear, despite the fact that they serve to legitimate these same structural differences. State action is examined simply in terms of state revenues, but not in terms of state organization.

In Germany the apparent practical duties of the state were essentially reduced only in the economic sphere, contrary to the postulates of liberal thought, while elsewhere the expansion of state administration continued unabated in the nineteenth century. Hence the problem of control over state power became ever more urgent. To some extent the problem was resolved on the basis of the constitutional idea through the separation and mutual regulation of the state's sectional powers, but this system of mutually limiting powers could be effective only insofar as all state action was subject to law and subject to judicial review. The saying prevalent in the 'policing state' that 'government matters are not matters for the judiciary' had to be eliminated and replaced by the idea of justiciable public law (Grimm 1987b). The distinction between public and private law (which, as opposed to the Anglo-Saxon tradition of 'government', is so characteristic of the continental European state tradition; see Dyson [1980]) represents the institutional embodiment of the conceptual distinction between state and civil society that henceforward became a premise of all subsequent discourse about the role of the state.

The self-limitation of the state serves its transition to autonomy at the same time. This is facilitated by the codification of law and the ensuing changeability of legal regulation, as well as through the idea of the constitutional state, not only protecting the system of private law but subjecting all state action to (public) law. The juridification and guarantee of all state procedures emphasize what was new about this state development. This is what is meant by the rule of law as 'the assured trust in the existence of law and its neutral and fair application' (Scholz 1955: 3).

According to liberal discourse, the role of the state lies in protecting the freedom and reliability of civil transactions and thereby facilitating social progress. The converse is that the state should refrain from any concern for the happiness and well-being of its citizens because they can (if their rights are protected) best care for themselves. This idea, unimaginable in pre-Enlightenment times, places belief in the potential and organizing capabilities of alternative models of non-statist systems as first developed in Adam Smith's notion of the 'invisible hand' (see Kittsteiner 1984). The idea that cooperation between individuals without state involvement could lead to productive outcomes that could be beneficial for all the participants (and possibly even for non-participating third parties) was unintelligible to the early modern era's fearful image of humanity as 'fallen nature' (see Delumeau 1967). It was only the civilizing effects of self-interest working in the context of state territorial pacification that enabled the emergence of a new attitude towards life (Hirschman 1977).

The idea that the interaction of private interests – steered by the invisible hand – was more beneficial than state provision for human welfare was what Hegel conceptualized as 'civil society', as differentiated from the state and the family (1821/2008: § 157). The liberal theory of the state not only adopts this distinction but posits a division between the spheres of state and society, as expressed in the postulates of economic freedom and the division of church and state, while disregarding Hegel's inclusion of the family. Sociological theory took this idea's historical power into account in ideas of structural autonomy and the functional specialization of social subsystems (see introduction).

The Welfare State

The internal dynamic of civil societies liberated to a greater or lesser degree from state custodianship, in combination with the belief in progress and reason of that period, unleashed unprecedented forces. However, these did not at the same time lead to an improvement in the situation of both rich and poor (as Adam Smith had presumed) but instead to new structures of social inequality chiefly associated with the ownership or non-ownership of the means of production. Before the middle of the nineteenth century, German observers of the rush of English and French developments had already identified the not merely temporary but structural nature of the current forms of exploitation and poverty, and thus unmasked the liberal vision of an upcoming society of bourgeois property owners as an illusion. Engels and Marx assumed that the state was an instrument of the ruling classes and that its repression of the protesting masses would bring exploitation to a head, thus paving the way for the revolution. But while Lorenz von Stein came to a similar diagnosis of class antagonisms, he saw the state as the power with the capability, as a 'social state', to alter the conditions of antagonistic class interests through the introduction of universal suffrage and the creation of a 'social administration', thereby promoting insight by both the propertied and unpropertied classes into the complementary character of their interests (see chapter 2). This expressed an important new basic idea that would lead to the reformulation of the understanding of the state, though not until the twentieth century. The idea of politically actuated social reform was also expressed, albeit with different emphases, in France by Sismondi and in England by Bentham and J.S. Mill (see chapter 1).

The practicalities of the politics and administration were never confined to the tight limits drawn by the liberal theory of the state. Thus most of the European states drew up laws and took steps to control the problematic consequences of industrialization and urbanization. Because these consequences were initially expressed in very disparate ways, the different European states varied widely in the priorities they accorded to social policy measures and their implementation (see Alber 1982; Ashford 1986; Kaufmann 2003c). At first these were largely only occasional interventions, but over time they gained in intensity and scope. In turn they led to the emergence of specialized administrations, and frequently to new organizational forms at the boundaries between the state and civil society. Typical of such organizational forms were those found particularly in the sphere of income maintenance for the loss of working ability or employment (social security), and also in the development of services for education, health and personal social services. After the first world economic crisis had exposed the fragility of purely market-driven methods of provision, and after the Allies had committed themselves, in the 1941 Atlantic Charter, to public responsibility for the welfare of citizens, the long period of economic prosperity after the Second World War brought with it a massive expansion in organizations of these kinds in almost every country in Europe.

These institutional developments were only very gradually absorbed into theories of the state. Although both the term social policy and the term welfare state, coined by Adolph Wagner in 1876, became established as part of the political language of the Weimar Republic, the welfare state programme of the Weimar Reich Constitution (largely based on the 'class compromise' of the Stinnes-Legien Agreement of 15 November 1918) lacked any corresponding resonance in jurisprudence because, Grimm suggests, the basic social rights

> failed to restrict the state in the same way that classic basic rights did, but instead promoted social action, they did not appear to be directly applicable but instead required statutory authorisation. But the legislative jurists were not prepared even to consider them as constitutional objectives or as guides to the interpretation of statute, but simply declared them to be no law. They therefore appear as mere declarations of intent, located in the constitution but without any practical role in expressing its intentions. (Grimm 1987a: 155)

Even after the Second World War, the Federal Constitution's references to the 'social' character of the state (articles 20.I and 28.I) only gradually took constitutional shape (Zacher 1987). The German term *Wohlfahrtsstaat* was now used polemically to differentiate the German model of semi-autonomous bodies of social protection from the British and Scandinavian model of centralized state provision for all citizens. Only during roughly the past three decades have the terms social state and welfare state widely come to be treated as synonymous, not least because cross-national comparisons are becoming increasingly important in the process of European integration.

The jurisprudential interpretations of the constitution in Germany describe the role of the social state as the protection of 'the social conditions for the realisation of constitutional freedoms' (Böckenförde 1976a: 238) and try, by reference to the underlying intentions of the liberal concept of the state, to overcome the asserted tensions between social aims and constitutionality. In this way the constitutional outlines of a social order are constructed, relating the social responsibility of the state to other responsibilities, and while this does not lead to any tangible legal rights or binding demands on legislators, it is, however, possible to derive evaluative perspectives and criteria for interpreting statute (Zacher 1980, 2004).

The articulation of the role of the welfare state thus takes place not at a constitutional level but through legislation, which reveals further typical differences in respect of the substance and conditions for implementation of the new legal subject matter. First, it results in an inflation of administrative law and its growing differentiation, in which the growing distinction between legal intervention and services becomes increasingly important. This distinction is based on the ideal-type opposition between the legal state and the welfare state (Forsthoff 1968) and reflects them at the level of administrative law. Ideally, interventions limited by private law can be differentiated from beneficial forms of state action. But this differentiation does not coincide with that between the protection of law and order on the one hand, and on the other social policies where, for instance, levying social security contributions or supervising industry definitely falls under the administration of interventions. Similarly, the assurance of services such as subsidies or the provision of children's day care also represents interventions in a social context (the economy or the family), as first clarified by the economic analysis of interventionism (Küng 1956).

The decisive difference between the older concept of the rule of law and the newer idea of a *social* rule of law refers to the relationship between the state and the other spheres of life loosely called 'society'. Not only can the state now act as guarantor of (civil) society as basically organized by private law and to that degree distinct from it, but its measures now also aim to influence social relations, though within constitutional limits and no longer in the blanket sense claimed by the older authoritarian state. This recognizes the structural self-determination of social subsystems and the basically independent legal status of individuals and collective actors in those contexts, but tries to correct or compensate for the undesired effects of the ensuing internal dynamics. Such undesired effects are treated as social or political problems, or in other words are interpreted in ways to stimulate the state to resolve them; the desired effects are typically associated with population groups identified as socially weak or disadvantaged, so that the state can appear to act in their favour and in the name of social justice. However, according to the economic concept of the social market economy, such state activities are constrained by the conditions imposed by functionally effective competition (Blum 1980).

Social theory uses the term inclusion to address an important associated problem, social change in the individual's conditions of life, which was previously treated as an aspect of industrialization but nowadays comes under the heading of modernization. It refers to the fact that the old caring associations have dissolved in the course of the structural differentiation of functionally specialized treatment systems. These associations used to ensure that the individual's essential needs were met, albeit in limited ways and varying according to social rank, though focused on the individual's total situation. With the transformation of society into functionally specialized structures, this total perspective has been lost from view, so that it now falls upon the individual him- or herself to secure what is necessary for and conducive to a good life (see introduction) by participating in a variety of disparate systems. Ensuring that these participatory opportunities are available to everybody is increasingly becoming the responsibility of the welfare state, served by instruments for the specification of human rights. This is what originally lay behind the demand for social security – until, as social policy developed, that concept was reduced to denoting merely income maintenance (see chapter 5).

The legitimation of sociopolitical interventions is not found in a generalized interest in social order but rather in the particular effects on individuals that are expected to result from them. The effects of specific measures cannot be determined within the political process; instead, the effectiveness or lack of effect of measures taken, including their often unforeseen side effects, only becomes apparent in the process of implementation and its consequences (see chapter 6). Moreover, policy measures sometimes seem to have been adopted on the assumption (or even the hopes of some interested parties) that they will not work, in order at least to give the impression that political action has been taken (see Edelman 1967). But to assert the effectiveness of the proposed measures, the political discourses demanding constructive state action cannot avoid identifying the problems to be alleviated. In that case, the demand for state action cannot usually be based on legal infringements but instead requires the assertion of a specific state competence to alter particular conditions or solve particular problems. However, this assertion often remains only implicit in the discourse. The political argument confines itself to dramatizing the problem and appealing to state responsibility, an appeal that gains plausibility the more that governments have previously acted on these problems. But even here, the desired effects – often described as the objectives of some action – still remain the rational core of the argument.

However, governments generally have to feel considerable pressure from a problem to undertake new interventions, which invariably entail elaborate legislative procedures and, where the interventions or services are controversial, additional judicial supervision. The state's capacity for intervention is constrained, not only by lack of funding but also by lack of the time and attention needed by the political process, thus putting pressure on political priorities to give effect less to the facts of the case and more to entrenched interests and political influence. Europe only developed social policy, and thereby transformed capitalism, under the pressure of the growing workers' movement. This happened not simply because of this pressure and the changes in ruling interests that accompanied it, but in the context of the contemporary ideas of freedom and social justice whose intellectual background (Christianity and the Enlightenment) allied the ruling classes with the social movements (Heimann 1929).

The state's 'interference' in social relations, which from then on was accepted as inherently legitimate, changed the relationship between state and society in terms of policy inputs and policy outputs alike. Because socially constitutive state interventions necessarily conflict with existing interests, those who are liable to be affected by such interventions develop a political desire to influence state decision-making processes and choices. Hence actors with similar interests form themselves into associations struggling by various means to acquire political leverage (see Ritter 1988). The result is that the theoretical distinction between state and society is broken; social forces aim for direct influence not only over parliament but even over government administration.

But state actions, too, blur the borders between state and society. In trying to affect social relations, the state increasingly makes use of non-governmental actors by establishing institutions under public or even private law (Schuppert 1981; Hood 1986), or by empowering, contracting or subsidizing genuinely non-governmental actors such as associations or commercial firms. Ultimately even the classic character of the state has changed at the level of service provision:

> The methods employed by the state in this process are those of tax policy, budget policy, monetary policy and distributive policy. Most of them do not affect the individual directly as orders or prohibitions, but instead indirectly as incentives, reliefs or greater or lesser redistributions. Thus they fall almost entirely outside legal forms and judicial controls. (Böckenförde 1976b: 425–26)

The traditional distinction between state and (civil) society thus becomes an oversimplified way of thinking, but nonetheless the difference it reflects has not in principle been negated.

The System-regulating State

Although the theory of the state has not completely assimilated the emergence of the welfare state, the most recent discourse on the role of the state already seems to have moved on to new questions and problems (see Grimm 1994). What is already historically existent is of course easier to identify and describe than what is nascent. It would nevertheless be heuristically productive to suggest there is a fourth stage of discourse of state roles, and to attempt its characterization. That permits not only elucidation of novel elements in recent debate but also clarification of characteristics drawn from earlier stages.

The new trends in political challenges to state action can be outlined as follows:

(a) New responsibilities will obviously be formulated in the field of the protection of natural resources. Environmental protection itself is not new, as it is completely consistent with modern urban renewal policies, but the concept of the environment has itself changed, becoming international and arguably even global, especially in respect of potential climatic disasters. The focus of attention is no longer on individuals or social groups threatened by environmental pollution; instead it is 'nature under threat', conceived of as the ecological system endangered by human activity. In that context the state is expected to influence individual behaviour and economic organizations so that essential environmental protection is guaranteed (see Kirchgässner 1994).

(b) To an increasing degree, the state's responsibility for not only social policy but crime and economic policy is shifting away from regulation, correction and compensation towards preventive action. The state is assigned the capacity (or is even required) not only to take steps to avoid damage or deal with its consequences, but to prevent the damage arising by acting against its sources or causes (Preuß 1994). In social policy this finds expression in, for instance, the growing importance of social services that offer skills, advice or prevention, and generally in a shift of emphasis away from cash transfers to transfers in kind, which are seen as more effective. In fighting crime, preventive interventions to hinder crime are increasingly acclaimed as cure-alls. In economic policy the demand that global regulation compensate for the internal dynamics of the economic cycle is giving way to demands for forward-looking economic development and technology policies (see Kitschelt 1994).

(c) New kinds of state action are being studied and to some extent promoted, though less in political practice than in the discourses of law and state theory, starting from diagnoses of the unwanted side effects or inefficiencies of conventional forms of state action, especially the coercive forms, in resolving current policy problems. The state is diagnosed as suffering from a regulatory deficit, although that is very variably assessed. Many political scientists, on the one hand, deplore the erosion of the state's sovereign role as well its growing dependence on the cooperation of civil actors, and they fear the weakness of statutory forms of regulation in the face of new challenges (see Böckenförde 1976d; Grimm 1994a). On the other hand, social scientists tend to emphasize the state's new, non-official regulatory potential (Kaufmann, Majone and Ostrom 1986; Teubner 1989; Schuppert 1994).

(d) A reduction in the sovereignty of the state is foreseeable in terms of not only its domestic social environment but also international relations. Under international law states continue to remain supreme, but they do so less on the premise of autarky than of their increasing integration in international and sometimes supranational contexts. Social connections transcend the boundaries of the nation state with increasing intensity, while the interdependence of nations tends towards globalizing structures. Hence it is not only the more or less voluntary commitments under international law that have a direct effect on a state's roles and budgets, but the completely involuntary dependence on global developments, such as the world economic cycle, oil prices or some third world nations' technology policies, that do so through the medium of developments in economic growth and full employment (see chapter 13). These contexts are not entirely new, but they seem to intensify unceasingly and have only very recently entered into general consciousness. This has encouraged some states or supranational associations such as the EU to adopt a new mercantilism with attempts to improve their international competitiveness by setting national standards for the promotion of business and technology (Willke 1991).

It is likely that these developmental trends are connected. The new roles of the state can be characterized as demonstrating clearly the inadequacy of traditional interpretations of state action, or at least the need to supplement them. The terminological shift from intervention to regulation is symptomatic. What is called for is no longer more or less isolated local state interventions to correct violations of the law, to avoid hazards or ameliorate the position of some social groups; instead the demand is for action to manage systems, no longer linked to sanctioning individual behaviour but to the assumptions on which the behaviour is based (see chapter 7).

To grasp this problem shift requires recourse less to political theory of the state and more to social theory. What older social scientists simply used to call 'society' – as opposed to 'the state' – is nowadays increasingly understood not only by sociology but even public awareness as an institutionally complex locus of social relations and communications, highly organized and better explained in terms of systems theory. What the older theories (with the notable exception of market theory) treated as only the implicit hypothetical emergence of a new order in the non-state sphere as well (Adam Smith's 'invisible hand') is now analysed reflexively. For precisely that reason, the state's influence on social relations constituted through its legal system is conceptualized as system regulation and no longer as mere intervention. Since most social actors in a system behave according to its premises, isolated interventions from outside the system are generally at best rendered only partially effective. This applies especially because the addressees of state regulation are increasingly organized as collective actors who owe their existence to the national or transnational (EU) regulations of corporate law. These collectivities exist subject to internal organizational and external institutional rules that make their activities more predictable than those of individuals (Geser 1990).

What is new about the expectations of the state's fulfilment of its roles is that the state intervenes not merely as sovereign authority in social relations, but now is also to reflect the specific features of each field of intervention and the interests of the targeted actors as essential conditions for the efficacy of its own intervention. As official behaviour is based on imperatives and prohibitions necessarily typified by considerable inflexibility, it tends to provoke defensive and evasive strategies by disaffected actors. Opportunities for evasion multiply with the complexity of situations and especially with the openness of national frontiers. In addition, prescriptive policies in some fields, such as social services, environmental protection or business promotion, often have counterproductive consequences. Hence the state is advised to make use of softer strategies such as incentive programmes (Mayntz 1983) or the creation of consultative systems, educational campaigns, procedural or reflexive legislation, or contextual management (Teubner and Willke 1984).

But this outline of the new discourses still fails to explain sufficiently what has brought about the shift in themes. It can be dated historically to around the mid 1970s, when the first report of the Club of Rome, *Limits of Growth,* was published (Meadows et al. 1972) and the subsequent oil crisis created, for the first time, a widespread awareness of the global interdependence of modern states and their populations. The economic recession that followed similarly created political awareness of the fiscal limits of the welfare state, and at the same time other limits on the state's capacity to solve problems became labelled as a crisis. But once most Western states had managed to weather their apparent lack of capability, the social science rhetoric of crisis was soon superseded by more complex theories of social contingency. Nonetheless, public anxieties have not receded. The concept of risk, or even of risk society (Beck 1992), focuses on features of modern social contexts whose own inherent dynamic seems a hazard to itself and to others; hence risk prevention is claimed to be a state responsibility (Preuß 1994).

Precautionary avoidance of hazard prevention is (like environmental protection) by no means a new demand on government, as Preuß shows. As such, the description of the state's new role as preventive government exaggerates the problem. The heart of the matter is that prevention of some problems is impossible because there are no adequate explanatory models for some real hazards. 'To be honest, global effects and contingent effects are very hard to attribute to single decisions ... however good the decision maker's calculations are, one knows (and he knows) that in the interaction of many decisions, aggregate effects and unexpected coincidences defy prediction' (Luhmann 1990: 41). This disturbing perspective – that the 'threat of unforeseeable outcomes' that might cause widespread damage should be seen as 'a systematic feature of modern developments' (Preuß 1994: 534) – understandably leads to demands on the modern state to promote collective renunciation of running risks with unpredictable consequences, by collectively binding decisions.

The new imposition on the state arising from the problems sketched above no longer concerns simply the obligation to uphold conformity to law (as in constitutional or legal discourse) or the assurance of individual welfare for citizens (as in welfare state discourse) but also responsibility for the protection of non-damaging interaction of the inherent dynamics of the various social systems (Willke 1994). What is therefore required of the state is to regulate these systems so as to keep the external effects of their inherent dynamics under control without calling into question their capacity for self-management, something seen as indispensable. This is why I suggest that this discourse about state roles be conceptualized as the system-regulating state (*Steuerungsstaat*).[2]

These expectations of government action that can be described as a state responsibility concern relations between the state and society's other functional fields that are no longer seen as givens but as matters for continuous reflexive shaping through policy decisions. The practical expression of this formative state power is the public sector – the structurally differentiated outcome of distinct state policies such as those for health, education, science or technology. A large number of non-state actors work in these fields, pursuing defined goals under the presumption of national organizational and procedural regulation, and sometimes state-regulated funding as well. The substance and legitimation of these sectoral policies do not derive only from the government but arise in the continuous process of negotiation between the participating actors.[3] The associated processes of decision-making mostly take place in the pre-parliamentary arena, but they nonetheless depend on governmental legitimation to become binding. To that extent the government is neither simply *primus inter pares* (Willke), nor even merely the notary to the agreement reached between the social actors. Admittedly the balance of power between governmental and non-governmental actors varies from country to country and from policy sphere to policy sphere, but as a rule the social actors would be completely unable to reach long-lasting agreement without state procedural regulation – and, not infrequently, under pressure from government. On the other hand, for a variety of reasons (see Schuppert 1994) the state is not capable on its authority alone of taking decisions about the complex management problems looming ahead. Expansion of the state's capacity for effective regulation thus depends on newer adaptable forms of political decision-making (see Kaufmann 1991b).

Conclusions

The subject of this discussion is not the development of political structures and actions as they historically took place and currently do so, but the sequence of typical discourses about the roles of the state. There are of course grounds for assuming that changes in the discourses also reflect changes in the state's actual roles, but these changes are by no means as radical as the differences between the discourses of theories of the state. The appearance of a new discourse on the roles of the state always concerns the degree to which the state has fulfilled its roles so far, and instead of calling it into question, the new discourse puts it into relative perspective. New discourses on the role of the state reflect changes in the conceptualization of relations between the state and the fields within which it acts.

While the policing state discourse takes the object of state concerns to be the totality of living conditions in its territorial dominions, the constitutional state discourse reduces state roles to ensuring national security and the rule of law as the foundation for every citizen's completely free development. The state's field of operations here is limited to passing, administering and implementing statute, while other social relations – subsumed under the residual category of civil society – do not count as matters for state action at all. This reductivist concept of state roles can be understood as a reaction against the undifferentiated all-purpose prerogatives of the policing state discourse. The welfare state discourse then develops in a critical controversy with the liberal assumptions of the constitutional discourse. The welfare state discourse conceives the state's field of activity to be citizens' social relationships and conditions of life, which means reducing the power differentials and compensating for the social disadvantages that result from the free play of social (and especially economic) forces. These goals are to be achieved by granting individuals rights of protection and state or indirect state services. Finally, the system-regulating state discourse arises from the insight that the reliability of law and the targeted individualization of state procedures are not alone sufficient to ensure citizens' well-being. The self-imposed limits the state sets, by allowing growing differentiation and self-management of the increasingly organized fields of societal action, give rise to systematic dynamics of their own. Their consequences in other fields of operation, as well as for the population as a whole, can lead to disadvantages that cannot be ascribed to either individuals or particular groups. Hence the state is increasingly called on to regulate these systemic relationships.[4]

The precise consequences these changes in ascription of state roles will have for understanding the state and its activities has scarcely been studied so far but doubtless will become a research topic for both social and political science. What must be kept in mind is that the appearance of these new discourses of state roles does not render the fulfilment of the state's current roles redundant. On the contrary, we can assume that the emergence of new discourses is a sign that the postulates of the previous discourses have become embedded in state practice. These policies must continue, even as they produce a constant need for readjustment. But they are debated chiefly at the level of separate policy fields and not in terms of discourses of state roles.

In the sphere of jurisprudential scholarship, there clearly is considerable dissatisfaction with these recent demands for system regulation. From this perspective the state seems overloaded with an unceasing flood of demands for regulation whose fulfilment, even partially, largely eludes statutory scrutiny. The most recent developments in social theory treat the state as no longer an entity set against 'society' but a social subsystem beside others. Theorists of the state fear – and some sociologists have concurred with these fears in their critical expressions on the subject – that the sovereign functions of a state singled out in this way could become lost vis-à-vis the influence of other social subsystems. Indeed, Luhmann's theory does not recognize a hierarchical relationship among social subsystems (as Anglo-Saxon social science has always done), but at best a historically changeable 'functional primacy'.

This does not, however, negate the constitutive role of the state for modern, highly complex social contexts. The specific function of the political subsystem that cannot be replaced by the provisions of any other subsystem is the production and communication of collectively binding decisions that apply as national law, not only to the state but equally to all other social subsystems. State law contributes to the stabilization of other emergent social systems such as the market economy, health and education services or even the family, a fact always recognized by the liberal theory of the state. It follows that the state's non-substitutable functions also include the production of binding law, the protection of law, the expression of law and the punishment of infractions of the law. The state is accorded a constitutive function with respect to ordering modern social relations because almost all other configurative forms are dependent on statutory norms and organizational potentialities (e.g. the various forms of legal person) framed by the state. This classical state role takes on an additional specific character in the light of the new state roles.

The traditional distinction between public and private law is based on the idea that laws committing states on the one hand, and legal frameworks ordering relations between individuals on the other, represent two separate spheres comprising the entire scope of law. The inadequacy of this idea is already obvious in the fields of commercial, labour and social law, where the effects of the norms of public and private law interact with each other. The distinction between public and private law becomes completely redundant where the state takes over regulation of complete sectors such as health or technology policy, whose services are supplied almost entirely by non-governmental actors and their associates.

However, none of this applies to the satisfaction of the immediate necessities of life (private households), the production of cultural patterns of meaning (art, knowledge, religion) or the reproduction of the population (family), all of which have a similarly constitutive importance for the continuance of human history. They remain largely state-free realms that are usually kept free of direct political influence for good reason. To the extent that state rule imposes borders on an identifiable part of the earth's surface and its inhabitants and thus creates a space for greater interdependence and therefore collective fates, which symbolically represent the cultural meaning of collective identity (e.g. 'France') and functional connections, the state becomes the guarantor of social coherence including these provisions. It also becomes the locus and the arena of sometimes bitter conflicts among social groups (Vogel 2007).

Discourses on state roles refer to these politically and legally constituted social relations, and in the process of differentiation and debate on the state's unending new roles, two propositions emerge more clearly. One is the interdependence of state and non-state activities, or even the necessary synergy between them; the other is the loss of autonomy, the fragmenting of such state socialization in the context of the emergent 'global society'.[5] The fact that states are no longer sovereign actors is shown not only by their interdependence with other subsystems but also by the growing interdependence of states and their citizens internationally and even globally in marginal cases. The belief in the sovereign state derived its historical plausibility from the pacificatory and integrative functions of early modern state development, where the establishment and defence of national borders were necessary conditions for a higher stage of the organization of social relations and the extension of trade links, as noted by Norbert Elias. However, as the national-state stage of order became the norm, trade links extended farther and exchange relations expanded beyond national borders in so many ways and to such an extent that national borders gradually ceased to act as barriers to interdependence (see chapter 13). The state thus necessarily loses its sovereignty and functionally becomes a kind of organizational centre for the collectivities it has itself constituted; only through them can it still be understood as a bounded entity.

A theory of the state capable of addressing these new challenges must in my view divorce itself explicitly from the premise of sovereignty and start from the consequences of the ineluctable loss of sovereignty. The roles of the state have to be understood as functions in a transnational context in a double sense: first, with regard to the further development of the state-constituted collectivities, including those beyond the political subsystem; second, regarding international and transnational relations into which states mesh as politically constituted collectivities.

The 'new insecurity', which nowadays is discussed as an aspect of risk society or of demands for state protection against risk, is primarily a problem of what Habermas (1985) called *'die neue Unübersichtlichkeit'* – a new lack of clarity, the experience of the non-transparency or opacity of the real world. The old hypotheses, such as those of the causal determinism of reality or state sovereignty, by which early modern man tried to assert his position as 'master and owner of nature' (Descartes) are ever more obviously bound to fail. However, because trade relations have expanded and their increasingly complexity can be represented by scientific research, opportunities for oversight and understanding of the consequences, and for influencing them through deliberate decisions, have grown greatly. It is not that dangers to humanity have increased (a glance at the worldwide increases in life expectancies reveals the absurdity of this suggestion) but rather that the risks have, specifically the unpredictability of the possible outcomes of decisions and thus uncertainty about the future (Luhmann 1990).

Inasmuch as the state still remains and represents the accepted organizational model for producing collectively binding decisions, it becomes increasingly aware of being dependent on an uncontrollable future and of the potential for influencing the contexts of action. Under these conditions the state necessarily has not only a political but a highly significant cultural function. The belief in the necessarily beneficial virtues of the 'invisible hand' has faded just as much as has the belief in the omnipotence of the strong state. Collective expectations must become more modest but also more differentiated, and must pay more attention to the coexistence of a variety of institutional modes of coordination of human actions and the potential for learning embodied in them (see chapter 8). If the future is still full of surprises but the predictable outcomes of decisions spread ever more widely, the horizons of time and matter in political decisions must expand as far as knowledge allows. This could for instance be done by institutionalizing the 'rights of future generations' in a constitutional framework. It is also essential to increase the political system's ability to learn and adapt through institutional provisions. In terms of widely debated major technological risks, this means that if actions are known to have unpredictable outcomes, then the relevant political decisions must be open to revision (Preuß 1994). If the decisions' predictable consequences appear so irreversible that revision could not avert possible damage (and thresholds of scale would have to be set), this would be an indicator that the rights of future generations are being damaged.

Summary

The dominant conceptions of what the scope of political rule should be have frequently changed in the course of the modern development of the state. They are summarized as four discourses here – policing state, constitutional state, welfare state and system-regulating state – related sequentially to the growing structural autonomy and functional specialization of society's subsystems. The most recent theorizations of state roles no longer assign the state merely problem-solving intervention but also directive system-driving action. This has lasting effects on state theory and practice. Outdated ideas of sovereignty and rigid claims to authority must be replaced by types of political decision-making processes that are capable of learning, and by a reflective use of law as the organizational tool of the state.

The essays collected in the first part of this book concern the philosophical antecedents and intellectual foundations of ideas about the social or welfare state. This forms a basis for the second part, which reflects on a political system trying to solve social problems by applying isolated statute on a case-by-case basis. But the reference to 'second-order social policy' (chapter 7) shows that the accumulation of interventions leads to subsequent problems that themselves necessitate a more systematic approach to intervention and systematic grasp of their relations. Germany attempted to meet this need chiefly by creating a 'social budget' and a 'code of social law'. Chapters 8 and 10 then develop a theoretical apparatus, based on the perspectives outlined in the introduction, with which to examine welfare state developments from the perspective of the growing interconnectedness between various kinds of welfare production and the consequent interdependence of social subsystems.

Chapters 11 to 13 concern specific challenges to welfare-state configurations posed by actual developments to date. They reflect serious challenges to democratically legitimized welfare state politics. In this final chapter, the outline offered for a new approach to the state commensurate with the scale of these problems has had to remain highly abstract. Instead of the state having blanket responsibility for all the emergent problems in detail, government and parliament are now expected to take responsibility in principle for the constitution and control of the specialized and self-governing subsystems. Here the role of the systems-stabilizing state consists in essence of minimizing the damaging effects of the subsystems' own internal processes (e.g. excessive costs or environmental damage), mediating the demands of the other subsystems (e.g. the claims of economy with respect to research, education and training) and ensuring system performance for the whole population (e.g. through social rights, consumer protection and a well-functioning legal and judicial system).

In the spirit of this perspective, the distinction drawn from the outset is between the political responsibility for welfare as a task for government, and the institutionalized welfare sector as a collective term for individual social service systems. While the welfare sector's systems may be part of the state administration, they do not have to be. They may be managed primarily by a hierarchical bureaucracy, but they do not have to be, and they may be corporatized or marketized. There are even signs that the inclusion of other modes of coordinating actions into the political design often improve system efficiency and effectiveness under conditions of increasing scarcity. But these questions are best dealt with in particular national contexts and political systems, which is not this book's intention. The aim here is simply to advance concepts that will allow more exact studies to be undertaken, and to relate them to each other so that they will better facilitate the understanding of the variety of welfare state developments from country to country. That, it seems to me, is what theory is meant to be for.

Notes

1. Another discourse level not discussed here concerns the term 'sovereignty'. This represented an attempt to establish a metaphysical legitimation of state rule, which originally was oriented to a god-given idea of absolute higher power. Discourses on the functions or responsibilities of the state became relevant to the legitimation problem only to the extent that the 'political theology' of sovereignty lost credibility.
2. Referring more directly to welfare issues, Vogel (2007) draws a cognate distinction between the caring welfare state and the guaranteeing welfare state. The latter is meant to guarantee social rights even if those who perform the task are not part of the state administration any longer.

3. The structure of the relationship that sustains this negotiating process varies according to the political system. In many states in continental Europe, the dominant arrangement appears to be corporatist, that is, a relatively close network linking state authorities responsible for particular policy fields and certain privileged actors. By contrast, in the U.S. the relevant networks would appear looser and more accessible to outside parties (see Windhoff-Heritier 1994).

4. Luhmann (1990: 29, 37–38) differentiates three social models of articulating the double contingency inherent in social actions: norms, scarcity and risk. Referring to the typology of state discourses above, the norm model corresponds to the constitutional discourse, the scarcity model to the welfare state, and the risk model to the system-regulating state.

5. For a good compendium of the discussions about global society see Heintz, Münch and Tyrell (2005). For the transformation of national states see Leibfried and Zürn (2005) and Hurrelmann et al (2008).

BIBLIOGRAPHY

Achinger, H. 1958: *Sozialpolitik als Gesellschaftspolitik – Von der Arbeiterfrage zum Wohl-fahrtsstaat*. 2nd enl. ed. Frankfurt a. M. 1971.
———. 1966: 'Soziologie und Sozialreform', in A. Busch (ed.) *Soziologie und moderne Ge-sellschaft*. 2nd ed. Stuttgart: 39–52.
Aidukaite, J. 2004: *The Emergence of the Post-Socialist Welfare State. The Case of the Baltic States: Estonia, Latvia and Lithuania*. Huddinge.
Alber, J. 1982: *Vom Armenhaus zum Wohlfahrtsstaat*. Frankfurt and New York.
———. 1995: 'A Framework for the Comparative Study of Social Services', *Journal of European Social Policy* 5: 131–149.
———. 2001: 'Hat sich der Wohlfahrtsstaat als soziale Ordnung bewährt?' in K.-U. Mayer (ed.), *Die beste aller Welten?* Frankfurt and New York: 59–111.
Alcock, A. 1971: *History of the International Labour Organisation*. London.
Alexander, E. 1953: 'Church and Society in Germany: Social and Political Movements and Ideas in German and Austrian Catholicism 1789–1950', in J. Moody (ed.), *Church and Society: Catholic Social and Political Thoughts and Movements 1789–1950*. New York: 325–583.
Allmendinger, J. and S. Leibfried. 2002: 'Bildungsarmut und Sozialstaat', in G. Burkart and J. Wolf (eds), *Lebenszeiten. Erkundungen zur Soziologie der Generationen*. Opladen: 287–315.
Anderson, M.L. 1981: *Windthorst: A Political Biography*. Oxford.
Andreß, H.-J., T. Heien and D. Hofäcker. 2001: *Wozu brauchen wir noch den Sozialstaat? Der deutsche Sozialstaat im Urteil seiner Bürger*. Wiesbaden.
Anheier, H.K. and W. Seibel (eds). 1990: *The Third Sector: Comparative Studies of Non-profit Organizations*. Berlin and New York.
Arnold, D.R., M.J. Graetz and A.H. Munell (eds). 1998: *Framing the Social Security De-bate: Values, Politics, and Economics*. Washington, D.C.
Ashford, D.E. 1986: *The Emergence of the Welfare State*. Oxford.
Ashley, W. 1969: *Introduction to John Stuart Mill: Principles of Political Economy* (1909). (Reprint, New York.)
Assmann, J. 2003: *Die Mosaische Unterscheidung oder der Preis des Monotheismus*. Munich.

Atkinson, A.B. 1989: *Poverty and Social Security*. New York.

Baader, F. von 1835: 'Über das dermalige Missverhältnis der Vermögenslosen oder Proletairs zu den Vermögen besitzenden Klassen der Sozietät in Betreff ihres Auskommens, sowohl in materieller, als intellektueller Hinsicht, aus dem Standpunkt des Rechts betrachtet'. (Reprint in E. Pankoke (ed.), *Gesellschaftslehre*. Frankfurt a. M. 1991: 320–339.)

Bachem, K. 1929: *Vorgeschichte, Geschichte und Politik der deutschen Zentrumspartei*, vol. 4. Cologne. (Reprint Aalen 1967).

Badura, B. and C. von Ferber (eds). 1981: *Selbsthilfe und Selbstorganisation im Gesundheitswesen*. Munich and Vienna.

Baker, D. (ed.). 1975: *Church, Society and Politics*. Oxford.

Baldwin, P. 1990: *The Politics of Social Solidarity*. Cambridge.

Barker, P. 1984: *Founders of the Welfare State*. London.

Bauer, C. 1931: 'Wandlungen der sozialpolitischen Ideenwelt im deutschen Katholizismus des 19. Jahrhunderts', *Görres-Gesellschaft zur Pflege der Wissenschaft im katholischen Deutschland, Veröffentlichungen der Sektion für Wirtschafts- und Sozialwissenschaft* 2: 11–46.

Baumol, W.J. 1965: *Welfare Economics and the Theory of the State. With a New Introduction: Welfare and the State Revisited*. Cambridge, MA.

Bayertz, K. (ed.). 1998: *Solidarität. Begriff und Problem*. Frankfurt a.M.

Beck, U. 1992: *Risk Society: Towards a New Modernity*. London.

Becker, G.S. 1991: *A Treatise on the Family*. Enl. ed. Cambridge.

Beckert, J., J. Eckert, M. Kohli and W. Streeck (eds.) 2004: *Transnationale Solidarität – Chancen und Grenzen*. Frankfurt/Main.

Beck-Gernsheim, E. 1983: 'Vom Dasein für andere zum Anspruch auf ein Stück „eigenes Leben"', *Soziale Welt* 34: 307–340.

Bell, D. 1973: *The Coming of Postindustrial Society*. New York.

Bendix, R. 1964: *Nation-Building and Citizenship: Studies on our Changing Social Order*. New York.

Berman, H.J. 1983: *Law and Revolution: The Formation of the Western Legal Tradition*. Cambridge, MA.

Berner, F. 2009: *Der hybride Wohlfahrtsstaat. Die Neuordnung von öffentlich und privat in der sozialen Sicherung*. Frankfurt and New York.

Beveridge, W.H. 1942: *Social Insurance and Allied Services*. Report, London.

———. 1943: *The Pillars of Security and Other Wartime Essays and Addresses*. London.

Beyreuther, E. 1962: *Geschichte der Diakonie und inneren Mission in der Neuzeit*. 2nd ed. Berlin.

Bielefeldt, H. 1998: *Philosophie der Menschenrechte: Grundlagen eines weltweiten Freiheitsethos*. Darmstadt.

Blackburn, D. 1980: *Class, Religion and Social Politics in Wilhelmine Germany*. London.

Blanke, K., M. Ehling and N. Schwarz. 1996: *Zeit im Blickfeld. Ergebnisse einer repräsentativen Zeitbudgeterhebung*. Stuttgart.

Bleses, P. and M. Seeleib-Kaiser. 2004: *The Dual Transformation of the German Welfare State*. Basingstoke.

Blum, R. 1980: 'Marktwirtschaft, soziale', in W. Albers (ed.), *Handwörterbuch der Wirtschaftswissenschaft*. Vol. 5. Stuttgart: 153–166.

Böckenförde, E.-W. 1976a: *Staat, Gesellschaft, Freiheit*. Frankfurt a. M.

———. 1976b: 'Die Bedeutung der Unterscheidung von Staat und Gesellschaft im demokratischen Sozialstaat der Gegenwart', in E.-W. Böckenförde (ed.), *Staat und Gesellschaft*. Darmstadt: 395–431.

————. 1976c: 'Lorenz von Stein als Theoretiker der Bewegung von Staat und Gesellschaft zum Sozialstaat', in E.-W. Böckenförde, *Staat, Gesellschaft, Freiheit*. Frankfurt a. M.: 146–184.

————. 1976d: 'Die politische Funktion wirtschaftlich-sozialer Verbände und Interessenträger in der sozialstaatlichen Demokratie', *Der Staat* 15: 457–483.

Böckenförde, E.-W. et al. (eds). 1981: *Soziale Grundrechte*. Heidelberg and Karlsruhe.

Bortkiewicz, L. von. 1899: 'Der Begriff „Sozialpolitik"', *Jahrbücher für Nationalökonomie und Statistik* 17: 332–349.

Boulding, K. 1971: *Collected Papers*. Vol. 1. Boulder, CO.

Bourdieu, P. 1970: *La réproduction: Éléments pour une théorie du système d'enseignement*. Paris.

————. 1973: 'Cultural Reproduction and Social Reproduction', in R. Brown (ed.), *Knowledge, Education, and Cultural Change*. London: 71–112.

Bradley, J. 1976: *The Call to Seriousness: The Evangelical Impact on the Victorians*. London.

Brakelmann, G. 1966: *Kirche und Sozialismus im 19. Jahrhundert*. Witten.

————. 1971: *Die soziale Frage des 19. Jahrhunderts*. 4th ed. Witten.

————. 1977: *Kirche, soziale Frage und Sozialismus*. Gütersloh.

Bremme, G. 1961: *Freiheit und soziale Sicherheit. Motive und Prinzipien sozialer Sicherung, dargestellt an England und Frankreich*. Stuttgart.

Brentano, L. 1879: *Die Arbeiterversicherung gemäß der heutigen Wirtschaftsordnung*. Leipzig.

Brettschneider, S. 2007: 'Jenseits von Leistung und Bedarf. Zur Systematisierung sozialpolitischer Gerechtigkeitsdiskurse', *Zeitschrift für Sozialreform* 53: 365–389.

Briefs, G. 1925: 'Die wirtschafts- und sozialpolitischen Ideen des Katholizismus', in N.J. Bonn and M. Palyi (eds), *Die Wirtschaftswissenschaft nach dem Kriege: Festgabe für Lujo Brentano zum 80. Geburtstag*. Munich und Leipzig: 195–226.

Briggs, A. 1961: 'The Welfare State in Historical Perspective', *Archives européennes de sociologie* 2: 221–258.

————. 1978: *The Age of Improvement 1783–1867*. 3rd ed. London.

Brock, D. and M. Junge. 1995: 'Die Theorie gesellschaftlicher Modernisierung und das Problem gesellschaftlicher Integration', *Zeitschrift für Soziologie* 24: 165–182.

Brunkhorst, H. 2002: *Solidarität. Von der Bürgerfreundschaft zur globalen Rechtsgenossenschaft*. Frankfurt a. M..

Bundesministerium für Arbeit und Soziales und Bundesarchiv (eds), *Geschichte der Sozialpolitik in Deutschland seit 1945*. 11 Volumes, Baden-Baden.

Bundesministerium für Familie und Senioren (ed.). 1994: *Familie und Familienpolitik im geeinten Deutschland – Zukunft des Humanvermögens. Fünfter Familienbericht*. Bonn.

Burns, E.M. 1956: *Social Security and Public Policy*. New York.

Calzonetti, F.J. and R.T. Walker. 1991: 'Factors Affecting Industrial Location Decisions: A Survey Approach', in H.W. Herzog Jr. and A.M. Schlottmann (eds), *Industry Location and Public Policy*. Knoxville, TN: 221–240.

Cassin, R. 1951: *La déclaration universelle et la mise en oeuvre des Droits de l'Homme*. Paris.

Castel, R. 1995: *Métamorphoses de la question sociale*. Paris.

Castles, F.G. 1978: *The Social Democratic Image of Society*. London.

Castles, F.G. et al. (eds). 2010: *The Oxford Handbook of the Welfare State*. Oxford.

Cerych, L. and P. Sabatier. 1986: *Great Expectations and Mixed Performance: The Implementation of Higher Education in Europe*. Trentham.

Clar, G., J. Doré and H. Mohr. *Humankapital und Wissen: Grundlagen einer nachhaltigen Entwicklung*. Berlin and Heidelberg.

Clarke, G.R.G. 1995: 'More Evidence on Income Distribution and Growth', *Journal of Development Economics* 47: 403–427.

Clayton, R. and J. Pontusson. 1998: 'Welfare State Retrenchment Revisited: Entitlement Cuts, Public Sector Restructuring, and Inegalitarian Trends in Advanced Capitalist Societies', *World Politics* 51: 67–90.

Cohen, W.J. and M. Friedman. 1972: *Social Security: Universal or Selective?* Washington, D.C.

Coleman, J.S. 1974: *Power and the Structure of Society*. New York.

———. 1988: 'Social Capital in the Creation of Human Capital', *American Journal of Sociology* 94 (supplement): 95–120.

Committee on Economic Security. 1937: *Social Security in America: The Factual Background of the Social Security Act as Summarized from Staff Reports to the Committee on Economic Security*. Washington, D.C.

Conze, W. 1984: 'Sicherheit, Schutz', in O. Brunner, W. Conze and R. Koselleck (eds), *Geschichtliche Grundbegriffe. Historisches Lexikon zur politisch-sozialen Sprache in Deutschland*. Vol. 5. Stuttgart: 831–862.

Corwin, R.G. 1973: *Reform and Organizational Survival: The Teachers' Corps as an Instrument of Educational Change*. New York.

Coughlin, B.J. 1965: *Church and State in Social Welfare*. New York and London.

Crick, B. 1962: *In Defence of Politics*. Chicago.

Dahl, R.A. and Lindblom C.E. 1976: *Politics, Economics, and Welfare: Planning and Politico-Economic Systems Resolved into Basic Social Processes*. Chicago and London.

Dahme, H.-J. and D. Grunow. 1983: *Persuasive Programme als Steuerungsinstrument des Wohlfahrtsstaates*. Bielefeld.

Dann, O. 1975: ‚Gleichheit', in O. Brunner, W. Conze and R. Koselleck (eds), *Geschichtliche Grundbegriffe. Historisches Lexikon zur politisch-sozialen Sprache in Deutschland*. Vol. 2. Stuttgart: 997–1046.

Deacon, B. 1997: *Global Social Policy*. London.

De la Chapelle, P. 1967: *La déclaration universelle des droits de l'homme et le catholicisme*. Paris.

De Laubier, P. 1978a: *L'âge de la politique sociale. Acteurs, idéologies, réalisations dans les pays industrialisés depuis 1800*. Paris.

———. 1978b: 'Sismondi: Théoricien de la politique sociale', in P. de Laubier, *L'âge de la politique sociale*. Paris: 27–67.

Delumeau, J. 1967: 'Réinterprétation de la Renaissance: Les progrès de la capacité d'observer, d'organiser et d'abstraire', *Revue d'Histoire moderne et contemporaine* 14: 296–314.

———. 1978: *La Peur en Occident*. Paris.

Dempf, A. 1937: *Christliche Staatsphilosophie in Spanien*. Salzburg.

De Swaan, A. 1988: *In Care of the State*. Cambridge.

Deutsch, K.W. 1963: *The Nerves of Government*. New York.

Dewey, J. 1929: *The Quest for Certainty*. New York.

'Dignity of the Human Being and Human Rights'. 1999. *The Journal of Oriental Studies* 9 (special issue), Tokyo.

Dipper, C. 1992. 'Sozialreform – Geschichte eines umstrittenen Begriffs', *Archiv für Sozialgeschichte* 32: 323–351.

Döhler, M. and P. Manow-Borgwardt. 1992a: 'Gesundheitspolitische Steuerung zwischen Hierarchie und Verhandlung', *Politische Vierteljahresschrift* 33: 571–596.

———. 1992b: 'Korporatisierung als gesundheitspolitische Strategie', in *Staatswissenschaften und Staatspraxis* 3: 64–106.

———. 1995: 'Staatliche Reformpolitik und Verbände im Gesundheitssektor', in R. Mayntz and F.W. Scharpf (eds), *Gesellschaftliche Selbstregelung und politische Steuerung*. Frankfurt and New York: 140–168.

Domscheit, S. and M. Kühn. 1984: *Die Kindergartenreform. Eine Fallstudie bundesdeutscher Sozialpolitik*. Frankfurt and New York.

Donzelot, J. 1984: *L'invention du social. Essai sur le déclin des passions politiques*. Paris.

Dorwart, R.A. 1971: *The Prussian Welfare State before 1740*. Cambridge, MA.

Durkheim, E. 1960: *The Division of Labour in Society*. New York. (In French 1893).

Dyson, K. 1980: *The State Tradition in Western Europe*. Oxford.

Easton, D. 1965a: *A System Analysis of Political Life*. New York.

————. 1965b: *A Framework for Political Analysis*. Englewood Cliffs, NJ.

Ebertz, M.N. and F. Schultheis (eds). 1986: *Volksfrömmigkeit in Europa*. Munich.

Edelman, M. 1967: *The Symbolic Uses of Politics*. Urbana, IL.

Edgerton, D. 2006: *Warfare State: Britain 1920–1970*. Cambridge.

Eisenstadt, S.N. 2000: 'Multiple Modernities', *Daedalus* 129: 1–29.

Ekelund, R. and R.D. Tollison. 1987: 'J.S. Mills neue politische Ökonomie: Mittel und Wege zu sozialer Gerechtigkeit', in G. Claeys (ed.), *Der soziale Liberalismus John Stuart Mills*. Baden-Baden: 221–245.

Elias, N. 1969: *Die höfische Gesellschaft*. Neuwied and Berlin.

————. 1994: *The Civilizing Process*. Oxford. (First in German 1939).

Elkana, Y. et al. (eds). 2002: *Unraveling Ties: From Social Cohesion to Cartographies of Connectedness*. Frankfurt and New York.

Esping-Andersen, G. 1985: *Politics Against Markets: The Social-Democratic Road to Power*. Princeton, NJ.

————. 1990: *The Three Worlds of Welfare Capitalism*. Cambridge.

———— (ed.). 1996: *Welfare States in Transition: National Adaptations in Global Economies*. London.

————. 2002: *Why We Need a New Welfare State*. Oxford.

Etzioni, A. 1971: *The Active Society*. New York.

Evans, P.B., D. Rueschemeyer and T. Skocpol (eds). 1985: *Bringing the State Back In*. New York.

Evers, A. 2008: 'Investiv und aktivierend oder ökonomistisch und bevormundend? Zur Auseinandersetzung mit einer neuen Generation von Sozialpolitiken', in A. Evers and R.G. Heinze (eds), *Sozialpolitik, Ökonomisierung und Entgrenzung*. Wiesbaden: 229–249.

Evers, A. and T. Olk (eds). 1996: *Wohlfahrtspluralismus. Vom Wohlfahrtsstaat zur Wohlfahrtsgesellschaft*. Opladen.

Éwald, F. 1986: *L'état providence*. Paris.

Ewerhart, G. 2001: 'Humankapital in Deutschland: Bildungsinvestitionen, Bildungsvermögen und Abschreibungen auf Bildung', *Beiträge zur Arbeitsmarkt- und Berufsforschung* 247. Nuremberg.

————. 2002: 'Bildungsinvestitionen, brutto und netto – Eine makroökonomische Perspektive', in S. Hartard and C. Stahmer (eds), *Magische Dreiecke. Berichte für eine nachhaltige Gesellschaft*, vol. 3: *Sozio-ökonomische Berichtsysteme*. Marburg: 217–246.

————. 2003: 'Ausreichende Bildungsinvestitionen in Deutschland? Bildungsinvestitionen und Bildungsvermögen in Deutschland 1992–1999', *Beiträge zur Arbeitsmarkt- und Berufsforschung* 266. Nuremberg.

Exner, G. 2004: 'Rudolf Goldscheid (1870–1931) and the Economy of Human Beings', *The Vienna Yearbook of Population Research* 2004: 283–301.

Ferber, C. von and F.-X. Kaufmann (eds). 1977: *Soziologie und Sozialpolitik*. Special issue 19 of *Kölner Zeitschrift für Soziologie und Sozialpsychologie*. Opladen.

Flora, P. (ed.). 1986: *Growth to Limits: The Western European Welfare States since World War II*. Vol. 1: *Scandinavia*. Berlin.

Flora. P. and A. Heidenheimer (eds). 1981: *The Development of Welfare States in Europe and America*. New Brunswick NJ and London.

Flora, P. et al. 1983: *State, Economy and Society in Western Europe 1815–1975*. Vol. 1. Frankfurt, London and Chicago.

Fogarty, M.P. 1957: *Christian Democracy in Western Europe 1820–1953*. London. (Reprint Westport, CT, 1974).

Forsthoff, E. (ed.). 1968: *Rechtsstaatlichkeit und Sozialstaatlichkeit*. Darmstadt.

Fourastié, J. 1949: *Le grand éspoir du XXe siècle*. Paris.

Frankenberg, G. 1997: *Die Verfassung der Republik. Autorität und Solidarität in der Zivilgesellschaft*. Frankfurt a. M.

Franz, J. 1991: 'Interorganizational Policy Coordination: Arrangements of Shared Government', in F.-X. Kaufmann (ed.), *The Public Sector: Challenge for Coordination and Learning*. Berlin and New York: 460–499.

Frazer, D. 1984: *The Evolution of the British Welfare State*. 2nd ed. London.

Frerich, J. and M. Frey. 1996: *Handbuch der Geschichte der Sozialpolitik in Deutschland*. 2nd ed., 3 vols. Munich and Vienna.

Fröbel, J. 1847: *System der socialen Politik*. (Reprint ed. R. Koch, Aalen 1975.)

Fry, G.K. 1979: *The Growth of Government*. London.

Gabriel, K. (ed.). 2001: *Herausforderungen kirchlicher Wohlfahrtsverbände*. Berlin.

Gabriel, K., A. Herlth and K.P. Strohmeier (eds). 1997: *Modernität und Solidarität, Konsequenzen gesellschaftlicher Modernisierung*. Freiburg.

Galant, H. 1955: *Histoire politique de la sécurité sociale française 1945–1952*. Paris.

Galtung, J. 1981: 'Structure, Culture, and Intellectual Style: An Essay Comparing Saxonic, Teutonic, Gallic and Nipponic Approaches', *Social Science Information* 20(6): 817–856.

Gartner, A. and F. Riessman. 1974: *The Service Society and the Consumer Vanguard*. New York.

Geck, L.H.A. 1950: *Sozialpolitische Aufgaben*. Tübingen.

———. 1963: *Über das Eindringen des Wortes 'sozial' in die deutsche Sprache*. Göttingen.

Gehlen, A. 1964: *Urmensch und Spätkultur*. 2nd ed. Frankfurt a. M.

Genschel, P. and B. Zangl. 2008: 'Metamorphosen des Staates: Vom Herrschaftsmonopolisten zum Herrschaftsmanager', *Leviathan* 36: 430–454.

George, V. 1968: *Social Security: Beveridge and After*. London.

Geser, H. 1990: 'Organisationen als soziale Akteure', *Zeitschrift für Soziologie* 19: 401–417.

Gestrich, A., L. Raphael and H. Uerlings (eds). 2009: *Strangers and Poor People*. Frankfurt a. M.

Giddens, A. 1990: *The Consequences of Modernity*. Cambridge.

Gide, C. and C. Rist. 1948: *A History of Economic Doctrines from the Time of the Physiocrats to the Present Day*. 2nd ed. London. (First in French 1909; English translation from the 7th ed. 1947).

Gilbert, N. 1983: *Capitalism and the Welfare State: Dilemmas of Social Benevolence*. New Haven, CT, and London.

———. 2002: *Transformation of the Welfare State*. Oxford and New York.

Gilbert, N. and B. Gilbert. 1989: *The Enabling State*. Oxford and New York.

Girvetz, H.K. 1968: 'Welfare State', in D.L. Sills (ed.), *International Encyclopedia of the Social Sciences*. Vol. 16. New York: 512–521.

Goldscheid, R. 1908: *Entwicklungswerttheorie, Entwicklungsökonomie, Menschenökonomie*. Leipzig.

Göschel, A. et al. 1979: 'Infrastrukturdisparitäten und soziale Segregation', in F.-X. Kaufmann (ed.), *Bürgernahe Sozialpolitik*. Frankfurt and New York: 219–294.

Götting, U. 1998: *Transformation der Wohlfahrtsstaaten in Mittel- und Osteuropa: eine Zwischenbilanz*. Opladen.

Gottschall, K. 2004: 'Vom Statuserhalt zur Sozialinvestition? Erziehung und Bildung als Sozialstaatstransformation', *Zeitschrift für Sozialreform* 50: 126–146.

Gregg, P. 1967: *The Welfare State*. London.

Greschat, M. 1980: *Das Zeitalter der industriellen Revolution: Das Christentum vor der Moderne*. Stuttgart.

Grimm, D. 1986: 'The Modern State: Continental Traditions', in F.-X. Kaufmann, G. Majone and V. Ostrom (eds), *Guidance, Control, and Evaluation in the Public Sector*. Berlin: 89–109.

———. 1987a: 'Die sozialgeschichtliche und verfassungsrechtliche Entwicklung zum Sozialstaat', in D. Grimm, *Recht und Staat der bürgerlichen Gesellschaft*. Frankfurt a. M.: 138–161.

———. 1987b: 'Zur politischen Funktion der Trennung von öffentlichem und privatem Recht in Deutschland', in D. Grimm, *Recht und Staat der bürgerlichen Gesellschaft*. Frankfurt a. M.: 84–103.

———. 1994a: 'Der Wandel der Staatsaufgaben und die Zukunft der Verfassung', in D. Grimm (ed.), *Staatsaufgaben*. Baden-Baden: 613–646.

———. (ed.). 1994b: *Staatsaufgaben*. Baden-Baden.

Grimm, D. and W. Maihofer (eds). 1988: *Gesetzgebungstheorie und Rechtspolitik. Jahrbuch für Rechtssoziologie und Rechtstheorie* 13. Opladen.

Gronemeyer, A. 2007: 'Social Problems, Politics of', in *The Blackwell Encyclopedia of Sociology*, vol. 9: 4502–4507.

Große Kracht, H.-J. 2003: *Solidarität institutionalisieren. Arenen, Aufgaben und Akteure christlicher Sozialethik*. Münster.

Grün, K. 1845: *Die soziale Bewegung in Frankreich und Belgien*. (Reprint Hildesheim 1974).

Grunow, D. and F. Hegner. 1979: 'Organisatorische Rahmenbedingungen der Gewährung persönlicher und wirtschaftlicher Sozialhilfe und ihre Auswirkungen auf „Bürgernähe"', in F.-X. Kaufmann (ed.), *Bürgernahe Sozialpolitik*. Frankfurt and New York: 349–408.

Grunow, D., F. Hegner and F.-X. Kaufmann. 1978: *Steuerzahler und Finanzamt*. Frankfurt and New York.

Gurvitch, G. 1931: *Le Temps présent et l'idée du droit social*. Paris.

———. 1932: *L'idée du droit social*. (Reprint Aalen 1972).

———. 1946: *La déclaration des droits sociaux*. Paris.

Habermas, J. 1981: *Theorie des kommunikativen Handelns*. 2 vols. Frankfurt a. M.

———. 1985: 'Die Krise des Wohlfahrtsstaats und die Erschöpfung utopischer Energien', in J. Habermas, *Die neue Unübersichtlichkeit*. Frankfurt a. M.: 141–163.

———. 1992: *Faktizität und Geltung*. Frankfurt a. M.

Habisch, A. 1997: 'Sozialpolitik als Sozialvermögenspolitik', *Jahrbuch für Christliche Sozialwissenschaften* 38: 192–212.

Hamilton, B. 1963: *Political Thought in Sixteenth-Century Spain*. Oxford.

Hauser, R. 2007: 'Verteilung von Zukunftsrisiken als Problem der Alterssicherung', in U. Becker et al. (eds), *Alterssicherung in Deutschland*. Baden-Baden: 17–42.

Hauser, R., H.Cremer-Schäfer and V.U. Nouverté. 1981: *Armut, Niedrigeinkommen und Unterversorgung in der Bundesrepublik Deutschland*. Frankfurt a. M.

Head, J.G. 1969: 'Merit Goods Revisited', *Finanzarchiv* NF 28: 214–225.

Heclo, H. 1974: *Modern Social Politics in Britain and Sweden*. New Haven, CT, and London.

Hegel, G.W.F. 1821: *Grundlinien der Philosophie des Rechts oder Naturrecht und Staatswissenschaft im Grundrisse*. (In English: *Outlines of the Philosophy of Right*, ed. S. Houlgate, trans. T.M. Knox. Oxford 2008).

Hegner, F. 1976: 'Die Entwicklung des sozialwisssenschaftlichen Klassenbegriffffs bei den Frühsozialisten und bei Lorenz von Stein', *Archiv für Rechts- und Sozialphilosophie* 62: 401–422.

———. 1991: 'Comparing Solidarity, Hierarchy, and Markets: Institutional Arrangements for the Coordination of Actions', in F.-X. Kaufmann (ed.), *The Public Sector: Challenge for Coordination and Learning*. Berlin and New York: 417–439.

Heidenheimer A. 1981: 'Education and Social Security Entitlements in Europe and America', in P. Flora and A. Heidenheimer (eds), *The Development of Welfare States in Europe and America*. New Brunswick, NJ and London: 269–304.

Heidenheimer, A.J. 1983: 'Secularization Patterns and the Westward Spread of the Welfare State, 1883–1983', *Comparative Social Research* 6: 3–38.

Heimann, E. 1929: *Soziale Theorie des Kapitalismus – Theorie der Sozialpolitik*. (Reprint with a preface by Bernhard Badura, Frankfurt a. M. 1980)

Heintz, B., D. Müller and H. Schiener. 2006: 'Menschenrechte im Kontext der Weltgesellschaft. Die weltgesellschaftliche Institutionalisierung von Frauenrechten und ihre Umsetzung in Deutschland, der Schweiz und Marokko', *Zeitschrift für Soziologie* 35: 424–448.

Heintz, B., R. Münch and H. Tyrell (eds). 2005: *Weltgesellschaft*. Special issue of *Zeitschrift für Soziologie*. Stuttgart.

Heinze, R.G. (ed.). 1986: *Neue Subsidiarität: Leitidee für eine künftige Sozialpolitik?* Opladen.

Heinze, R.G. and C. Offe (eds). 1990: *Formen der Eigenarbeit*. Opladen.

Heitzer, H. 1979: *Der Volksverein für das katholische Deutschland im Kaiserreich 1890–1918*. Mainz.

Heller, H. 1970: *Staatslehre*. 4th ed. Leiden.

Henderson, W.O. 1983: *Friedrich List: Economist and Visionary*. London.

Hepple, B. (ed.). 1986: *The Making of Labour Law in Europe*. London and New York.

Heuss, T., E. Salin and J.A. Schumpeter. 1965: *Friedrich List (1789–1846)*. Cologne.

Heyde, L. 1919: *Das Weltarbeiterrecht im Völkerbund*. N.p.

Hinrichs, C. 1977: 'Der Hallesche Pietismus als politisch-soziale Reformbewegung des 18. Jahrhunderts', in Martin Greschat (ed.), *Zur neueren Pietismusforschung*. Darmstadt: 243–258.

Hirschman, A.O. 1970: *Exit, Voice, and Loyalty*. Cambridge, MA.

———. 1977: *The Passions and the Interests: Political Arguments for Capitalism before its Triumph*. Princeton, NJ.

Hochschild, A. 1997: *The Time Bind: When Work Becomes Home and Home Becomes Work*. New York.

Höffe, O. 1987: *Politische Gerechtigkeit. Grundlegung einer kritischen Philosophie von Recht und Staat*. Frankfurt a. M.

———. 1995: *Moral als Preis der Moderne. Ein Versuch über Wissenschaft, Technik und Umwelt*. Frankfurt a. M.

Höffner, J. 1972: *Kolonialismus und Evangelium. Spanische Sozialethik im goldenen Zeitalter*. 3rd ed. Trier.

Hofmann, E. 1848: *Woher und Wohin? Eine populaire Schrift zur Aufklärung über die socialpolitische Bewegung der Neuzeit*. Königsberg.

Hofmann, H. 1999: *Die Entdeckung der Menschenrechte: Zum 50. Jahrestag der Allgemeinen Menschrechtserklärung vom 10. Dezember 1948*. Berlin and New York.

Hofmann, W. 1970: *Ideengeschichte der sozialen Bewegung des 19. und 20. Jahrhunderts*. Berlin.

Homburg, S. 1995: 'Humankapital und endogenes Wachstum', *Zeitschrift für Wirtschafts- und Sozialwissenschaften* 115: 339–336.

Hondrich, K.O. and C. Koch-Arzberger. 1992: *Solidarität in der modernen Gesellschaft.* Frankfurt a. M.

Hood, C. 1991: 'The Hidden Public Sector: The "Quangocratization" of the World?' in F.-X. Kaufmann (ed.), *The Public Sector: Challenge for Coordination and Learning.* Berlin and New York: 165–188.

———. 1994: 'Umkehrung der Theorie wachsender Staatstätigkeit', in D. Grimm (ed.), *Staatsaufgaben.* Baden-Baden: 93–124.

Huber, E. and J.D. Stephens. 2001: *Development and Crisis of the Welfare State: Parties and Policies in Global Markets.* Chicago and London.

Huf, S. 1998: *Sozialstaat und Moderne. Modernisierungseffekte staatlicher Sozialpolitik.* Berlin.

Humboldt, W. von. 1982: *Ideen zu einem Versuch, die Wirksamkeit des Staates zu bestimmen* (1792). Stuttgart.

Humphrey, J.P. 1979: 'The Universal Declaration of Human Rights: Its History, Impact and Juridical Character', in B.G. Ramcharan (ed.), *Human Rights: Thirty Years After the Universal Declaration.* The Hague: 21–37.

———. 1984: *Human Rights and the United Nations: A Great Adventure.* New York.

Hurrelmann, A. et al. (eds). 2008: *Zerfasert der Nationalstaat?* Frankfurt and New York.

Janowitz, M. 1976: *Social Control of the Welfare State.* New York.

Jellinek, G. 1900: *Allgemeine Staatslehre.* (Reprint 3rd ed., Bad Homburg 1966).

———. 1904: *Die Erklärung der Menschen- und Bürgerrechte. Ein Beitrag zur modernen Verfassungsgeschichte.* 2nd ed. Leipzig.

Jenks, C.W. 1970: *Social Justice in the Law of Nations: The ILO Impact After Fifty Years.* Oxford.

Jessop, B. 1994: 'Veränderte Staatlichkeit', in D. Grimm (ed.), *Staatsaufgaben.* Baden-Baden: 43–73.

———. 2002: *The Future of the Capitalist State.* Cambridge.

Johnson, H.M. 1961: *Sociology.* London.

Johnston, G.A. 1970: *The International Labour Organization: Its Work for Social and Economic Progress.* London.

Jöhr, W.A. 1976: 'Die kollektive Selbstschädigung durch Verfolgung des eigenen Vorteils, erörtert aufgrund der „Tragik der Allmende", des „Schwarzfahrerproblems" und des „Dilemmas der Untersuchungsgefangenen"', in *Wettbewerb, Konzentration und wirtschaftliche Macht. Festschrift für Helmut Arndt.* Berlin: 127–159.

Jonas, F. 1976: *Geschichte der Soziologie.* 2 vols. Reinbek bei Hamburg.

Jostock, P. 1965: *Wilhelm Emanuel von Ketteler der Arbeiterbischof.* Osnabrück.

Juster, F.T. and K.C. Land (eds). 1981: *Social Accounting Systems.* New York and London.

Kaelble, H. 2004: 'Das europäische Sozialmodell – eine historische Perspektive', in H. Kaelble and G. Schmid (eds), *Das europäische Sozialmodell.* Berlin: 31–50.

Kaelble, H. and G. Schmid (eds). 2004: *Das europäische Sozialmodell. Auf dem Weg zum transnationalen Sozialstaat.* Jahrbuch 2004 des Wissenschaftszentrums Berlin. Berlin.

Kahl, S. 2005: 'The Religious Roots of Modern Poverty Policy: Catholic, Lutheran, and Reformed Protestant Traditions Compared', *European Journal of Sociology* 45(1): 91–126.

———. 2006: *The Religious Foundations of the Welfare State: Poverty Regimes, Unemployment, and Welfare-to-Work in Europe and the United States.* Dissertation, Humboldt-Universität Berlin.

Kant, I. 1997: 'On the Common Saying that May be Correct in Theory, But It is as of No Use in Practice' (in German 1793), in M.J. Gregor (ed.), *Immanuel Kant, Practical Philosophy.* Cambridge: 273–310.

————. 1795: 'Zum ewigen Frieden. Ein philosophischer Entwurf'. (English: 'Principles of Lawful Politics: Immanuel Kant's Philosophic Draft "Toward Eternal Peace"', trans. and ed. W. Schwarz. Aalen 1988).

Kapp, W.K. and F. Vilmar (eds). (1972): *Sozialisierung der Verluste? Die sozialen Kosten eines privatwirtschaftlichen Systems*. Munich.

Kaube, J. 2003: 'Das Reflexionsdefizit des Wohlfahrtsstaates', in S. Lessenich (ed.), *Wohlfahrtsstaatliche Grundbegriffe – Historische und aktuelle Diskurse*. Frankfurt and New York: 41–54.

Kaufmann, F.-X. 1973: *Sicherheit als soziologisches und sozialpolitisches Problem*. 2nd rev. ed., Stuttgart.

————. 1977: 'Sozialpolitisches Erkenntnisinteresse und Soziologie. Ein Beitrag zur Pragmatik der Sozialwissenschaften', in C. von Ferber and F.-X. Kaufmann (eds), *Soziologie und Sozialpolitik*. Special issue 19 of *Kölner Zeitschrift für Soziologie und Sozialpsychologie*. Opladen: 35–75. (Revised version in Kaufmann 2005b: 31–68.)

———— (ed.). 1979: *Bürgernahe Sozialpolitik. Planung, Organisation und Vermittlung sozialer Leistungen auf örtlicher Ebene*. Frankfurt and New York.

————. 1980: 'Social Policy and Social Services: Some Problems of Policy Formation, Program Implementation, and Impact Evaluation', in D. Grunow and F. Hegner (eds), *Welfare or Bureaucracy? Problems of Matching Social Services to Clients' Needs*. Cambridge, MA: 29–43.

————. 1982: 'Wirtschaftssoziologie, allgemeine', in W. Albers et al. (eds), *Handwörterbuch der Wirtschaftswissenschaften*, vol. 9. Göttingen: 238–267.

————. 1983: 'The Churches and the Emergent Welfare State in Germany', in *Acts of the 17th International Conference for the Sociology of Religion*. Paris: 227–241.

————. (ed.). 1984a: *Ärztliches Handeln zwischen Paragraphen und Vertrauen*. Düsseldorf.

————. 1984b: 'Solidarität als Steuerungsform – Erklärungsansätze bei Adam Smith', in F.-X. Kaufmann and H.G. Krüsselberg (eds), *Markt, Staat und Solidarität bei Adam Smith*. Frankfurt and New York: 158–184.

————. 1985: 'Rechtsgefühl, Verrechtlichung und Wandel des Rechts', in J. Lampe (ed.), *Das sogenannte Rechtsgefühl. Jahrbuch für Rechtssoziologie und Rechtstheorie* 10: 185–199.

————. 1986: 'The Blurring of the Distinction "State versus Society" in the Idea and Practice of the Welfare State', in F.-X. Kaufmann, G. Majone and V. Ostrom (eds), *Guidance, Control, and Evaluation in the Public Sector*. Berlin and New York: 127–138.

————. 1987: 'Prevention and Intervention in the Analytical Perspective of Guidance', in K. Hurrelmann, F.-X. Kaufmann and F. Lösel (eds), *Social Intervention: Chances and Constraints*. Berlin and New York: 3–20.

————. 1988a: 'Christentum und Wohlfahrtsstaat', *Zeitschrift für Sozialreform* 34: 65–89.

————. 1988b: 'Steuerung wohlfahrtsstaatlicher Abläufe durch Recht', in *Gesetzgebungstheorie und Rechtspolitik. Jahrbuch für Rechtssoziologie und Rechtstheorie* 13: 65–108.

————. 1989: *Religion und Modernität*. Tübingen.

————. 1990: *Zukunft der Familie*. Munich. 2nd enl. ed.: *Familie im vereinten Deutschland: Gesellschaftliche und politische Bedingungen*. Munich 1995.

————. 1991a: 'Introduction: Issues and Context', in F.-X. Kaufmann (ed.), *The Public Sector: Challenge for Coordination and Learning*. Berlin and New York: 3–28.

———— (ed.). 1991b: *The Public Sector: Challenge for Coordination and Learning*. Berlin and New York.

————. 1991c: 'The Relationship of Guidance, Control, and Evaluation', in F.-X. Kaufmann (ed.). *The Public Sector: Challenge for Coordination and Learning*. Berlin and New York: 213–234.

————. 1991d: 'Wohlfahrtskultur – ein neues Nasobem?' in R. Nippert et al. (eds), *Kritik und Engagement*. Munich: 9–27.

————. 1992: *Der Ruf nach Verantwortung. Risiko und Ethik in einer unüberschaubaren Welt*. Freiburg i. Br.

————. 1993: 'Familienpolitik in Europa', in Bundesministerium für Familien und Senioren (ed.), *40 Jahre Familienpolitik in der Bundesrepublik Deutschland – Rückblick/Ausblick*. Neuwied: 141–167.

————. 1994: 'Lässt sich Familie als gesellschaftliches Teilsystem begreifen?' in A. Herlth et al. (eds), *Abschied von der Normalfamilie? Partnerschaft kontra Elternschaft*. Heidelberg: 42–63.

————. 1997a: *Herausforderungen des Sozialstaates*. Frankfurt a. M.

————. 1997b: 'Schwindet die integrative Funktion des Sozialstaates?', *Berliner Journal für Soziologie* 7: 5–22.

————. 1997c: 'Was hält die Gesellschaft heute zusammen?' *Frankfurter Allgemeine Zeitung* 4 November 1997, 11–12.

————. 1998a: 'Globalisierung und Gesellschaft', *Aus Politik und Zeitgeschichte. Beilage zur Wochenzeitung Das Parlament*, B 18/98: 3–10.

————. 1998b: 'Normative Conflicts in Germany: Basic Consensus, Changing Values, and Social Movements', in P.L. Berger (ed.), *The Limits of Social Cohesion: Conflict and Mediation in Pluralist Societies*. Boulder, CO: 84–111.

————. 1999: 'Die Entwicklung der korporatistischen Steuerungsstrukturen der ambulanten Krankenversorgung in Deutschland und ihre verteilungspolitischen Implikationen', in G. Igl and G. Naegele (eds), *Perspektiven einer sozialstaatlichen Umverteilung im Gesundheitswesen*. Munich: 27–49.

————. 2000a: 'Globalisierung, Europäisierung und Sozialstaat', *Jahrbuch für christliche Sozialwissenschaften* 41: 32–50.

————. 2000b: *Wie überlebt das Christentum?* Freiburg i. Br.

————. 2002a: '"Bindung": Exploring the Issues', in Y. Elkana et al. (eds), *Unraveling Ties: From Social Cohesion to Cartographies of Connectedness*. Frankfurt and New York: 25–52.

————. 2002b: 'Sozialpolitik zwischen Gemeinwohl und Solidarität', in H. Münkler and K. Fischer (eds), *Gemeinwohlrhetorik und Solidaritätsverbrauch. Integrationsprobleme moderner Gesellschaften*. Berlin: 19–54.

————. 2003a: 'Sicherheit: Das Leitbild beherrschbarer Komplexität', in S. Lessenich (ed.), *Wohlfahrtsstaatliche Grundbegriffe*. Frankfurt and New York: 73–104.

————. 2003b: *Sozialpolitisches Denken. Die deutsche Tradition*. Frankfurt a. M. (English: *Thinking about Social Policy: The German Tradition*. Vol. 1 of L. Leisering (ed.), *German Social Policy*. Heidelberg 2012.)

————. 2003c: *Varianten des Wohlfahrtsstaats. Der deutsche Sozialstaat im internationalen Vergleich*. Frankfurt a. M. (English: *Variations of the Welfare State: Great Britain, Sweden, France and Germany Between Capitalism and Socialism*. Vol. 5 of L. Leisering (ed.), *German Social Policy*. Heidelberg 2012.)

————. 2005: *Schrumpfende Gesellschaft. Vom Bevölkerungsrückgang und seinen Folgen*. Frankfurt a. M.

————. 2007: 'Alterssicherung und Nachwuchssicherung', in U. Becker et al. (eds), *Alterssicherung in Deutschland*. Baden-Baden: 245–270.

————. 2008: 'Sozialstaat und Gerechtigkeit', in C. Leggewie and C. Sachße (eds), *Soziale Demokratie, Zivilgesellschaft und Bürgertugenden*. Frankfurt and New York: 35–64.

————. 2009: *Was kann die Sozialstaatstheorie vom Sonderforschungsbereich 600 lernen?* Trier.

Kaufmann, F.-X. and H.G. Krüsselberg (eds). 1984: *Markt, Staat und Solidarität bei Adam Smith*. Frankfurt and New York.

Kaufmann, F.-X., G. Majone and V. Ostrom (eds). 1986: *Guidance, Control, and Evaluation in the Public Sector*. Berlin and New York.

Kaufmann, F.-X. and B. Rosewitz. 1983: 'Typisierung und Klassifikation politischer Maßnahmen', in R. Mayntz (ed.), *Implementation politischer Programme II: Ansätze zur Theoriebildung*. Opladen: 25–49.

Kaufmann, F.-X. and P. Schäfer. 1977: 'Bürgernahe Gestaltung der sozialen Umwelt: Ein Bezugsrahmen zur Problemexposition', in F.-X. Kaufmann (ed.), *Bürgernahe Gestaltung der sozialen Umwelt*. Meisenheim am Glan: 1–44.

Kaufmann, F.-X. and C. Stahmer. 2007: 'Stiefkind Humanvermögen', *Frankfurter Allgemeine Zeitung*, 20 December 2007, 8.

Kaufmann, F.-X. and K.P. Strohmeier. 1981: 'Evaluation as Meaningful Social Research', in R. A. Levine et al. (eds), *Evaluation Research and Practice*. Beverly Hills, CA, and London: 149–167.

Keller, P. 1945: *Dogmengeschichte des wohlstandspolitischen Interventionismus*. Winterthur.

Kern, T. 2005: *Südkoreas Pfad zur Demokratie. Modernisierung, Protest, Regimewechsel*. Frankfurt and New York.

Kersbergen, K. van. 1995: *Social Capitalism: A Study of Christian Democracy and the Welfare State*. London and New York.

Kersbergen, K. van and P. Manow (eds). 2009: *Religion, Class Coalitions, and Welfare States*. Cambridge.

Kersting, W. 2003: 'Gerechtigkeit: Die Selbstverewigung des egalitaristischen Sozialstaats', in S. Lessenich (ed.), *Wohlfahrtsstaatliche Grundbegriffe*. Frankfurt and New York: 105–135.

Kirchgässner, G. 1994: 'Umweltschutz als Staatsaufgabe', in D. Grimm (ed.), *Staatsaufgaben*. Baden-Baden: 453–485.

———. 1995: 'Soziale Gerechtigkeit: Produktivkraft, Illusion oder regulative Idee?' in A. Brandenberg (ed.), *Standpunkte zwischen Theorie und Praxis. Handlungsorientierte Problemlösungen in Wirtschaft und Gesellschaft*. Bern: 173–192.

Kirchgässner, G. and L.P. Feld. 2001: *The Impact of Corporate and Personal Income Taxes on the Location of Firms and on Employment: Some Panel Evidence for the Swiss Cantons*. CESifo Working Paper Series 455. St. Gallen.

Kitschelt, H. 1994: 'Technologiepolitik als Lernprozeß', in D. Grimm (ed.), *Staatsaufgaben*. Baden-Baden: 391–425.

Kittsteiner, H.-D. 1984: 'Ethik und Teleologie: Das Problem der „unsichtbaren Hand" bei Adam Smith', in F.-X. Kaufmann and H.G. Krüsselberg (eds), *Markt, Staat und Solidarität bei Adam Smith*. Frankfurt and New York: 41–73.

Klauder, W. 1992: 'Wirtschaftliche und gesellschaftliche Bedeutung der Frauenerwerbstätigkeit heute und morgen', *Zeitschrift für Bevölkerungswissenschaft* 18: 435–463.

Koch, B.A. 1992: *Die Sachhaftung*. Berlin.

Kogan, M. 1978: *The Politics of Educational Change*. Glasgow.

Kohl, J. 1985: *Staatsausgaben in Westeuropa*. Frankfurt and New York.

Köhler, P.A. 1987: *Sozialpolitische und sozialrechtliche Aktivitäten in den Vereinten Nationen*. Baden-Baden.

Kohli, M. 1985: 'Die Institutionalisierung des Lebenslaufs', *Kölner Zeitschrift für Soziologie und Sozialpsychologie* 37: 1–29.

Kolberg, J.E. 1991: 'The Gender Dimension of the Welfare State', in J.E. Kolberg (ed.), *The Welfare State as Employer*. Armonk, NY, and London: 119–148.

Koselleck, R. 1973: *Kritik und Krise. Eine Studie zur Pathogenese der bürgerlichen Welt*. Frankfurt a. M.

Koslowski, S. 1995: 'Vom sozialen Staat zum Sozialstaat: Aufstieg und Niedergang einer Vision', *Der Staat* 34: 221–241.

Koss, S. 1975: *Nonconformity in Modern British Politics*. London.

Kouri, E.J. 1984: *Der deutsche Protestantismus und die soziale Frage 1870–1919*. Berlin.

Krappmann, L. 1988: *Soziologische Dimensionen der Identität*. 7ᵗʰ ed. Stuttgart.

Krause, P. 1981: 'Die Entwicklung der sozialen Grundrechte', in G. Birtsch (ed.), *Grund- und Freiheitsrechte im Wandel von Gesellschaft und Geschichte*. Göttingen: 402–431.

Krüsselberg, H.G. 1977: 'Die vermögenstheoretische Dimension in der Theorie der Sozialpolitik', in C. von Ferber and F.-X. Kaufmann (eds), *Soziologie und Sozialpolitik*. Opladen: 232–259.

———. 2002: 'Ökonomische Analyse der werteschaffenden Leistungen von Familie im Kontext von Wirtschaft und Gesellschaft', in H.-G. Krüsselberg and H. Reichmann (eds), *Zukunftsperspektive Familie und Wirtschaft*. Grafschaft: 87–130.

Kuczynski, J. 1960: *Bürgerliche und halbfeudale Literatur aus den Jahren 1840–1847 zur Lage der Arbeiter*. Berlin.

Kulawik, T. 1999: *Wohlfahrtsstaat und Mutterschaft. Schweden und Deutschland 1870–1912*. Frankfurt and New York.

Küng, E. 1956: 'Interventionismus', *Handwörterbuch der Sozialwissenschaften*. Vol. 5. Stuttgart u.a.: 321–329.

Künzler, J. 2002: 'Paths Towards a Modernization of Gender Relations, Policies, and Family Building', in F.-X. Kaufmann et al. (eds), *Family Life and Family Policies in Europe*, vol. 2: *Problems and Issues in Comparative Perspective*. Oxford, 252–298.

Kurer, O. 1991a: *John Stuart Mill: The Politics of Progress*. New York and London.

———. 1991b: 'John Stuart Mill and the Welfare State', *History of Political Economy* 23(4): 713–730.

Lampert, H. 1996: *Priorität für die Familie. Plädoyer für eine rationale Familienpolitik*. Berlin.

Lampert, H. and J. Althammer. 2007: *Lehrbuch der Sozialpolitik*. 8ᵗʰ ed. Berlin and Heidelberg.

Lamping, W. 2009: 'European Union Social Policy: Towards a Post-National Welfare State', in K. Schubert, S. Hegelich and U. Bazant (eds), *The Handbook of European Welfare Systems*. London: 495–510.

Lane, D. 1985: *Soviet Economy and Society*. Oxford.

Lash, J.P. 1976: *Roosevelt and Churchill 1939–1941: The Partnership That Saved the West*. New York.

Lauterpacht, H. 1945: *An International Bill of the Rights of Man*. New York.

Lavergne-Peguilhen, M. von. 1838–41: *Grundzüge der Gesellschaftswissenschaft*. 2 vols. Königsberg.

———. 1863: *Sozialpolitische Studien*. Berlin.

Lawson, E. (ed.). 1991: *Encyclopedia of Human Rights*. New York.

Lee, E. 1994: 'The Declaration of Philadelphia: Retrospect and Prospect', *International Labour Review* 133: 467–484.

Leibfried, S. 2009: 'Through the Funhouse Looking Glass: Europe's Ship of States', *German Law Journal* 10(4): 311–333.

Leibfried, S. and S. Mau. 2008: 'Introduction', in S. Leibfried and S. Mau (eds), *Welfare States: Construction, Deconstruction, Reconstruction*, vol. 1: *Analytical Approaches*. Cheltenham and Northampton: xi–lxiv.

Leibfried, S. and P. Pierson (eds). 1995: *European Social Policy: Between Fragmentation and Integration*. Washington, D.C.

Leibfried, S. and U. Wagschal (eds). 2000: *Der deutsche Sozialstaat: Bilanzen – Reformen – Perspektiven*. Frankfurt and New York.

Leibfried, S. and M. Zürn (eds). (2005): *Transformation of the State?* Cambridge.

Leisering, L. 1992: 'Selbststeuerung im Sozialstaat – Zur Verortung der Rentenreform 1992 in der Sozialpolitik der 80er Jahre', *Zeitschrift für Sozialreform* 38: 3–39.

———. 1997: 'Wohlfahrtsstaatliche Dynamik als Wertproblem', in K. Gabriel, A. Herlth and K.P. Strohmeier (eds), *Modernität und Solidarität*. Freiburg: 251–273.

———. 2002: 'Entgrenzung und Moralisierung – Alterssicherung und Generationenbeziehungen im globalisierten Wohlfahrtskapitalismus', *Zeitschrift für Gerontologie und Geriatrie* 35: 343–354.

———. 2003: 'Government and the Life Course', in J.T. Mortimer and M.J. Shanahan (eds), *Handbook of the Life Course*. New York: 205–225.

———. 2004a: 'Desillusionierung des modernen Fortschrittsglaubens: „Soziale Exklusion" als gesellschaftliche Selbstbeschreibung und soziologisches Konzept', in T. Schwinn (ed.), *Differenzierung und soziale Ungleichheit. Die zwei Soziologien und ihre Verknüpfung*. Frankfurt a. M.: 238–268.

———. 2004b: 'Paradigmen sozialer Gerechtigkeit. Normative Diskurse im Umbau des Sozialstaats', in S. Liebig, H. Lengfeld and S. Mau (eds), *Verteilungsprobleme und Gerechtigkeit in modernen Gesellschaften*. Frankfurt and New York: 29–68.

———. 2007a: 'Gibt es einen Weltwohlfahrtsstaat?' in M. Albert and R. Stichweh (eds), *Weltstaat und Weltstaatlichkeit. Beobachtungen globaler politischer Strukturbildung*. Wiesbaden: 185–205.

———. 2007b: 'Privatisierung der Alterssicherung als komplexe Ordnungsbildung – Zur Entstehung von Wohlfahrtsmärkten und regulativer Staatlichkeit', in U. Becker et al. (eds), *Alterssicherung in Deutschland*. Baden-Baden: 189–219.

Lerner, D. 1968: 'Modernization I: Social Aspects', in D.L. Sills (ed.), *International Encyclopedia of the Social Sciences*. Vol. 10. New York: 386–395.

Lessenich, S. (ed.), 2003: *Wohlfahrtsstaatliche Grundbegriffe – Historische und aktuelle Diskurse*. Frankfurt and New York.

Lindbeck, A. 1995: 'Welfare State Disincentives with Endogenous Habits and Norms'. *Scandinavian Journal of Economics* 97: 477–494.

Lipponen, P. 2005: 'Warum wir Finnen Pisa-Sieger sind', *Die Zeit*, 18 August 2005, 6.

List, F. 1927: *Das natürliche System der politischen Ökonomie* (Manuscript in French 1837). Berlin.

———. 1928: *The National System of Political Economy*. London. (First in German 1841).

———. 1985: *Die Welt bewegt sich. Über die Auswirkungen der Dampfkraft und der neuen Transportmittel auf die Wirtschaft, das bürgerliche Leben, das soziale Gefüge und die Macht der Nationen* (Zweite Pariser Preisschrift 1837). Ed. Eugen Wendler. Göttingen.

Lowe, R. 1993: *The Welfare State in Britain since 1945*. London.

Luard, E. 1982: *A History of the United Nations*, vol. 1: *The Years of Western Domination, 1945–1955*. London and Basingstoke NJ.

Luhmann, N. 1965: *Grundrechte als Institution*. Berlin.

———. 1968: *Zweckbegriff und Systemrationalität: Über die Funktion von Zwecken in sozialen Systemen*. Tübingen.

———. 1975: 'Interaktion, Organisation, Gesellschaft. Anwendungen der Systemtheorie', in *Soziologische Aufklärung*, vol. 2: *Aufsätze zur Theorie der Gesellschaft*. Opladen: 9–20.

———. 1977: 'The Differentiation of Society', *Canadian Journal of Sociology* 2: 29–53.

———. 1980: *Gesellschaftsstruktur und Semantik*. Vol. 1. Frankfurt a. M.

———. 1981a: *Politische Theorie im Wohlfahrtsstaat*. Munich and Vienna.

————. 1981b: 'Subjektive Rechte: Zum Umbau des Rechtsbewußtseins für die moderne Gesellschaft', in N. Luhmann, *Gesellschaftsstruktur und Semantik*. Vol. 2. Frankfurt a. M.: 45–104.

————. 1981c: 'Wie ist soziale Ordnung möglich?' in N. Luhmann, *Gesellschaftsstruktur und Semantik*. Vol. 2. Frankfurt a. M.: 195–285.

————. 1984: *Soziale Systeme. Grundriss einer allgemeinen Theorie*. Frankfurt.

———— (ed.). 1985a: *Gesellschaftliche Differenzierung. Zur Geschichte einer Idee*. Opladen.

————. 1985b: 'Zum Begriff der sozialen Klasse', in N. Luhmann (ed.), *Soziale Differenzierung: Zur Geschichte einer Idee*. Opladen: 119–162.

————. 1990: *Risiko und Gefahr*. St. Gallen.

————. 1997: *Die Gesellschaft der Gesellschaft*. Frankfurt a. M.

Luhmann, N. and K.E. Schorr. 1979: *Reflexionsprobleme im Erziehungssystem*. Stuttgart.

Lutz, B. 1984: *Der kurze Traum immerwährender Prosperität*. Frankfurt and New York.

Lynd, R.S. and H.M. Lynd. 1937: *Middletown in Transition*. New York.

Mackenroth, G. 1954: *Die Verflechtung der Sozialleistungen*. Berlin.

Madeley, J. 1977: 'Scandinavian Christian Democracy: Throwback or Portent?' *European Journal of Political Research* 5: 267–286.

————. 1982: 'Politics and the Pulpit: The Case of Protestant Europe', *West European Politics* 5: 149–171.

Madison, B.Q. 1968: *Social Welfare in the Soviet Union*. Stanford, CA.

————. 1980: *The Meaning of Social Policy: The Comparative Dimension in Social Welfare*. London.

Majone, G. 1993: 'The European Community Between Social Policy and Social Regulation', *Journal of Common Market Studies* 31: 153–170.

Makropoulos, M. 1995: 'Sicherheit', in J. Ritter and K. Gründer (eds), *Historisches Wörterbuch der Philosophie*. Vol. 9. Basel: 745–750.

Mangoldt, H. von and V. Rittberger (eds). 1995: *The United Nation System and its Predecessors*, vol. 1: *The United Nations System*. Bern and Munich.

Manow, P. 2001: 'Ordoliberalismus als ökonomische Ordnungstheologie', *Leviathan* 29: 179–198.

————. 2002: '"The Good, the Bad, and the Ugly": Esping-Andersen's Regime Typology and the Religious Roots of the Western Welfare State'. Max Planck Institute for The Study of Societies, Working Paper 04/3, Cologne. (In German in *Kölner Zeitschrift für Soziologie und Sozialpsychologie* 54: 203–225).

————. 2009: *Religion und Sozialstaat. Die konfessionellen Grundlagen europäischer Wohlfahrtsstaatsregime*. Frankfurt and New York.

Maritain, J. 1940: *De la justice politique. Notes sur la présente guerre*. Paris. (Reprint in *Jacques et Raissa Maritain: Oeuvres complètes*, vol. 7, Freiburg and Paris 1988: 283–332.)

————. 1942: *Les droits de l'homme et la loi naturelle*. New York. (Reprint in *Jacques et Raissa Maritain: Oeuvres complètes*, vol. 7, Freiburg and Paris 1988: 617–695.)

Marlo, K. (= Winkelblech, K.-G.). 1850: *Untersuchungen über die Organisation der Arbeit oder System der Weltökonomie, Band I, 1. Abt.: Historischer Teil*. Kassel.

Marshall, T.H. 1950: 'Social Class and Citizenship', in T.H. Marshall, *Citizenship and Social Class and Other Essays*. Cambridge.

————. 1964: *Class, Citizenship and Social Development*. New York.

Marx, K. 1859: 'Zur Kritik der politischen Ökonomie', in Institut für Marxismus-Leninismus beim ZK der SED (ed.), *Karl Marx und Friedrich Engels Werke*. Vol. 13. Berlin: 3–160.

————. 1968: 'Nationalökonomie und Philosophie' (1844), in S. Landshut (ed.), *Karl Marx – Die Frühschriften*. Stuttgart: 225–316.

Mayer, K.-U. and W. Müller. 1989: 'Lebensverläufe im Wohlfahrtsstaat', in A. Weymann (ed.), *Handlungsspielräume. Untersuchungen zur Individualisierung und Institutionalisierung von Lebensläufen in der Moderne*. Stuttgart: 41–60.

Mayntz, R. (ed.). 1980: *Implementation politischer Programme. Empirische Forschungsberichte*. Königstein.

———— (ed.). 1983: *Implementation politischer Programme II. Ansätze zur Theoriebildung*. Opladen.

————. 1987: 'Politische Steuerung und gesellschaftliche Steuerungsprobleme – Anmerkungen zu einem theoretischen Paradigma', *Jahrbuch zur Staats- und Verwaltungswissenschaft* 1: 89–110.

————. 1990: 'Politische Steuerbarkeit und Reformblockaden: Überlegungen am Beispiel des Gesundheitswesens', *Staatswissenschaften und Staatspraxis* 1: 283–307.

Mayntz, R. and B. Rosewitz. 1988: 'Ausdifferenzierung und Strukturwandel des deutschen Gesundheitssystems', in R. Mayntz et al., *Differenzierung und Verselbständigung. Zur Entwicklung gesellschaftlicher Teilsysteme*. Frankfurt and New York: 117–179.

Mayntz, R. and F.W. Scharpf (eds). 1995: *Gesellschaftliche Selbstregelung und politische Steuerung*. Frankfurt and New York.

Mayntz, R. et al. 1988: *Differenzierung und Verselbständigung. Zur Entwicklung gesellschaftlicher Teilsysteme*. Frankfurt and New York

Mazmanian, D.A. and P.A. Sabatier (eds). 1981: *Effective Policy Implementation*. Lexington, MA.

McInerny, R. 1995: 'Maritain, Jacques', *The Cambridge Dictionary of Philosophy*. Vol. 6. Cambridge: 101–105.

Meadows, D.H. 1972: *Limits to Growth*. New York.

Metz, K.H. 1985: 'Liberalismus und soziale Frage. Liberales Denken und die Auswirkungen der Industrialisierung in Großbritannien des 19. Jahrhunderts', *Zeitschrift für Politik* 32: 375–392.

Meyer, A. 1864: 'Zum Begriffe der Socialpolitik', *Preußische Jahrbücher* 14: 315–330.

Mill, J.S. 1909: *Principles of Political Economy*. Ed. W. Ashley. (Reprint New York 1969.)

————.1992: *On Liberty and Utilitarianism* (1859–63). London.

Miller, D. 1999: *Principles of Social Justice*. Cambridge MA and London.

Mockenhaupt, H. 1977: *Weg und Wirken des geistlichen Sozialpolitikers Heinrich Brauns*. Paderborn.

Mohl, R. von. 1835: 'Über die Nachteile, welche sowohl den Arbeitern selbst, als dem Wohlstande und der Sicherheit der gesamten bürgerlichen Gesellschaft von dem fabrikmäßigen Betriebe der Industrie zugehen und über die Notwendigkeit gründlicher Vorbeugungsmittel', in F. Fürstenberg (ed.), *Industriesoziologie 1*. 2nd ed. Neuwied, 1966: 273–310.

————. 1851: 'Gesellschaftswissenschaften und Staatswissenschaften', *Zeitschrift für die gesamte Staatswissenschaft* 7: 3–71.

Mohr, H. 1997: 'Die Bedeutung des Sozialkapitals', in G. Clar, J. Doré and H. Mohr, *Humankapital und Wissen: Grundlagen einer nachhaltigen Entwicklung*. Berlin and Heidelberg: 97–101.

Montesquieu, C. de Secondat. 1745: *De l'ésprit des lois*. (English: *The Spirit of Laws: A Compendium of the First English Edition*, ed. D.W. Carrithers. Berkeley, CA, 1977).

Moody, J.N. 1953: *Church and Society: Catholic Social and Political Thoughts and Movements 1789–1950*. New York.

Moore, B. 1978: *Injustice: The Social Basis of Obedience and Revolt*. White Plains, NY.

Morgan, E.S. 1988: *Inventing the People: The Rise of Popular Sovereignty in England and America*. New York and London.

Morin, E. 1974: 'Complexity', *International Social Science Journal* 26: 555–582.

Morris, J. (ed.). 1956: *From the Third Programme: A Ten-Years' Anthology*. London.

Müller, H. 1967: *Ursprung und Geschichte des Wortes Sozialismus und seiner Verwandten*. Hanover.

Murray, C. 1984: *Losing Ground: American Social Policy 1950–1980*. New York.

———. 1988: *In Pursuit of Happiness and Good Government*. New York.

Musgrave, R.A. 1959: *The Theory of Public Finance*. New York.

Myrdal, A. 1945: *Nation and Family*. London.

Myrdal, A. and G. Myrdal. 1934: *Kris i Befolkningsfragan*. Stockholm.

Myrdal, G. 1960: *Beyond the Welfare State*. London.

Narr, W.-D. and C. Offe. 1975: 'Einleitung', in W.-D. Narr and C. Offe (eds), *Wohlfahrtsstaat und Massenloyalität*. Cologne: 9–46.

Nelson, B. 1977: *Der Ursprung der Moderne*. Frankfurt a. M.

Nettl, J.P. 1968: 'The State as a Conceptual Variable', *World Politics* 20(4): 559–592.

Noble, C. 1997: *Welfare As We Knew It: A Political History of the American Welfare State*. New York.

Norman, E.R. 1976: *Church and Society in England 1770–1970*. Oxford.

Nullmeier, F. 2003: 'Anerkennung: Auf dem Wege zu einem kulturalen Sozialstaatsverständnis', in S. Lessenich (ed.), *Wohlfahrtsstaatliche Grundbegriffe*. Frankfurt and New York: 395–418.

Nußberger, A. 2005: *Sozialstandards im Völkerrecht*. Berlin.

Obinger, H. et al. (eds). 2010: *Transformations of the Welfare State*. Oxford.

OECD. 1985: *Social Expenditure 1960–1990: Problems of Growth and Control*. Paris.

Oestreich, G. 1969: 'Strukturprobleme des europäischen Absolutismus', in G. Oestreich, *Geist und Gestalt des frühmodernen Staates*. Berlin: 179–197.

Offe, C. 1972: *Strukturprobleme des kapitalistischen Staates*. Frankfurt a. M.

———. 1984: *Contradictions in the Welfare State*. Ed. J. Keane. London.

Ogorek, R. 1975: *Untersuchungen zur Entwicklung der Gefährdungshaftung im 19. Jahrhundert*. Cologne.

O'Neill, J. 1994: *The Missing Child in Liberal Theory*. Toronto.

Oorschot, W. van, M. Opielka and B. Pfau-Effinger (eds). 2008a: *Culture and Welfare State: The Value of Social Policy*. Cheltenham.

Oorschot, W. van, M. Opielka and B. Pfau-Effinger. 2008b: 'The Culture of the Welfare State: Historical and Theoretical Arguments', in W. van Oorschot et al. (eds), *Culture and Welfare State: The Value of Social Policy*. Cheltenham: 1–26.

Opielka, M. 2008: 'Christian Foundations of the Welfare State: Strong Cultural Values in Comparative Perspective', in W. van Orschot et al. (eds), *Culture and Welfare State*. Cheltenham: 89–114.

Opitz, D. 1969: *Der christlich-soziale Volksdienst. Versuch einer protestantischen Partei in der Weimarer Republik*. Dusseldorf.

Osborn, R.J. 1970: *Soviet Social Policies: Welfare, Equality, and Community*. Homewood IL.

Osmani, S.R. 2009: 'The Sen System of Social Evaluation', in B. Kaushik and R. Kanbur (eds), *Arguments for a Better World*. Vol. 1. Oxford: 15–34.

Ostrom, V. 1991: *The Meaning of American Federalism*. San Francisco, CA.

Ostrom. E. 1990: *Governing the Commons: The Evolution of Institutions for Collective Action*. Cambridge.

Ozbekhan, H. 1969: 'Towards a General Theory of Planning', in E. Jantsch (ed.), *Perspectives of Planning*. Paris.

Pankoke, E. 1970: *Sociale Bewegung – Sociale Frage – Sociale Politik. Grundfragen der deutschen 'Socialwissenschaft' im 19. Jahrhundert*. Stuttgart.

————. 1977: 'Sozialpolitik zwischen staatlicher Systematisierung und situativer Operationalisierung', in C. von Ferber and F.-X. Kaufmann (eds), *Soziologie und Sozialpolitik*. Opladen: 76–97.

———— (ed.). 1991: *Gesellschaftslehre*. Frankfurt a. M..

Parsons, T. 1971: *The System of Modern Societies*. Englewood Cliffs, NJ: Prentice Hall.

————. 1977: 'Some Problems of General Theory in Sociology', in T. Parsons, *Social Systems and the Evolution of Action Theory*. New York: 229–269.

Pesch, H. 1920–26: *Lehrbuch der Nationalökonomie*. 5 vols. Freiburg i. Br.

Pfaller, A., I. Gough and G. Therborn (eds). 1991: *Can the Welfare State Compete? A Comparative Study of Five Advanced Capitalist Countries*. Basingstoke and London.

Philippovich, E. von. 1908: 'Das Eindringen der sozialpolitischen Ideen in die Literatur', in *Die Entwicklung der Volkswirtschaftslehre im neunzehnten Jahrhundert*. Vol. 2. Leipzig: 1–51.

Pierson, C. and M. Leimgruber. 2010: 'Intellectual Roots', in F.G. Castles et al. (eds), *The Oxford Handbook of the Welfare State*. Oxford: 32–44.

Pierson, P. 1994: *Dismantling the Welfare State? Reagan, Thatcher, and the Politics of Retrenchment*. Cambridge.

————. 1996: 'The New Politics of the Welfare State', *World Politics* 48(2): 142–179.

————. 1998: 'Irresistible Forces, Immovable Object: Post-industrial Welfare States Confront Permanent Austerity', *Journal of European Public Policy* 5: 539–560.

Pinker, R. 1971: *Social Theory and Social Policy*. London.

Plünnecke, A. and S. Seyda. 2004: 'Bildung', in Institut der deutschenWirtschaft (ed.), *Perspektive 2050 – Ökonomik des demographischen Wandels*. Cologne: 121–143.

Polanyi, K. 1944: *The Great Transformation*. New York.

————. 1957: 'The Economy as Instituted Process', in K. Polanyi, K.M. Arensberg and H.W. Pearson (eds), *Trade and Market in the Early Empires*. Glencoe, IL: 243–270.

Popenoe, D. 1988: *Disturbing the Nest: Family Change and Decline in Modern Societies*. Berlin.

Popper, K. 1982: *Unended Quest: An Intellectual Autobiography*. Glasgow.

Preller, L. 1949: *Sozialpolitik in der Weimarer Republik*. (Reprint Kronberg and Düsseldorf 1978.)

Pressman, J. and A. Wildawsky. 1973: *Implementation*. Berkeley.

Preu, P. 1983: *Polizeibegriff und Staatszwecklehre*. Göttingen.

Preuß, U.K. 1994: 'Risikovorsorge als Staatsaufgabe', in D. Grimm (ed.). *Staatsaufgaben*. Baden-Baden: 523–551.

Priddat, B. 1990: *Hegel als Ökonom*. Berlin.

————. 2003: 'Umverteilung: Von der Ausgleichssubvention zur Sozialinvestition', in S. Lessenich (ed.), *Wohlfahrtsstaatliche Grundbegriffe*. Frankfurt and New York: 373–394.

Prisching, M. 2003: 'Solidarität: Der vielschichtige Kitt gesellschaftlichen Zusammenlebens', in S. Lessenich (ed.), *Wohlfahrtsstaatliche Grundbegriffe*. Frankfurt and New York: 157–190.

Putnam, R. 1995: 'Bowling Alone: America's Declining Social Capital', *Journal of Democracy* 6: 65–78.

Quesel, C. 1989: *Soziologie und soziale Frage. Lorenz von Stein und die Entstehung der Gesellschaftswissenschaft in Deutschland*. Wiesbaden.

Randak, H. 1972: *Friedrich List und die wissenschaftliche Wirtschaftspolitik*. Basel and Tübingen.

Rassem, M. 1992: 'Wohlfahrt, Wohltat, Wohltätigkeit, Caritas', in O. Brunner, W. Conze and R, Koselleck (eds), *Geschichtliche Grundbegriffe. Historisches Lexikon zur politisch-sozialen Sprache in Deutschland*. Vol. 7. Stuttgart: 595–636.

Ratzinger, G. 1884: *Geschichte der kirchlichen Armenpflege*. 2nd ed. Freiburg.

Rauscher, A. (ed.): 1981–82: *Der soziale und politische Katholizismus – Entwicklungslinien in Deutschland 1803–1963*. 2 vols. Munich.

Rawls, J. 1999: *A Theory of Justice*. Oxford.

———. 2001: *Justice as Fairness*. Cambridge, MA.

Reidegeld, E. 1996: *Staatliche Sozialpolitik in Deutschland. Historische Entwicklung und theoretische Analyse von den Ursprüngen bis 1918*. Opladen.

Reinicke, W. 1998: *Global Public Policy: Governing without Government?* Washington, D.C.

Richter, E. 1992: *Der Zerfall der Welteinheit. Vernunft und Globalisierung in der Moderne*. Frankfurt and New York.

Riedel, M. 1979: 'Gesellschaft, bürgerliche', in O. Brunner, W. Conze and R. Koselleck (eds), *Geschichtliche Grundbegriffe. Historisches Lexikon zur politisch-sozialen Sprache in Deutschland*. Vol. 2. Stuttgart: 719–800.

Rieger, E. 1992a: *Die Institutionalisierung des Wohlfahrtsstaates*. Opladen.

———. 1992b: ,T.H. Marshall: Soziologie, gesellschaftliche Entwicklung und die moralische Ökonomie des Wohlfahrtsstaates', in *T. H. Marshall: Bürgerrechte und soziale Klassen*. Frankfurt and New York: 7–32.

Rieger, E. and S. Leibfried. 1999: 'Wohlfahrtsstaat und Sozialpolitik in Ostasien. Der Einfluß von Religion im Kulturvergleich', in G. Schmidt and R. Trinczek (eds), *Globalisierung. Ökonomische und soziale Herausforderungen am Ende des zwanzigsten Jahrhunderts*. Baden-Baden: 413–499.

———. 2001: *Grundlagen der Globalisierung – Perspektiven des Wohlfahrtsstaates*. Frankfurt a. M.

———. 2003: *Limits to Globalization: Welfare States and the World Economy*. Cambridge.

———. 2004: *Kultur versus Globalisierung. Sozialpolitische Theologie in Konfuzianismus und Christentum*. Frankfurt a. M.

Riehl, W.H. 1854: *Die Naturgeschichte des Volkes als Grundlage einer deutschen Social-Politik*, vol. 1: *Land und Leute*. Stuttgart and Tübingen.

Rifkin, J. 2000: The age of access: the new culture of hypercapitalism, where all of life is a paid-for experience. New York.

Rimlinger, G.V. 1971: *Welfare Policy and Industrialization in Europe, America, and Russia*. New York.

Rinderle, P. 2000: *John Stuart Mill*. Munich.

Ritter, E. 1954: *Die katholisch-soziale Bewegung Deutschlands im 19. Jahrhundert und der Volksverein*. Cologne.

Ritter, G.A. 1988: 'Der Übergang zum Interventions- und Wohlfahrtsstaat und dessen Auswirkungen auf Parteien und Parlamente im deutschen Kaiserreich', in W. Treue (ed.), *Geschichte als Aufgabe*. Berlin: 437–459.

Ritter, G.A. 1989: *Der Sozialstaat. Entstehung und Entwicklung im internationalen Vergleich*. Munich.

Roberts, B. 1979: *Paternalism in Early Victorian England*. London.

Rodrik, D. 1997: *Has Globalization Gone Too Far?* Washington, D.C.

Rokkan, S. 1975: 'Dimensions of State Formation and Nation-Building', in C. Tilly (ed.), *The Formation of National States in Western Europe*. Princeton, NJ: 562–600.

Roller, E. 1992: *Einstellungen der Bürger zum Wohlfahrtsstaat der Bundesrepublik Deutschland*. Opladen.

Romer, P.M. 1994: 'The Origins of Endogenous Growth', *Journal of Economic Perspectives* 8: 3–22.

Roosevelt, F.D.: *The Public Papers and Adresses*. Compiled with special material and explanatory notes by S.I. Rosemann. Vols 3 (1934) and 9–11 (1940–42). New York.

Rosenstock-Huessy, E. 1938: *Out of Revolution*. London.

Roth, G. 1968: 'Stein, Lorenz von', in D.L. Sills (ed.), *International Encyclopedia of the Social Sciences* 15: 257–259.

Rothfels, H. 1927: *Theodor Lohmann und die Kampfjahre der staatlichen Sozialpolitik 1871– 1905*. Berlin.

Rubinow, I.M. 1934: *The Quest for Security*. New York.

Russell, R. 1958: *A History of the United Nations Charter: The Role of the United States 1940–1945*. Washington, D.C.

Sachße, C. and F. Tennstedt (eds). 1986: *Soziale Sicherheit und soziale Disziplinierung*. Frankfurt a. M.

———. 1988: *Geschichte der Armenfürsorge in Deutschland*, vol. 1: *Vom Spätmittelalter bis zum 1. Weltkrieg*. 2nd enl. ed. Stuttgart.

Schäfer, D. 2004: 'Unbezahlte Arbeit und Bruttoinlandsprodukt 1992 und 2001', *Wirtschaft und Statistik* 9: 960–978.

Schambeck, H. 1969: *Grundrechte und Sozialordnung*. Berlin.

Scharpf, F.W. 1987: *Sozialdemokratische Krisenpolitik in Europa*. 2nd ed. Frankfurt and New York.

———. 1993: 'Verhandeln, wo nicht regiert werden kann. Handlungsfähigkeit und Legitimation der Politik am Ende des zwanzigsten Jahrhunderts', in *30 Jahre Beirat für Wirtschafts- und Sozialfragen*. Vienna: 23–41.

Scharpf, F.W., F. Reissert and F. Schnabel. 1976: *Politikverflechtung: Theorie und Empirie des kooperativen Föderalismus in der Bundesrepublik*. Kronberg.

Scharpf, F. and V.A. Schmidt (eds). 2000: *Welfare and Work in the Open Economy*, vol. 1: *From Vulnerability and Competitiveness*, vol. 2: *Diverse Responses to Common Challenges*. Oxford.

Schick, M. 1970: *Kulturprotestantismus und soziale Frage*. Tübingen.

Schieder, W. 1984: 'Sozialismus', in O. Brunner, W. Conze and R. Koselleck (eds), *Geschichtliche Grundbegriffe. Historisches Lexikon zur politisch-sozialen Sprache in Deutschland*. Vol. 5. Stuttgart: 923–996.

Schiekel, H. 1955: *Deutsche Sozialpolitik*. Munich.

Schimank, U. 2007: *Theorien gesellschaftlicher Differenzierung*. 3rd ed. Wiesbaden.

Schluchter, W. 1979: *Die Entwicklung des okzidentalen Rationalismus*. Tübingen.

Schmidt, K. 1964: 'Zur Geschichte der Lehre von den Kollektivbedürfnissen', in N. Kloten et al. (eds), *Systeme und Methoden in den Wirtschafts- und Sozialwissenschaften*. Tübingen: 335–362.

Schmidt, M. 1978: *Pietismus*. 2nd ed. Stuttgart.

Schmidt, M.G. 2005: *Sozialpolitik in Deutschland – Historische Entwicklung und internationaler Vergleich*. 3rd enl. ed. Wiesbaden.

Schmoller, G. 1867: 'Lorenz Stein', *Preußische Jahrbücher* 19: 245–270.

Schnabel, Franz. 1965: *Deutsche Geschichte im 19. Jahrhundert: Die protestantischen Kirchen in Deutschland*. Freiburg i. Br.

Schneider, M. 1981: 'Kirche und soziale Frage im 19. und 20. Jahrhundert unter besonderer Berücksichtigung des Katholizismus', *Archiv für Sozialgeschichte* 21: 533–553.

———. 1982: *Die christlichen Gewerkschaften 1894–1933*. Bonn.

Scholl, S.H. (ed.). 1966: *Katholische Arbeiterbewegung in Westeuropa*. Bonn.

Scholz, F. 1955: *Die Rechtssicherheit*. Berlin.

Schröder, J. and U. van Suntum. 1996: *Internationales Beschäftigungs-Ranking 1996*. Gütersloh.

Schubert, K., S. Hegelich and U. Bazant (eds). 2008: *Europäische Wohlfahrtssysteme*. Wiesbaden.

Schulte, B. 2004: 'Die Entwicklung der Sozialpolitik der Europäischen Union und ihr Beitrag zur Konstituierung des europäischen Sozialmodells', in H. Kaelble and G. Günter (eds), *Das europäische Sozialmodell*. Berlin: 75–103.

Schultheis, F. 1988: *Sozialgeschichte der französischen Familier.politik*. Frankfurt and New York.

Schultz, T.W. 1961: 'Investment in Human Capital', *American Economic Review* 51: 1–17.

———. 1968: 'Capital, Human', in D.L. Sills (ed.), *International Encyclopedia of the Social Sciences* 2: 278–286.

——— (ed.). 1974: *Economics of the Family: Marriage, Children, and Human Capital*. Chicago and London.

———. 1981: *Investing in People: The Economics of Population Quality*. Berkeley, CA, Los Angeles, and London.

Schulze, H.-J. and W. Wirth. 1996: *Who Cares? Social Service Organizations and their Users*. London and New York.

Schuppert, G.F. 1981: *Die Erfüllung öffentlicher Aufgaben durch verselbständigte Verwaltungseinheiten*. Göttingen.

———. 1994: 'Institutional Choice im öffentlichen Sektor', in D. Grimm (ed.), *Staatsaufgaben*. Baden-Baden: 647–683.

Schütt, F. 2003: 'The Importance of Human Capital for Economic Growth', *Materialien des Wissenschaftsschwerpunktes 'Globalisierung der Weltwirtschaft'* 27, Universität Bremen.

Schwinn, T. 1995: 'Funktion und Gesellschaft: Konstante Probleme trotz Paradigmenwechsel in der Systemtheorie Niklas Luhmanns', *Zeitschrift für Soziologie* 24: 196–214.

Scott, W.R. 1992: *Organizations: Rational, Natural, and Open Systems*. 3rd. ed. Englewood Cliffs, NJ.

Seidel, F. 1971: *Das Armutsproblem im deutschen Vormärz bei Friedrich List*. Cologne.

Sen, A. 1970: 'The Impossibility of a Paretian Liberal', *Journal of Political Economy* 72: 152–157.

———. 1982: 'Equality of What?' in S. Sen, *Choice, Welfare and Measurement*. Cambridge, MA: 353–369.

———. 1985: *Commodities and Capabilities*. Amsterdam.

———. 2001: *Development as Freedom*. Oxford.

Senghaas, D. 1975: 'Friedrich List und die Neue internationale ökonomische Ordnung', *Leviathan* 3: 292–300.

———. 1989: 'Friedrich List und die moderne Entwicklungsproblematik', *Leviathan* 17: 561–573.

Senti, M. 2002: *Internationale Regime und nationale Politik. Die Effektivität der Internationalen Arbeitsorganisation (ILO) im Industrieländervergleich*. Bern.

Shanahan, W.O. 1962: *Der deutsche Protestantismus vor der sozialen Frage 1815–1871*. Munich.

Sharp, W. 1969: *The United Nations Economic and Social Council*. New York and London.

Siegel, N.A. 2002: *Baustelle Sozialpolitik. Konsolidierung und Rückbau im internationalen Vergleich*. Frankfurt and New York.

Siep, L. (ed.). 1997: *G.W.F. Hegel – Grundlinien der Philosophie des Rechts*. Berlin.

Simmel, G. 1890: *Über sociale Differenzierung. Sociologische und psychologische Untersuchungen*. (Reprint in Simmel, *Gesamtausgabe*, vol. 2. Frankfurt a. M. 1989: 109–295.)

Sinn, H.-W. et al. 2001: *EU-Erweiterung und Arbeitskräftemigration: Wege zu einer schrittweisen Annäherung des Arbeitsmarktes*. Munich.

Sinzheimer, H. 1976: 'Theorie des sozialen Rechts', in H. Sinzheimer, *Arbeitsrecht und Rechtssoziologie. Gesammelte Aufsätze und Reden*. Vol. 2. Frankfurt and Cologne: 164–187.

Sismondi, J.C.L. Simonde de. 1991: *New Principles of Political Economy: Of Wealth in Its Relation to Population*. Trans. and annotated R. Hyse, New Brunswick, NJ, and London. (French 1819, 2nd ed. 1827.)

Skocpol, T. 1992: *Protecting Soldiers and Mothers: The Political Origins of Social Policy in the United States*. Cambridge, MA, and London.

Smith, A. 1759: *The Theory of Moral Sentiments*. (Reprint: *The Glasgow Edition of the Works and Correspondence of Adam Smith*, vol. 1. Oxford 1976.)

Smith, A. 1776: An *Inquiry into the Nature and Causes of the Wealth of Nations*. (Reprint: *The Glasgow Edition of the Works and Correspondence of Adam Smith*, vol. 2. Oxford 1979.)

Stadt Reutlingen. 1989: *Friedrich List und seine Zeit. Katalog und Ausstellung zum 200. Geburtstag*. Reutlingen.

Stafford, W. 1998: *John Stuart Mill*. London and New York.

Stahmer, C. 2002: 'Das unbekannte Meisterwerk – Sir Richard Stone und sein System of Social and Demographic Statistics', in S. Hartard and C. Stahmer (eds), *Magische Dreiecke – Berichte für eine nachhaltige Gesellschaft*, vol. 3: *Sozio –ökonomische Berichtssysteme*. Marburg: 13–88.

Stahmer, C., G. Ewerhart and I. Herrchen. 2003: *Monetäre, physische und Zeit-Input-Output-Tabellen*, vol. 1: *Konzepte und Beispiel*. Wiesbaden.

Stahmer, C., I. Mecke and I. Herrchen. 2002: *Zeit für Kinder, Betreuung und Ausbildung von Kindern und Jugendlichen*. Wiesbaden.

Statistisches Bundesamt (ed.). 1995: *Im Blickpunkt: Familien heute*. Stuttgart.

————. 2004: *Alltag in Deutschland – Analysen zur Zeitverwendung*. Wiesbaden.

Stegmann, F.-J. 1978: *Der soziale Katholizismus und die Mitbestimmung in Deutschland*. 2nd ed. Paderborn.

Stein, Lorenz (von). 1842: *Der Socialismus und Communismus des heutigen Frankreich*. Leipzig.

————. 1850: *Geschichte der sozialen Bewegung in Frankreich von 1789 bis auf unsere Tage*. 3 vols. (Reedited by G. Salomon, Munich 1921. Reprint Hildesheim 1959.)

————. 1964: *The History of the Social Movement in France 1789–1850*. Introduced, ed. and trans. K. Mengelberg. Totowa, NJ.

————. 1856: 'Der Begriff der Gesellschaft und die Lehre von den Gesellschaftsklassen', in *System der Staatswissenschaft, Band 2: Die Gesellschaftslehre, 1. Abteilung*. Stuttgart and Augsburg.

————. 1876: *Die Verwaltungslehre*, vol. 2: *Die Lehre von der inneren Verwaltung*. (Reprint Aalen 1975.)

————. 1888: *Handbuch der Verwaltungslehre*. 3rd ed., part 3: *Die Verwaltung und das gesellschaftliche Leben*. Stuttgart.

Stichweh, R. 2000: 'Zur Theorie der politischen Inklusion', in K. Holz (ed.), *Staatsbürgerschaft, soziale Differenzierung und politische Inklusion*. Opladen: 159–170.

Stichweh, R. and P. Windolf (eds). 2009: *Inklusion und Exklusion: Analysen zur Sozialstruktur und sozialen Ungleichheit*. Wiesbaden.

Stolleis, E.P. 1931: *Das internationale Arbeitsschutzrecht*. Kallmünz.

Stolleis, M. 2011: *Historical and Legal Foundations: Social Policy in Germany before 1945*. Vol. 2 of L. Leisering (ed.), *German Social Policy*. Heidelberg.

Stone, R. and G.S. Stone. 1959: *Social Accounting and Economic Models*. London.

Strohmeier, K.P. and C.W. Matthiessen (eds). 1992: *Innovation and Urban Population Dynamics: A Multi-Level-Process*. Aldershot.

Tczerclas von Tilly, H. 1924: *Internationales Arbeitsrecht*. Berlin and Leipzig.

Teichert, V. 1993: *Das informelle Wirtschaftssystem*. Opladen.

Temple, W. 1941: *Citizen and Churchman*. London.

Tennstedt, F. 1981a: *Sozialgeschichte der Sozialpolitik in Deutschland*. Göttingen.

————. 1981b: 'Vorgeschichte und Entstehung der kaiserlichen Botschaft vom 17. November 1881', *Zeitschrift für Sozialreform* 27: 663–710.

Tessaring, M. 1986: 'Educational Accounting in the Federal Republic of Germany', in D.L. Parkes, B. Sellin and M. Tessaring (eds), *Education/Training and Labour Market Policy*. Gravenhage.

Teubner, G. 1989: *Recht als autopoietisches System*. Frankfurt a. M.

Teubner, G. and H. Willke. 1984: 'Kontext und Autonomie: Gesellschaftliche Selbststeuerung durch reflexives Recht', *Zeitschrift für Rechtssoziologie* 5: 4–35.

Therborn, G. 1993: 'The Politics of Childhood: The Rights of Children in Modern Times', in F.C. Castles (ed.), *Families of Nations: Patterns of Public Policy in Western Democracies*. Dartmouth, MA: 241–281.

————. 1995: *European Modernity and Beyond, The Trajectory of European Societies 1945–2000*. London.

Thomas, W.I. 1966: 'Motivation: The Wishes' (1928), in *Social Organisation and Social Personality: Selected Papers of W.I. Thomas*. Ed. Morris Janowitz. Chicago and London: 117–139.

Thompson, J.D. 1967: *Organizations in Action*. New York.

Titmuss, R.A. 1958: 'The Social Division of Welfare', in R.A. Titmuss, *Essays on 'The Welfare State'*. London: 34–55.

Tomka, B. 2004: 'Wohlfahrtsstaatliche Entwicklung in Ostmitteleuropa und das europäische Sozialmodell, 1945–1990', in H. Kaelble and G. Schmid (eds), *Das europäische Sozialmodell*. Berlin: 107–139.

Tönnies, F. 1963: *Community and Society (Gemeinschaft und Gesellschaft*, 1887). New York.

Tragl, T. 2000: *Solidarität und Sozialstaat*. Munich.

Treitschke, H. von. 1859: *Die Gesellschaftswissenschaft. Ein kritischer Versuch*. Leipzig.

Ullrich, C.G. 1996: 'Solidarität und Sicherheit. Zur sozialen Akzeptanz der gesetzlichen Krankenversicherung', *Zeitschrift für Soziologie* 25: 171–189.

————. 2000: 'Die soziale Akzeptanz des Wohlfahrtsstaates', *Soziale Welt* 51: 131–151.

Ulrich, G. 1994: *Politische Steuerung: Staatliche Intervention aus systemtheoretischer Sicht*. Opladen.

UNESCO. 1951: *Um die Erklärung der Menschenrechte*. Zürich.

United Nations. 1975: *Towards a System of Social and Demographic Statistics*. New York.

Valticos, N. 1969: 'Fifty Years of Standard-Setting Activities by the International Labour Organization', *International Labour Review* 100: 201–237.

Veit-Wilson, J. 2000: 'States of Welfare: A Conceptual Challenge', *Social Policy and Administration* 34(1): 1–25.

————. 2002: 'States of Welfare: A Response to Charles Atherton', *Social Policy and Administration* 36(3): 312–317.

————. 2007: 'Some Social Policy Implications of a Right to Social Security', in J. van Langendonck (ed.), *The Right to Social Security*. Antwerp: 57–83.

Verdoot, A. 1964 : *Naissance et signification de la déclaration universelle des droits de l'homme*. Louvain.

Vobruba, Georg (ed.). 1989: *Der wirtschaftliche Wert der Sozialpolitik*. Berlin.

————. 2003: 'Freiheit: Autonomiegewinne der Leute im Wohlfahrtsstaat', in S. Lessenich (ed.), *Wohlfahrtsstaatliche Grundbegriffe*. Frankfurt and New York: 137–155.

Vogel, B. 2007: *Die Staatsbedürftigkeit der Gesellschaft*. Hamburg.

Voigt, U. (ed.). 1998: *Die Menschenrechte im interkulturellen Dialog*. Frankfurt a. M.

Vom Bruch, R. 1985: *,Weder Kommunismus noch Kapitalismus'. Bürgerliche Sozialreformen in Deutschland vom Vormärz bis zur Ära Adenauer*. Munich.

Wagar, W.W. 1961: *H.G. Wells and the World State*. New Haven, CT.

Wagner, A. 1876: *Allgemeine oder theoretische Volkswirtschaftslehre*, vol. 1: *Grundlegung*. Heidelberg.

———. 1891: 'Über soziale Finanz- und Steuerpolitik', *Archiv für soziale Gesetzgebung und Statistik* 10: 1–81.

Wahl, R. 2003: 'Zwei Phasen des öffentlichen Rechts nach 1949', in R. Wahl, *Verfassungsstaat, Europäisierung, Internationalisierung*. Frankfurt a. M.: 411–435.

Wallin, M. 1969: 'Labour Administration: Origins and Development'. *International Labour Review* 100: 51–110.

Walzer, M. 1983: *Spheres of Justice*. Oxford.

Wattler, T. 1978: *Sozialpolitik der Zentrumsfraktion zwischen 1877 und 1889 unter besonderer Berücksichtigung interner Auseinandersetzungen und Entwicklungsprozesse*. Cologne.

Weir, M, A.S. Orloff and T. Skocpol. 1988a: 'The Future of Social Policy in the United States: Political Constraints and Possibilities', in Weir et al. (eds), *The Politics of Social Policy in the United States*. Princeton, NJ: 421–445.

——— (eds). 1988b: *The Politics of Social Policy in the United States*. Princeton, NJ.

Weisser, G. 1956: 'Distribution (II) Politik', *Handwörterbuch der Sozialwissenschaften*. Vol. 2. Göttingen: 635–654.

Wells, H.G. 1940a: *The New World Order: Whether it is Attainable, How it can be Attained, and What Sort of World a World at Peace will Have to Be*. London.

———. 1940b: *The Rights of Man – Or What Are We Fighting For?* Harmondsworth and New York.

———. 1941: *Guide to the New World*. London.

Wiebringhaus, H. 1982: 'La charte sociale européenne: vingt ans après la conclusion du traité', *Annuaire français de droit international* 28: 934–947.

Wildt, A. 1996: 'Solidarität', in J. Ritter and K. Gründer (eds), *Historisches Wörterbuch der Philosophie*. Vol. 9. Basel: 1004–1015.

Wilensky, H.L. 1985: *Comparative Social Policy: Theories, Methods, Findings*. Berkeley, CA.

Willke, Helmut. 1991: 'Le droit comme instrument de guidage neomercantiliste de l'état', in C.-A. Morand (ed.), *L'état propulsif. Contribution á l'étude des instruments d'action de l'état*. Paris: 95–106.

———. 1992: *Ironie des Staates*. Frankfurt a. M.

———. 1994: 'Die Steuerungsfunktion des Staates aus systemtheoretischer Sicht', in D. Grimm (ed.), *Staatsaufgaben*. Baden-Baden: 685–711.

Wilson, T.A. 1969: *The First Summit: Roosevelt and Churchill at Placentia Bay 1941*. Boston, MA.

Winch, D. 1984: 'Adam Smith als politischer Theoretiker', in F.-X. Kaufmann and H.G. Krüsselberg (eds), *Markt, Staat und Solidarität bei Adam Smith*. Frankfurt and New York: 95–113.

Windhoff-Héritier, A. 1994: 'Der aktive Staat: Umweltpolitik in den USA', in D. Grimm (ed.). *Staatsaufgaben*. Baden-Baden: 427–451.

Windhoff-Héritier, A. et al. 1990: *Verwaltungen im Widerstreit von Klientelinteressen. Arbeitsschutz im internationalen Vergleich*. Wiesbaden.

Wirth, W. 1982: *Inanspruchnahme sozialer Dienste: Bedingungen und Barrieren*. Frankfurt and New York.

————. 1991a: 'Coordination of Administrative Controls: Institutional Challenges for Operational Tasks', in F.-X. Kaufmann (ed.), *The Public Sector: Challenge for Coordination and Learning*. Berlin and New York: 235–256.

————. 1991b: 'Responding to Citizens' Needs: From Bureaucratic Accountability to Individual Coproduction in the Public Sector', in F.-X. Kaufmann (ed.), *The Public Sector: Challenge for Coordination and Learning*. Berlin and New York: 69–85.

Wissenschaftlicher Beirat für Familienfragen. 1979: *Leistungen für die nachwachsende Generation in der Bundesrepublik Deutschland*. Stuttgart.

Wronka, J. 1992: *Human Rights and Social Policy in the 21st Century*. Lanham, MD, and London.

Zacher, H.F. 1976: 'Einleitung', in H.F. Zacher (ed.), *Internationales und Europäisches Sozialrecht. Eine Sammlung weltweiter und europäischer völkerrechtlicher und supranationaler Quellen und Dokumente*. Percha am Starnberger See: v–xxvii.

————. 1977: 'Sozialstaatsprinzip', in W. Albers et al. (eds), *Handwörterbuch der Wirtschaftswissenschaften*. Vol. 7. Stuttgart: 152–160.

————. 1978: 'Der Sozialstaat als Prozeß'. (Reprint in H.F. Zacher, *Abhandlungen zum Sozialrecht*. Heidelberg 1993: 73–93.)

————. 1980: *Sozialpolitik und Verfassung im ersten Jahrzehnt der Bundesrepublik Deutschland*. Berlin.

————. 1987: 'Das soziale Staatsziel'. (Reprint in H.F. Zacher, *Abhandlungen zum Sozialrecht*. Heidelberg. 1993: 3–72.)

———— (ed.). 1991: *Alterssicherung im Rechtsvergleich*. Baden-Baden.

————. 2004: 'Das soziale Staatsziel', in J. Isensee (ed.), *Handbuch des Staatsrechts, Band II Verfassungsstaat*. Heidelberg: 659–784.

Zapf, W. 1972: 'Zur Messung von Lebensqualität', *Zeitschrift für Soziologie* 1: 353–376.

————. 1984: 'Welfare Production: Public versus Private', *Social Indicators Research* 14: 263–274.

Zürn, M. 1996: 'Über den Staat und die Demokratie im europäischen Mehrebenensystem', *Politische Vierteljahresschrift* 37: 27–55.

Zwiedineck-Südenhorst, O. von. 1911: *Sozialpolitik*. Leipzig and Berlin.

INDEX OF NAMES

INDEX OF SUBJECTS